DUNKIRK

DUNKIRK

Operation "Dynamo" 26th May – 4th June 1940

An Epic of Gallantry

BRITANNIA NAVAL HISTORIES OF WORLD WAR II

BMT Press
Britannia Museum Trust Press

This edition first published in the United Kingdom in 2020 by Britannia Museum Trust Press, Britannia Royal Naval College, Dartmouth, TQ6 0HJ, United Kingdom.

ISBN: 978-1-838017-1-3

© Britannia Museum Trust, 2020 © The Devonshire Press™ 2020

A CIP catalogue record of this book is available from the British Library.

Publisher: Paul Honeywill
Editorial Assistants: Charlotte Bailey, Abigail Joyce, Saffron Saunderson and Anna Young
Series Editors: G. H. Bennett, J. E. Harrold, R. Porter and M. J. Pearce

Pages 8-9. At the start of World War II, Charles Ernest Cundall, RA RWS RP was given a commission as an Admiralty artist. Cundall was best known for the painting, *The Withdrawal from Dunkirk*, June 1940, which was commissioned by the War Artists' Advisory Committee. *This painting hangs at Britannia Royal Naval College, Dartmouth.*

Cover image © Edward Stables 2020. *Lady Cable* picking up passengers before World War II at Babbacombe pier, Torquay, Devon.

Britannia Royal Naval College

A majestic landmark, which towers above the harbour town of Dartmouth in Devon, Britannia Royal Naval College was designed by royal architect Sir Aston Webb to project an image of British sea power. A fine example of Edwardian architecture, the College has prepared future generations of officers for the challenges of service and leadership since 1905.

The Britannia Museum opened in 1999 to safeguard the College's rich collection of historic artefacts, art and archives and promote greater public understanding of Britain's naval and maritime heritage, as a key element in the development of British history and culture. It also aims to instil a sense of identity and ethos in the Officer Cadets that pass through the same walls as their forbears, from great admirals to national heroes to royalty.

www.royalnavy.mod.uk/The-Fleet/Shore-Establishments/BRNC-Dartmouth

"... What began as a miserable blunder, a catalogue of misfortunes ended as an **epic of gallantry**. We have a queer habit – and you can see it running through our history – of conjuring up such transformations ..."

J B Priestley, Postscript, BBC, 5 June 1940

Contents

Foreword 12

Introduction 17

PART I

Illustrations 60

PART II Battle Summary No. 41

Introduction 116

Preliminary Events 10th-18th May 1940 119

The week before Operation "Dynamo," 19th-25th May, 1940 126

Operation "Dynamo" is Commenced, Sunday, 26th May, 1940 142

Monday, 27th May 148

Tuesday, 28th May 160

Wednesday 29th May 173

Thursday, 30th May 203

Friday, 31st May – Evacuation Reaches its Zenith 217

Saturday 1st June – Germans Renew their Heavy Air Effort 245

The Night of the 1st-2nd June Daylight to Dusk on 2nd 261

The Night 2nd-3rd June – B.E.F. Evacuated 2330/2 277

The Final Night, 3rd-4th June 288

Analysis of the Operation 300

Notes for following Disembarkation Records 310

Record of Troop Numbers Lifted from Dunkirk 312

Record of British Ships Lifting Troops from Dunkirk 318

Record of other Ships Lifting Troops from Dunkirk 324

Summary of Operation Dynamo 328

Appendices A-Z 330

Dunkirk Sources 415

Biographies 418

Britannia Naval Histories of World War II 421

Admiral Sir Bertram Ramsay, KCB, KBE, MVO

Bertram Ramsay joined the Royal Navy in 1898. He was given his first command in August 1915, a small monitor M25. He was promoted Commander in June 1916 and took over command of the Dover based destroyer HMS *Broke*. He saw action in the second Ostend raid, which was a follow up to the Zeebrugge Raid for which he was mentioned in despatches.

He retired from the Royal Navy in 1938 but was persuaded out of retirement by Churchill to help deal with the Axis Threat. He was promoted to Vice Admiral and became Vice Admiral, Dover on 24th August 1939.

As Vice Admiral Dover he was responsible for Operation "Dynamo" directing operations from the tunnels beneath Dover Castle.

After his success in rescuing the thousands of British and Allied Troops from the beaches of Dunkirk he was asked to personally report on the Operation to King George VI which resulted in him being made Knight Commander of the Order of the Bath.

Following Operation Dynamo for the next two years he was responsible for the defence of the waters off Dover against the expected German invasion and was again mentioned in despatches.

He was appointed Naval Force Commander for the invasion of Europe on 29th April 1942 but because of the postponement of the invasion he was transferred to become Deputy Naval Commander of the Allied invasion of North Africa.

He played a major role in Operation Husky (the invasion of Sicily) in July 1943 as Naval Commanding Officer, Eastern Task Force preparing for the amphibious landings. In 1944 he was promoted to the rank of Admiral and appointed Naval Commander-in-Chief of the Allied Naval Expeditionary Force (Operation Neptune). He masterminded this invasion from Southwick House, where he is pictured in the portrait in the drawing room where the master plan of the invasion is hanging on the wall, where it can still be seen to this day.

A portrait by Sir Oswald Birley from a collection of portraits painted by Birley just after WWII.

The nineteen portraits housed at BRNC are all WWII Commanders-in-Chief and were formerly displayed at the RNC Greenwich.

The historian Correlli Barnett described the operation as a 'never surpassed masterpiece of planning' which required the commanding and co-ordinating of nearly 7,000 vessels and deliver the men onto the beaches of Normandy for the D-Day invasion.

Both Churchill and the King expressed a wish to accompany and observe the D-Day invasion and heated discussions were held between the two of them. Ramsay defused the situation by intervening and saying that he could not ensure their safety and that they would both be needed in London.

Admiral Sir Bertram Ramsay met an untimely death on 2nd January 1945 aged 61 when he died when the aircraft in which he was travelling crashed on take off at Toussus-le-Nable Airpot south west of Paris, *en route* to a conference in Brussels with General Montgomery.

Foreword

Admiral Sir James Burnell-Nugent

Imagine

Imagine spending the early part of your career on a round the world deployment in the cruiser HMS *Durban*, followed by 3 years on the China Station in another cruiser, HMS *Suffolk*. Much time spent in white uniform, on gunnery practice, winning inter-ship sailing regattas and on diplomatic activity ashore. The 1937 Coronation Fleet Review for King George VI is something of a pinnacle for that era of the Royal Navy. In sharp contrast to what was about to happen, it was attended by the German Pocket Battleship *Graf Spee*. You then choose to serve in destroyers – becoming a so called "Salt Horse", that is not specialising for example in gunnery or torpedoes – and by 1940 you are in your third command, one of the Navy's newer destroyers, HMS *Havant*.

On the 29th May 1940 you are ordered to collect troops from Dunkirk under Operation "Dynamo". Proud of your ship handling, something of a cult amongst Salt Horses, you are one of the first destroyers alongside The Mole, being frustrated with the exposure of slow embarkation across the beach. On the morning of 1st June HMS *Havant* was on her fourth such trip to retrieve members of the British Expeditionary Force. That same morning Major McCracken of the 7th Field Regiment, Royal Artillery, had written on behalf of his men to thank HMS *Havant* for taking them off the previous day. *"I am writing to express our admiration for what you did and our most grateful thanks to you personally and all ranks under your command. We know if it is humanly possible you will today be embarking the rearguard which remained."* When half way across the English Channel, returning at best speed to The Mole, Signalman Pattinson brings to the Captain on the open bridge of HMS *Havant*, a message from the Admiralty ordering withdrawal from Operation "Dynamo", because the risks have become too great for the valuable large destroyers. With this immense challenge to his sense of duty – to the Admiralty or to the men on the beach – the Captain quietly tears up the message, deciding to "press on" one more time.

With a full load of troops, heading back to Dover at Full Ahead, whilst weaving between the sandbanks off Dunkirk and engaging a shore battery with her 4.7in guns, HMS *Havant* was repeatedly bombed by Stukas which came so low pulling out of their near vertical dive that "you could hit them with a shotgun." Even as she was sinking and transferring survivors to other vessels alongside her, the bombing continued. The Captain, my father Lieutenant Commander A.F. Burnell-Nugent, had to order "Abandon Ship." There were two large holes on the starboard side, one large hole below the waterline on the port side, split bulkheads in the engine rooms, most stern compartments

Memorial to HMS *Havant*, St. Faith's Church, Havant

flooded, two large fires and the port side of the upper deck almost awash. All in the machinery spaces were killed and there were significant numbers of dead and wounded on the upper deck, but most on board survived.

Just imagine the physical, mental and personal transition from those globetrotting peacetime years in tropical uniform, to 69 minutes of carnage from the moment the first bombs hit to stepping across to a rescuing tug. Of course such a shocking experience was not unique to destroyers, the little ships, our airmen or the hundreds of thousands of soldiers on the beach. Most were too young to have been in the First World War; most had only served for a few peacetime years; most had never been shot at or bombed.

Just imagine. How traumatic this must have been for individuals, their families and other citizens at home, and how traumatic for us as a nation. Churchill, who had been Prime Minister for less than a month, gave his famous "We shall fight them on the beaches" speech to the House of Commons on 4th June. This legendary rhetoric was the start of a long and dark journey to victory.

For myself, having had the good fortune to have Rear Admiral's command at sea as Commander UK Maritime Forces and later been Commander-in-Chief Fleet, it is impossible not to look back at Dunkirk from the senior officer's perspective of command and control. I would not presume to claim similarity between Dunkirk in 1940 and the Al Qaeda attack on the Twin Towers in New York on 11th September 2001, but there are some common features in terms of the impact on higher levels of command. On that September morning I was in command of a Royal Navy Task Group of over 50 units, ranging from nuclear submarines, destroyers and frigates, to mine warfare vessels, amphibious ships, Royal Marine Commandos and air squadrons. My flagship was HMS *Illustrious* and we were, coincidentally, on our way to the Gulf for a major joint exercise in Oman. On the basis that the slowest ships had to start earlier so we would all arrive together, on 11th September the mine warfare vessels were in the Red Sea, the Amphibious Group off Turkey and the Flagship with her escorts mid-Mediterranean. I had taken the trouble to meet as many of the Task Group Commanding Officers as possible before we deployed – but this was certainly widely distributed command and control. Unsurprisingly, the MoD and indeed the whole machinery of Westminster and Whitehall were busy facing the geopolitical nature of the crisis. So for me in HMS *Illustrious*, as for Vice-Admiral Ramsay in Dover Castle, it was a classic moment for mission command and improvisation. A key difference was that the flames of the town of Dunkirk burning in 1940 could be seen from Dover, but Al Qaeda 61 years later was a pervasive threat on a new scale that had been revealed to the world on live television.

It was no good waiting for further instructions. I had to issue short personal messages to all units under my command directing them to "press on", but with unprecedented levels of such an unknown threat. And plenty of potentially vulnerable moments ahead, such as the Suez Canal, the Bab-el-Mendeb Straits at the southern end of the Red Sea, and the Straits of Hormuz. Brevity and clarity as the critical components of mission command were key. A civilian aircraft, maybe even quite small, crash diving onto a warship out of a clear blue sky was not at that time something in any drill book, with any training or procedures, or with rules of engagement for use prior to the ultimate moment of self-defence. Equally true for a fast small boat packed with explosives. Unlike 1940, we were not at war. We would pass through international and territorial waters as we progressed East. International maritime law demands that warships proceed on "innocent passage" when in another nation's territorial waters. Is that possible when "the enemy" are undeclared, largely invisible and certainly not in uniform? In fact who were the enemy? In such confusing circumstances I also attached great importance to signal messages having a personal touch. With apologies to many brilliant staff officers over the years, even the most junior commanding officer can tell the difference between a message from the Admiral and a message written by a staff officer, purporting to be from the Admiral. As I am sure Admiral Ramsay did, I adhered to such key principles throughout the operation. By November, working largely with the US Marine Corps, this Royal Navy Task Group had ejected the Taliban Government from Kabul – but that is another story.

The many readers who I hope will immerse themselves or perhaps just refer to this excellent book in the Britannia Naval History series, will do so from different perspectives. Some, like me, will have a family connection. Others will be associated with the many Services, military and civilian, that played their part in showing the original "Dunkirk Spirit". For readers who aspire to leadership roles, or maybe already in such a position in any modern work setting, I would encourage you as you read, to do so through the lens of leadership at Dunkirk. By all means consider the leadership pressures on the King, the newly appointed Prime Minister after a vote of no confidence in his predecessor, or any of the Chiefs of Staff. Or at the other end of the spectrum, view the events as seen by an Army NCO who can only find half his men, or RAF ground crew still trapped in France, or maybe a Leading Seaman in charge of a private pleasure craft commandeered by the Admiralty with only the most sketchy instructions. If ever there was a need to focus on essentials, give brief and clear instructions, take courage and "press on", it was there and then at Dunkirk. From grand strategy to selfless individual bravery, there is something for all of us in this Epic of Gallantry.

James Burnell-Nugent.

February 2020
Admiral Sir James Burnell-Nugent KCB CBE MA

Introduction

Michael Pearce

The successful evacuation of the British Expeditionary Force from Belgium and northern France through the port of Dunkirk and across adjacent beaches is rightly regarded as one of the most significant episodes in the nation's long history, although Winston Churchill sagely cautioned in Parliament on 4th June that the country "must be careful not to assign to this deliverance the attributes of a victory. Wars are not won by evacuations".[1] Nevertheless, the Dunkirk evacuation, Operation "Dynamo", was a victory and, like many others before it, it was a victory of sea power. The Royal Navy achieved what it set out to do, despite grievous losses, in the teeth of determined opposition. It denied an aggressive and ruthless continental power a potentially war-winning total victory that could have changed the direction of civilization for generations to come. The loss of the main British field army would have enfeebled the nation militarily and psychologically, prompting political upheaval, potentially resulting in a negotiated peace with Nazi Germany on unfavourable terms dictated by Adolf Hitler. The undeniable success of the evacuation was certainly a crucial naval and military achievement but its positive effect on the nation's morale was just as important, instilling confidence in the eventual outcome of the war, whatever the immediate future might hold, and creating optimism in the face of adversity that added "the Dunkirk spirit" to the English language. Several major movies have been made between 1958 and 2017 retelling the story and many others have set their own against its background, while the exploits and achievements of 'the little ships' have attained an almost mythical status, with many people today being certain that the entire BEF was lifted from Dunkirk's beaches and brought home by hundreds of small craft, whereas the greater part of the army was embarked from Dunkirk harbour in destroyers and large personnel vessels.

This volume of the Britannia Naval Histories of World War 2 (BNHWW2) marks the 80th anniversary of the operation and comprises an original Admiralty document, Battle Summary No 41, 'The Evacuation From Dunkirk', that was issued in small numbers in 1949 for internal use only, as part of the official Naval Staff History of the Second World War. Classified under the Official Secrets Act until the 1970s, it is particularly rich in detail and is a scarce and important historical source today. This introduction seeks to describe the naval side of the campaign that included the Dunkirk evacuation and also place the operation in context, showing that it did not happen in isolation. It presents,

---

1 Hansard, 5th Series, vol 361, cols 787-96. Quoted in Jenkins, Roy, (2001), *Churchill*, Macmillan, p.597. Also in Lord, Walter, (1983), *The Miracle of Dunkirk*, Allen Lane, p.271.

in chronological order, events prior to Operation "Dynamo", additional operational and background information and also covers the lesser known major evacuations from other French ports, carried out after Operation "Dynamo" had been concluded on 4th June 1940 but before the French armistice with Nazi Germany became effective on 25th, as these operations were a similar consequence of France's defeat and an essential sequel to Operation "Dynamo".

Winston Churchill became Prime Minister of a cross-party National Government on 10th May 1940, when the United Kingdom was beset by grave political and military crises. An angry House of Commons had reflected the nation's dissatisfaction with the previous Government's conduct of the War, making abundantly clear to Neville Chamberlain that he could not continue as Premier; any hopes he may have had of clinging to power were dashed by several prominent parliamentarians, culminating in Leo Amery's speech, when he quoted Oliver Cromwell from nearly 300 years earlier: "You have sat too long here for any good you have been doing. Depart, I say, and let us have done with you. In the name of God, go."[2] If this were not bad enough from a fellow Conservative, the Labour opposition refused to serve in a National Government headed by Chamberlain. His fellow pre-War appeaser, Viscount Halifax, then Foreign Secretary, declined to offer himself as successor, nominally on the grounds that he could not manage the Government's Parliamentary business from the House of Lords but also said he was not the best man for the job – at that time. Therefore, King George VI asked Winston Churchill to form a Government. After Chamberlain's resignation as Premier, and until ill-health intervened in September, he served loyally in Churchill's small War Cabinet, certainly more loyally than the pessimistic and defeatist Halifax but on 9th November, only six months after leaving Downing Street, Neville Chamberlain's cancer killed him. Six weeks later, Halifax bowed to Churchill's inexorable pressure and accepted the vacant post of British Ambassador in Washington, leaving the War Cabinet and being replaced as Foreign Secretary by Anthony Eden. Churchill may have calmed the worst of the domestic political turmoil but his immediate task was to deal with a serious military situation that worsened daily.

On 10th May, the day Churchill became Prime Minister, Nazi Germany attacked France, and invaded the neutral nations of Luxembourg, the Netherlands and Belgium, swiftly making significant military and territorial gains. Luxembourg was overrun in hours, becoming part of the Third Reich, while the Netherlands initially fought back fiercely, despite a gravely

---

2 Jenkins, Roy, (2001), *Churchill*, Macmillan, p.579.

outnumbered army and air force with outdated equipment. The Belgian army, based on static defences as a result of the country's strict pre-war neutrality, also resisted, even though their key frontier fortress of Eben-Emael fell to German glider-borne troops as early as 11th May. At this time, bitter fighting still raged in Norway, where British, French and Polish forces had been fighting to support the resolute but tiny Norwegian military since 9th April. Despite some notable British and Norwegian naval successes, it was becoming increasingly clear that, lacking adequate air support, Allied forces would be unable to defeat the well-planned, heavily resourced German invasion and their evacuation began on 4th June, the last day of Operation "Dynamo".

On 13th May, Churchill entered the House of Commons for the first time as Prime Minister, to an unenthusiastic reception but gave the first of his passionate and emotive wartime speeches, saying: "I have nothing to offer but blood, toil, tears and sweat". But promising: "victory, victory at all costs, victory in spite of all terror, victory, however long and hard the road may be."[3] Parliament's reaction was subdued but Churchill's words caught the imagination of the press and public and became a rallying cry, stiffening the nation's resolve.

Also, on 13th May, Queen Wilhelmina of the Netherlands boarded the destroyer HMS *Hereward*, under heavy air attack, and took passage to Britain, followed that evening by her government in HMS *Windsor*. The country's gold and bullion reserves and a fortune in diamonds were also evacuated, while many ships of the Royal Netherlands Navy, including several incomplete vessels towed across the Channel by Dutch tugs, reached Britain to fight on. Royal Navy and Dutch demolition teams destroyed port facilities, while oil stocks in Amsterdam and Rotterdam were set ablaze and Belgian oil stocks at Antwerp rendered unusable. A force of Royal Marines and Irish and Welsh Guards protecting the demolition teams, was evacuated from the Hook of Holland on 14th May, the day that the Luftwaffe razed the centre of Rotterdam. Overwhelmed, the Netherlands surrendered on 15th but, by then, the Royal Navy had taken to Britain 50 tugs and more than 600 coastal and inshore craft, including many Dutch schuyts, small, shallow draught motor coasters, called 'skoots' by the British, that proved invaluable at Dunkirk less than two weeks later.

On 15th May, France's Prime Minister, Paul Reynaud, telephoned Churchill, to say that the Germans had broken through in the Ardennes, a French counter-attack had failed and the road to Paris was open. In a state of high emotion, Reynaud felt that the battle was lost and France might have to end the war.

---

3 Jenkins, Roy, (2001), *Churchill*, Macmillan, p.591.

On 16th, as Churchill flew to France to meet Reynaud, the Chief of Staff of the British Expeditionary Force telephoned the War Office after visiting the French 1st Army HQ, saying that the French army's collapse was so complete that the BEF, sent to France in 1939 to support the much larger French armies, might require evacuation. Acknowledging this possibility, Vice Admiral Bertram Ramsay, commanding at Dover, assumed operational control of contingency planning on 19th, when the loss of French airfields necessitated the withdrawal of the surviving 66 RAF Hurricane fighters, after Fighter Command had lost a quarter of its strength fighting in France.

Following the outbreak of war, many coastal excursion vessels and paddle steamers were requisitioned for naval service, being commissioned as armed patrol vessels, auxiliary minesweepers and AA ships, all manned by RN personnel, and the Admiralty put these on stand-by for a possible evacuation. Vice Admiral Ramsay was convinced that the outlook for the BEF was bleak and its evacuation unavoidable; at a conference with the War Office and Ministry of Shipping on 20th May, he emphasised the urgent need for additional coastal passenger vessels and paddle steamers to transport large numbers of troops across the Channel. He added that even greater numbers of much smaller craft would be required to transfer troops from shallow waters off Dunkirk's gradually shelving beaches to deeper draught vessels compelled to remain offshore by up to a mile and a half of sand extending seawards at low tide but completely submerged at high water.

At this time the Luftwaffe already constituted a serious threat to allied shipping off the Channel ports; on 21st May, the French destroyer *L'Adroit* was bombed in the approaches to Dunkirk and damaged so seriously that she was beached at Malo-les-Bains where she burned uncontrollably until her forward magazine detonated, destroying the fore part of the ship and blowing off her bows. Her burned out broken wreck could be reached easily on foot at low tide and her stark profile became a grim backdrop to the evacuation, demonstrating to troops waiting on the beaches, the lethal effects of air attack on the ships they were looking to for rescue.

There was shock and disbelief in London and within the BEF, at the sudden French military collapse, feelings shared for very different reasons by the Germans as leading elements of 2nd Panzer Division reached the coast at Noyelles on 21st May, isolating the BEF and large numbers of French troops to the north. The armoured thrust from the Ardennes to the Channel ports, known as the 'Sickle Cut' (*Sichelschnitt*) strategy, was devised by General Erich von Manstein, then Chief of Staff to Army Group A, although Hitler later claimed it as his own personal idea. But, also on 21st, the seemingly inexorable German advance through northern France, received a sharp, if temporary, setback at Arras, when a hastily assembled force of British armour and infantry, with limited French support, counter-attacked General Erwin Rommel's 7th Panzer Division. Although the attack ran out of steam, losing many of its tanks, it inflicted over 400 casualties, took several hundred prisoners, and caused significant damage, dismay and even short-lived panic among some German units, notably the SS Totenkopf (Death's Head) Division, until Rommel took charge of the front line, at considerable personal risk, and restored the situation, using the formidable 88mm 'flak 36' AA gun in the anti-tank role. Nevertheless, the unexpected attack prompted an already apprehensive German High Command on 24th May to order the armoured spearheads to halt their advance towards the Channel ports until supporting infantry could secure their exposed flanks. The panzer divisions were already weakened by armoured vehicle losses during their rapid and continuous advance, while their crews were exhausted, notwithstanding millions of Pervitin methamphetamine tablets officially issued to sustain the blistering pace of the *Sichelschnitt* by obviating the need for sleep. German commanders recorded that Pervitin also instilled a sense of euphoria and self-confidence in their troops, increasing aggression. Now known as crystal meth, it is considered a dangerous and illegal substance.

The panzer commanders vehemently opposed the halt order but Hitler not only confirmed it, he extended the delay to three days. Hitler may have been influenced by factors other than immediate tactical and logistical considerations: a determination to impose his authority on his generals by curbing their independent action; a wish to conserve his panzer strength for future actions; the lure of capturing Paris; the perceived unsuitability for armour of the rain-soaked terrain and web of waterways around Dunkirk; and, not least, vigorous lobbying from Hermann Goering, gripped by his inflated ego and morphine-fuelled false optimism, for his Luftwaffe to be allowed the honour of destroying the trapped BEF from the air. It has also been postulated that Hitler sought to influence possible peace negotiations with the British, as he had not planned or expected war with Britain in 1939 and had not intended it until several years later. Nevertheless, he informally admitted to panzer group commander General Paul von Kleist, shortly after the Dunkirk evacuation, that halting the advance might have been a mistake. But whatever its cause, the effect of the halt order, particularly in delaying the advance on Dunkirk by 10th Panzer Division, would be critical to the survival of the BEF.

Although the Allies hoped to hold the Channel ports of Calais and Boulogne in addition to Dunkirk, Vice Admiral Ramsay sent the destroyer HMS *Venomous* to Calais on 21st May, to remove classified anti-submarine detection equipment and specialist RN personnel from the secret 'loop station' at Sangatte. While alongside in Calais under heavy air attack, the *Venomous* also embarked some 200 British refugees, 50 nurses from the Base Hospital, and four deliberately anonymous sacks containing platinum spinning jets worth over £1,000,000, hurriedly removed from the town's Courtaulds rayon factory in a clandestine operation organised by British Intelligence. On 22nd May, when Reynaud was quoted as saying "only a miracle can save France", and Churchill flew to France for a second time to meet the new French Commander-in-Chief, General Maxime Weygand, the RN manned many of the shallow-draught Belgian and Dutch schuyts moored on the Thames and in Poole harbour, in preparation for an evacuation. But on 22nd, as Calais was reinforced by a rifle battalion and a tank battalion, with two more rifle battalions landing the following day, 10th Panzer Division was only nine miles from the town, with their sights set on Dunkirk 30 miles beyond.

It became clear on 22nd May that Boulogne, not previously garrisoned by the British, was imminently threatened by the advance of 2nd Panzer Division. Vice Admiral Ramsay despatched demolition teams with 200 naval personnel and Royal Marines, to take charge of Boulogne docks, while the two Guards battalions evacuated from the Netherlands a week before were landed with an anti-tank battery, in the hope that Boulogne could be held. They joined 1500 men of the Auxiliary Military Pioneer Corps, who, cut off, had conducted a fighting retreat into the town, despite a lack of military training and small arms. Large numbers of wounded, refugees and the rear GHQ were evacuated on 22nd but the following day, German troops with tanks and artillery, supported by dive bombers, attacked in force, driving the over-matched defenders back and raking the port area with continuous small-arms, mortar and artillery fire, although this did not prevent naval demolition teams wrecking docks and harbour facilities. Realising that Boulogne could not be held, Ramsay despatched all the destroyers at his disposal and two, the flotilla leader HMS *Keith* (sunk nine days later off Dunkirk) and HMS *Vimy*, were already alongside on 23rd May when the evacuation order came, while others shelled German positions from seawards.

Destroyers went alongside Boulogne's quays in pairs, taking aboard wounded, British refugees, support troops and lastly fighting troops, while their main armament hotly engaged German artillery at very close range. The captains of both HMS *Keith* and HMS *Vimy* were killed on their bridges by machine gun fire as the ships embarked wounded; when they sailed, their places alongside were taken by HMS *Whitshed* and the AA destroyer HMS *Vimiera*, which took over 1100 troops with them when they departed, guns blazing at German artillery. They were replaced by HMS *Wild Swan* and HMS *Venomous* as the Germans closed in; both ships proved 4.7 inch naval guns were highly effective anti-tank weapons, obliterating German armour at point-blank range, while their lighter weapons, augmented by rapid rifle fire from their ships' companies and troops already embarked, successfully repelled advancing German troops as the ships took aboard another 1000 defenders. Another destroyer, HMS *Venetia*, waiting inside the harbour mouth for her turn to berth, was seriously damaged and set ablaze by seven heavy shells from German-manned coastal artillery attempting to sink her and block the port but, shrouded in smoke, she safely jettisoned her torpedoes and was extricated from the port stern first by a Sub Lieutenant, her other bridge officers having been killed or seriously wounded. HMS *Venomous* swiftly turned her 4.7 inch guns on the fort mounting the heavy artillery that had so nearly sunk her sister ship, rapidly blowing away large sections of the walls, which tumbled down the hillside, taking parts of the guns with them. When the *Wild Swan* and *Venomous* finally sailed, British troops were still resolutely holding the port area, while the Germans had withdrawn temporarily to regroup, enabling the destroyer HMS *Windsor* to steam into Boulogne without hindrance shortly before midnight, to embark the naval demolition teams and 600 Welsh Guards. Finally, HMS *Vimiera*, ordered back by Vice Admiral Ramsay to evacuate as many as possible of the remaining defenders, steamed into an eerily quiet Boulogne in the early hours of 24th May, her stealthy arrival lit by a full moon and the crackling fires of burning vehicles. She embarked 1400 British troops, together with Polish refugees and Jewish civilians, dangerously overloading the ship and making her so unstable that no more than five degrees of helm could be applied during her return to Dover, where she arrived at dawn, despite a German bomber missing her by only 20 yards on the return voyage. Even so, over 800 British troops from various units could not reach the quays and remained in Boulogne; they fortified the town's Gare Maritime and fought on until 1300 on 25th May, four and a half hours after the French commanding general surrendered Boulogne with its citadel and garrison of 6,000.

During the early morning of 24th, London told Brigadier Nicholson, commanding the four British battalions defending the contracting perimeter in Calais, they would be evacuated the following day. However, the French land commander, with fewer forces at his disposal in Calais than Nicholson, had this decision overturned, even though 1500 French naval gunners manning coastal batteries, having engaged the besieging Germans vigorously from first light, obeyed orders to spike their guns in the late morning and report aboard French ships in the harbour, which promptly evacuated them. Their elderly commandant, with some 50 volunteers, refused to comply and remained defending a strongpoint until Calais was finally overrun, although the commandant himself died from a heart attack on 26th May. On 24th, Allied destroyers bombarding German positions around Calais were subjected to very heavy air attack that sank HMS *Wessex* and the French *Chacal* and seriously damaged HMS *Vimiera* and the Polish *Burza*. Vice Admiral Sir James Somerville, then the Admiralty's Director of Anti-Aircraft Weapons and Devices, arrived in Calais overnight on 24th/25th May, aboard the destroyer HMS *Verity* under fire from heavy shore batteries, nominally to investigate using naval 12 pounder guns ashore as anti-tank weapons. However, he woke an exhausted Brigadier Nicholson to confirm the unwelcome news transmitted to Calais from the War Office two hours earlier, that his battalions would have to fight on, notwithstanding previous messages to the contrary, because the French command had ordered that there would be no evacuation of Calais and the British had to comply to maintain Allied solidarity. However, Somerville also conveyed a personal telephone message from the Prime Minister, received by the admiral before he left Dover, that it was essential for Nicholson to hold Calais for as long as possible, to delay advancing German units trying to cut off the BEF from Dunkirk. Although the AA destroyer HMS *Wolfhound*, was already alongside in Calais as a communications link, Somerville told Nicholson that both she and the *Verity* must sail before daybreak or be sunk. After the *Verity* sailed, Somerville organised an alternative shoreside communications link for Nicholson before leaving Calais in the *Wolfhound* shortly before dawn on 25th, having reached the obvious conclusion that it was far too late for 12 pounder naval guns to save Calais.

During the morning of 25th, Nicholson rejected surrender terms offered by the besieging Germans, who were anxious to take Calais without further delay and press on to Dunkirk, replying that if they wanted Calais they would have to fight for it. Savage fighting for the town paused again later when the Germans offered Nicholson a further opportunity to surrender, which he again refused, having received a message from Anthony Eden, Secretary of State for War, emphasising that defending Calais to the last was critical to the survival of the BEF. Notwithstanding the cruisers HMS *Arethusa* and HMS *Galatea* bombarding German positions on 26th May, the French commander surrendered Calais during that afternoon, leaving Nicholson and the surviving British troops little choice but to follow suit, nevertheless their stubborn resistance had further delayed the German advance on Dunkirk. During the night, the 200 ton requisitioned motor yacht *Gulzar*, once used by the Duke and Duchess of Windsor for their first wedding anniversary Mediterranean cruise, crept into Calais, having been hastily repainted as a hospital ship and sent by Vice Admiral Ramsay to embark wounded. Unaware that the burning town had already fallen, she secured alongside but was heavily fired on and cut her mooring ropes to make a rapid withdrawal, taking 51 British soldiers who jumped aboard from the town's eastern jetty as she passed.

During the night of 25th May, while Nicholson's brigade still held Calais, Anthony Eden informed the BEF commander, General Viscount Gort VC, of the War Cabinet's view that the army should fall back to the Channel coast for evacuation from Dunkirk, as the predominant consideration was to save as much as possible of Britain's main field army. But senior BEF commanders did not view the prospect of evacuation with confidence; on 26th May, as the French Prime Minister, Paul Reynaud, flew to London to meet with Churchill, Lt Gen Alan Brooke commanding II Corps, wrote: "It is going to be a very hazardous enterprise and we shall be lucky if we save 25% of the BEF!."[4] But Hitler's order to halt the Panzer formations after the British counter attack at Arras, together with the delay inflicted on the advance of 10th Panzer Division by the dogged defence of Calais, gave Lord Gort the time needed to withdraw into Dunkirk most of his army, together with large numbers of French troops at similar risk of encirclement, setting up a defensive perimeter before the Wehrmacht could reach the town.

Casualties and support troops had been withdrawn through Dunkirk from mid-May but at 1857 on Sunday 26th, the Admiralty ordered Vice Admiral Ramsay to commence Operation "Dynamo", the evacuation of the BEF, in the hope that up to 45,000 troops could be brought home in the two days envisaged before the Germans occupied Dunkirk and the beaches. However, Ramsay had anticipated the formal order by despatching 'personnel vessels', requisitioned passenger ships, and the Isle of Man packet *Mona's Queen*, already alongside at Dunkirk, was the first sailing to Dover under Operation "Dynamo", carrying over 1300 troops but, early on 29th as she returned, she was sunk a mile east of

---

4 Danchev, Alex and Todman, Daniel (Eds), (2001), *War Diaries 1939-1945, Field Marshal Lord Alanbrooke*, Weidenfeld & Nicolson, p.70.

Dunkirk by a magnetic mine; these, laid by Luftwaffe aircraft, were a constant threat throughout the operation. Her near sister, the naval-manned *Mona's Isle*, completed the first round trip early on 27th followed by a procession of similar vessels embarking BEF troops from Dunkirk harbour, after first unloading urgently needed cargoes of water in two-gallon cans, following destruction of Dunkirk's water supply. The port was relatively undamaged at that time and Ramsay made haste to berth personnel ships alongside the harbour quays to embark large numbers of troops swiftly while it was still possible, knowing the situation would not last when air attacks developed.

Ramsay had been working almost around the clock for days and was becoming exhausted but on 27th, he was joined in his headquarters tunnels under Dover Castle by Vice Admiral Somerville, whose energetic voluntary assistance allowed Ramsay to sleep for a few hours most nights, while six additional RN captains and commanders were added to his staff.

Ships using the direct route to and from Dover, along the coast to the west of Dunkirk, found themselves under damaging fire from German shore batteries around Calais, requiring Ramsay to establish two safer but longer routes through numerous offshore sandbanks; these routes were quickly surveyed and swept of mines. The anticipated heavy air attacks on Dunkirk began on 27th, progressively demolishing the town and port facilities, targeting evacuation vessels offshore, and sinking shipping alongside, choking the harbour with wrecks. Ramsay's plan to lift troops from Dunkirk's beaches needed to be implemented urgently, as no-one knew how long the defensive perimeter would hold, although the war diary of General Georg-Hans Reinhardt's XLI Panzer Corps says of British troops at this time: 'The enemy fights with determination and stays in his positions until the last moment; if he is expelled from one point, he appears a little later at some other and takes up the fight again.'[5]

During the afternoon of 27th, Captain William Tennant RN, appointed as Senior Naval Officer Dunkirk, went ashore from the AA destroyer HMS *Wolfhound* in the inner harbour with 162 naval personnel to organise evacuation from the beaches, which began that evening. Lack of small boats to ferry troops from the beaches to larger vessels offshore handicapped initial efforts by destroyers, the AA cruiser HMS *Calcutta* and an increasing number of paddle minesweepers, drifters and coasters, all using their own boats to ferry troops from the shore, a slow and inefficient process. But the outlook was better than

---

5 War diary of XLI Panzer Corps. Quoted in Thompson, Julian, (2008), *Dunkirk: Retreat to Victory*, Sidgewick & Jackson, p.217.

Ramsay and his staff might have feared; two weeks previously a call had gone out to owners of self-propelled boats between 30 and 100 feet in length to declare them to the Admiralty for "general naval purposes", while officers from the Small Vessels Pool and appointed agents scoured coastal and Thames-side boatyards and moorings, assessing small craft and requisitioning those suitable for service. In addition, the Commanders-in-Chief at Portsmouth and the Nore (Chatham) were identifying all manner of small craft: paddle steamers, car ferries, tugs, barges, lighters, lifeboats, naval picket boats, and oared cutters and whalers. In addition, a small number of newly developed 'Assault Landing Craft' (later known as LC(A)s) were available and eight of these were loaded aboard the cargo ship SS *Clan Macalister*, to be launched from her derricks and cranes off Dunkirk's beaches, effectively making her a prototype Infantry Landing Ship, or LS(I), a type of amphibious warfare vessel that later became indispensable.

While small craft were being assembled in England, Tennant reported to Ramsay that the ¾ mile long stone-built breakwater or mole at the eastern side of Dunkirk harbour was undamaged and that ships could berth there. The structure had not been designed for that purpose and had only a narrow wooden causeway built above it on wooden piles but berthing there would avoid rescue ships negotiating Dunkirk's increasingly wreck-strewn harbour and enable far greater numbers of troops to be embarked than was possible from the beaches. Tennant asked the master of the excursion vessel MV *Queen of the Channel* to attempt to secure alongside the seaward end of the mole to see if a large personnel ship could do so. The *Queen of the Channel* was successful, becoming the first of many, and she sailed early on 28th, having embarked over 900 troops, only to be bombed and sunk on the voyage to Dover, most of those aboard being rescued by other ships. Having proved embarkation from the mole, or east pier, to be a practicable proposition, Tennant's naval beach parties directed troops there, to form a seemingly endless but orderly queue shuffling forward along the narrow wooden causeway, to board the stream of personnel ships and destroyers ordered there by Ramsay. At a later stage, on 30th May, embarkation became so rapid that, for a while, troops moved along the causeway at the double.

On 28th, in response to Ramsay's urgent request, the Admiralty ordered every destroyer in the Western Approaches and Portsmouth commands to Dunkirk, while the auxiliary paddle minesweeper HMS *Brighton Belle*, formerly a popular south coast excursion ship for more than 30 years, struck a submerged wreck while returning from Dunkirk on 28th and sank stern first after her troops transferred to two other paddle steamers in company, the *Medway Queen* and

Sandown. By then, a thick pall of smoke, easily visible from Dover, was rising many thousands of feet over Dunkirk from the burning oil refinery and town. This gave some local respite from bombing, while several days of extensive cloud cover also helped to reduce the number and effectiveness of air attacks.

Luftwaffe operations were further disrupted by RAF Fighter Command deploying Spitfire squadrons on a large scale for the first time over France. The elegant fighter startled Luftwaffe pilots with its speed and manoeuvrability, although interceptions and subsequent aerial combats nearly always took place inland, unseen by troops on the beaches, giving rise to misplaced bad feeling that the RAF was not doing enough to protect them. This misconception has persisted in some quarters, with the question "where were the RAF at Dunkirk?" still being asked today. In fact, Fighter Command dedicated 16 squadrons to cover the evacuation during daylight hours, most pilots flying two or three sorties each day. The RAF lost 177 aircraft, 106 of them fighters, during the nine days of the Dunkirk evacuation and flew almost 2800 fighter sorties. RAF fighter operations were aided by the Government Code and Cypher School at Bletchley Park breaking the Luftwaffe's new Enigma 'Red' key on 22nd May and passing the resulting intelligence to the RAF in a special cypher via a Secret Intelligence Service (MI6) protected communications link. Further intelligence support came from the 'Y Service' signals interception and traffic analysis organisation, which also successfully jammed German dive bomber communications and supplied information from Luftwaffe intercepts that helped Ramsay's staff at Dover to control shipping off Dunkirk. The Royal Navy's Fleet Air Arm also operated over Dunkirk during Operation "Dynamo", using the obsolescent but still effective Skua dive bomber against German troops attacking the defensive perimeter, while its misconceived turret fighter derivative, the Roc, scored the type's only kill on 1st June, shooting down a Ju88. In addition, Swordfish and Albacore biplanes flew anti-submarine and anti-shipping patrols, as well as bombing advancing Wehrmacht units.

On 28th May King Leopold of Belgium surrendered with his army, against the wishes of his government, although the Belgian naval trawler *A4* already had brought to Britain the final 40 tonnes of the Belgian national gold reserves. The breaking of the Belgian line and their subsequent capitulation could have left a wide gap on the left flank of the Allied defensive perimeter but Lord Gort, advised by Lt Gen Alan Brooke, commanding II Corps, cancelled a planned counter attack and moved two divisions to fill the gap, after an aggressive British infantry patrol ambushed the staff car of a senior liaison officer with Army Group B on

25th May, and captured two highly classified German documents. One exposed German intentions to outflank the BEF by pushing through Belgian positions but Gort's rapid redeployment of British troops blocked this move and was key to the BEF's survival. The second, of less immediate tactical value, presented a strategic overview of the Wehrmacht's organisation and structure, which the War Office kept updated for the remainder of the war from intelligence provided by Bletchley Park's regular decrypts of Enigma signals traffic. BEF HQ at La Panne was linked to the War Office in London via an insecure cross-Channel telephone line and army staff officers maintained a level of security by using Indian dialects, in a precursor to the later and better known US practice of using native American Navajo speakers in the Pacific theatre.

German naval strength had been considerably reduced by significant warship losses during the Norwegian campaign and the most notable Kriegsmarine successes against Dunkirk evacuation ships came during the misty night of 28th/29th May, when 'Schnellboote', fast coastal torpedo boats known to the British as 'E(nemy)-Boats', operating out of Antwerp, torpedoed the destroyer HMS *Wakeful* shortly after midnight; she immediately broke in two and sank with the loss of all but one of the 640 soldiers on board and over 160 of her ship's company. About two hours later, the submarine U62 torpedoed the destroyer HMS *Grafton* and broke her back, fortunately all but 16 of her ship's company transferred to the personnel ship *Malines* and to the destroyer HMS *Ivanhoe* before the derelict *Grafton* was sunk by gunfire.

The Wehrmacht made a major effort to break into the Dunkirk perimeter on 29th May, leading to two days of fierce and costly fighting, particularly around the key town of Furnes where some units of Major General Bernard Montgomery's 3rd Division suffered severely, but the perimeter held along its entire length and the evacuation continued. On 29th alone, over 40,000 troops were taken off, the majority from the east pier, despite a significant number of ships being lost and many more damaged. The rate of attrition increased over the following days but without stemming the constant flow of rescue ships; as one vessel was sunk or disabled offshore, another took its place at the mole or off the beaches. The Luftwaffe offensive against evacuation ships was matched by similar attacks on the troops gathering in increasing numbers on the beaches and in the dunes but here bombers were less effective, particularly Ju87 Stuka dive bombers with their howling sirens, as their bombs penetrated deeply into the sand, which smothered the explosions and reduced casualties, although machine gun and cannon fire from strafing aircraft caused significant loss of life among the troops waiting patiently to embark, some up to their necks in water as the tide rose.

Around midday on 29th May, the first of the 'little ships' arrived, mainly larger power boats, often brought over independently from England by their owner/skippers, volunteers who had been "signed on" for a month's temporary naval service. They were pressed into immediate service off the beaches, collecting abandoned smaller boats, ferrying troops out to larger vessels and even transporting them directly to England, despite having to cope with air attack, as well as all manner of floating debris, derelict vehicles and other navigational hazards submerged at high tide. One boat was the 58 foot motor yacht *Sundowner*, owned and skippered by Charles Lightoller, formerly Second Officer of the RMS *Titanic* and the senior surviving officer of her sinking in 1912. Lightoller, aged 66, was retired by 1940 when the Admiralty requisitioned the *Sundowner* for Operation "Dynamo" but insisted on taking her to Dunkirk harbour himself, crewed by his eldest son and a sea scout. The *Sundowner* could officially hold only 21 but Lightoller packed in 127 soldiers, almost capsizing at Ramsgate when they began disembarking too enthusiastically. The *Sundowner*, now 108 years old, has been restored and is still afloat at the Ramsgate Maritime Museum, 80 years after Operation "Dynamo".

Notwithstanding the welcome arrival of such craft, the shortage of small boats to ferry troops from the shallows to larger craft offshore continued to slow the rate of evacuation from the beaches and most embarkations were still from the east pier. However, it occurred to several people at more or less the same time that makeshift jetties could be improvised from discarded army lorries. They were driven down the beaches to the sea's edge at low tide, arranged side by side in long lines, the largest vehicles farthest out, lashed together, weighted down with sandbags, their tyres shot out and planked over where possible, to form rickety jetties from which troops could embark directly onto smaller rescue ships that came alongside as the tide rose. Soon there were ten of these ramshackle structures along Dunkirk's beaches and this simple expedient significantly increased the rate of embarkation from the shore.

During 29th, Vice Admiral Ramsay despatched additional destroyers and trawlers and rescue ships berthed on both sides of the east pier but air attacks intensified during the afternoon, despite five RAF fighter squadrons engaging the Luftwaffe almost constantly within ten miles of Dunkirk. Several ships were bombed alongside the mole, including the destroyer HMS *Grenade*, which burned fiercely until a magazine explosion sank her, and the Isle of Man packet

Fenella, both of which were towed clear before they sank, to preserve access for other rescue vessels. The new large destroyer HMS *Jaguar* was bombed and disabled, being towed clear by another destroyer, HMS *Express*, which also took aboard her troops. The *Jaguar* later repaired her engines and restored her steering, returning to Dover at reduced speed. The large oil-fired Thames paddle steamer HMS *Crested Eagle*, an auxiliary AA ship, was sunk in particularly tragic circumstances at this time; she took aboard 600 troops and the crew from the sinking *Fenella* and cast off from the mole but was herself immediately hit by four bombs that ignited her fuel oil and wooden upperworks. About half those onboard died in the raging fires and many survivors suffered appalling burns; she was run ashore in shallow water west of Bray, where she burned out; 80 years later her twisted remains still can be seen at low tide.

During the morning of 29th, the SS *Clan Macalister* anchored in shallow water about 1½ miles off the beaches west of Dunkirk, and hoisted out six of her eight landing craft before three bombs quickly struck her, her large size – almost 7,000 tons – making her an obvious target. Naval vessels took off her troops and crew and she was abandoned, sinking on an even keel in water so shallow that her burning upperworks remained well above the surface, giving the impression that the ship was still afloat. She became a useful decoy over the next few days, providing an irresistible target for Luftwaffe bombers, tempting them away from smaller rescue ships, to waste tons of bombs on her burning hulk. Her six assault landing craft gave sterling service throughout Operation "Dynamo", proving the soundness of their concept and design; only three survived, including ALC5 which lifted over 2,000 troops from the beach at La Panne, while others not only ferried troops from the beaches but carried them directly across the Channel, before returning for more, operating over distances for which they were never intended.

The paddle minesweeper HMS *Waverley*, a former Clyde excursion ship, left Dunkirk in the afternoon of 29th with more than 600 troops aboard, but was attacked by 12 aircraft, taking a bomb through the stern that holed her bottom plating, quickly sinking her; over half those on board were lost despite survivors being rescued by the French destroyer *Cyclone*, the auxiliary AA paddle steamer HMS *Golden Eagle*, and several other vessels. In the evening, the personnel ship *Lorina*, a Southern Railway Channel Islands packet, approached Dunkirk harbour to embark troops but was struck amidships by four bombs that broke her back and split open her hull, leaving her hunched wreck grounded in shallow water, a jagged vertical crack several feet wide from upper deck to keel, aft of the second funnel. Nevertheless, seamen from the destroyer HMS *Winchelsea* boarded the abandoned derelict on 31st and released undamaged lifeboats from their davits, using them to ferry troops from the beaches to rescue ships offshore.

About the time the *Lorina* sank, the escort sloop HMS *Bideford* came as close inshore as the shallow waters off Bray dunes allowed and, under heavy air attack, used her own boats to collect previously abandoned small boats. She used them to embark mainly French troops but then was twice hit right aft, a bomb detonating one of her depth charges, blowing off 40 feet of her stern, causing serious casualties among those aboard and sinking landing craft ALC16 alongside. With much of her upper deck wrecked, the ship caught fire and was unable to steam or steer; she grounded when her magazine was flooded to prevent explosion, her troops being taken off by the minesweeper HMS *Kellett*. During the night, after she extinguished her fires, a towing line from HMS *Locust*, a river gunboat commissioned only two weeks earlier, was secured aboard the battered vessel before she refloated on the tide and took aboard over 400 French and British troops. The shallow-draught *Locust*, only half the tonnage of the *Bideford* and already carrying 620 troops from the beaches at La Panne, commenced towing around dawn on 30th. The towline parted several times but both ships reached Dover at mid-day on 31st after a remarkable display of determination and fine seamanship during a 32 hour channel crossing at less than three knots. The *Bideford* was under repair for 15 months but returned to service as a convoy escort, while the *Locust* immediately returned to Dunkirk and was back in the shallow waters off the Bray dunes during the night of 1st/2nd June, successfully engaging German artillery.

Before midnight on 29th, while the *Crested Eagle* still burned in the shallows, the 340 ton naval-manned schuyt *Patria*, approached the shore by the light of the paddle steamer's fires; her commander, a retired Lt Cdr, gently ran her aground on the soft sand, enabling columns of troops to wade out and scramble aboard. Remarkably, in little over two hours she took aboard 1200, including a number of badly burned survivors from the *Crested Eagle*, the *Fenella* and the destroyer *Grenade*. Although seriously overloaded, the *Patria* refloated on the tide, landing her passengers safely at Margate the following morning. The *Patria* herself later served as an Allied transport during the Normandy landings and returned to commercial service in 1945, being scrapped in 1989 after 52 years service.

Late on 29th May, the significant losses of destroyers during the operation so far and the ongoing risk to the remainder, prompted the Admiralty to order the withdrawal of the most modern destroyers of the H, I and J classes but Vice

Admiral Ramsay telephoned the First Sea Lord, Admiral Sir Dudley Pound, during the afternoon of 30th, protesting vigorously that these ships were vital to the success of the evacuation and, after a robust exchange, Admiral Pound agreed to their return.

During 30th, many more troops arrived on the beaches, including ever-increasing numbers of French soldiers and it was fortunate that coastal mist provided a temporary respite from air attack. However, with so many evacuation ships offshore, the task of coordinating the evacuation expanded to such an extent that Captain Tennant, as Senior Naval Officer Dunkirk, and his teams could not adequately control activities afloat as well as ashore, where his primary responsibility was to organise troop embarkations. Therefore, early on 30th May, the Admiralty appointed Rear Admiral Wake-Walker to take command afloat as Rear Admiral Dover, with two retired vice admirals, serving as acting commodores, to assist him. Wake-Walker needed to stay at sea off the beaches but was reluctant for any ship nominated as his flagship to be prevented from evacuating troops, so, first hoisting his flag in the minesweeper HMS *Hebe*, he moved from ship to ship, as availability and operations allowed. During the afternoon of 30th the French destroyer *Bourrasque* sailed from Dunkirk harbour heavily overloaded with French troops who had rushed aboard so rapidly, and in such numbers, that no head-count could be made. Steaming at 25 knots, she sought to avoid sandbanks and minefields, while keeping out of range of German shore batteries at Nieuport but was shaken by a violent mine explosion aft that left her dead in the water, listing to port and settling by the stern. There was panic among the troops aboard as the ship began to capsize; survivors were picked up by two drifters and the French torpedo boat *Branlebas* but the number lost in her sinking will never be known.

In the early hours of Friday 31st May, the French destroyer *Siroco*, sister-ship of the *Bourrasque,* was torpedoed and sunk by E-boats, her survivors picked up by the Polish destroyer *Blyskawica*, the coastal escort sloop HMS *Widgeon* and two trawlers. By morning, sea conditions had worsened, with rising surf hindering evacuation from the beaches until the afternoon when the weather moderated. Rear Admiral Wake-Walker decided to speed up embarkation of troops waiting at La Panne by beaching a ship as a jetty. The auxiliary paddle minesweeper HMS *Devonia*, a former excursion steamer launched in 1905, was selected following previous bomb damage, and was run ashore at speed but later suffered such severe damage from further bombing and German shellfire that she was abandoned where she lay, high and dry at low water. Her rusted ribs and lower hull plating are still visible 80 years later, protruding from the sand at low tides.

During 31st, 15 Belgian and eight French fishing vessels sailed from England to reinforce the Dunkirk rescue fleet, but the major development throughout the afternoon was the arrival from midday onwards of hundreds of the 'little ships', collected and assembled by the Royal Navy and towed or shepherded across the Channel in convoys to the beaches of Dunkirk. There were all sorts of unlikely small craft: cabin cruisers, motor launches, motor boats, yachts, Thames passenger launches, naval power boats, Thames sailing barges, fishing smacks, drifters, river lighters, Thames Estuary cockle boats and Norfolk wherries, most entirely unsuitable for the open sea but many manned by their owners or peace-time crews, or by volunteers from yacht clubs, riverside towns and fishing villages, others by naval personnel. At least 13 bore the traditional seaside boat's name of *Skylark*, while a shallow-draught Thames fire boat, the *Massey Shaw*, was manned by volunteers from the London Fire Brigade. Some boats came independently from as far west as Devon, brought voluntarily by their owners or skippers, including the 40 foot masted open launch *Lady Cable*, built in 1923 by Morgan Giles, a famous yacht and boat builder at Teignmouth. The *Lady Cable* was used pre-war for local excursions from Torquay harbour, including trips along the River Dart to view Britannia Royal Naval College on its dominating hilltop position overlooking the town of Dartmouth. She reportedly made two cross-Channel voyages from Ramsgate to Dunkirk; the first under her peacetime skipper when she made seven trips ferrying troops from the beaches to vessels offshore, before returning to Ramsgate with a full load of troops to refuel; the second in the charge of a 19 year old trainee, probably a Royal Navy midshipman, when she made four more ferry trips from the beaches to larger ships before finally returning on 2nd June loaded with French soldiers, having transported an estimated total of 630 troops to larger vessels offshore. Her young temporary skipper was certain that she was the last 'little ship' to leave Dunkirk's beaches. The *Lady Cable* still exists but ashore in South Devon and far from seaworthy as she awaits restoration.

Vice Admiral Ramsay and the Admiral Superintendent at Portsmouth, each sent across their own personal admiral's barges; sadly, neither of these spotless and gleaming craft survived the operation but the picket boat sent from the battleship HMS *Nelson* was more fortunate, returning under her own power, laden with troops. Most importantly perhaps for the troops on the beaches, was the arrival of the first of 18 tugs towing formations of open boats, including ships' lifeboats stripped from merchant ships in London's docks and ships' boats from warships under refit or repair in naval dockyards. The boats were lashed together to get them across the Channel to act as shallow-water ferries under the charge of junior naval ratings to take troops from the beaches to ships waiting offshore. On arrival off the beaches, the little ships were immediately subjected to air attack and to artillery fire from the east, which was beginning to menace rescue ships off the beaches, damaging the destroyer HMS *Vivacious*, while from the west, German shells were now reaching Dunkirk harbour itself.

During the morning of 31st, the BEF's II Corps was withdrawn from the contracting perimeter for evacuation and on arrival at Dover, Lieutenant-General Alan Brooke, commanding II Corps, briefed Vice Admiral Ramsay on the situation ashore, giving his view that evacuation would take several more days. The War Cabinet formally ordered a reluctant Lord Gort to return to London after handing over command of the remaining units of the BEF to Major General Harold Alexander of I Corps and, in late afternoon, Lord Gort boarded the minesweeper HMS *Hebe*. He waited on the bridge as the ship continued to embark troops until he transferred to a fast anti-submarine boat that took him to Dover. During the night, heavy shelling from German artillery to the east forced the abandonment of La Panne and troops there marched westwards to Dunkirk through a new defensive perimeter at the Franco-Belgian frontier to the east of Bray dunes.

Major General Alexander's instructions were to keep his three depleted divisions defending the perimeter alongside General Fagalde's French formations for as long as possible, hopefully until French intentions for evacuating their troops became clear. They were waiting in the hope that French Army units encircled at Lille and elsewhere might be able to withdraw into the Dunkirk perimeter, as some French III Corps troops had done two days previously. However, Alexander telephoned Anthony Eden, Secretary of State for War, saying that keeping British I Corps troops in the line for more than an additional day could jeopardise their evacuation. After an emergency meeting of the War Cabinet's Defence Committee, Alexander's written instructions were that he "should withdraw remaining British troops as rapidly as possible on a 50-50 basis with the French ... aiming at completion by the night of 1st/2nd June."[6] The French had wanted the Dunkirk perimeter to be defended indefinitely, as a thorn in the Wehrmacht's side, and were reluctant to organise their troops for

---

6 Sebag-Montefiore, Hugh, (2006 and 2015), *Dunkirk, Fight to the Finish*, Viking/Penguin, p.410.

evacuation. But, at a meeting of the Supreme War Council in Paris, Winston Churchill, Paul Reynaud and the French C.-in-C., General Weygand, agreed that the Dunkirk defensive perimeter would be held only until it was clear that no more French troops were able to reach it; later that evening news was received that the 35,000 French troops surrounded at Lille had surrendered. Nonetheless, Churchill in Paris and Alexander on the spot had to deal with the bone of contention that the majority of troops evacuated so far had been British. Churchill sought to diffuse bad feeling by making an emotional undertaking in his famously appalling French, that British and French troops would leave Dunkirk arm-in-arm and it was agreed that they would be evacuated on an equal basis.

On 31st, Alexander informed Admiral Abrial, the overall French commander of Dunkirk that, in accordance with his instructions from the War Cabinet, the remaining British troops would hold their allocated sector of the perimeter until midnight the following day – 1st June – and would then withdraw for evacuation during 2nd. At the same time, he made it clear that French troops could share on an equal basis the British shipping that would be waiting. But, during 1st, as British I Corps troops prepared to disengage from the perimeter, heavy losses inflicted on ships lifting troops already awaiting rescue, compelled Ramsay to restrict ship movements to the short Summer night to prevent further prohibitive losses from Luftwaffe attacks during daylight on 2nd. This essential constraint made clear that final evacuation could not be achieved in the planned timescale. Alexander, always pragmatic, accepted the delay and informed the French that I Corps troops would stay in the line until 2nd when they would pull out and be evacuated overnight on 2nd/3rd June by British ships which would also be available to French troops. Admiral Abrial and General Fagalde accepted this, confident that their troops could hold the contracting perimeter, although Fagalde decided in the morning of 2nd that most of his troops would not leave that night; he informed his subordinate French commanders but did not tell the British.

1st June was a costly day for the rescue ships. E-boats sank two anti-submarine trawlers around midnight and, after first light, Rear Admiral Wake-Walker's current flagship, the destroyer flotilla leader HMS *Keith*, already dangerously short of AA ammunition, became the focus of unrelenting Stuka dive bombing attacks that continued unabated for two hours until, disabled and burning, the *Keith* finally sank. Just before she rolled over, Wake-Walker transferred to MTB 102, which became his flagship, flying a makeshift Rear

The wreck of the destroyer HMS *Basilisk*, sunk by waves of Ju87 Stuka dive bombers and finally demolished with gunfire and torpedo by HMS *Whitehall*.

Admiral's flag made from a white dishcloth daubed with red paint. MTB 102 survived the war and has been comprehensively restored, so that, 80 years later, she not only appears as she did in 1940 but is in excellent running order. While the *Keith* was in her death throes, the fleet minesweeper HMS *Skipjack*, half a mile away, took several direct bomb hits in rapid succession and immediately capsized with about 275 embarked troops below decks, few of whom survived. The destroyer HMS *Basilisk* was ordered to stand by the *Keith* and finish her off if necessary but relentless attacks by nine Stukas dropping 45 bombs on and close around the *Basilisk*, almost broke the ship in two, totally disabling her and causing severe casualties. As attempts were made to take her in tow, more bombs sank her and she settled in shallow water with her upper deck awash; she was abandoned shortly after mid-day and the destroyer HMS *Whitehall* set her upperworks ablaze with gunfire and then torpedoed her hull for good measure. During the *Basilisk's* ordeal, the destroyer HMS *Ivanhoe*, having embarked some 1,000 troops from the beaches, sailed for Dover but was dive-bombed off Dunkirk harbour, disabled and set on fire, suffering 26 dead and many injured. The new destroyer HMS *Havant*, having already taken over 2,000 troops to Dover in three previous trips, left her berth in Dunkirk harbour, went alongside the drifting *Ivanhoe* with the fleet minesweeper HMS *Speedwell* on the other beam and took off the embarked troops before leaving at speed for Dover. However, the *Havant* was immediately attacked by a combination of high level, low level and dive bombers inflicting serious damage that killed many of the engine-room personnel and badly holed her hull, leaving her dead in the water. The minesweeper HMS *Saltash* and naval-manned motor yacht HMS *Grive* came alongside, one on each quarter, under continual air attack and took off all the troops. The *Saltash* took the destroyer in tow but she was taking in water rapidly, her list to port increasing until her remaining ship's company had to be transferred to the naval-manned schuyt *Aegir* before the *Havant* capsized and sank. HMS *Grive* was totally destroyed by a mine explosion off Dunkirk later in the day. HMS *Ivanhoe*, the destroyer HMS *Havant* had gone to assist, extinguished her fires, was towed back across the Channel by the tug *Persia* and repaired, only to be mined and sunk three months later.

Other ships lost to Luftwaffe bombers on 1st June included the river gunboat HMS *Mosquito*, the French destroyer *Foudroyant*, and the auxiliary paddle minesweeper HMS *Brighton Queen* carrying French colonial troops whose survivors transferred to the minesweeper HMS *Saltash* before the well-known former excursion ship sank. When the passenger steamer *Scotia*, carrying 2,000 French troops, was bombed and sunk in shallow water, the destroyer HMS *Esk* went alongside and took off 1,000 of her embarked troops, while vigorously engaging and driving off German aircraft that were machine-gunning survivors clinging to the hulk. Many other rescue ships suffered serious bomb damage and casualties: the destroyer HMS *Worcester* crept back to Dover at 10 knots with 46 dead and 180 injured; the oldest paddle steamer to take part in Operation "Dynamo", the auxiliary paddle minesweeper HMS *Westward Ho*, launched in 1894, became the target of 90 bombs while carrying French troops but survived without being hit, although she had casualties from strafing attacks, while the large personnel ship *Prague* suffered severe bomb damage aft, requiring most of the 3000 French troops aboard to be transferred to other ships. The listing *Prague* just managed to limp back across the Channel on one engine but had to be beached off the Kent coast to prevent her from sinking.

Notwithstanding the heavy losses, rescue ships continued throughout the day to evacuate large numbers of troops from the east pier, including over 2000 boarding the destroyers *Icarus*, *Vanquisher* and *Windsor*, across the Southern Railway steamer *Maid of Orleans* as she lay alongside the mole for six hours under frequent air attack, before sailing for Dover fully loaded with almost 2000 troops. A remarkable achievement was packing over 2,500 troops onto the Isle of Wight ferry *Whippingham*, seriously overloading the little paddle steamer until her sponsons were only a foot above water. Designed for the sheltered waters of the Solent, she was in very real danger of capsizing when German shells exploded close on her starboard beam and the troops aboard shifted rapidly to the port side, until they were urgently redistributed by ship's personnel, enabling her to reach Margate.

After daylight evacuations ceased, efforts in the few hours of darkness focussed on the east pier and the beaches at Malo-les-Bains but also utilised the west pier on the opposite side of Dunkirk harbour, hitherto less used because it was connected to the burning oil refinery that partially restricted access. Overnight on 1st, destroyers and large personnel vessels continued to sail laden with troops, while power boats and small drifters picked their way between the semi-submerged hazards of sunken wrecks and tangled debris to rescue soldiers from the near-derelict inner harbour. After sailing from Ramsgate, the requisitioned Thames tug *Fossa* embarked troops from the east pier, casting off before dawn towing a loaded motor boat and an open naval cutter full of French troops but was hit by a shell from German artillery, went ashore at Bray and had to be abandoned after the shallow draught river gunboat HMS *Locust* could not refloat her. Her troops were transferred to other vessels and the *Fossa* was eventually salvaged by the Germans. Large numbers of British and French fishing vessels and other small craft lifted troops from Malo beach, covered by accurate gunfire from HMS *Locust*, which tenaciously engaged Wehrmacht artillery from close inshore off Bray. However, by first light on Sunday 2nd June, the east pier was still crowded with troops awaiting rescue and Ramsay ordered the destroyers to continue to embark them until 0700, accepting the dangers of sailing in daylight but, protected by RAF fighter patrols, all the destroyers reached Dover safely.

As the remaining British troops disengaged and withdrew on 2nd for overnight evacuation, General Alexander made an urgent request for 'hospital carriers', small hospital ships for the short-term transport of seriously wounded, to pick up large numbers of stretcher cases from Dunkirk. His message was sent en clair, to enable the Germans to read it and leave the ships unmolested. The two selected were former cross-Channel passenger vessels, *Worthing* and *Paris*, both unarmed and already clearly painted as hospital ships in accordance with the provisions of the Geneva Convention: all white hulls, upperworks and funnels, with a broad green band around the hull, interspersed with large red crosses. They sailed from Dover separately during the afternoon of 2nd June, in the expectation that the Germans would respect their non-combatant humanitarian status under the Geneva Convention and allow them safe passage. However, 12 Ju88 bombers attacked the *Worthing*, the first to sail, nine bombs exploding close enough to damage her hull and engines, forcing her to limp back to Dover, reaching port just as the *Paris* sailed. When she was about 15 miles out from Dunkirk, the *Paris* was attacked by two or three bombers and disabled by near misses but a second attack by 15 Luftwaffe aircraft caused more extensive damage and she had to be abandoned. Her crew and the nurses aboard were towed in the ship's lifeboats by a motor boat until they were transferred to a tug and taken to Dover. The ship herself, listing heavily to starboard, was taken in tow by another tug but capsized and sank in the early hours of 3rd June. These attacks on ships that should have been protected by the provisions of international law, precluded more hospital carriers being sent and large numbers of seriously injured British casualties were left behind in Dunkirk with their medical staff, to fall into German hands.

During daylight on 2nd June, destroyers, personnel ships, minesweepers and many smaller vessels alongside in Dover, waited to sail for what they understood would be the final effort to evacuate the BEF and their French allies. To make optimum use of limited berths, sailings were arranged for ships to reach Dunkirk at allocated times during the night of 2nd/3rd June, embark the maximum number of troops in the shortest possible time and return to Dover before the Luftwaffe could interfere. These well-organised night operations went without hindrance from the Germans, although the historically fair weather and smooth sea conditions that had prevailed throughout the previous days of Operation "Dynamo" took a turn for the worse. An easterly wind made berthing difficult and small craft acted as berthing tugs to push destroyers and personnel vessels against the east pier. Rear Admiral Wake-Walker's diminutive flagship shared this mundane duty, holding the destroyer HMS *Venomous* close alongside against wind and tide, allowing her to embark 4th and 5th battalions of the Green Howards. Although both battalions were depleted in numbers, the *Venomous* embarked over 1300 men and was about to cast off, when a hail from the mole asked if she had room for some senior officers and their staff. General Alexander and his staff came aboard, having previously toured the beaches and east pier with Captain Tennant, checking all British troops were clear, and were initially accommodated in the captain's cabin until Alexander joined him on the bridge for the voyage back to Dover. General Alexander was among the last British soldiers to be evacuated from Dunkirk; the destroyer HMS *Winchelsea* sailed from Dunkirk at 2300 with only 152 stragglers aboard. At 2330 on 2nd June, Vice Admiral Ramsay received a succinct but very welcome signal from Captain Tennant in Dunkirk: "BEF Evacuated. "

Ramsay had expected to evacuate at least 10,000 French troops overnight on 2nd/3rd June, alongside the BEF, and sent over rescue ships with sufficient capacity to take that number and more but the French did not appear and many vessels, including several destroyers, waited for three hours or more before having to return to Dover empty. Nevertheless, personnel ships and small craft did embark some French troops from the west pier, despite General Fagalde's decision over 12 hours earlier not to evacuate his troops during the night of 2nd/3rd June. Dover and London had not been made aware of Fagalde's decision and neither had they been informed of increasing intensity in fighting around the perimeter and the consequential need for the French to hold back troops for a counter attack. British frustration with the non-appearance of the French army overnight on 2nd/3rd, resulted in Churchill sending a forthright and impatient message on 3rd, reminding the French commanders that rescue ships had waited throughout the previous night at considerable risk but to no avail, and encouraging them to ensure that the French army took advantage of the ships standing by during the coming night. The First Sea Lord, Admiral Sir Dudley Pound, and the Chief of the French Naval Staff, Admiral Francois Darlan (later to be assassinated in North Africa as a Vichy collaborator), agreed in an exchange of personal signals that the final evacuation would be completed that night, 3rd/4th June, Darlan estimating that there were 30,000 French troops remaining to be rescued. Vice Admiral Ramsay signalled the worn out ships and exhausted men under his command, explaining why another night's effort was required, saying: "We cannot leave our Allies in the lurch".[7]

After the BEF withdrew the German army increased pressure on the contracting Dunkirk perimeter, pinning French front-line soldiers in their defensive positions and fierce fighting developed at several points but the French troops stood their ground and even made a courageous, if poorly organised, counter attack. This staunch defence blunted the German assaults and relieved pressure on the perimeter, enabling Fagalde to allocate his units specific times during the night of 3rd/4th June to withdraw from their positions in the final defence lines, leaving only thin screens as rearguards until early on 4th, when they, too, could withdraw. After leaving the line, the French units were to make their way to the east pier and Malo-les-Bains beach, where rescue ships would be waiting. But the front-line French troops, who had borne the brunt of the fighting in the final hours of the defence of Dunkirk, found themselves

---

7 Chalmers, Rear Admiral W S, (1959), *Full Cycle, The Biography of Admiral Sir Bertram Home Ramsay KCB, KBE, MVO*, Hodder and Stoughton, p.93.

obstructed by large numbers of demoralised and seemingly leaderless French troops from second-line and support units in the town, on the beaches, and already queueing for rescue ships. Some French officers of front-line units, whose men were making an orderly withdrawal after fighting on the perimeter, accused these troops of skulking in the cellars of the town or in the dunes to avoid being sent into action when they had been needed most and then emerging only for evacuation at a time when fighting troops should have priority. As more and more French troops withdrew from the perimeter, joined finally by the last rearguards, the numbers to be evacuated increased beyond anything expected. Although the rescue ships had the capacity to lift them, time was running out to embark them before daylight and before the German army marched into an undefended Dunkirk.

It was reported that some French troops already awaiting rescue became disorderly and indisciplined, making it increasingly difficult for front-line troops to reach and board rescue ships.[8] The ships did their best; the Isle of Man packet *Tynwald* sailed with over 3,000 aboard, 1,000 more than her usual capacity, and the ubiquitous destroyer HMS *Venomous* took over 1,100. Finally, when the destroyer HMS *Shikari*, carrying French troops and the last large ship to leave Dunkirk, sailed as dawn broke at 0340 under heavy German artillery fire, over 30,000 French soldiers had to be left behind, many of them the courageous and well-disciplined front-line troops who had defended Dunkirk to the last. The final act of the *Shikari*'s captain was to sink three blockships in the entrance to the harbour after other large-scale destruction of Dunkirk's harbour facilities had been carried out by Anglo-French demolition teams. Admiral Abrial and General Fagalde embarked with their staffs in a French motor torpedo boat in the early hours of 4th June and sailed for Dover but the vessel was disabled after colliding with wreckage *en route* and the passengers completed their journey in the destroyer flotilla leader HMS *Malcolm*. Even after the departure of the *Shikari*, British power boats and other small craft continued to manoeuvre around sunken wrecks and dangerous obstacles in Dunkirk's ruined inner harbour, embarking as many French soldiers as they could until they eventually were forced to withdraw by small-arms fire at close range from advancing German troops. Intensive RAF fighter patrols protected vessels carrying French soldiers that continued to arrive in Dover and other south coast ports during 4th June, but Operation "Dynamo" was finally terminated at 1423 on 4th, although, on 5th, intensive air and sea

---

8 Sebag-Montefiore, Hugh, (2006 and 2015), *Dunkirk, Fight to the Finish*, Viking/Penguin, p.454.

patrols swept the Channel between Dover and Dunkirk for stragglers, bringing in another 1,000. An official total of more than 338,000 troops were evacuated, 198,000 British and 140,000 French, although there are other sets of statistics that give slightly different totals.

An astonishing number of troops had been evacuated, compared with the 45,000 originally hoped for, but a sobering fact was that many soldiers reached England without even their rifles and all the BEF's vehicles, tanks, guns, equipment and ammunition had been left behind, littering Dunkirk's beaches, foreshore and the streets of the shattered town, turning the whole area into a jumbled scrapyard of abandoned military detritus.

The Royal Navy absorbed similar professional lessons from Operation "Dynamo" as from the fighting in Norway's fjords. Firstly: ships operating in waters dominated by hostile air power were extremely vulnerable, particularly to dive bombers, and serious losses were inevitable if essential objectives had to be achieved. Secondly: fighter cover was indispensable to reduce losses to a tolerable level, although it was accepted that the RAF had done all it could over Dunkirk, given the limited number of fighters available and the fact that they were operating at the limit of their range. Thirdly: the AA armament of pre-war ships was largely ineffective, being too little and too light. It needed urgent augmentation with greater numbers of more powerful modern AA weapons such as 40mm Bofors and 20mm Oerlikon guns, although little could be done about the main armament of most ships being unable to elevate sufficiently to engage aircraft, until the development of dual-purpose medium calibre guns. However, from 1943, deployment of the Proximity, or VT, Fuse (invented in Britain and developed in the US), delivered reasonable prospects of success against attacking aircraft, as seen over southern England against V1 flying bombs and in the Pacific during 1944/45.

Up to 40,000 British troops in the Dunkirk area could not reach the beaches or town to be evacuated and became prisoners of war, suffering the privations of five years in captivity, including forced marches, ill-treatment and near starvation. Other British troops in the rearguard were not even offered the dubious privilege of becoming PoWs: on 27th May, 99 members of the Royal Norfolk Regiment at Le Paradis ran out of ammunition and surrendered to a unit of the Waffen SS 'Totenkopf' Division but were machine-gunned and bayoneted to death, although two survived wounded under the bodies of their dead comrades. Taken prisoner later and given medical treatment by regular Wehrmacht troops, they survived to give evidence at a 1948 war crimes trial that resulted in the SS unit commander being hanged. Another similar massacre occurred a day later when members of the Waffen SS Leibstandarte Division herded a similar number of British and French PoWs into a barn at Wormhoudt and hurled stick grenades into the building after them, following up with indiscriminate automatic fire, killing 91, for which no-one was ever held to account. Other similar incidents were alleged but could not be followed up due to lack of evidence from survivors or witnesses.

French confidence, morale and resolve had been severely shaken by the speed and success of the German *Sichelschnitt* assault and it became Winston Churchill's primary concern to keep the French in the war. He visited Prime Minister Paul Reynaud in France six times during May and June 1940, although it became increasingly unlikely that the French could be persuaded to fight on, particularly when the ageing, defeatist Marshal Philippe Petain became deputy Prime Minister. On 11th June, Italy's fascist dictator Benito Mussolini, added to French woes with a cynical and opportunistic declaration of war on France and Britain, with the intention of gaining a share of the spoils following the expected Allied defeat. However, to Mussolini's embarrassment, his armies advancing into southern France were stopped by resolute French resistance; he was additionally confounded soon after by Britain robustly refusing to surrender and choosing to fight on, come what may.

Notwithstanding the success of Operation "Dynamo", more than 140,000 British troops remained further south in France, as part of the Allied army facing the advancing Wehrmacht. This number included newly arrived reinforcements that continued to be sent to France between 7th and 14th June, with additional RAF fighter and bomber squadrons, in an attempt to bolster the French and keep them in the war. This force, known as 2nd BEF, was commanded by the bluntly out-spoken, stubbornly determined but highly competent General Sir Alan Brooke, recently brought home from Dunkirk after commanding II Corps, to be knighted, promoted and quickly sent back to France. General Brooke had no illusions about his chances of success, given the dire state of the French Army, and he stated his view forcefully to the War Office before and after he re-crossed the Channel, that no more British troops should be risked to support France. Following a meeting with the French Commander in Chief, General Weygand, Brooke told Winston Churchill by telephone on 14th that 'the French army was, to all intents and purposes, dead.'[9] Finally, on 14th, it was accepted that no more

9 Danchev, Alex and Todman, Daniel (Eds), (2001), *War Diaries 1939-1945, Field Marshal Lord Alanbrooke*, Weidenfeld & Nicolson, p.81.

British troops would be sent to France.

It became increasingly likely that France would sue for peace, no matter what support Britain provided, and evacuation plans – Operation "Cycle" – were put in place from 9th June for British formations most in danger of being isolated by the rapid German advance. The first to be considered was the 51st Highland Division and its attached units, commanded by Major General Victor Fortune, that was holding an unfeasibly broad front on the left of French IX Corps, part of 10th Army. IX Corps, unable to halt the German advance, was being continually outflanked and cut off from its intended lines of retreat. The situation was aggravated by the unrealistic expectations of General Weygand, who seemed unaware of, or unwilling to accept, the true gravity of the military position and placed unreasonable demands on 10th Army and the IX Corps commander, General Marcel Ihler. However, the British always remained conscious of the delicate politics involved and that the primary objective was to keep the French fighting. The 51st Division was an integral part of the French 10th Army and no matter how desperate the military situation became, the British were unwilling to summarily withdraw the Division without French command authority, which was not forthcoming, particularly from General Weygand.

Nevertheless, the British expected military necessity and political persuasion to convince the French to relent and authorise evacuation of 51st Division. Initial expectations were that they would be brought out through Le Havre, therefore on 9th June, General Fortune detached a force of about 4,000 men (known as 'Ark Force') to secure a line of retreat for the rest of 51st Division and defend the port. However, the bulk of the Division was quickly cut off from Le Havre by the speed of the German advance, and on 10th, it became apparent that the Germans had broken through to the coast. British ships seeking alternative evacuation points for 51st Division between Le Havre and Dieppe were fired on by German shore batteries that hit the destroyer HMS *Ambuscade*, while JU87 Stukas severely damaged two other destroyers, sister ships HMS *Boadicea* and HMS *Bulldog*, which had taken aboard over 100 members of the 51st Division and other evacuees from beaches near St Valery. The crippled ships survived only because a blanket of thick fog suddenly descended and obscured them, while the Divisional History of the 51st records one officer writing:

> As trained soldiers we were deeply impressed on board Boadicea by the conversational tone in which the Royal Navy restored order from brief chaos, so that within an hour of the explosion, without any voice being

raised above drawing-room pitch, the ship had collision mats over holes, the list had been reduced to a more or less even keel, wounded had received first-aid, the ship lightened, and the bulkheads shored up. As a show of casual ability to cope it impressed us to the point where speech failed.[10]

The alternative to Le Havre as an embarkation port for 51st Division was the fishing port of St Valery-en-Caux, east of Le Havre between Fecamp and Dieppe, and General Fortune withdrew there, accompanied by much of French IX Corps, establishing a defensive perimeter, while Admiral Sir William James, C.-in-C. Portsmouth, after visiting the coast personally, despatched destroyers, personnel vessels and coasters towing small craft. Over 50 wounded and a small number of fit troops were evacuated by the newly commissioned corvette HMS *Gardenia* early on 11th June, while naval parties put ashore reported that the bulk of 51st Division would be ready to embark during the night of 11th/12th. Rescue ships were therefore ordered offshore until nightfall because shipping and the burning town were under increasing Luftwaffe attack during daylight hours. However, the Wehrmacht was moving rapidly against little opposition from the French army; by midday on 11th, St Valery was within range of German artillery and by early afternoon, Rommel's 7th Panzer Division, advancing to the coast from Rouen, reached the cliff top heights of Le Tot, overlooking St Valery from the west. German artillery batteries, quickly established in this commanding position, dominated the harbour, its seaward approaches and the town itself. Nonetheless, General Fortune still had hopes of the Navy extricating his division during the night as he had finally, if obliquely, obtained French authority for its evacuation, not from the French army but from the French naval command at Le Havre. However, Fortune underestimated the serious threat posed to shipping by the German cliff top artillery batteries. Just after midnight, the first four of nine small craft entered the harbour in fog; all were sunk within minutes, while a storm of artillery fire forced the remainder to withdraw or suffer the same fate. The captain of the destroyer flotilla leader HMS *Codrington* (who had evacuated over 5,400 troops from Dunkirk a week earlier), reported that the beach and harbour were being swept by machine guns as well as artillery fire and that St Valery had become "quite impractical as a place for evacuation". She and the destroyer HMS *Saladin* moved three miles eastwards along the coast to the small village of Veules-les-Roses, where personnel ships, cargo vessels

---

10 https://51hd.co.uk/accounts/action_off_st_valery. Divisional History of 51st Highland Division – Viewed Jan 2020

and schuyts waited with ten small French vessels, picking up troops who had descended precipitous chalk cliffs 300 feet high to reach the beach, some being killed, or incurring serious injuries in doing so, and others who had made their way under fire along the beach from St Valery. They were ferried out to larger vessels, mainly in ships' boats, but at 0930, long after dawn, German shellfire from the west was joined by new batteries, positioned to the east above Veules. This lethal concentration of German artillery fire sank the French auxiliary naval patrol vessel *Cerons* 300 yards offshore in shallow water – her wreck still can be seen at low spring tides – and hit the RN-manned schuyt *Twente* several times, fortunately on the waterline, making her roll over and quickly sink before her cargo of petrol and ammunition exploded. Another schuyt, the *Kaap Falga*, was damaged, as was the personnel ship *Duke of York* and the cargo ship *Guernsey Queen*, while a grounded schuyt, the naval-manned *Hebe 2*, already damaged by shellfire, was unable to refloat before being captured by German soldiers advancing along the beach. This forced the rescue ships to withdraw, taking with them 2,137 British and 1,184 French troops, a total of 3,321 evacuated in difficult circumstances.

In St Valery, General Fortune prepared to attack the German artillery batteries on the Le Tot cliff top heights above and to the west of the town in the hope that silencing them would enable his division to be evacuated the next night but his hopes were dashed when General Ihler surrendered the town and some 30,000 troops of IX Corps at 0800. A furiously angry General Fortune initially refused to comply with Ihler's order to surrender but 51st Division's position was untenable; they were very short of ammunition and all French troops had ceased fire, allowing the Wehrmacht into the burning town without hindrance. He had no choice but to cancel the Highlanders' assault on the German artillery and reluctantly surrender the remaining 8,000 men of the 51st Division just after 1030 on 12th June. However, the 4,000 men detached from the Division as 'Ark Force' to defend Le Havre, were successfully evacuated from the port on 12th and 13th, in company with another 7,300 British troops, shortly before the Wehrmacht entered the city, the last ships sailing at 0500 on 13th. Several of the personnel vessels involved, including the *Lady of Mann*, *Canterbury* and *Tynwald* were veterans of the Dunkirk evacuation.

The last of Churchill's six meetings with Reynaud was on 13th June, when Churchill flew to Tours, then the latest temporary seat of the French Government, for a meeting of the Allied Supreme War Council. Having landed on the bomb-damaged airfield in a thunderstorm, the British party was left to its own devices and had to borrow a car to get to the meeting in the Prefecture, nevertheless arriving some time before the French Government. When the French did arrive, they were profoundly dispirited, appearing to focus only on the possibilities of an armistice with Germany. But this would require Britain to release France from the specific obligation enshrined in their joint agreement for neither nation to seek a separate peace, something that Churchill was not prepared to do in any circumstances and the meeting achieved nothing before Churchill flew home that evening. Another meeting was planned to take place three days later but was cancelled by the French.

Winston Churchill's determination to do all in his power to support France and keep the nation fighting began to soften after the loss of the bulk of the 51st Highland Division, for which he blamed the French, saying at a meeting of the War Cabinet during the afternoon of 12th, that the French 'had let us down badly'[11] and that British commanders in the area should not accept any further orders from them. After it was finally agreed on 14th June that no more British troops would be sent to France to prop up the crumbling French army, it fell to General Sir Alan Brooke to persuade the War Office and particularly Churchill himself, that all British troops already in France should be evacuated without further delay, to avoid their loss in the event that the French military collapse became a sudden political capitulation, which the presence or absence of British troops was unlikely to affect. Brooke's fears were realised on 17th June when Petain announced a ceasefire, without first informing the British, to allow him to negotiate an armistice but Brooke, fortunately anticipating this eventuality, had already withdrawn RAF ground crews and large numbers of support troops with their equipment to the nearest French ports, nominally to rationalise 2nd BEF's lines of communication but, in reality, to facilitate their evacuation when approval was forthcoming.

Following completion of the Operation "Cycle" evacuation from Le Havre on 13th June, plans were finally approved as Operation "Aerial", to evacuate the large number of British troops already in, or withdrawing to, major French ports further south, commencing on 15th. Initially, 133 ships of all types, from ocean liners to coasters, were allocated to embark troops and equipment, while, in addition, a large fleet of fishing vessels and other small craft was assembled in south coast ports of Devon and Cornwall in case it became necessary to use minor French ports or to bring troops off beaches.

---

11 Sebag-Montefiore, Hugh, (2006 and 2015), *Dunkirk, Fight to the Finish*, Viking/Penguin, page 481.

At Cherbourg, the task of evacuating more than 30,000 troops and large quantities of equipment was considered particularly challenging, given the limited time available after Petain's sudden announcement of a ceasefire and the likelihood of imminent French surrender. Nevertheless, in four days from 15th June, all personnel, more than 200 artillery pieces and AA guns, over 2,000 vehicles (including 22 tanks) and 45 tons of stores were successfully evacuated in over 50 different ships from ocean liners to coasters. However, 1,200 vehicles remained and these were burned, immobilised or pushed off the quaysides. In the early afternoon of 18th June, the last troops departed in three personnel ships, leaving another, the *Manxman*, to bring out senior naval and military staff and the rearguard, whose men quickly set up their Bren and Lewis light machine guns on her decks, as a makeshift defence against Luftwaffe attacks. By late afternoon the port came under artillery fire from the advancing Wehrmacht and the *Manxman*, wreathed in smoke from burning British army lorries, cast off hurriedly, going astern to avoid the wreckage of vehicles that had been dumped off the quays. As she departed, Cherbourg shook to huge explosions as demolition charges wrecked docks and port facilities, toppling cranes into harbour basins, and destroying the French submarine *Roland Morillot*, almost ready for launching. With Rommel's 7th Panzer Division less than three miles away, the teams embarked in the destroyer HMS *Sabre* and the brand new escort destroyer HMS *Fernie*, completed only two weeks earlier. The *Fernie* became the last ship to leave Cherbourg, after returning alongside to collect some newly arrived British troops, preventing them from becoming PoWs.

Evacuation from St Malo of an estimated 28,000 troops, including the recently arrived 1st Canadian Division, began early with two personnel ships landing 2,500 at Southampton on 15th June, while other personnel ships, freighters and naval-manned schuyts loaded with troops sailed on 16th and 17th. The destroyer *Wild Swan*, arrived early on 17th with naval demolition teams from Portsmouth, having called at Jersey, requisitioning an additional seven small cargo vessels and bringing St Helier Yacht Club volunteers to assist with the St Malo evacuation. This was largely completed by nightfall on 17th but on 18th two French tugs sailed for Plymouth with civilian evacuees, while the demolition teams, having wrecked dock gates, port infrastructure and oiling facilities, embarked with some stragglers in the small Jersey harbour launch *Duchess of Normandy* and the even smaller Jersey Rescue Boat *RFC113*; both were overloaded but sailed for Jersey in a force six wind, as the Wehrmacht entered St Malo.

On 15th, a major effort began at Brest to evacuate an estimated 23,000 British troops. Already alongside were three cargo ships that had arrived on 14th carrying artillery and vehicle reinforcements for 2nd BEF; these ships were not unloaded and returned to England with their cargoes intact, having embarked such troops as they could accommodate on their upper decks and in any other available spaces. The personnel ships *Canterbury*, *Lady of Mann* and *Manx Maid*, began loading more than 6,000 troops on 15th but Luftwaffe minelaying delayed their sailing until the following afternoon. It became clear after 13,500 troops had departed, that the initial estimate of troops in Brest had been too low, as over 18,000 remained and a wide variety of vessels were employed to evacuate them. These ranged from the large, graceful, three-funnelled P&O liner *Strathaird* that swiftly embarked 6,500 troops and sailed for Plymouth, to the collier *Blairangus*, which discharged her cargo of coal and immediately embarked 1,200 troops, whose passage to Falmouth in her hold spaces must have been dirty and uncomfortable. The heavy cargo vessel *Bellerophon*, sent out to save vehicles and artillery, managed to load 36 guns and four RAF lorries loaded with classified material before time ran out and she had to sail, the remaining guns, vehicles and equipment being destroyed on the quayside. The personnel ship *Ulster Monarch* arrived to land French and Polish troops but the 400 Poles elected to stay aboard and returned to England when she sailed late on 17th, carrying British rearguard troops. The destroyer HMS *Mackay*, having taken charge of organising shipping in Brest roadstead, followed with senior naval and military personnel, while British and French demolition teams wrecked harbour facilities, scuttled the British freighter *Dido*, dry-docked for repairs, the damaged French destroyer *Cyclone*, under repair after being torpedoed by an E-boat off Dunkirk, and four French submarines in dockyard hands: *Achille*, *Agosta*, *Ouessant* and *Pasteur*, the first two drydocked and partly dismantled. Two trawlers remained to pick up stragglers, transferring them to the Belgian passenger vessel *Prinses Josephine Charlotte* waiting offshore, before she too departed on 18th, leaving the destroyer HMS *Broke* to sail with the demolition teams on 19th June.

The powerful new French battleship *Richelieu*, under construction at Brest and almost complete, put to sea under air attack on 19th, shortly before the port fell, carrying 250 midshipmen from the Ecole Navale and a substantial shipment of gold from the Bank of France, sailing to Dakar in French West Africa, which later declared for the collaborationist Vichy government, when the still unfinished *Richelieu* became a thorn in the side of the Allies until the end of

1942, when all Vichy French ships joined the Allied cause and she sailed for an extensive refit in the US.

At Nantes, 30 miles up the River Loire from St Nazaire, BEF stores were withdrawn on 15th and 17th in five colliers still loaded with most of their cargoes of coal. Evacuation from the area then continued from St Nazaire at the river's mouth, where there were an estimated 44,000 British troops and large quantities of military vehicles, equipment and stores. Another brand new escort destroyer, HMS *Berkeley*, completed only ten days earlier, brought a naval embarkation team on 16th, when four large troopships, former ocean liners, also arrived: the Cunard-White Star *Georgic*, the Canadian Pacific *Duchess of York* and the Polish Gdynia-Amerika Line *Batory* and *Sobiesky*, which took aboard 17,000 troops between them and sailed that night with a destroyer escort. The hospital ship *Somersetshire* followed just after dawn, as two more ocean liners, Cunard's *Lancastria* and the Orient Line's *Oronsay*, anchored in the Loire estuary. Destroyers and smaller vessels transferred troops and evacuees from the port and the *Lancastria* initially kept a tally of the numbers embarking but, as more and more arrived on board, the recording system broke down; the final number is not known with any certainty and estimates vary from 7,500 to 11,000. The ship's master was reportedly overheard ordering embarkation to cease after the next boatload when he was told there were already 6,700 aboard; troops, RAF personnel and British civilians, including women and children, in addition to 330 crew. The *Lancastria* and *Oronsay* were to have sailed together but in the early afternoon, Luftwaffe attacks developed and a bomb partially destroyed the *Oronsay*'s bridge but without endangering the ship. Another air raid in the mid-afternoon targeted the *Lancastria*, hitting her with four bombs, one of which was said to have gone down her funnel, the others penetrated the upper deck, blowing large holes in the ship's side and setting her on fire. Down by the bows, she listed to port, until she was on her side, starboard propeller above water, then capsized and sank, only 20 minutes after the bombing. Luftwaffe aircraft strafed survivors struggling in thick fuel oil and it was reported that some tried to ignite the floating oil but, mercifully, were largely unsuccessful. Some 3,700 survivors were picked up by several ships, including the destroyers HMS *Beagle* and HMS *Havelock*, which took over 1,000 between them and the damaged *Oronsay*, which rescued over 1,500. The final loss of life will never be known, estimates varying from under 3,000 to nearly 7,000, but is likely to have been at least 4,000, making the sinking of the *Lancastria* on 17th June the worst disaster in British maritime history.

Despite this tragedy, the evacuation from St Nazaire continued, although a cargo ship, the *Teiresias*, was also bombed and sunk, fortunately with only one casualty. In the early hours of 18th, the hospital ship *Dorsetshire* sailed, followed during the day by a convoy of eight large cargo vessels, carrying about 3,000 troops each, even though they were intended as vehicle transports. One of these ships was the almost new fast freighter *Clan Ferguson*, which later became a mainstay of Malta convoys, taking part in no less than 11 before she was sunk in August 1942 when part of the vital Operation "Pedestal" convoy. Another was the previously bomb-damaged *Floristan* that was targeted by a Ju88 bomber during the night; the *Floristan's* master handled his ship skilfully, avoiding the bombs, while army bren-gunners aboard opened fire enthusiastically and accurately, shooting down the bomber, cheered on by other ships in the convoy. Also, on 18th, the trawler HMS *Manor* evacuated senior naval staff, while General Sir Alan Brooke and his staff had an uncomfortable passage to Plymouth on another, the *Cambridgeshire*, her decks still slimy with oil from rescuing survivors of the *Lancastria*. Finally, after 54,000 troops had been evacuated, operations terminated with the departure of the cargo ship *Harpathian* at 1100 on 18th June; although many vehicles and military stores were destroyed, much was abandoned. However, in response to intelligence reports, five British destroyers returned the following day to successfully embark 2,000 newly arrived Polish troops for Plymouth.

The unfinished French battleship *Jean Bart*, sister ship of the *Richelieu* at Brest, was under construction at St Nazaire but even further from completion, with only half her propulsion machinery and armament installed. Nevertheless, after days of round the clock working she was made ready for sea early on 19th and, although damaged by Luftwaffe bombers as she sailed, she escaped to Casablanca before German forces occupied St Nazaire, having declined a Royal Navy offer to escort her to a British port. She remained at Casablanca incomplete but was seriously damaged by US forces during the 1942 Operation "Torch" invasion and not completed until after WW2.

Further south at La Pallice, were RAF maintenance personnel and AA gun crews with their weapons and, on 17th June, two requisitioned cargo ships embarked all the British servicemen, some 2,300, together with civilian evacuees, but were unable to load most of the guns and heavy equipment before sailing in the early hours of 18th. On 19th, following intelligence reports of Polish troops approaching the port, the cargo ship *Alderpool* manoeuvred around numerous wrecks in the harbour to embark all 4,000, sailing at dawn on 20th, as French demolition teams began to destroy port facilities, sink remaining shipping and set fire to the oil stocks. On 22nd, the destroyer HMS *Vanquisher* put in to La Pallice, followed on 23rd by the cargo ship *Clan Ross*; neither found any further troops in the burning port.

By 16th June, the French government had moved to Bordeaux and the cruiser HMS *Arethusa* was sent to Le Verdon at the mouth of the Gironde estuary, while the escort destroyer HMS *Berkeley*, sailed up river to Bordeaux to provide communications between the governments. A cargo vessel with the unlikely name of *Rhineland* was requisitioned at Bordeaux and sailed for Falmouth on 17th, carrying British nurses and troops, while on 19th some 900 British civilian evacuees left in five Dutch vessels. Polish and Czech troops embarked in two Belgian ships, while HMS *Arethusa* took aboard 250 civilian evacuees, including the Polish president, Wladyslaw Raczkiewicz and staff from the British Embassies in Brussels and Paris, sailing for Plymouth on 20th. The personnel ship *Royal Scotsman*, with the fast freighter *Clan Ferguson*, back in French waters after landing troops from St Nazaire, took aboard more than 3,800 Polish troops and sailed for Liverpool on 22nd, while other vessels were diverted further south to Bayonne and St Jean-de-Luz. The destroyer HMS *Beagle*, which took over the communications link on 20th, sailed from Bordeaux on 23rd, carrying more than 80 naval and military evacuees, together with important equipment and demolition stores, while the freighter *Delius*, escorted by HMS *Berkeley*, left Le Verdon carrying the final 2,000 troops from the area. On 24th, the French scuttled the incomplete large sloop *Beautemps-Beaupre* in the Gironde to prevent her capture by advancing German forces.

The concentration of shipping further south was necessary for the evacuation of a large proportion of the Polish army that had continued fighting in France under their Commander-in-Chief, General Wladyslaw Sikorski, after the invasion and occupation of their own country by Nazi Germany and the Soviet Union. Several thousand Polish soldiers had been evacuated previously from St Nazaire, Bordeaux and other French ports during Operation "Aerial" but many units, fighting on while the French army disintegrated around them, could not reach embarkation ports. Determined not to surrender, the Polish units maintained their cohesion and customary high standards of morale and discipline as they withdrew in good order down the length of France, fighting when and where necessary, finally reaching the Atlantic coast of the Basque country, close to the Spanish border. The port initially identified for their evacuation was Bayonne but that soon changed to the smaller town of St Jean-de-Luz, with its sheltered natural harbour, where they waited with nearly 2,000 Polish Air Force personnel.

Appropriately, two Polish troopships, the passenger liners, *Batory* and *Sobiesky*, with a nominal maximum capacity of 3,000 troops each, were first to anchor off the port, having returned from the St Nazaire evacuation. Local fishing boats ferried to the ships some 9,000 of their compatriots, mainly soldiers and airmen but also Polish diplomats and government officials, as well as some French who wanted to continue the fight abroad. The *Batory* and *Sobiesky* sailed for Plymouth on 21st June and the following day another troopship, the almost new P&O *Ettrick*, arrived and embarked about 1,100 British evacuees, together with 300 Polish troops transferred from the cruiser HMS *Galatea*, arriving from Le Verdon. The *Galatea* then embarked the British ambassador, together with the Canadian and South African ministers with all their staffs and sailed for Plymouth in the early hours of 24th, being replaced at St Jean-de-Luz by the AA cruiser HMS *Calcutta*. Before the *Ettrick* sailed for Plymouth on 24th, she took aboard the exiled King Zog of Albania and his family who had been living in France since the Italian invasion of his country in April 1939. As the *Ettrick* departed, another troopship, the large and elegant Blue Star line passenger ship *Arandora Star*, replaced her, embarked 4,000 Polish army and air force personnel – well beyond her normal capacity – and sailed on 24th, her size, draught and the state of the tide causing some difficulty in the shallow harbour. Nine days later, having delivered her Polish passengers safely to England, the *Arandora Star*, by then carrying German and Italian internees from Liverpool to Canada, was torpedoed and sunk by U47 with heavy loss of life. The much smaller freighter *Kelso* arrived in St Jean-de-Luz harbour on 24th and continued to embark Polish servicemen, joined by two other cargo ships, the *Baron Kinnaird* and the *Baron Nairn*. All three ships sailed in the early afternoon of 25th, carrying British refugees and more than 3,200 Polish personnel between them, as German artillery was sighted setting up on a hill overlooking the harbour entrance. The evacuation from St Jean-de-Luz was made easier by overcast weather conditions restricting large scale interference from the Luftwaffe, although the freighter *Clan Ross* was bombed and damaged on passage to St Jean-de-Luz from La Pallice, forcing her return to England. Sadly, the conclusion of Operation "Aerial" was marred by a night collision off the Gironde between the AA cruiser HMS *Calcutta* and the destroyer HMCS *Fraser*, when the Canadian ship was cut in two and sunk; both ships suffering serious casualties. Overall, 211,000 people were evacuated from French ports during the 11 days of Operation "Aerial", including 140,000 British, 24,000 Polish, 17,000 French and 5,000 Czech servicemen, the balance being civilian evacuees.

On 16th June, as Operation "Aerial" got underway, last ditch diplomatic efforts continued in an effort to keep France fighting. The seemingly imminent capitulation of France and its government's inability to offer any policies for the continuation of the war, led to the British War Cabinet approving an astonishing offer to be made to France. This was to unite the British and French nations as one state, the people of both countries having common citizenship. That such an extraordinary proposal should have been put together and approved so quickly indicates the paramount importance attached by the British Government to keeping France in the war and the lengths to which the War Cabinet was prepared to go to try to achieve this. Britain's proposal was presented to Reynaud by the French War Minister, Major General Charles De Gaulle, but despite it gaining Reynaud's support, the French cabinet rejected it during the evening of 16th. Reynaud resigned as Prime Minister and was replaced by Petain, who immediately began preparations to surrender to the Germans, broadcasting to the French people on 17th that France would stop fighting while he negotiated an armistice. De Gaulle flew back to England to lead the exiled Free French forces, who fought the Axis throughout the remainder of the war. He made a radio broadcast on 18th, exhorting the French to continue the fight against Nazi Germany, later leading to the collaborationist Vichy French government sentencing him, in absentia, to death for treason. On 22nd June, France accepted and signed a harsh armistice that became effective after midnight on 25th June, exactly one month after Operation "Dynamo" began.

Overwhelmed by self-satisfaction and wallowing in vindictive pleasure at the depth of France's humiliation, a jubilant Adolf Hitler expected Britain to follow the French example and seek an armistice. As the flattery and adulation of his fawning acolytes fed his hubris, Hitler dismissed the growling defiance and eloquent scorn of Winston Churchill, failing to realise the significance of the Royal Navy's control of the sea that had snatched more than half a million mainly fighting soldiers from his grasp, confirmed in the British an indomitable determination not to give in, and sowed the seeds of his own final defeat. He also dismissed the English Channel as merely a wide river, a narrow strip of water of no significance, failing to realise that Britain's moat, having saved its army, would foil his ambition to create a 'thousand-year Reich'.

Bibliography

Printed Sources

Beevor, Antony, (2012), *The Second World War*, Weidenfeld & Nicolson.

Brann, Christian, (1989), *The Little Ships of Dunkirk*, Collectors' Books,

Bush, Captain Eric, (1958), *Bless Our Ship*, George Allen and Unwin.

Chalmers, Rear Admiral W S, (1959), *Full Cycle, The Biography of Admiral Sir Bertram Home Ramsay KCB, KBE, MVO*, Hodder and Stoughton.

Chesneau, Roger (Ed), (1980), *All the World's Fighting Ships 1922-1946*, Conway Maritime Press.

Cooksey, Jon, (2001), *Calais 1940, A Fight to the Finish*, Leo Cooper.

Couhat, Jean Labayle, (1971), *French Warships of World War II*, Ian Allan.

Danchev, Alex and Todman, Daniel (Eds), (2001), *War Diaries 1939-1945, Field Marshal Lord Alanbrooke*, Weidenfeld & Nicolson.

Hinsley, F H et al, (1979), *British Intelligence in the Second World War, Vol 1*, HMSO.

Jackson, Robert, (1976), *Dunkirk, The British Evacuation, 1940*, Cassell.

Jenkins, Roy, (2001), *Churchill*, Macmillan.

Jordan, John and Dumas, Robert, (2009), *French Battleships 1922-1956*, Seaforth Publishing.

Jordan, J and Moulin Jean, (2015), *French Destroyers 1922-1956*, Seaforth Publishing.

Knowles, David J, (2000), *Escape From Catastrophe, 1940 Dunkirk*, Knowles Publishing.

Lenton, H T, (1998), *British and Empire Warships of the Second World War*, Greenhill Books.

Levine, Joshua, (2019), *Dunkirk and Operation Fortitude*, William Collins.

Lord, Walter, (1983), *The Miracle of Dunkirk*, Allen Lane.

Mace, Martin (Ed), (2017), *The Royal Navy at Dunkirk*, Frontline Books.

Macintyre, Captain Donald, (1961), *Fighting Admiral, The Life and Battles of Admiral of the Fleet Sir James Somerville GCB GBE DSO*. Evans.

McCarthy, Peter and Syron, Mike, (2002), *Blitzkrieg. The Rise and Fall of Hitler's Panzer Divisions*, Constable.

Ministry of Home Security, (1940), *Silhouettes of German Aircraft*, HMSO.

Moore, Robert J and Rodgaard, John A, (2010), *A Hard Fought Ship, The Story of HMS Venomous*, Holywell House.

Morton, Andrew, (2015), *17 Carnations*, Grand Central Publishing.

Murland, Jerry, (2016), *Retreat and Rearguard, Dunkirk 1940, The Evacuation of the BEF to the Channel Ports*, Pen and Sword.

Ohler, Norman, (2016), *Blitzed: Drugs in Nazi Germany*, Allen Lane.

Pearce, M J and Porter, R (Eds), (2012), *Fight for the Fjords; The Battle for Norway 1940*, University of Plymouth Press.

Plummer, Russell, (1990), *The Ships That Saved An Army*, Patrick Stephens.

Preston, Antony, (1971), *V and W Class destroyers, 1917-1945*, Macdonald.

Ranger, Alan, (2017), *Dunkirk 1940 Through a German Lens*, Stratus.

Sebag-Montefiore, Hugh, (2006 and 2015), *Dunkirk, Fight to the Last Man*, Penguin.

Simpson, Michael (Ed), (1995), *The Somerville Papers*, Scholar Press for the Naval Records Society.

Stone, William, (2009), *Hero of the Fleet*, Mainstream Publishing.

Symonds, Craig L, (2018), *World War II At Sea; A Global History*, Oxford University Press.

Takle, Patrick, (2009), *The British Army in France After Dunkirk*, Pen and Sword.

Thompson, Julian, (2008), *Dunkirk: Retreat to Victory*, Sidgewick & Jackson.

Williams, David L, (2002), *Paddle Steamers*, Ian Allan Publishing.

Winser, John de S, (1999), *BEF Ships, Before During and After Dunkirk*, World Ship Society.

Winton, John (Ed), (1967), *Freedom's Battle, Vol 1: The War at Sea 1939-45*, Hutchinson.

On-Line Sources

https://codenames.info/operation/ordnance/ – viewed Dec 2019

http://www.naval-history.net/xDKWW2-4005-14MAY02.htm – viewed Dec 2019

https://www.naval-history.net/xDKWDa-Aerial.htm – viewed Feb 2020

https://www.naval-history.net/xDKWW2-4006-19JUN01.htm – viewed Feb 2020

http://www.historyofwar.org/articles/operation_aerial.html – viewed Jan 2020

https://www.bbc.co.uk/history/ww2peopleswar/stories/48/a3144548.shtml - viewed Dec 2019

https://www.navalairhistory.com/2017/07/24/the-fleet-air-arm-over-dunkirk/ – viewed Jan 2020

https://www.rafbf.org/news-and-blogs/rafs-vital-role-dunkirk-evacuation – viewed Jan 2020

http://dunkirk1940.org/index.php?&p=1_151 – viewed Dec 2019

http://www.adls.org.uk/t1/content/lady-cable – viewed Feb 2020

https://www.wrecksite.eu/wreck.aspx?141 – viewed Feb 2020

https://www.normandythenandnow.com/the-other-dunkirk-british-army-bravery-and-surrender-in-1940-normandy/ – viewed Jan 2020

http://dunkirk1940.org/index.php?&p=1_21 - viewed Dec 2019

https://51hd.co.uk/accounts/ – viewed Feb 2020

http://www.wildwood.org.nz/david/exhibits/ronald-hall-his-majesty-s-minesweepers.pdf – viewed Jan 2020

https://uboat.net/allies/merchants/ship/3272.html – viewed Jan 2020

http://www.paddlesteamers.info/RoyalEagle.htm – viewed Jan 2020

http://www.paddlesteamers.info/MedwayQueen.htm – viewed Feb 2020

https://www.tracesofwar.com/articles/4452/Dutch-contribution-to-Operation-Neptune.htm – viewed Feb 2020

PART I

The beach at Dunkirk, troops await evacuation.

Illustrations

The Britannia Museum archive has supplied unusual photographs taken by, or for, German occupation forces as 'trophy' pictures immediately after the fall of Dunkirk on 4th June 1940. They portray the ruins of the town, abandoned British and French vehicles and military equipment, shipwrecks off the beaches, sunken ships blocking the harbour, and the remains of shot down aircraft. They often show Wehrmacht personnel inspecting or posing by the subject. The German armed forces appear to have encouraged the taking of personal photographs, unlike the British, who regarded it as a breach of security and punishable as a disciplinary offence. Many front-line German soldiers carried high-quality cameras into action with them and there appears to have been no shortage of Agfa film and photographic paper at that early stage of the war. The occupation forces also permitted local photographers to produce, very quickly after the event, packs of 10 or 20 snapshots for commercial sale as souvenirs. Today, all these photographs form a valuable, important and sometimes unique historical record of the immediate aftermath of the evacuation.

Other illustrations depict many of the ships that played a significant part in the Dunkirk evacuation, particularly those that were sunk during Operation Dynamo. There is also a pre-War photograph of the liner RMS *Lancastria*, whose sinking as a troopship during Operation Aerial constitutes the worst disaster in British maritime history, because of the huge loss of life. The photographs have been selected mainly from original pre-WW2 photographs, also in the archive of the Britannia Museum, supplemented by a small number taken from copyright-free photographs now in the public domain.

In addition, there are two pages of silhouettes of the Junkers Ju87 Stuka dive bomber and Ju88 twin-engined bomber, the aircraft types that inflicted most losses and damage on Operation Dynamo rescue vessels. They are reproduced from a then-classified recognition booklet, 'Silhouettes of German Aircraft', issued in 1940 by the Ministry of Home Security to roofwatchers and other official personnel who needed to identify hostile aircraft.

Top Right. Thought to be the wreck of the cargo ship SS *Clan Macalister*, pictured a few months after the German occupation. Bombed and sunk in shallow water to the west of Dunkirk on 29th May, while hoisting out some of the first Assault Landing Craft.

Bottom Right. Wreck of the personnel vessel SS *Lorina*, a Southern Railway Channel Island packet, bombed and run ashore in shallow water on her first trip to Dunkirk on 29th May. Four bombs broke her back and split open her hull; a jagged crack from the upper deck to well below the water line can be seen aft of the second funnel in this German photograph taken about the middle of June, after the occupation.

Panorama of Dunkirk's beaches looking west from La Panne, showing Dunkirk harbour in left background and (left to right) Thames barges *Lark* and *Ethel Everard* ashore, wreck of personnel ship *Lorina* in shallow water, lorry jetty and abandoned vehicles

Beach looking west from La Panne some weeks after German occupation, showing wreck of SS *Lorina* breaking up, one funnel fallen, and lorry jetty already disappeared.

Thames tug *Fossa* damaged and aground on Bray beach, with a German army officer posing in front of her. She was salvaged, repaired and put back into service by the German authorities.

French anti submarine patrol craft *Chasseur 9* (Ch9), run ashore east of Dunkirk harbour after being bombed 22nd May.

Wreck of French destroyer L'Adroit
on Malo-les-Bains beach, bombed
21st May; in foreground is abandoned
British army lorry loaded with artillery
ammunition.

Closer view of wreck of French
destroyer *L'Adroit*.

Top and Bottom. Wreck of French destroyer *L'Adroit* showing site of forward magazine explosion.

Wreck of French Destroyer *L'Adroit* high and dry at low tide, pictured on 21st June 1940, large number of German troops sightseeing alongside.

Malo-les-Bains beach from former casino, ruined ice-cream parlour in foreground used as control point during evacuation. Wreck of French destroyer *L'Adroit* in background.

Beach at Bray with German personnel in front of derelict vehicles, showing, to left, wreck of Belgian river launch Ambleve and, to right, an abandoned and beached cabin cruiser, one of the Little Ships, as yet unidentified.

Lorry jetty composed of derelict British army lorries of various makes; note German "driver".

Lorry jetty, stretching down the beach from high tide line to the sea's edge at low tide.

Bottom Left. Vickers Mark VI B light tank abandoned on Malo-les-Bains beach, shown at low tide, wreck of French destroyer *L'Adroit* in the background.

Malo-les-Bains beach with abandoned motorcycles. Wreck of French destroyer *L'Adroit* in distant background.

Bottom Right. Abandoned vehicles on esplanade at Bray, Thames barge *Ethel Everard* and tug *Fossa* ashore in background.

Abandoned vehicles on esplanade at Bray, tug *Fossa* ashore in background.

Top Right. Line of Vickers Mark VI B light tanks in the foreground and Universal Carriers in the background, separated by a solitary Matilda Mark 1 infantry tank, abandoned to the west of Dunkirk harbour.

2nd Royal Ulster Rifles awaiting evacuation at Bray Dunes. Grounded paddle steamer Devonia in background.

Top Left. Abandoned vehicles on Bray beach, Renault ambulance in foreground, Thames barge *Ethel Everard* and tug *Fossa* ashore in background.

Scattered remains of a Junkers Ju88 twin engined bomber crashed on the beach to the west of Dunkirk harbour.

RAF Hawker Hurricane fighter crash-landed on beach, pictured after being partially stripped for souvenirs by German troops.

Top Right. RAF Fairey Battle light bomber crash-landed on the beach to the west of Dunkirk harbour, being examined by three German personnel.

Bottom Right. French Naval Air Force Chance Vought V-156-F reconnaissance bomber, a modified US SB2U-2 Vindicator, crashed-landed inland of Dunkirk, partially stripped for souvenirs, German personnel in cockpit.

Top Left. Bridge in Dunkirk harbour destroyed by Allied demolition parties before evacuation.

Bottom Left. Demolition charges exploding in Dunkirk harbour, likely to have been photographed on 3rd June during the final German advance on the town.

Top Right. French cargo ship SS *Cap Tefelneh* completed in 1920, bombed and sunk in Dunkirk's inner harbour. Salvaged by Germans, survived the war, returned to her owners 1946 and put back into service, not scrapped until 1975.

Top Left. French cargo ships, as yet unidentified, bombed and sunk in Dunkirk's inner harbour, showing the dangerous obstacles of sunken wrecks and tangled debris facing rescue ships.

Bottom Left. Blockship SS *Edvard Nissen* completed in 1921, one of three sunk in the main entrance to Dunkirk harbour by the captain of the destroyer HMS *Shikari*, as Operation Dynamo terminated.

Top Right. Eight of a flotilla of 12 harbour and canal tugs, all sunk alongside the Quai des Hollandais in the Bassin de Commerce in Dunkirk's inner harbour. Most were refloated and taken into German service.

Top Left. Burned out and abandoned vehicles on esplanade.

Bottom Left. Bombed ruins of Dunkirk town with damaged Allied vehicles, including a lorry carrying oil/petrol drums, partly unloaded.

Top Right. Bombed ruins of Dunkirk town with burned out British and French vehicles.

Bombed ruins of Dunkirk town, note burned out vehicles in photograph at upper left.

Burned and disabled vehicles in the town, with an apparently undamaged British motorcycle placed neatly on its stand.

Allied vehicles on the western outskirts of Dunkirk, destroyed by burning.

Top and Bottom Right. Allied vehicles comprehensively destroyed by fire and explosives to prevent use by German forces. These on the outskirts of the town are unrecognisable but many others were abandoned almost undamaged.

Destroyer HMS *Havant*, fully loaded with troops, coming alongside a French minesweeper in Dover on 31st May; she was bombed and sunk the following day.

Top Left. AA destroyer HMS *Wolsey* alongside in Dover.

Top Right. Destroyer HMS *Icarus* coming alongside Admiralty Pier Dover, fully loaded with troops.

Bottom Right. Coaster *Lady Sheila* coming alongside French trawlers at Admiralty Pier Dover, minesweeper HMS *Skipjack* (bombed and sunk 1st June) in background.

.

Personnel Vessel SS *Mona's Queen,* an Isle of Man packet and the first ship to sail from
Dunkirk harbour after the commencement of Operation "Dynamo", carrying 1,312
troops. On her return voyage, a German magnetic mine broke her back and she sank
about a mile east of Dunkirk. This photograph captures the moment when the mine
exploded under her hull. The destroyer HMS *Vanquisher* picked up her master and 31
of her crew.

Top Left. Three of the armada of "little ships".

Top Right. Disembarking at Dover.

Bottom Right. Some of the "little ships" used during the evacuation of Dunkirk being towed back along the River Thames past Tower Bridge, 9th June 1940.

Top Left. **HMS *Albury*** Minesweeper completed 1919, scrapped 1947. Made six round trips to Dunkirk between 29th May and 4th June, rescuing 1,851 troops.

Bottom Left. **HMS *Codrington*** Destroyer Flotilla Leader completed 1930, bombed and sunk in Dover Harbour 27th July 1940. Made eight round trips to Dunkirk between 28th May and 3rd June, rescuing 5,450 troops. Subsequently took part in Operation "Cycle" evacuation from St Valery.

Top Right. **HMS *Basilisk*** Fleet Destroyer completed 1931, bombed and sunk off Dunkirk 1st June 1940. Previously made two round trips to Dunkirk, rescuing 695 troops. Illustration taken from an unusual memorial postcard.

Bottom Right. **HMS *Havant*** Fleet Destroyer completed 1939, bombed and sunk off Dunkirk 1st June 1940. Previously made three round trips to Dunkirk, rescuing 2,105 troops. Illustration taken from an unusual memorial postcard.

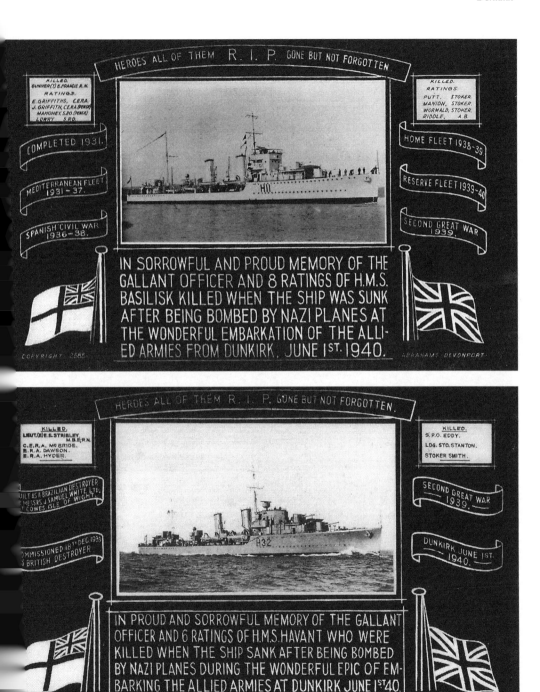

HEROES ALL OF THEM R. I. P. GONE BUT NOT FORGOTTEN

KILLED.
GUNNER (T) E. FRANCIS R.N.
RATINGS.
E. GRIFFITHS, C.E.R.A.
J. GRIFFITH, C.E.R.A. (PENSR)
MAHONEY, S.P.O. (PENSR)
LOWRY, S.B.O.

KILLED.
RATINGS.
PUTT, STOKER.
MANION, STOKER.
WORMALD, STOKER.
RIDDLE, A.B.

COMPLETED 1931.

HOME FLEET 1938-39.

MEDITERRANEAN FLEET
1931-37.

RESERVE FLEET 1939-40

SPANISH CIVIL WAR
1936-38.

SECOND GREAT WAR
1939.

IN SORROWFUL AND PROUD MEMORY OF THE GALLANT OFFICER AND 8 RATINGS OF H.M.S. BASILISK KILLED WHEN THE SHIP WAS SUNK AFTER BEING BOMBED BY NAZI PLANES AT THE WONDERFUL EMBARKATION OF THE ALLIED ARMIES FROM DUNKIRK, JUNE 1ST. 1940.

COPYRIGHT 2585

ABRAHAMS·DEVONPORT·

HEROES ALL OF THEM R. I. P. GONE BUT NOT FORGOTTEN.

KILLED.
LIEUT.(E) E.S.STRIBLEY
M.B.E.R.N.
C.E.R.A. McBRIDE.
E.R.A. DAWSON.
E.R.A. HYDER.

KILLED.
S.P.O. EDDY.
LDG. STO. STANTON.
STOKER SMITH.

UILT AS A BRAZILIAN DESTROYER
MESSRS. J. SAMUEL WHITE LTD.
T COWES ISLE OF WIGHT.

SECOND GREAT WAR
1939.

OMMISSIONED 18TH DEC. 1939
S BRITISH DESTROYER

DUNKIRK JUNE 1ST.
1940.

IN PROUD AND SORROWFUL MEMORY OF THE GALLANT OFFICER AND 6 RATINGS OF H.M.S. HAVANT WHO WERE KILLED WHEN THE SHIP SANK AFTER BEING BOMBED BY NAZI PLANES DURING THE WONDERFUL EPIC OF EMBARKING THE ALLIED ARMIES AT DUNKIRK JUNE 1ST '40.

COPYRIGHT 2582

ABRAHAMS·DEVONPORT·

93

Top Left. **HMS Esk** Fleet Destroyer completed 1934, mined and sunk off Texel 31st August 1940. Made six round trips to Dunkirk between 30th May and 3rd June, rescuing 3,100 troops.

Bottom Left. **HMS Grenade** Fleet Destroyer completed 1936, bombed in Dunkirk Harbour 29th May 1940 and sank after magazine explosion. Previously made one round trip on 29th May, rescuing 871 troops. Sister ship astern.

Top Right. **HMS Icarus** Fleet Destroyer completed 1936, scrapped 1946; sank four U-boats between 1939 and 1945. Made six round trips to Dunkirk between 29th May and 2nd June, rescuing 4,396 troops.

Bottom Right. **HMS Jupiter** Large Fleet Destroyer completed 1939, under repair during Operation "Dynamo", identical sister ship of HMS *Jaguar* and *Javelin*, both damaged off Dunkirk but rescued 1,623 troops between them in three round trips.

Top Left. **HMS Keith** Destroyer Flotilla Leader completed 1931, bombed and sunk off Dunkirk 1st June as flagship of Rear Admiral Wake-Walker. Made one round trip to Dunkirk on 31st May, rescuing 992 troops.

Bottom Left. **HMS Leda** Fleet Minesweeper completed 1938, torpedoed and sunk by U435 in north Atlantic 20th Sept 1942. Made six round trips to Dunkirk between 29th May and 4th June, rescuing 2,857 troops.

Top Right. **HMS *Malcolm*** Destroyer Flotilla Leader completed 1919, scrapped 1945. Made seven round trips to Dunkirk between 29th May and 4th June, rescuing 5,991 troops, more than any other warship.

Bottom Right. **HMS *Shikari*** Destroyer completed 1924, scrapped 1945. Made seven round trips to Dunkirk between 29th May and 4th June, rescuing 3,349 troops. Last large ship to leave Dunkirk, shown disarmed for training, rearmed 1939.

Top Left. **HMS Skipjack** Fleet Minesweeper completed 1935, bombed and sunk with heavy loss of life off Dunkirk 1st June. Previously made three round trips to Dunkirk, rescuing 959 troops.

Bottom Left. **HMS Venomous** Destroyer completed 1919, scrapped 1948. Made five round trips to Dunkirk between 31st May and 4th June, rescuing 3,128 troops. Previously fought at Calais and at Boulogne against German armour and forts.

Top Right. **HMS *Vivacious*** Destroyer completed 1917, scrapped 1948. Made four round trips to Dunkirk between 28th May and 1st June, rescuing 1,649 troops, damaged by artillery on 31st May.

Bottom Right. **HMS *Wakeful*** Destroyer completed 1917, torpedoed and sunk by schnellboote (E-boat) S30 east of Dunkirk 29th May with heavy loss of life. Made one round trip to Dunkirk on 28th May, rescuing 631 troops.

Top Left. Schnellboote (E-boat) completed 1938-40, used in night attacks on ships off Dunkirk, sinking two destroyers and many other craft. A contemporary Third Reich Kriegsmarine propaganda photograph.

Bottom Left. **HMS *Windsor*** Destroyer completed 1918, scrapped 1949. Made six round trips to Dunkirk between 30th May and 3rd June, rescuing 3,991 troops. Previously evacuated troops from Boulogne.

Top Right. **HMMTB 102** Motor Torpedo Boat completed 1938, restored to original appearance and seaworthy running condition (2020). Became flagship of Rear Admiral Wake-Walker after sinking of destroyer flotilla leader HMS *Keith*.

Bottom Right. **L'Adroit** Destroyer completed 1927, bombed 21st May, caught fire and beached in shallow water off Dunkirk where her forward magazine exploded. Wreck high and dry at low tide, becoming a favourite German 'trophy' photo after Dunkirk.

Top Left. **MV *Royal Daffodil*** General Steam Navigation Co Excursion Ship completed 1939, scrapped 1967. Made five round trips to Dunkirk between 28th May and 2nd June, then bombed and seriously damaged. Rescued 7,461 troops.

Bottom Left. **SS *Lorina*** Southern Railway Cross Channel Steamer completed 1919, bombed and sunk in shallow water 29th May approaching Dunkirk on her first trip, wreck still partly visible (2020).

Top Left. **SS *Maid of Orleans*** Southern Railway Cross Channel Steamer completed 1918, mined and sunk 28 June 1944 in the Channel. Made four round trips to Dunkirk between 27th May and 1st June, rescuing 5,503 troops

Bottom Left. **SS *Mona's Queen*** Isle of Man packet completed 1934, sunk by magnetic mine 29th May returning to Dunkirk. First ship to leave Dunkirk harbour under Operation "Dynamo", carrying 1,312 troops.

Top Left. **SS *Clan Macalister*** Clan Line freighter completed 1930, used to transport and launch assault landing craft, bombed and sunk 29th May in shallow water west of Dunkirk, wreck still partly visible (2020).

Bottom Left. **PS *Brighton Belle*** Auxiliary Paddle Minesweeper, 1940, formerly P&A Campbell excursion ship completed 1900, sank 28th May after striking submerged wreck off Dunkirk.

Top Right. **PS *Crested Eagle*** Auxiliary AA Ship, 1940, formerly General Steam Navigation Co Thames excursion ship completed 1925, bombed 29th May and caught fire with serious loss of life, beached off Dunkirk, wreck still visible (2020).

Bottom Right. **PS *Brighton Queen*** Auxiliary Paddle Minesweeper, 1940, formerly P&A Campbell excursion ship completed 1905, bombed and sunk off Dunkirk 1st June having completed one round trip to Dunkirk rescuing 160 troops.

Top Left. **MV Queen of the Channel** New Medway Excursion Ship completed 1935, bombed and sunk 28th May. Took part in Boulogne evacuation, first ship to berth alongside Dunkirk's east pier but sunk on way to Dover carrying over 900 troops.

Bottom Left. **PS Devonia** Auxiliary Paddle Minesweeper, 1940, formerly P&A Campbell excursion ship completed 1905, bombed 31st May and beached as a jetty 1st June, abandoned after additional bomb and shell damage, wreck still visible (2020).

Top Right. **PS Golden Eagle** Auxiliary AA Ship, 1940, formerly General Steam Navigation Co Thames excursion ship completed 1909, scrapped 1951. Made three round trips to Dunkirk between 30th May and 3rd June, rescuing 1,751 troops.

Bottom Right. **PS Medway Queen** Auxiliary Paddle Minesweeper, 1940, formerly Medway Steam Packet excursion ship completed 1924. Made seven round trips to Dunkirk between 28th May and 4th June, rescuing 2,914 troops.

Top Left. **PS *Royal Eagle*** Auxiliary AA Ship, 1940, formerly General Steam Navigation Co Thames excursion ship completed 1932, scrapped 1953. Made four round trips to Dunkirk between 30th May and 2nd June, rescuing 4,015 troops.

Bottom Left. **PS *Waverley*** Auxiliary Paddle Minesweeper, 1940, formerly London and North Eastern Railway Clyde excursion ship completed 1899, bombed and sunk off Dunkirk 29th May with serious loss of life.

Top Right. **PS Whippingham** Southern Railway Isle of Wight Ferry completed 1930, requisitioned by RN as auxiliary AA Ship in 1942, scrapped 1963. Made one round trip to Dunkirk on 1st June, rescuing 2,500 troops.

Bottom Right. **RMS Lancastria** Cunard liner completed 1920, used as a troopship during Operation "Aerial" evacuation from St Nazaire. Sunk 17th June with such heavy loss of life that her sinking constitutes the worst disaster in British maritime history.

Wreck of Thames paddle steamer (anti-aircraft) *Crested Eagle* sunk 29th May 1940.
P/T/Lt. Cdr. Bernard Ralph Booth, RNR.

Wreck of paddle minesweeper *Devonia* sunk 30th May 1940.
T/Lt. John Brotchie, RNVR.

Ramsgate, 4th April 2010. *Sundowner*.

Restored *Medway Queen*, Gillingham Pier, Kent. Photograph
Clem Rutter, Rochester, Kent. 2nd October 2016.

Junkers JU 87B
Stuka dive bomber
Wing span: 13.79m
Length: 10.77m
Height: 3.86m

Junkers Ju87 'Stuka' dive bomber, entered service 1936. Highly effective as a close support aircraft, or 'flying artillery', and in the anti-shipping role. Very vulnerable to fighters if unescorted but continued in service until the end of WW2.

These two Luftwaffe aircraft types inflicted most of the losses and damage to rescue vessels during the evacuation from Dunkirk.

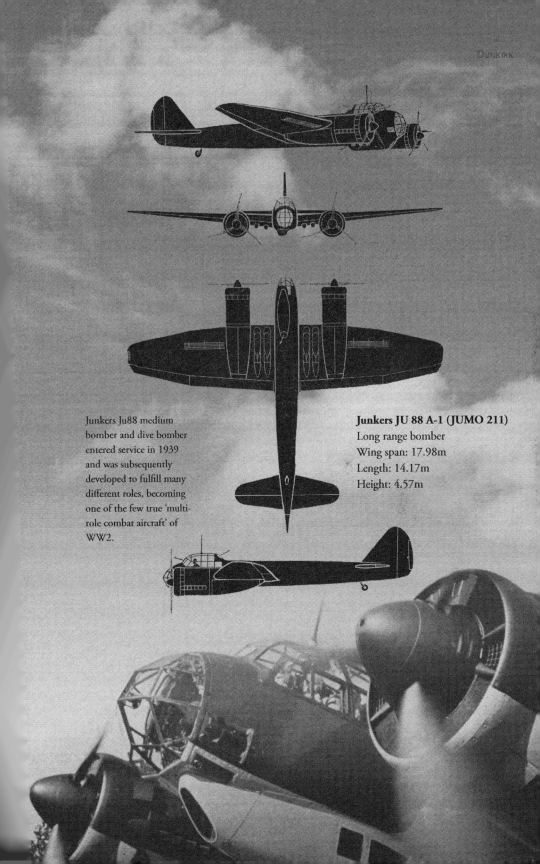

Junkers Ju88 medium
bomber and dive bomber
entered service in 1939
and was subsequently
developed to fulfill many
different roles, becoming
one of the few true 'multi-
role combat aircraft' of
WW2.

Junkers JU 88 A-1 (JUMO 211)
Long range bomber
Wing span: 17.98m
Length: 14.17m
Height: 4.57m

PART II

NAVAL STAFF HISTORY
SECOND WORLD WAR

BATTLE SUMMARIES No 41

The Evacuation from Dunkirk
Operation "Dynamo"
26th May – 4th June 1940

T.S.D. 21/46
Training and Staff Duties Division (Historical Section), Naval
Staff, Admiralty, S.W.1

Introduction

The Dunkirk evacuation looms large in the history of the war. It involved the dual problem of lifting a mass of hard-pressed troops from a continually shrinking perimeter under uncertain conditions of wind and sea, the menace of heavy attacks by air, and the onrush of a great hostile army; and then of transporting them to England in the face of air attacks, shore bombardments, torpedoes, mines, and the dangers of unlit shoals and wreck-strewn channels.

Despite the heavy losses suffered from all these perils, no less than 239,000 troops were embarked from the shattered quays of a wreck-encumbered harbour; while some 99,000 more were lifted from the 10 miles stretch of shoaling beach north-east of the harbour. This was no light task. The evacuation from the beaches was performed by many hundreds of shallow-draught motor boats, fishing craft, lighters, barges, sailing and pulling boats, manned partly by civilian volunteers – which ferried the weary troops to the destroyers, mine-sweepers, skoots, personnel vessels, tugs and other ships lying off in deeper water.

Operation "Dynamo" was essentially a combined operation, requiring the devoted co-operation of the Royal Navy and the Royal Air Force, and the cheerful courage and steadiness of an exhausted Army waiting on the beaches with hardly anything to eat or drink.

It must at once be said that the stupendous success which crowned Operation "Dynamo," in the face of the determined onslaught of numbers of hostile bombers, could not have been achieved without the air cover provided by Fighter and Coastal Command,[1] which performed its task almost invariably

---

1 The following five naval aircraft squadrons also operated under Coastal Command:

801 and 806 Skuas

815 and 825 Swordfish

826 Albacore

against superior numbers, and with the serious handicap of having no base nearer than England. In spite of the most strenuous efforts, however, the inadequate numbers of aircraft available precluded the possibility of continuous cover, and it is significant that the losses of ships by air attacks were greater than the aggregate of losses from all other enemy action, while their severity varied proportionately with the strength of our fighter cover at the time.

These aircraft were the only available British dive bombers. They carried out attacks on tanks, transport, batteries, gun emplacements, enemy positions in the Calais and Dunkirk areas, and E-boats. In spite of their relative inadequacy for the purpose the Skuas were also detailed for fighter escort for ships. (M.011883/40) The incidence of losses by enemy action is given in the two following tables:

Ships Sunk or Lost

Destroyers 5^A Air Attack, 3^A E-Boats or s/ms, 1^B Shore Guns

Gunboats 1 Air Attack

Minesweepers 5 Air Attack

Armed boarding vessels 1 Air Attack

Trawlers 6^E Air Attack, 2 E-Boats or s/ms, 5^A mines, 1^C Shore Guns

Special Service vessels 1 Air Attack

Drifters 2 Air Attack, 1 Shore Guns

Yachts 1 Mines

Skoots 1 Air Attack, 1^D Shore Guns

Personnel vessels 6 Air Attack, 1 Mines

Hospital carriers 1 Air Attack

Seaplane tender 1 Air Attack

Tugs 2 Air Attack

Cockle Bawley boat 1 Mines

Total 32 Air Attack, 5 E-Boats or s/ms, 8 Mines, 4 Shore Guns

Ships Damaged and put out of Action

Destroyers 8 Air Attack, 1^F E-Boats or s/ms

Sloops 1 Air Attack,

Minesweepers 2 Air Attack,

Trawlers 1 Shore Guns

Personnel vessels 2 Air Attack, 2 Shore Guns

Hospital carriers 2 Air Attack, 1 Mines

Total 15 Air Attack, 1 E-Boats or s/ms, 1 Mines, 3 Shore Guns

^A Including 1 French

^B French. Driven on to Allied minefield where she struck a mine.

^C Driven on to Allied minefield where she struck a mine.

^D Damaged and had to be abandoned.

^E Including 3 French.

^F French.

Something must now be said of the Army Movements

The *active* operations of the British Expeditionary Force in northern France and Belgium began on 10th May, 1940, when Germany invaded the Low Countries. The first phase of these operations (see Plan 1) was the advance to the River Dyle, from 10th-16th May; the second-phase, from 17th-26th May (see Plan 2), the withdrawal from the Dyle to the River Escaut, the defence of the Belgian frontier, and of the southern and western flanks; and the third and final phase was the withdrawal into the Dunkirk perimeter and the embarkation of the B.E.F., from 26th May – 4th June.[2]

In the following day-by-day account may be discerned, first, the rapid sequence of events which resulted in the desperate task imposed on the Royal Navy on 26th May, and second, the supreme difficulty of co-ordinating naval measures with an ever-changing military situation. That situation it is not intended to present in detail, but only so far as the sudden onrush of military events affected the course of naval dispositions.

---

2 Lord Gort's Second Despatch, para. 1.

Preliminary Events 10th–18th MAY 1940

(Plan 1, pages 124–125)

10th May – Germany Invades Holland and Belgium

On the 10th May, following the invasion of Holland and Belgium, the Franco-British forces under General Georges, commanding the French Front of the North East, crossed the Belgian frontier and began their advance to the River Dyle,[1] according to plan.

11th May – Allies reach River Dyle

During the afternoon and evening of the 11th May the leading infantry brigades reached the Dyle.

The news from the Belgian Army, of which King Leopold had assumed command on the outbreak of war, was not good. At Maastricht the Belgians had been unable to demolish important bridges over the Albert Canal and the river Meuse, and the enemy had begun to move across them; whilst the Belgian anti-tank obstacle eastward had been reconnoitred by the French Cavalry Corps and found to be not only badly sited but unfinished.[2]

12th May – German Thrust on French 9th Army Front

The Allied advance to the Dyle was successfully completed by the 12th May. The B.E.F. was in position between Wavre and Louvain, with the French 7th Army (General Giraud) on its left and the French 1st Army (General Blanchard) on its right. On the right of the French 1st Army was the French 9th Army (General Corap) of the French Southern Command. Disquieting news was, however, received from the south, where a German thrust with at least two armoured divisions[1] was reported as developing on the front of the French 9th Army.

This thrust eventually proved to be the beginning of the German breakthrough and their sweep westward, which cut off the Allied northern forces from the

---

1 Lord Gort's Second Despatch, para. 18.

2 Lord Gort's Second Despatch, para. 19.

main French forces in the south, led to the capture of Boulogne and Calais, and culminated in the evacuation of Dunkirk.

General Billotte was in command of the French First Group of Armies, which included the French 1st Army (with the French Cavalry Corps), and the French 7th Army. Between these two armies lay the Belgian Army (under the independent command of their King), and the B.E.F., which, though under the command of General Georges, was not under that of General Billotte. On this day, however, it was agreed to co-ordinate the action of the British, French and Belgian forces, and General Billotte was appointed to perform this task.[3]

13th May – Occupation of Walcheren and Zuid Beveland Imminent

Movements of the main bodies of the French 1st and 7th Armies continued in accordance with their plans, and by the 13th May, units of the latter were north of Antwerp on the Dutch border. It was, however, becoming increasingly evident that they would be unable to prevent the enemy occupation of Walcheren and Zuid Beveland, which was developing from the north-east.

During the day and the following night the Belgians were withdrawing their northern forces to the general line Louvain-Antwerp.[3]

14th May – Germans cross Meuse

May the 14th was crucial, for on that day the enemy penetrated the French 9th Army front, and crossed the Meuse between Sedan and Mézières.[3] *(See Plan 1)*.

15th May – Dutch Army Surrenders

On the 15th May the Dutch Army laid down its arms. The immediate effect of this on the operations of the B.E.F. was small, but "I anticipated ..." says Lord Gort, "that this would come as a shock to the Belgian Army".[4]

The French 7th Army withdrew its advanced formations to the neighbourhood of Antwerp, and the French divisions on the B.E.F.'s left flank were ordered to move across the British rear to fill the gap which had been created on the French 9th Army's front. This move did not, however, actually take place till some 3 days later,[4] and it then left the Belgian Army responsible for the security of the British left flank.

---

3 Lord Gort's Second Despatch para. 22.

4 Lord Gort's Second Despatch, para. 23.

On the British front the day passed quietly on the whole. The 1st Corps [Lt.-Gen. M. G. H. Barker] was not attacked in strength; 3rd Division [Maj.-Gen. B. L. Montgomery] of 2nd Corps [Lt.-Gen. A. F. Brooke] was attacked north-west of Louvain, and its forward positions were penetrated, but a counterattack successfully restored the original line.[5]

At about 1800, however, the enemy penetrated the French 1st Army's front, and, in spite of British support, some ground was lost.

16th May – Allies Withdraw to River Escaut

By the 16th May it became clear that a prolonged defence of the Dyle position was impracticable,[5] because the French 1st Army on the B.E.F.'s right flank were unlikely to make good the ground lost on the previous day and a further withdrawal seemed likely to be forced on them by events in the south.[5]

It was therefore decided to withdraw to the River Escaut, spending one day on the River Senne and one day on the River Dendre. Accordingly, on the night of 16th-17th May, the 15 to 20 miles withdrawal to the Senne positions began.

Preliminary Events 17th May

French 9th Army Front Broken

By the early morning of the 17th May, the situation on the French 9th Army's front had become grave. The French line was broken, and enemy armoured and mobile forces had crossed the river Oise. East of St. Quentin, there was a gap of at least 20 miles in which there appeared to be no organised resistance.[5] The enemy break-through was now offering an imminent threat to the British rear G.H.Q. at Arras, to the communications over the Somme at Amiens and Abbeville, and to the base areas. To meet this, every available man and weapon were collected. A mobile bath unit, for example, took part in the defence of St. Pol; General Construction Companies of the Royal Engineers, and many units of the Royal Army Service Corps, set to work to place their localities in a state of defence, and manned them until overwhelmed, relieved or ordered to withdraw. These numerous delaying actions, though small in themselves, all contributed to gain the time required for the withdrawal of the main forces.[6] A force was also organised to guard against a more immediate threat to the B.E.F.'s right flank;

---

5 Lord Gort's Second Despatch, para. 24.

6 Lord Gort's Second Despatch, para. 25.

and, as a further precaution against the risk of being out-flanked on the right, the withdrawal to the Dendre and thence to the Escaut was continued without pause.[7]

18th May – Allied Rail Communications Severed

By the morning of the 18th May the Belgians had effected a junction with the B.E.F. left flank at Alost, on the Dendre. From the B.E.F.'s right flank the French line ran through Mons and Maubeuge.

During the day, the enemy, pounding westward, had penetrated as far as Amiens in sufficient strength to sever rail communications with the Allies' bases.

On the night of the 18th-19th May, the 1st, 2nd and 3rd Corps of the B.E.F. completed their withdrawal to the line of the Escaut without interference, and prepared to defend the line of that river. (The French 1st Army completed its withdrawal by the following day and was in touch with the right of the British 1st Corps).

Meanwhile, inundations were being carried out southward by the French; unfortunately however, without regard to the front of the B.E.F., where it was soon found that the level of water in the Escaut was becoming so low that the river was fast ceasing to form a serious obstacle.

After a conference that night with General Billotte, Lord Gort formed the opinion that there was an imminent danger of the forces in the north-eastern area – that is the French forces next to the sea, the Belgian Army, the B.E.F. and the bulk of the French 1st Army on its right – being irretrievably cut off from the main French forces in the south.[8] The event three days later showed this opinion to have been fully justified.

---

7 Lord Gort's Second Despatch, para. 26.

8 Lord Gort's Second Despatch, para. 30.

Plan 1. Centre page detail, 124-125

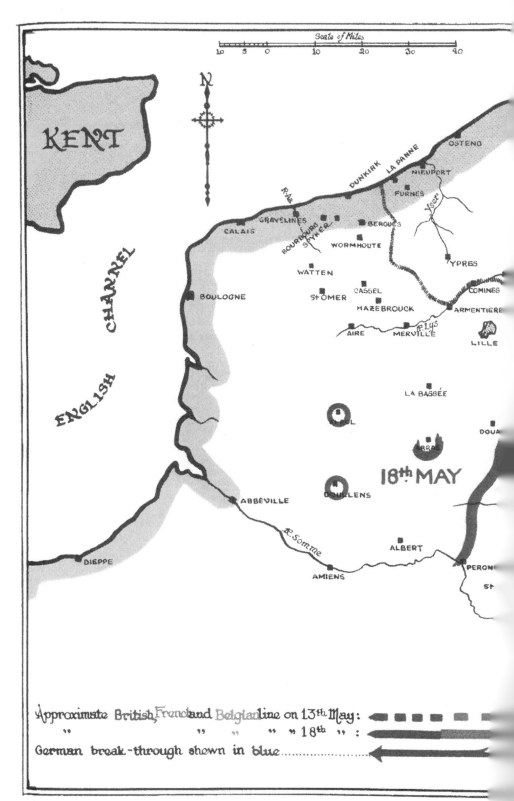

Scale of Miles

KENT

N

OSTEND
LA PANNE
DUNKIRK
NIEUPORT
FURNES
Ysar
R. Aa
GRAVELINES
CALAIS
BOURBOURG
SPYKER
BERGUES
WORMHOUTE
YPRES
WATTEN
CASSEL
ST OMER
HAZEBROUCK
COMINES
ARMENTIERE
AIRE
MERVILLE
P LYS
LILLE

CHANNEL

ENGLISH

BOULOGNE

LA BASSÉE

DOUA

L

ARRAS

18th MAY

ABBEVILLE

DOULLENS

R. Somme

DIEPPE

ALBERT

PERON
St

AMIENS

Approximate British, French and Belgian line on 13th May: ▬ ▬ ▬ ▬
     ,,   ,,   ,,   ,, ,, 18th ,, : ▬▬▬▬▬
German break-through shown in blue................. ◀▬▬▬▬

C.B.H. 16675- Wt.41534 - Dd. D.8188 -625- 6/49

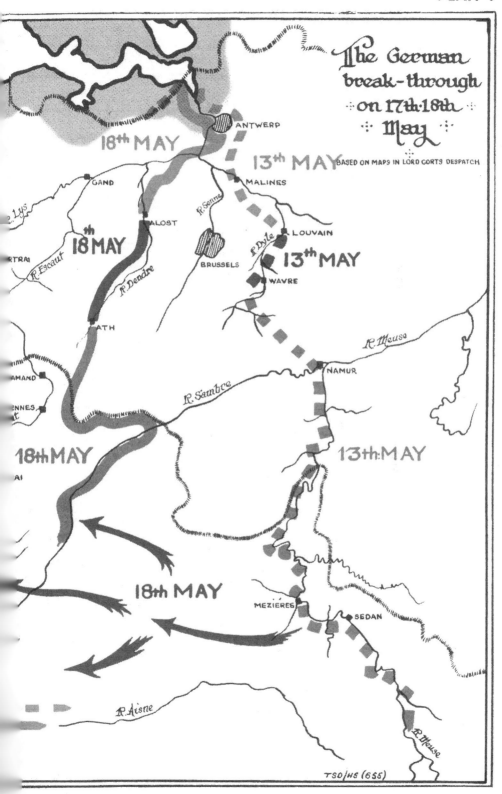

The German
break-through
on 17th-18th
May

BASED ON MAPS IN LORD GORT'S DESPATCH

18th MAY

13th MAY

ANTWERP

GAND

MALINES

R.Senne

ALOST

LOUVAIN

R.Lys

18 MAY

R.Dyle

13th MAY

R.Escaut

BRUSSELS

WAVRE

RTRAI

R.Dendre

ATH

R.Meuse

AMAND

NAMUR

R.Sambre

ENNES

18th MAY

13th MAY

AI

MEZIERES

SEDAN

18th MAY

R.Aisne

R.Meuse

TSO/HS (655)

The week before Operation "Dynamo," 19th–25th May, 1940

19th May – Compulsory Withdrawal of B.E.F. Foreseen

A crisis was now approaching. After considering various alternatives, Lord Gort was forced to the conclusion that the possibility of a compulsory withdrawal of the B.E.F. from the Continent must be faced, and so his Chief of the General Staff, Lieut-General H. R. Pownall, telephoned to the Director of Military Operations and Plans at the War Office and discussed this possibility.[1]

On this 19th day of May communications by road and rail over the Somme at Abbeville were still holding, but there was little doubt that enemy armoured forces in that area would shortly break through to the coast. The force could then no longer be supplied through the ports south of the Somme, and the great bulk of the reserves, which were in the rearward areas, would shortly cease to be available for maintaining replacements.[1]

R.A.F. Component Begins Return to England

The growing failure of communications had now made it impracticable for the British air organisation to function, and by the evening orders had to be given for a large proportion of the R.A.F. Component of the B.E.F. (Air Vice-Marshal C. H. B. Blount) to return to England.

Equally serious was the fact that, by the evening, German troops had arrived in Amiens. The picture was no longer that of a line bent or temporarily broken, but of a besieged fortress.[2]

Vice–Admiral, Dover, Represented at War Office Conference

Meanwhile, in London, following the receipt of General H. R. Pownall's message, a meeting had been held at the War Office at which Vice-Admiral B. H. Ramsay (Vice-Admiral, Dover), was represented.

---

1 Lord Gort's Second Despatch, para. 30.

2 Lord Gort's Second Despatch, para. 31.

This meeting discussed the temporary maintenance of the B.E.F. – and the evacuation of its personnel through Dunkirk, Calais and Boulogne. Among other questions considered was the possiblity of "the hazardous evacuation of very large forces." So little, apparently, was the true military situation then known in London that this problem was regarded as "unlikely," though only seven days later it developed into Operation "Dynamo". "The main decision of this meeting," says Vice-Admiral Ramsay, "was that the control must be delegated to the Vice-Admiral Dover, and available shipping placed at his disposal."

Channel Ports the German objective

On the 20th May the breach south of Arras deepened and widened; the enemy armoured forces appeared to be directed on two main objectives – one down the valley of the Somme on Abbeville, the other doubtless making for the Channel ports.[3]

General Weygand Directing Allied Operations

During this day also, Lord Gort became aware that Allied operations were actually being directed by General Weygand (successor to General Gamelin), who announced later, on 23rd May, that he was Commander-in-Chief in all theatres of war.[4]

The first move in this so-called "Weygand plan," (see under 23rd-24th May), now became apparent when General Sir Edmund Ironside, the Chief of the Imperial General Staff, arrived at Lord Gort's G.H.Q. with instructions from the British Cabinet that the B.E.F. was to move southward upon Amiens, attacking all enemy forces encountered and taking station on the left of the French Army.[1] This move, Lord Gort pointed out, was impracticable because it would involve the disengagement of seven British divisions which were actually in close contact with the enemy on the Escaut, and would be immediately followed up by the enemy. In any case, owing to the prospective interruption by the enemy of the B.E.F.'s line of supply, imminent at any moment, it was unlikely that the B.E.F. could undertake sustained offensive operations.

Lord Gort had, however, already made plans to counter-attack with two divisions southward of Arras, and now proposed that they should make this attack on the following day. The C.I.G.S. agreed with this action.[1]

3 Lord Gort's Second Despatch, para, 32.

4 Lord Gort's Second Despatch, para. 32.

R.A.F. Component to Set Up Rear H.Q. at Hawkinge

Meanwhile, the evacuation of the R.A.F. Component was proceeding, and it was decided to set up its rear headquarters at Hawkinge, in England.[5]

Naval Staff at Dover Considers Large-scale Evacuation

At Dover, the possiblity of a large-scale evacuation was now definitely foreseen for a meeting of the Naval Staff was held there during the day to consider the emergency evacuation across the channel of very large forces. This meeting, which was attended by Liaison Officers from the War Office Movement Control and the Ministry of Shipping, considered the number of personnel vessels and small craft available; it agreed that the air protection of sailings, embarkations and disembarkations was to be arranged by Vice-Admiral, Dover, direct with Fighter Command; and it called attention to the necessity, in the event of evacuation, for a large number of small boats to carry the troops from the very gradually shoaling beaches to the off-shore ships. Furthermore, as it was considered extremely doubtful whether the whole of the troops to be evacuated could be lifted from the beaches, it was urged that "if at all possible, the ports must be used as well".[6] It is evident that, at this date, it was not yet realised that the only port available for the evacuation would be Dunkirk.

Provision of Small Craft Considered

After this meeting at Dover, a long series of telephone conversations took place between the V-A. Dover, the Admiralty, the Ministry of Shipping and the C.-in-C. Nore, as to the provision of small craft for the final evacuation and the provision of naval personnel for manning the skoots[7] and small boats required for transport and ferrying.

21st May – Counter-attack South of Arras

The counter-attack with 2 divisions south of Arras planned by Lord Gort was begun this day under the command of Major-General H. E. Franklyn. He had the co-operation of the French Cavalry Corps and a French Light Mechanised Division, but the movements of the latter "did not develop so widely to the

---

5 R.A.F. Narrative.

6 D.R.

7 Dutch schuyts or coasters.

flanks as General Franklyn had hoped".[8] The hope that two divisions of the French 5th Corps would also attack southward from Douai, did not materialise. Furthermore, serious mechanical troubles developed in the British overworked tanks, whose tracks were now beginning to break through wear.[1]

Although the objectives of the day were therefore reached, it became clear that the attack would not maintain its momentum unless it was reinforced and supported by the French on its left.[1]

During the 22nd May General Franklyn held his ground, but on the 23rd enemy pressure compelled the Allied force to withdraw - and in an easterly direction.[1] "Thus concluded the defence of Arras," said Lord Gort, "… It had imposed a valuable delay on a greatly superior force against which it had blocked a vital road centre".[1]

Germans Approach Boulogne

In the meantime, the 21st May had marked a still more serious change in the military situation, for, in the afternoon, an enemy column of all arms was approaching Boulogne.[9] The military situation was rapidly deteriorating; the Germans were across the Somme[2] and had cut the railway at Abbeville, completely severing our line of communications.[10] A quarter of a million Allied troops now lay north of the Somme, cut off from the daily flow of 2,000 tons of ammunition and supplies essential to their maintenance." The decision to maintain the force through the northern ports", said Lord Gort, "was finally taken on 21st May and the headquarters of a Base Sub-Area established at Dunkirk …"[3]

A conference of the Allied Commanders was essential, and at 2000 Lord Gort went to Ypres where he met the King of the Belgians and General Billotte.[11] He explained the situation developing on the Escaut, where the water in the river was so low that it no longer formed a tank obstacle. It was thereupon decided that the Escaut should be abandoned on the night of 22nd-23rd May, and the line be withdrawn to the Belgian frontier defences.[12]

---

8 Lord Gort's Second Despatch, para. 33.

9 Lord Gort's Second Despatch, para. 36.

10 Lord Gort's Second Despatch, para. 37

11 General Billotte was fatally injured in a motor accident returning from this conference.

12 General Blanchard succeeded him in command of the French First Group of Armies.

As it was evident that sooner or later the Belgian Army would have to swing back to a line in rear, General Billotte asked the King of the Belgians whether, if he were forced to withdraw from the positions on the Lys, he would fall back on to the line of the Yser so as to continue to maintain touch with the left of the B.E.F.[5] His Majesty agreed that no alternative line existed, but five days later the Belgian command decided that the idea of the withdrawal to the Yser "must be ruled out".

Organisation of the Canal Line

On the 21st May, also, steps were taken to defend the south-western flank of the Allied force by organising the defence of the canal line from the Escaut to La Bassee, and to continue it to St. Omer and the sea at Gravelines.[13]

From this date all arrangements for air co-operation with the B.E.F. were made by the War Office in conjunction with the Air Ministry, the air liaison work being carried out in England at Hawkinge.[14]

Emergency Evacuation again Considered at the War Office

Meanwhile, in London, a meeting was held at the War Office at which, once again, the emergency evacuation across the channel of very large forces, now looming close ahead, was under consideration.[15]

22nd May – Canal Line Occupied

By the 22nd May the 85 miles of canal line from Gravelines, through St. Omer and Aire, to the Escaut (west of St. Amand) had been occupied, so far as was possible, with the 10,000 men available. This line was divided into sectors, for each of which a British commander was responsible,[1] but the number of anti-tank weapons was barely adequate to cover all the crossing places, and no effective watch could be kept against small parties of infantry crossing the canal between the bridges.[1]

Boulogne cut off, Calais Threatened

The ports of Boulogne and Calais were now no longer working and consequently the supply situation had grown worse than ever. It was found too that, at such

---

13 Lord Gort's Second Despatch, para. 34.

14 Lord Gort's Second Despatch, para. 29.

15 D.R.

short notice, the port of Ostend could not be adapted to military requirements.[16]

Boulogne was, in fact, by this time completely cut off, and by the evening enemy armoured forces were within 9 miles of Calais.[17] At Merville, the last remaining advanced landing ground available for the R.A.F. Component was abandoned.

On the night of 22nd/23rd May, according to plan, the Allied withdrawal to the Belgian frontier defences was carried out.[18]

The Operation ... will be known as "Dynamo"

Meanwhile, the Admiralty had begun to make definite preparations for an evacuation from the Continent. There were at this time, lying at Poole and in the Port of London, some 50 Dutch skoots (schuyts), 200 ton-motor coasters which had escaped from Holland. On the 22nd May the Admiralty, after allocating 8 of these vessels to the War Office for use as supply ships, directed the Commanders-in-Chief Portsmouth and the Nore to take over and man the remainder, arrange for their organisation and assembly, and report the names of the vessels as they became ready for service. At the same time it was intimated that, when ready, the skoots would be placed at the disposal of V-A. Dover.[19] It was added that the operation for which these ships were being prepared would be known as "Dynamo"[20], the first mention of the now famous word.

As a result of this direction, 40 skoots in all were commissioned; of these, 18 lying at Poole were commissioned by the C. in C. Portsmouth on the 25th May, and 22 lying at London were commissioned by the C. in C. Nore between the 25th and 27th May.

23rd May – Enemy within 20 miles of Dunkirk

Over in France, the situation on the canal line deteriorated during the 23rd May (see Plan 2), and the enemy established bridgeheads at Aire, at St. Omer ("which seems to have changed hands twice during the day"[21]), and near Watten. German tanks were reported harbouring in the forest of Clairmarais (immediately east of

16 Lord Gort's Second Despatch, para. 37.

17 Lord Gort's Second Despatch, para. 36.

18 Lord Gort's Second Despatch, para. 39.

19 Appendices F.1 and F.2.

20 Appendix F.3.

21 Lord Gort's Second Despatch, para. 39.

St. Omer), and, during the day, hostile armoured fighting vehicles came within 3 miles of Hazebrouck; and though by the evening these movements had been checked,[3] the enemy was then within some 20 miles of Dunkirk.

Calais cut off

Calais was now finally cut off, and, said Lord Gort, "the remainder of the gallant defence of Calais was conducted under the orders of the War Office".[3]

Dunkirk, though its water supply was destroyed,[22] was by this time the only port available for unloading supplies. Even the small supply by air of rations and small arms ammunition now ceased, as it had become impossible for aircraft to land. Accordingly, on the advice of the Quarter-Master-General (Lieut.-General W. G. Laidsell), Lord Gort put the B.E.F. on half rations.[4] During the day the evacuation of the R.A.F. Component of the B.E.F. was completed.

Naval demolition parties were ready at the Nore, and one was landed at Dunkirk during the day to prepare the locks for demolition. (Operation X D (E)).

Boulogne Evacuated

Early on the same day a demolition party (Operation XD (G)), under Lieut.-Comdr. A. E. P. Welman, D.S.O., D.S.C., R.N., (Retd.), was also despatched, in the destroyer *Vimy*, to Boulogne, together with a force known as "Force Buttercup", to restore control of the docks area and cover the demolition party ; Major C. F. L. Holford, R.M. was in command of this force, and it consisted of 4 platoons of seamen, 2 Marine platoons with a section of machine guns and a medical party. Two battalions of Irish Guards and an anti-tank battery had been sent on the previous day.

When "Force Buttercup" arrived, the town was under shell fire and being attacked by enemy tanks and infantry, and the Army forces were being withdrawn to the jetty in readiness for evacuation, although the War Office sent orders during the afternoon that the troops were to stay and fight it out.[23]

Communication with England was cut, and all messages had to be sent by destroyers.

By 1530 the Germans had occupied the whole of Boulogne except a bridgehead, all anti-tank guns were out of action, and half of Major Holford's

---

22 Lord Gort's Second Despatch, para. 37.

23 Admiralty Message 1422/23, *War Diary* 23.5.40, p. 356.

force were estimated to be casualties. The destroyers *Keith* (D. (19), Captain D. J. R. Simson) and *Whitshed*[24] went over to Boulogne during the afternoon, and were followed later by the *Venetia, Venomous, Vimiera, Wild Swan* and *Windsor*. The arrival of the first two destroyers was followed by an enemy air attack, together with close range mortar, machine gun and rifle fire, which caused damage and casualties, including Captain D. (19) who was killed, and necessitated breaking of the work of evacuating wounded and withdrawing temporarily from the port. Fortunately, No. 92 Squadron of the R.A.F. (12 Spitfires) soon encountered the large enemy formation and, with some loss to themselves and much to the enemy, gained a measure of control of the situation; and by 1955 the destroyers were back in harbour and carrying out the evacuation of the Welsh Guards. The *Keith* had received a signal at 1749 ordering all troops to be evacuated.

About 2000, while Lieut.-Comdr. Welman was on the point of firing the last of the demolition charges, German tanks towing field guns appeared over the hill north of the harbour and opened heavy fire at the three destroyers coming in to take off "Force Buttercup." An amazing engagement, described by eye-witnesses as magnificent, ensued between the German field guns and the destroyers. The *Venetia* was hit while in mid-channel, but she was got under control and out of the harbour, thus avoiding blocking in the *Venomous* and *Wild Swan* who were embarking "Force Buttercup" and the Irish Guards while engaging the enemy tanks and field guns with every gun they had.

It was low water when the destroyers eventually backed out of harbour, loaded down with troops. When the *Venomous* backed out her wheel jammed and she had to steer with her engines; the *Wild Swan*, following her, grounded for a moment, but both ships got off and both reached Dover safely. When, at 2234 some 3,000 troops had been brought off, the *Wild Swan* reported that although a considerable number remained further evacuation was impracticable.

The *Windsor*, however, which had been ordered at about 2030 to help in the evacuation, arrived after the rest of the destroyers had left; she entered the harbour after dark, filled to capacity and sailed again without damage or much difficulty. On clearing the harbour, the *Windsor* informed V.-A. Dover that further evacuation under cover of darkness was still possible and that two more destroyers could lift all the soldiers still left at Boulogne.

Vice-Admiral, Dover, therefore, despatched the *Vimiera* at 0015 on the 24th to try to bring off the remaining troops. She arrived at Boulogne at 0130, and

---

24 The *Whitshed* had been at Boulogne helping to evacuate wounded from 0630 to 1045 when she left with two transports for Calais.

found all silent. At length the Commanding Officer's hail was answered, and it was found that there were more than 1000 troops waiting for a ship. Going alongside the jetty, the destroyer was crowded to the tiller flat by 0230, the only space left being round the guns; and when she slipped at 0245 she was compelled to leave some 200 men behind. Five minutes later shore batteries opened fire on the jetty, and at 0255 a bomber passed close and a bomb exploded 20 yards away. The *Vimiera* was so over-loaded that even five degrees of helm made the ship list unpleasantly. She reached Dover safely at 0355 and landed some 1400 men, including Belgian and French troops and some refugees who got on board. The numbers evacuated by the destroyers concerned were approximately:

Keith 180
Vimy 150
Whitshed 580
Vimiera 1955 (in two trips)
Wild Swan 403
Windsor 600
Venomous 500

Total

The *Venetia*, damaged, did not get alongside a quay. During the night 22/23rd May, before the evacuation under fire, the *Verity* took off two General Officers and some 150 troops.

In addition to the *Venetia*, the *Wild Swan*, *Whitshed*, *Keith* and *Venomous* all received damage during the evacuation. The *Keith* lost Captain D. (19) and 7 ratings killed, and had 28 wounded; the *Vimy* had one officer killed and her Commanding Officer, Lieut.-Comdr. C. G. W. Donald R.N. was seriously wounded and died subsequently; the *Whitshed* lost one officer killed and had 12 ratings wounded; the *Venetia* had 20 ratings killed or missing and 11 wounded; the Commanding Officer of the *Verity*, Lt. Cdr. A. R. M. Black R.N. was wounded and subsequently died.

23rd–24th May – The "Weygand" Plan

In the midst of this changing panorama of events, on the 23rd May, General Weygand became "Commander-in-Chief in all theatres of war". He had, however, previously formulated the "Weygand plan". This plan contemplated a counter-offensive on a large scale[25] and, briefly, it consisted of 3 operations:

(a) An attack south-westward from the north, by the French 1st Army and the B.E.F., with the Belgian Cavalry Corps supporting the British right.
(b) An attack northward from the line of the Somme, which line the newly formed Third French Army Group was reported to be organising.
(c) Operations on the line of the Somme west of Amiens, by a new Cavalry Corps which was assembling south of the river near Neufchatel.

On the 23rd May Lord Gort received a telegram from the British Prime Minister to the French Prime Minister, M. Reynaud, of which the following is an extract:

"Strong enemy armoured forces have cut communications of Northern Armies. Salvation of these Armies can only be obtained by immediate execution of Weygand's plan."[1]

Not feeling sure that the situation developing for the Allied armies in the north could be accurately appreciated except on the spot, Lord Gort telegraphed to General Sir John Dill asking him to fly over that day.[1] On the following day (24th May), however, the Prime Minister again concerned with M. Reynaud and General Weygand in Paris; an extract is quoted below from the telegraphic report of this conference which Lord Gort received from the Secretary of State for War:

"Both are convinced that Weygand's plan is still capable of execution and only in its execution has [Plies] hope of restoring the situation. Weygand reports French VII Army is advancing successfully and has captured Peronne, Albert, and Amiens ... It is essential that you should make every endeavour to co-operate in this plan. Should however, situation on your communications make this at any time impossible you should inform us so that we can inform French and make Naval and Air arrangements to assist you should you have to withdraw on the north coast".

Lord Gort says that he "fully appreciated the importance of attacking early, before the enemy could bring up his infantry in strength, but facts had to be

---

25 Lord Gort's Second Despatch, para. 38

faced"[1]. These were some of the facts:

(a) General Weygand's report of the recapture of Peronne, Albert and Amiens was, says Lord Gort, "inaccurate"[1]. None of these three towns on the line of the Somme had been recaptured.

(b) Two British divisions were still closely engaged with the enemy, and three others were awaiting relief by the French and Belgians, and would not become available for a further 48 hours.[1]

(c) Only about 300 rounds per gun were immediately available to the B.E.F., and with communications cut the prospect of further supply was remote.[1]

(d) Serious losses in Allied tanks had already been suffered and could not be replaced.[1]

(e) The Belgian cavalry was unlikely to be able to engage, at short notice, in a battle 40 miles away, and on French soil.[1]

Nevertheless, after consultation with General Blanchard, Lord Gort agreed that in order to implement their share of the Weygand plan they should attack southwards with 2 British divisions, one French division and a French Cavalry Corps. The attack however, could not take place till the 26th May at the earliest, owing to the reliefs in progress and the need to assemble the 2 British divisions which were still closely engaged with the enemy.[1] Furthermore, Lord Gort emphasised, both to the Secretary of State and to General Blanchard, that the principal effort must come from the south, and that the operation of the northern forces could be nothing more than a sortie.

It will be seen therefore that the British and the French Governments were both urging a counter offensive on a large scale, barely 48 hours before the Dunkirk evacuation became a desperately urgent necessity.

24th May

The Allied position on the canal line was considerably strengthened during the 24th May. On this day also Lord Gort prepared for the proposed counter attack southwards on the 26th May, with the ultimate objective Plouvain – Marquion – Cambrai. In effect, this attack was never carried out.

Fighting Troops hold on at Calais

In the meantime the evacuation of Boulogne was completed. At Calais evacuation was limited to non-fighting personnel. The fighting troops held on, and a supply ship [the *Benlawers*] with stores and transport unloaded for them at Calais.

Defences of Dunkirk

It was now obvious that if the B.E.F. was to be evacuated the only port available would be Dunkirk[1]. Its local defences were under the Admiral du Nord, Admiral Abrial, whose command included Boulogne, Calais and Dunkirk, but on this day (24th May) he delegated the command of military forces in these areas to General Fagalde.

The French defences of Dunkirk extended only as far as the Belgian frontier, and comprised an inner and an outer sector; the inner on the line of the Mardyck Canal to Spyker, thence to Bergues to the frontier and so to the sea; the outer on the line of the river Aa to St. Omer, thence by Cassel and Steen-voorde to the frontier.[1]

The French now took over the British posts on the Aa and began to operate the inundations which formed part of the defence scheme of Dunkirk.[2]

Belgian line penetrated

In the late evening the enemy attacked the Belgian line on the Lys, penetrating to a depth of 1½ miles on a 13 mile front[3] and endangering the security of the British left flank.

It had become a matter of vital importance to keep open the B.E.F.'s line of communication to the coast through a corridor of withdrawal which was hourly narrowing. The penetration of the Belgian line made it certain that before long the whole area east of the Yser canal would be in the hands of the enemy, with the serious risk of the Belgian right becoming separated from the British left at Menin, and of the Belgian Army being forced to fall back in a northerly, rather than a westerly direction.[3]

25th May – Enemy Pincer Attack

On the 25th May enemy activity intensified. He was across the canal at St. Venant, and was developing the bridgeheads between that place and Aire and also at St. Omer, while further north the situation on the river Aa remained obscure.

During the day the Belgians continued to withdraw in a north-westerly direction under enemy pressure.

General Sir John Dill, who had now succeeded General Sir Edmund Ironside as C.I.G.S., visited Lord Gort in the morning. He then informed the Prime Minister and the Secretary of State for War that there could be no disguising the seriousness of the situation.[3]

By 1800, says Lord Gort, "I was convinced that the steps I had taken to secure my left flank would prove insufficient to meet the growing danger in the north." The pattern of the enemy pincer attack was becoming clearer. One movement from the south-west on Dunkirk had already developed, and was being held; the counterpart was now developing on the Belgian front. The gap between the British left and the Belgian right which had been threatening the whole day, might at any time become impossible to close; were this to happen, my last hope of reaching the coast would be gone".

In order to secure the British northern flank Lord Gort decided to issue orders for the occupation, as quickly as troops could be made available, of the line of the Ypres-Comines canal and the positions covering Ypres. In the absence of General Blanchard, who was visiting the Belgian G.Q.G. at Bruges, Lord Gort communicated this decision that evening to the Headquarters of the French First Group of Armies.[1]

The necessity of evacuation was becoming a matter of paramount immediacy.

British Destroyers Bombard Suburb of Calais

Meanwhile, on the 25th May, the trawler *Lord Howe* sailed to Calais with a cargo of ammunition. She entered the port and discharged part of her cargo in the face of heavy enemy fire from the dunes to the southward. In view of the risk involved, Commodore W. P. Gandell, R.N. (P.S.T.O., French Ports), who was on the quay, then ordered the *Lord Howe* to sail.

Outside Calais the destroyer *Greyhound* closed the *Lord Howe*, which was carrying a request for bombardment support of the town. At the same time, the *Greyhound* received a signal from the Vice-Admiral, Dover, ordering the bombardment of the Calais suburb of St. Pierre. The *Greyhound* opened fire, and at 2000, an H.A. battery east of Sangatte registered a hit on her, killing 2 and wounding 3. About this time the destroyer *Grafton* arrived and also opened fire. The 2 destroyers returned to Dover as darkness set in.

Evacuation of Calais Countermanded

At 2130 a force of seven trawlers, three yachts and two drifters, sailed for Calais road, ready to evacuate troops from Calais, the moment an order was received to do so. Five of the trawlers towed motor boats. Commander W. V. H. Harris, R.N. (Commander M/S, Dover), in the *Grey Mist*, was in command. The destroyers *Windsor* and *Verity* left Dover at 2300, to cover the withdrawal of this force.

On arrival off Calais, two of the motor boats were ordered into Calais harbour. At about 0300/26, a signal was received that Calais was to be held at all costs; furthermore, it was ordered that this signal was to be sent by hand to the Brigadier commanding on shore. The *Conidaw* went in to deliver the signal.

All ships were then ordered back to the Downs, but the *Botanic* and *Maretta* remained behind until the two motor boats and the *Conidaw* returned.

The *Botanic* and *Maretta* were damaged by gunfire when returning on the 26th May, and were unable to take part in Operation "Dynamo".

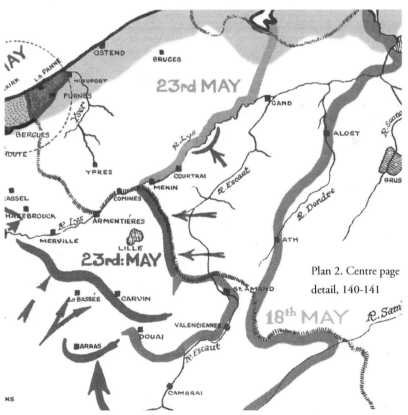

Plan 2. Centre page detail, 140-141

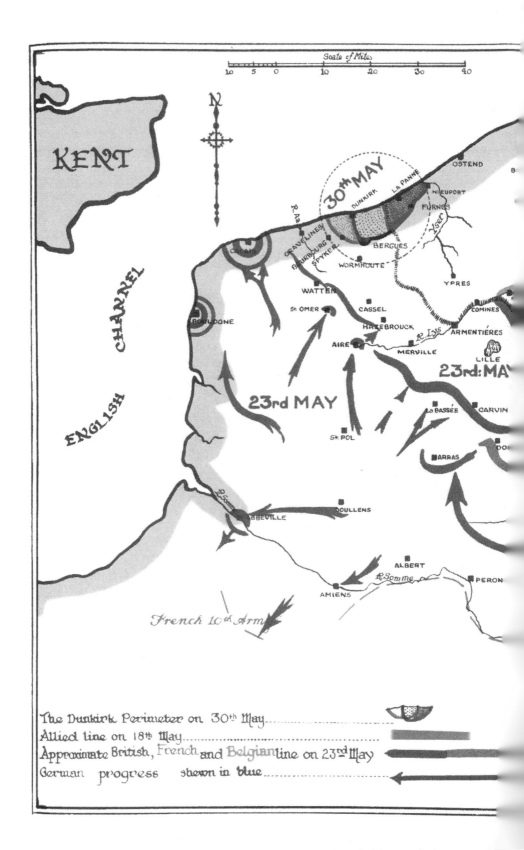

Scale of Miles
10 5 0 10 20 30 40

N

KENT

ENGLISH CHANNEL

OSTEND

30th MAY

LA PANNE
DUNKIRK   NIEUPORT
R. Aa   BERGUES   FURNES
GRAVELINES   Yser
CALAIS   BOURBOURG SPYKER
               WORMHOUTE
WATTEN   YPRES
St. OMER   CASSEL
BOULOGNE   HAZEBROUCK   COMINES
            AIRE   R. Lys   ARMENTIÉRES
               MERVILLE   LILLE

23rd MAY   23rd: MA'

La BASSÉE   CARVIN

St. POL   ARRAS   DO

R. Somme
ABBEVILLE   DOULLENS
                        ALBERT
                   R. Somme   PERON
            AMIENS

French 10th Army

The Dunkirk Perimeter on 30th May ....
Allied line on 18th May ....
Approximate British, French and Belgian line on 23rd May
German progress   shewn in blue ....

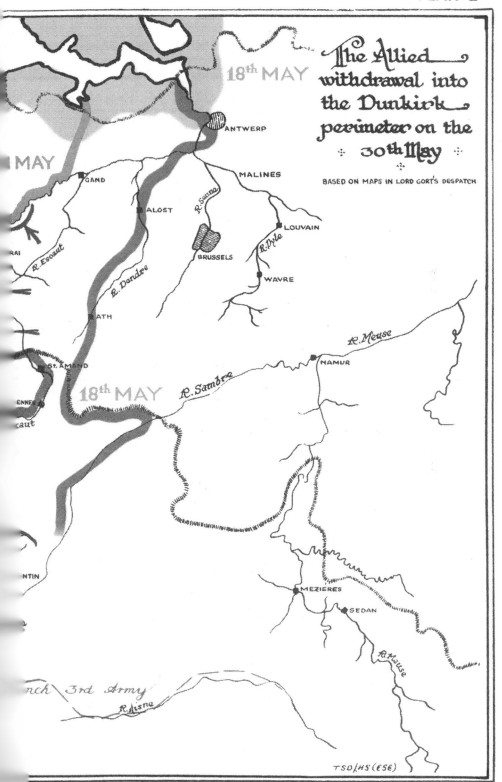

18th MAY

MAY

18th MAY

The Allied
withdrawal into
the Dunkirk
perimeter on the
⁙ 30th May ⁙
⁜
BASED ON MAPS IN LORD GORT'S DESPATCH

ANTWERP

MALINES

GAND

ALOST

LOUVAIN

R. Senne

R. Dyle

BRUSSELS

WAVRE

R. Escaut

R. Dendre

R. Meuse

ATH

NAMUR

RAI

St. AMAND

R. Sambre

ENNES

caut

NTIN

MEZIERES

SEDAN

R. Meuse

nch 3rd Army

R. Aisne

TSD/HS (E56)

Operation "Dynamo" is Commenced, Sunday, 26th May, 1940

Allied Decision to Withdraw

In the morning of Sunday, 26th May, Lord Gort was able to visit General Blanchard at his H.Q. The French general shared his view as to the impending collapse of the Belgian Army and felt that the time for the proposed combined French and British counter-attack southwards was past. It was agreed to withdraw the Allied main bodies behind the line of the Lys, subject to there being no further deterioration in the Belgian situation, and with this decision there vanished the last opportunity for a sortie.[1]

The disposition of the B.E.F. was beginning to take its final shape. Starting from what might be described as a normal situation with Allied troops on the right and left, there had developed an ever-lengthening defensive right flank. This had then become a semi-circular line with both flanks resting on the sea, manned by British, French and Belgians. Finally it had assumed the form of a corridor, with its southern end blocked by the French 1st Army, and each side manned, for the greater part of its length, by British troops; next to the sea were French troops on the west, and French and Belgian troops on the eastern flank.[1]

The Franco-British forces were now holding a front of 128 miles, of which 97 miles were held by British troops, though some of its sectors were held jointly with the French. The immediate problem was to shorten this front, and Lord Gort issued orders, in accordance with the agreement reached with General Blanchard that morning, for withdrawals north-westward to take place in successive stages, on the three coming nights.[1] These withdrawals would have the effect of shortening the Franco-British front by 58 miles, but there would still remain the possible necessity of having to occupy the 25 miles front from Ypres to the sea, at present the responsibility of the Belgian Army.[1]

---

1 Lord Gort's Second Despatch, para. 43.

H.M. Government Authorises Withdrawal to the Coast

So far Lord Gort had not discussed with General Blanchard a further withdrawal to the sea, and although he (Lord Gort) had foreseen the possibility of being forced to make this move, "up to now" he says, "no instructions had been given authorising me to undertake such an operation".[2] The tempo of events was, however, increasing rapidly, for at 1030 on 26th May, on returning to his H.Q., Lord Gort received a telegram from the Secretary of State for War which said, *inter alia*, " ... information ... goes to show ... French offensive from Somme cannot be made in sufficient strength ... only course open to you may be to fight your way back to west where all beaches and ports east of Gravelines will be used for embarkation. Navy will provide fleet of ships and small boats and R.A.F. would give full support ..."[2] This was the first intimation to Lord Gort that evacuation must be seriously considered.

Lord Gort replied that a plan for withdrawal north-westward had been agreed with the French that morning. He added that the news from the Belgian front was "disquieting," and concluded, "I must not conceal from you that a great part of the B.E.F. and its equipment will inevitably be lost even in best circumstances".

Later in the day Lord Gort received a further telegram from the War Office which said, *inter alia*, "... not ... possible for French ... to effect junction with Northern Armies ... no course open to you but to fall back upon the coast ... you are now authorised to operate towards the coast forthwith in conjunction with French and Belgian Armies".[3]

It will be remembered that on the evening of the 21st May the King of the Belgians had agreed that, if forced to abandon the Belgian positions on the Lys, he would withdraw to the Yser, maintaining touch with the left of the B.E.F. Now, however, late on the morning of the 26th May, a note was received from General Michiels, the Chief of the Staff of the Belgian Army, which said, *inter alia* "... the Belgian Army is being attacked with extreme violence ... and ... the lack of Belgian reserves makes it impossible to extend our boundaries ... we have no longer any forces available to fill the gap in the direction of Ypres. As regards the withdrawal to the Yser, the idea must be ruled out since it would destroy our units more quickly than the battle ..."[4]

---

2 *Ibid,* para. 44.

3 Lord Gort's Second Despatch, para. 44.

4 Lord Gort's Second Despatch, para. 45.

The Belgian collapse was impending, if it had not actually taken place, and the task of defending the Allied line as far as the sea had fallen on the British and French troops.[2]

Dunkirk Perimeter Organised

Faced with this critical situation Lord Gort, on the evening of the 26th May, put in hand his plans for withdrawing in to the bridgehead at Dunkirk.[5] Orders had already been given for the embarkation of certain key personnel, and now all units not required for battle were being withdrawn. It was possibly at this juncture that, "owing to a misunderstanding, the personnel of certain anti-aircraft units had been embarked instead of being retained for the defence of the port of Dunkirk".[6] The task of organising a bridgehead at Dunkirk was delegated to Lieut.-General Sir Ronald Adam, Bt., Commander of the 3rd Corps.[7]

The Admiralty Signals, Operation "Dynamo" is to Commence

Meanwhile, in the morning of 26th May, a meeting had been held at the Admiralty to give further consideration to the provision of small craft, and the crews for manning both them and the ex-Dutch skoots. The meeting also examined the number of craft available for the evacuation. The port of Dunkirk had already been so damaged by air attacks as to be no longer available for unloading supplies, which would now have to be landed on the beaches to the eastward.

Long before the operation was ordered, the Admiralty fully realised that large numbers of small craft would be required for a beach evacuation; but such was the secrecy of even the possibility of evacuation, that steps could not yet be taken to collect craft for the purpose.

During the afternoon of the 26th May, under the pressure of the acute military situation, the Admiralty informed the Vice-Admiral, Dover, that "it was imperative for 'Dynamo' to be implemented with the greatest vigour, with a view to lifting up to 45,000 of the B.E.F. within two days, at the end of which it was probable that evacuation would be terminated by enemy action".[8]

---

5 Lord Gort's Second Despatch, para. 47.

6 Lord Gort's Second Despatch, para. 55.

7 He handed over command of the 3rd Corps to Maj.-Gen. S. R. Wason.

8 D.R. page ii.

A further step was taken when, at 1800, Captain W. G. Tennant, M.V.O., R.N., was ordered by the Vice-Chief of the Naval Staff, Vice-Admiral T.S.V. Phillips, C.B., to proceed to Dunkirk to take control of the naval shore embarkation parties. Captain Tennant's appointment as S.N.O., Dunkirk, was promulgated, his duties to commence the following day[9], and beach masters and pier parties were ordered to proceed from the Nore to Dover.

Then, at 1857, there went out from the Admiralty, by teleprinter, the historic signal, "Operation Dynamo is to commence",[10] which was to save our Army in France, and to have the most momentous results for the Nation, the Empire and the World.

Mona's Isle Makes the First Round Trip

Except for the destroyer *Wolsey*, which left Dover at 1930 to act as W/T link ship, the first ship to sail on this great mission was the armed boarding vessel *Mona's Isle*, which left the Downs at 2116. After some delay with a fouled propeller she berthed at the Quai Felix Faure during an air attack, and embarked 1420 troops. On the return journey, she was straddled by shore guns off Gravelines, and shortly after, was heavily machine-gunned from the air; these attacks caused 83 casualties, including 23 dead. She reached Dover at noon on the 27th May escorted by the destroyer *Windsor*, which had put her doctor on board and landed her troops. Mona s Isle was the first ship to complete the round trip in Operation "Dynamo".

Mona's Queen First Ship Back on 27th May

This, however, was not the first passage on 26th May. Even before the Admiralty signal, the despatch of personnel vessels to Dunkirk had begun, a flow of 2 vessels every 4 hours having been accepted by the B.E.F.[11] The armed boarding vessel *King Orry* had sailed at 0930, and the *Mona's Queen* at noon. The *Maid of Orleans* had sailed at 1100 (with 6,000 two-gallon cans of water), but arriving off Dunkirk during an air attack was "unable to effect an entrance and returned to Dover"; she was sailed again at 1726, escorted by the destroyer *Wild Swan*, which had also taken out the *Canterbury* at 1728, and escorted her part of the way.

---

9 Appendix M. 2.

10 Appendix M. 1.

11 D.R.

The *Mona's Queen* (carrying 1200 troops) was the first of these ships to arrive back from Dunkirk, reaching Dover shortly after midnight on the 26th and 27th May; the *Canterbury* arrived at 0309/27 (with 1,340 troops), the store ship *Ngaroma* at 0500/27 (with a hundred troops), the *Maid of Orleans* at 0600/27 (with 980 troops), and the *King Orry* at 1100/27 (with 1,131). As a result of these sailings on the 26th May 6,083 troops were landed in England on the 27th May, of which *Mona's Isle* had contributed 1,420 towards the tentative Admiralty target of "lifting up to 45,000 of the B.E.F. within two days".

Hospital Carriers

The work of the hospital carriers was specially hazardous; their immunity under the Hague Convention was ignored, and their conspicuous white hull in blazing lights made them an easy target. On the 26th May the hospital carriers *St. Andrew* and *St. Julien* sailed at 1054 for Dunkirk, but coming under fire from the guns of Gravelines, they returned to Dover in company with the *Maid of Orleans*.

The hospital carriers *Isle of Guernsey* and *Worthing* sailed from Dover at noon and were bombed when off Calais; nevertheless, that night, flood-lit by the fires which raged in the docks and town of Dunkirk, they each embarked about 300 stretcher cases.

Admiralty call for Cutters and Whalers

All these troops and casualties, it should be noted, were lifted from the quays: Dunkirk harbour. Evacuation from the beaches did not commence until 24 hours later, and then only in a very small way, using ships' boats. On the 26th May, says Vice-Admiral Ramsay, "the only inshore craft available ... were Belgian passenger launches and the naval small craft of the Dover Command such as drifters, and motor boats from the Contraband Control Base at Ramsgate; the only ones capable of lifting personnel direct from a beach being the crafts from Ramsgate." The Admiralty had been asked for a supply of small crafts, especially whalers and cutters, but there remained the difficulty of arranging for the personnel to man them.[12] This request led at 2028, on 26th May, to an Admiralty signal to the Home Ports asking how many cutters and whalers could be made available for immediate service under Vice-Admiral, Dover.[13]

---

12 D.R. p. 1, para. 2.

13 Appendix G. 1

Sea and Air Patrols

Meanwhile, at 1937, C. in C. Nore had been requested to use all available forces to cover Operation "Dynamo" that night.

In conformity with these directions Allied fighters maintained continuous patrols, from 1700 to 2130, on the line Calais-Dunkirk.[14]

Germans Occupy Calais

That very night, however, the gallant defence of Calais came to an end. The yacht *Gulzar* had gone there with water and stretchers, to bring back wounded. She secured alongside the Gare Maritime and sent a party on shore to investigate. The town was found to be in German hands, and the *Gulzar* made a hasty departure under fire. On the way out, however, in response to hail, she stopped, and brought off 3 officers and 48 men from the end of the beakwater.[15]

---

14 R.A.F. Narrative, p. 315.

15 R.O. II, p. 513.

Monday, 27th May

The Dunkirk Perimeter (see plan 3, pages 274–275)

On the morning of 27th May, Lieut.-General Sir Ronald Adam commenced the organisation of the Dunkirk bridgehead. Its perimeter was to extend from Gravelines, south-eastward to the Canal de la Colme, along the canal to Bergues and thence by Furnes and Nieuport to the Belgian coast. In fact, however, the French were already evacuating Gravelines and the western part of the perimeter, and were falling back to the line of the Mardyck Canal, from the sea, to Spyker on the Canal de la Colme. The French were to be responsible for the defence of the western half of the perimeter as far as Bergues inclusive, and the British for the eastern half. The position of the Belgian Army was now so obscure that its inclusion in the bridgehead was not taken into account.[1]

The British sector of the Dunkirk perimeter had its right at Bergues, whence it followed the canals to Furnes and Nieuport. Immediately north of this line were the inundations; to the north of the inundations was low-lying land, and then the Dunkirk-Furnes Canal and the main lateral road from Furnes to Dunkirk; finally, there was the narrow strip of dunes giving way to a wide open beach running the whole length of the position and shelving very gradually to the sea. There were no quays or piers whatever, except those at Dunkirk itself. At intervals of from 3 to 4 miles along the shore (from east to west) lay the seaside resorts of Coxyde, La Panne, Braye-Dunes, and Malo-les-Bains (adjoining Dunkirk).

During the day troops and their transport began to withdraw into the perimeter on the fronts of all three British Corps. Where the troops had received the necessary orders, vehicles were disabled and abandoned in the assembly areas; but owing to the shortage of troops for traffic control a great number of British and French vehicles were able to enter the perimeter and the town of

---

1 Lord Gort's Second Despatch, para. 47.

Dunkirk,[2] causing grave congestion on the roads. Beaches were organised at La Panne, Bray-Dunes and Malo-les-Bains, one beach being allotted to each of the 3 British Corps.[3]

Dunkirk had been bombed for some days, but the town and port received their most serious damage on 27th May. At least 12 attacks were made on Dunkirk and the sea approaches between 0825 and 2000.[4] Lorry columns had been set on fire in the town and a pall of black smoke from the burning oil tanks hung continuously over the town and docks, impeding the air defence. Dunkirk was therefore cleared of all troops and they were sent to the dunes east of the town to await embarkation.[3]

The Belgian Armistice

During the 27th May Lord Gort received a further telegram from the Secretary of State for War which read, "... want to make it quite clear that sole task now is to evacuate to England maximum of your force possible."[5] No policy had yet been laid down by French G.O.G., or any other French higher authority, for a withdrawal northward of the Lys, and, says Lord Gort, "I had no idea what plans either he [General Blanchard] or Admiral Abrial had in mind".[1]

Lord Gort failed to contact General Blanchard either at La Panne, or at the French naval headquarters, situated at Bastion No. 32, Dunkirk. While at the Bastion, however, at 2300, he was informed in the course of conversation with General Koeltz (General Weygand's deputy) that the King of the Belgians had asked for an armistice from midnight that night. The British Commander-in-Chief thus found himself suddenly faced with an open gap of 20 miles between Ypres and the sea, through which enemy armoured forces might reach the beaches.[6]

Owing to congestion on the roads Lord Gort was unable to reach his headquarters at Houtkerque until 0430 on 28th May; he then found that a telegram had been received from the War Office at 0130/28 saying that the King of the Belgians was capitulating at midnight, 27th/28th May.[7]

---

2 Lord Gort's Second Despatch, para. 49.

3 Lord Gort's Second Despatch, para. 50.

4 R.A.F. Narrative, p.320.

5 Lord Gort's Second Despatch, para. 51

6 Lord Gort's Second Despatch, para. 49.

7 Lord Gort's Second Despatch 50.

This was the derelict situation facing Lord Gort in the early hours of the morning.

Dunkirk Locks Prepared for Demolition

On the 27th May, on the orders of Admiral Abrial, the Royal Naval demolition party which had arrived at Dunkirk on the 23rd May placed demolition charges at the New, the Trystram and the Guillain locks in Dunkirk harbour.

Route Z under Fire: Route Y Adopted: Route X Prepared

Owing to the great lack of inshore craft for beach work the main naval effort during the day had been confined to maintaining the flow of personnel vessels to Dunkirk at the rate of 2 every 3½ hours. Even this limited transport service had been seriously interrupted by the fire of shore batteries between Les Hemmes (east of Calais) and Gravelines. At 0623 the *Biarritz* and *Archangel*, en route for Dunkirk escorted by the destroyer *Verity*, were shelled 6 miles E.N.E. of Calais. The *Biarritz* was hit several times and had 1 killed and 2 wounded. The *Archangel* was also apparently damaged, and neither ship took any further part in "Dynamo". At 0640, the M/V *Sequacity* and the freighter *Yewdale* were also shelled off Calais, The *Sequacity* was hit four times, and at 1020, when north of Dunkirk channel, after the crew had been transferred to the *Yewdale*, the *Sequacity* went down by the head and sank. At 0750 the armed boarding vessel *Mona's Isle*, loaded with troops, suffered severe casualties and damage from shore guns off Gravelines, and also from an air attack shortly afterwards, and had to go into dock for repairs. At 0800 the H/C *Isle of Thanet* was shelled off Calais and returned to Dover. At 0900, the A.B/V *King Orry*, returning from Dunkirk loaded with troops also suffered casualties and damage from the Calais guns.

As a result of these happenings the Vice-Admiral, Dover, reported to the Admiralty that the normal or southern route, Dover to Dunkirk (later known as Route Z), was impracticable in daylight. Another, more northern route (later known as Route Y), via the Dyck Whistle buoy, Middelkerk buoy, and Zuydcoote Pass, was accordingly adopted. This, however, increased the round trip from 80 to 172 miles, and the route had to be swept before it could be used. Orders were therefore given for the establishment of a third, shorter route (the middle Route X), from the North Goodwin to the Ruytingen Pass, and thence into the Dunkirk road, and at 1140 work on this new route was commenced by the destroyer *Impulsive*, the minesweepers *Skipjack* and *Halcyon*, and the Trinity House Vessel *Patricia*. This route X had the great advantage of shortening the round trip from 172 to 108 miles.

Among the earliest ships to use the northern Route Y were the P/V's *St. Helier*[8] and *Royal Daffodil*, which left Dover at 1054 under escort of the destroyer *Vimy*; in company was the destroyer *Anthony*, escorting the S.S. *Kyno*.[9] The convoy was joined *en route* by the hospital carriers *St. Andrew* and *St. Julien*. Route Y was certainly, at that time, out of range of gunfire, but two bombing attacks were made on the hospital carriers between the West Hinder and Kwint Bank buoys, and when the convoy arrived off Dunkirk heavy air attacks were in progress there. The *Royal Daffodil* and the *St. Helier* entered the harbour, but the latter was ordered to withdraw, and she and the 2 hospital carriers returned empty to the Downs under escort of the *Vimy*. The *Royal Daffodil* embarked 840 troops before returning to Dover.

Sea and Air Patrols

The principal patrol line covered in the morning of the 27th May by Fighter Command, was Calais-Dunkirk, as it was not known that the Calais garrison had ceased fire. From 1450 onwards, however, Calais fell out of the picture, and it became possible to concentrate fighter protection more exclusively on the work of evacuation.[10] Sixteen squadrons, varying in strength from 9 to 20 aircraft, were engaged on these activities from 0500-2130; patrols were, however, limited to squadron strength. Most squadrons carried out 2 patrols, and 287 sorties in all were flown during the day.[11]

To cover the passage of ships between Dunkirk and the Downs destroyer patrols had been established to the northward during the forenoon, and Vice-Admiral, Dover, asked for 6 additional destroyers to strengthen the Dover forces. The Admiralty immediately ordered 4 destroyers from the Western Approaches Command, and 2 from the Portsmouth Command, to proceed to Dover.[12]

Ex-Dutch Skoots for Dunkirk

Other vessels were on their way to Dunkirk during the day, among them being 15

---

8 Eleven of the *St. Helier's* crew had been replaced by naval ratings.

9 Off R buoy the *Anthony*, with the *Kyno*, was ordered back to the Downs and subsequently to Portsmouth. The *Kyno* took no further part in Operation "Dynamo".

10 R.A.F. Narrative, p. 319.

11 R.A.F. Narrative, p. 320.

12 *Appendices D. 1 and D. 2. The Wakeful, Mackay, Worcester, Montrose, Shikari and Scimitar were sent.*

skoots.[13] Of these the *Lena*, *Hebe II*, and later the *Oranje*, arrived off the beaches and embarked troops during the night of 27th and 28th May; the *Abel Tasman*, *Alice* and *Kaap Falga*, loaded with ammunition and food, arrived off La Panne early in the morning of 28th May; the *Hilda* and *Doggersbank* reached Dunkirk by noon the 28th May, and were sent to the beaches; while the remainder,[14] in error, returned to the Downs, after having got within a few miles of Dunkirk.

The "build-up" of Small Craft Commences

Early on the 27th May, the Ministry of Sea Transport had been asked by the Admiralty to find between 40 and 50 small craft, which were to assemble; Sheerness "for a special requirement". The Director of the Small Vessels Pool (Vice-Admiral Sir Lionel Preston, K.C.B.) supplied a list of what were thought to be suitable vessels, but it was soon found that a great number of these were not in a fit state for service. A meeting was therefore held at the Admiralty which was attended by a representative of the Director of Sea Transport, Mr. H. C. Riggs. On Mr. Riggs' suggestion, Admiral Preston agreed to send some of his officers to the various boat-yards from Teddington to Burnham and Brightlingsea, to inspect and send to Sheerness all vessels fit for service.[15] Forty motor boats or launches were thus obtained, and arrangements made for them to reach Sheerness by 28th May.[16] Very few of these reached the Dunkirk beaches by the 29th May, but they were the forerunners: nearly 300 small craft, which were destined to play an important part in the embarkation from the beaches of some 99,000 troops, by ferrying them to waiting ships.

In the evening of the 27th the Naval Officer-in-Charge, Ramsgate, assumed by arrangement the duty of fuelling and despatching all small power boats with the attendant pulling boats forming the inshore flotilla.

Some delays occurred in the assembly at Ramsgate or in the Downs of small craft despatched from other commands, owing to many of them being routed to Dover in error, instead of to the Downs. Once despatched by the authorities no communication with these small vessels was possible until they arrived at their destination; this resulted in delays of up to 24 hours or more before assembly, because during the night misfortune befell many tows that came adrift owing to

---

13 The *Bornrif, Brandaris, Hondsrug, Jutland, Patria, Tilly* and *Twente*.

14 T.O. 9144/40.

15 T.O. 9144/40.

16 Appendix G. 3.

the moderate weather or collisions, and the business of rounding them up could not be effected until daylight.

"Dynamo Maintenance Officer" Appointed

To take charge of these small craft, Rear-Admiral, A. H. Taylor, O.B.E., with the acting rank of Commodore, after getting final instructions from the Vice-Admiral, Dover, proceeded to Sheerness on the 27th May to act as "Dynamo Maintenance Officer." He was responsible for the preparation of various vessels, small motor craft, and pulling boats, for service in Operation "Dynamo"; his staff comprised Cdr. H. R. Troup, R.N., and Lt. Cdr. D. E. Holland-Martin, R.N. The type of machinery fitted in many of the vessels and its defective state presented the Fleet Engineer Officer, Captain T. E. Docksey, R.N., and Sheerness Dockyard with some difficult problems; but within a week, under Commodore Taylor's general direction, no less than 100 motor boats, 10 self-propelled lighters, 7 skoots, 1 oil tanker, 6 paddle steamers, and numerous pulling boats, were prepared for service and sent out from sheerness.

B.N.L.O. Dunkirk Assumes Duty 1900/27

Meanwhile, at 1315, Captain Tennant left Dover for Dunkirk in the destroyer *Wolfhound*, with a naval beach and pier party of 12 officers and 160 ratings. The communications staff was also taken, as it was intended that the *Wolfhound* should relieve the *Wolsey* at Dunkirk as W/T link. The *Wolfhound* was attacked twice by dive-bombers *en route*, receiving some damage from near misses, and, on arrival at Dunkirk at 1655, found an air attack by 21 aircraft was in progress.

Captain Tennant proceeded ashore to the Bastion Naval Headquarters to investigate the local situation. The whole area of the docks and town was enveloped in a vast pall of smoke from the oil depots and refineries. The town was blazing, air raid casualties were lying about the streets, which were littered with masses of wreckage.

On arrival at the Bastion, Captain Tennant held a meeting with Brigadier Parminter; Colonel Whitfeld, Sub-Area Commandant; and Commander H. P. Henderson, R.N., the B.N.L.O. It was decided that the harbour was untenable, and that it was impracticable to retain the *Wolfhound* at Dunkirk as a W/T link.

At 1900 Captain Tennant assumed the duties of S.N.O. Dunkirk, and ordered the *Wolfhound* and *Wolsey* to proceed to the beach east of Dunkirk and embark troops, using their own boats. This they proceeded to do, but did not get away unscathed; the *Wolfhound* grounded as she left Dunkirk harbour and received further damage from a bomb which struck the jetty six feet away. She made no more trips to Dunkirk, but on that evening she and the *Wolsey* became the pioneers of beach evacuation.

Beach Evacuation Begins

Meanwhile, during the afternoon, four personnel vessels and two hospital carriers had sailed for Dunkirk.[17] Of these, the personnel vessels *Queen of the Channel* and *St. Seiriol* left Dover at 1330, by Route Y, and entered Dunkirk harbour at about 1930, during an air raid. The *Queen of the Channel* had barely embarked 50 troops when both ships were diverted to the beaches. At 2230, however, before the *St. Seiriol's* boats had started ferrying, S.N.O. Dunkirk signalled the *Wolfhound* to send a personnel ship to the east pier, Dunkirk, to embark 1,000 men. The *Wolfhound*, then with the *Wolsey* off the beaches passed this order to the *St. Seiriol* by megaphone and commandeered her boats, which were manned as necessary by naval ratings or towed by the destroyers' motor boats. The *Queen of the Channel*, using her own boats, embarked about 150 troops from the beach and then, returning to Dunkirk harbour, picked up a further 700 troops. She was the first ship, except the destroyers *Wolfhound* and *Wolsey*, to embark troops from the beaches, though she was unfortunately sunk by aircraft early next morning (May 28th) shortly after leaving Dunkirk.

"Evacuation Tomorrow Night is Problematical"

By 1958, on 27th May, only an hour after he had assumed the duties of S.N.O. Dunkirk, Captain Tennant had arrived at a very serious view of the local situation, and he sent this dramatic signal to the Vice-Admiral, Dover:

> "Please send every available craft to beaches east of Dunkirk immediately. Evacuation tomorrow night is problematical. T.O.0.1958."

This signal, delayed in transmission, was not received until 2055, but in the meantime at 2025, the Vice-Admiral, Dover, received another signal sent only. few minutes later:

> "Port continuously bombed all day and on fire. Embarkation possible

---

17 The *Queen of the Channel, St. Seiriol, Canterbury, Maid of Orleans, Isle of Thanet* and *Worthing.*

only from beaches east of harbour A.B.C.D.[18] Send all ships and passenger ships there to anchor. Am ordering *Wolfhound* to load there and sail. T.O.0.2005."

To the Vice-Admiral, Dover, the situation must have appeared critical when, later that evening, he received a report from two military officers from G.H.Q., that the plight of the B.E.F. was precarious and that the enemy might, indeed, succeed in cutting it off from Dunkirk.[19]

All Ships Diverted to the Beaches

Such was the grim picture presenting itself to the Vice-Admiral, Dover, that the B.E.F. was in grave and very real danger of being cut off altogether from Dunkirk, and possibly only a bare 24 hours available for its evacuation. Admiral Ramsay reacted to these dire tidings with characteristic drive and energy, a period of intense activity ensued. Every effort was concentrated on landing as many craft as possible to the beaches without delay[2]. Order followed order in rapid succession. Personnel ships were diverted to the beach, code letters A, B, C and D (i.e. Malo beach). Four paddle minesweepers[20] were sailed from the Downs to La Panne beach. Destroyers were rushed to the beaches and urged to embark as many British troops as possible, as this was his "last chance of saving them"; the *Gallant*, and *Vivacious*, then on patrol, the *Windsor*, *Vimy*, *Anthony*, *Impulsive*, *Sabre* and the cruiser *Calcutta*, were ordered to proceed with the utmost despatch to the beach at Malo-les-Bains and the beach at Zuydcoote, just east of it; the *Grafton* and *Greyhound*, on patrol between Fairy Bank and Kwint Bank buoys, and the *Wakeful*, just arrived at Dover from Plymouth, were hurried to the beach at La Panne.

---

18 These letters refer to an arrangement, whereby at the commencement of "Dynamo" the Dunkirk beaches were described by a letter code referring to Map G.S.G.S. 4040, Sheet 29, 1/50,000. The lengths of beach lying in each 1000 metre map square were lettered, west to east, commencing with "A" at square 2686 in sequence to "O" at iquare 3990. (Appx. N. 10). Under this arrangement, A.B.C.D. actually refers to the beach at Malo-les-Bains.

This arrangement appears to have fallen into disuse on and after 29th May, when the stretch of beach, one mile east of Dunkirk to one mile east of La Panne, was divided into equal parts, referred to as *La Panne*, *Bray* and *Malo*, from east to west, with a mile gap between each part. (Appendix O. 11).

19 D.R. page 3, para. 8.

20 The *Sandown*, *Medway Queen*, *Brighton Belle* and *Gracie Fields*.

The wording of some of the signals[21] conveying these orders reflects the desperation felt that night, a desperation which, in spite of the course of subsequent events, was at the time only too well-founded. "Had the situation appeared less critical," observes Admiral Ramsay, "an organised flow of large and small craft, working in reliefs, would have been arranged."[22]

Yet a further batch of vessels arrived off the beaches that evening; the 17 available flare-burning drifters of the Dover Auxiliary Patrol[23] had sailed for Dunkirk during the afternoon, and on arriving were diverted to the beaches by the *Wolfhound*, in accordance with a signal from the Vice-Admiral, Dover,[24] and anchored close inshore. The boats from the *Wolfhound* and *Wolsey*, and from the *St. Seiriol* and *Queen of the Channel*, in addition to the drifters' own dinghies, enabled these drifters to lift some 2,000 troops from Malo and Bray beaches during the night of the 27th/28th May.

Results of S.N.O. Dunkirk's 2005/27

As a result of the action taken on S.N.O. Dunkirk's signals, there were assembling off the beaches on the night of the 27th/28th May the *Wolfhound, Wolsey* and 6 other destroyers[25], 1 cruiser, 4 paddle-minesweepers, 17 drifters, 3 skoots (the *Lena, Hebe II* and *Oranje*) and 2 transports (the *Queen of the Channel* and the *St. Seiriol*). All these ships were ordered to use their own boats for ferrying, as no other small power boats, cutters, whalers or other pulling boats, were yet available.

S.N.O. Dunkirk's signals had therefore a big result; but owing to the difficulty of passing orders at night in a shattered harbour his decision to divert vessels to the beaches had unforeseen repercussions, and it was associated with a false report that Dunkirk had fallen, and the failure of one personnel vessel and 7 skoots to reach the beaches that night. The circumstances are described below.

The P/V *Canterbury* which had entered Dunkirk harbour at 2000, left at

---

21 See Appendices D. 3, D. 4, D. 5, D. 7, and D. 8.

22 D.R., p.3, para. 38.

23 They were the *Netsukis, Lord Howard, Lord Howe, Golden Sunbeam, Midas, Golden lift, Girl Pamela, Paxton, Boy Roy, Eileen Emma, Girl Gladys, Forecast, Ut Prosim, Yorkshire Lass, Young Mun, Shipmates* and *Torbay II*.

24 Appendix D.6

25 The situation having changed by the time they arrived, the Gallant and Wakeful went into Dunkirk. The Windsor remained on patrol. The Anthony had not yet returned from Portsmouth whither she had escorted the S.S. Kyno.

2058 with 457 troops, including 140 stretcher cases. Before leaving she was ordered by the "Sea Transport Officer"[26] "to turn back ships attempting to enter Dunkirk"; the order, evidently intended to divert ships to the beaches was misunderstood. In the Dunkirk road, the *Canterbury* passed the order to the P/V *Maid of Orleans* and to the H/C's *Isle of Thanet* and *Worthing*, and those vessels thereupon turned back to Dover. Later the order became definitely garbled, for the skoot *Tilly* (which was in the company with the 4 skoots *Hondsrug, Jutland, Patria* and *Brandaris*) met the *Canterbury* (in company with 2 hospital carriers) 8 or 9 miles from Dunkirk, and received from her the signal "Dunkirk is in enemy hands. Keep clear". This signal was variously recorded by some of the other skoots, as "Dunkirk has fallen. Return"; and all five of them, as well as the skoots *Bornrif* and *Twente*, did in fact return to the Downs, although the *Jutland* and the *Patria* first closed Nieuport Bank buoy in an unsuccessful endeavour to obtain more definite information. Some of the skoots, in turn, promulgated this false report to other ships, notably to the P/V *Dorrien Rose*; this ship, which received the signal "unsafe to approach Dunkirk," did at first alter course to the northward, but, shortly after, again set course for Dunkirk. It was subsequently thought by some of the vessels concerned that the false information had been passed by "fifth columnists," though there is very little proof of this.[27]

"Chronic Shortage" of Beaching Boats

Such was the beginning of the great build-up of ships[28] and of the inauguration of the beach evacuation. The successful development of the latter was necessarily dependent on the continuation of fine weather, and the making good of the "chronic shortage" of beach boats.[29] A wind of any strength in the northern sector between south-west and north-east would have made beach evacuation impossible; at no time did this happen, but it was not until the fifth day of the operation (May 30th) that small power boats and beach craft began to become available in adequate numbers.[30]

The reason for this is to be sought mainly in the need for secrecy enjoined by the British and French Governments, even after the operation had been ordered.

---

26 *Canterbury*'s report

27 See Appendicies H. 30 and H 32.

28 Appendices D, E and F.

29 D.R. page 3, para 11.

30 D.R. covering letter, No A.14/0/876/40, page 2, paras. 3 and 5.

The necessity for avoiding any action that might have given rise to talk rendered the collection of small craft slow. It was not until 31st May that the British public learnt from the press that evacuation had begun.

Disembarkation Ports Designated

In these early days the limiting factors seemed likely to be the scale of enemy attacks at Dunkirk and on the beaches, and the difficulty of concentrating the ships and troops at a common point or points.[31]

Meanwhile, in order to ensure air protection, Blenheims maintained a patrol by single aircraft over the Dunkirk area during the night.[32]

At 2330, the Vice-Admiral, Dover, promulgated the names of the ports for the disembarkation of troops in England as follows:

The *Calcutta* at Sheerness;
Destroyers at Dover;
Drifters, minesweepers, skoots, coasters at Margate or Ramsgate as directed by N.O.I.C. Ramsgate;
Personnel vessels at Folkstone.

Throughout the whole course of the operation the despatch of troops from the points of disembarkation in England was directed by the War Office Movements Control Organisation, and proceeded with great smoothness.[33]

Summary of Troops Evacuated

The ships which sailed from Dunkirk on the 26th May brought back 6,183 troops and 646 stretcher cases next day.

During the 27th May only two personnel vessels actually made the round trip, viz.: the *Royal Daffodil*, which brought back 840 troops from Dunkirk, and the *St. Helier*, which was ordered back before she could embark any troops. The destroyers *Wolsey* and *Wolfhound*, which embarked 206 and 130 troops respectively from Malo beach on the evening of 27th May, did not sail for England until shortly after midnight.

Thus the total number landed in England from the commencement of

---

31 D.R. page 3, para.11.

32 R.A.F. Narrative, page 320

33 D.R. covering letter, No A.14/0/876/40, page 2, para. 6.

Operation "Dynamo" to midnight 27th/28th May was:

26th May – Nil

27th May 7,669, all of whom were lifted direct from Dunkirk harbour.

Tuesday, 28th May

First Supplies Reach the Beaches

This was a day of tension. The first supplies of food, water and ammunition from England arrived at the beaches, and in spite of many losses by enemy action considerable quantities were landed at La Panne and at Coxyde to the north of it.[1]

Germans Reach Nieuport

Early on the 28th May the leading enemy mobile troops and tanks reached Nieuport, but the danger that the enemy forces, released by the Belgian armistice, might forestall the B.E.F.'s occupation of the perimeter had been foreseen,[2] and the measures taken by Lord Gort to meet a desperate situation and to delay the enemy proved successful.

At 1100 General Blanchard visited Lord Gort at his headquarters at Houtkerque. It then transpired that General Blanchard, having received no instructions from his Government regarding the evacuation of French troops, declined to contemplate any such operation. Later in the day, however, he consented, and orders were given for part of the French 1st Army to withdraw so as to arrive within the Dunkirk perimeter on 30th May.[3]

Lord Gort's Headquarters move to La Panne

Meanwhile, during the afternoon, Lord Gort moved his headquarters from Houtkerque to La Panne, which was in direct telephonic communication with London. There he received from Lt.-Gen. Sir Ronald Adam and the Quarter-Master-General, Lt.-General W. G. Laidsell, a very unfavourable report:

---

1 Lord Gort's Second Despatch, para. 50.

2 Lord Gort's Second Despatch, para. 53.

3 Lord Gort's Second Despatch, para. 52.

"No ships could be unloaded at the docks at Dunkirk, and few wounded could be evacuated. There was no water in Dunkirk and very little on the beaches. The Naval plans were not yet in full operation, and some 20,000 men were waiting to be taken off the beaches, 10,000[4] having been taken off in the last 2 days, chiefly from Dunkirk." Also, they stated it as their opinion that "given a reasonable measure of immunity from air attack, troops could be gradually evacuated ... If, however, intensive air attacks continued the beaches might easily become a shambles within the next 48 hours".[5]

Possibility of Surrender is Visualised

Lord Gort informed the C.I.G.S. of the gist of this report, and asked that H.M. Government should consider the policy to be followed if a crisis arose, "as well it might." He received this telegram in reply:

"H.M. Govt, fully approve your withdrawal to extricate your force in order to embark maximum number possible of B.E.F. If you are cut from all communication from us, and all evacuation from Dunkirk and beaches had, in your judgment, been finally prevented after every attempt to re-open it had failed, you would become sole judge of when it was impossible to inflict further damage to enemy".[2]

While a situation that could only mean surrender was now visualised in England as possibly a stark necessity, General Weygand sent an urgent telegram to Lord Gort appealing to him personally to ensure that the British Army took a vigorous part in any counter-attack thought necessary; the situation, said General Weygand, made it essential to hit hard.

Lord Gort, who saw the situation more clearly, observes, "when he [General Weygand] sent this message, he could have had no accurate information of the real position or of the powers of counter-attack remaining to either the British or French."

Germans take Ostend

That evening, at 2030, the Admiralty informed the Vice-Admiral, Dover, that Ostend was reliably reported to be captured. Dunkirk was the only port left in

---

4 Some of these had been taken off before Operation "Dynamo" commenced.

5 Lord Gort's Second Despatch, para. 54.

Allied hands.

Situation at Dunkirk Becomes Easier

Nor were the prospects at Dunkirk very hopeful. When the *Wolfhound* and the *Wolsey* left Malo beach for Dover just after midnight on the 27th May the whole of the port appeared to be ablaze.[6]

At 0125 the cruiser *Calcutta, en route* for La Panne, was missed by a torpedo 100 yards astern fired from an E-boat. No further attack took place, and the *Calcutta* arrived off La Panne beach an hour later to find that the destroyers *Grafton*, *Greyhound* and *Impulsive*, and the paddle-minesweepers *Sandown* and *Gracie Fields*, were already there.

Ever since 0030 destroyers making their first trip to the evacuation area had been arriving off the beaches, and only two – the *Gallant* and the *Wakeful* – went to Dunkirk. The *Vivacious* and the skoot *Hebe II* reached Malo beach at about 0030, and the *Sabre* at 0120. The *Hebe II*, unable to find any troops, entered Dunkirk harbour and embarked 150 from the east pier; the *Sabre* embarked troops from two drifters. At 0320 the *Vimy* arrived off the beach at Zuydcoote, 3 miles east of Dunkirk, and sent her boats to assist in filling up the minesweeper *Brighton Belle*, which was embarking troops with the assistance of the ex-Belgian canal boat *Yser* and a small pulling boat. The skoot *Lena* had been off Zuydcoote since the previous evening and in the early hours of the 28th May transferred the 120 troops she had embarked to a destroyer; the minesweeper *Medway Queen*, off La Panne since 2300/27, sailed with 600 troops on board.

By 0400 the situation in Dunkirk harbour appears to have eased, and at 0436 S.N.O. Dunkirk was asking for all vessels to go alongside the east pier. At 0445 the *Vimy*, leaving her boats with the *Brighton Belle*, went into Dunkirk harbour and embarked 613 troops. At 0955 the destroyer *Mackay* reached Dunkirk from the Irish Sea, and picked up 600 troops in an hour from the seaward end of Dunkirk east pier, giving up her berth to the destroyer *Montrose*. The *Sabre*, which had in the meantime returned to Dover with a load of 158 troops from Malo beach, berthed outside the *Montrose*. An hour later, the destroyers *Worcester* and *Anthony* arrived, and berthed ahead of the *Montrose*. The pier was crammed with troops and several aircraft, attempting to bomb it, were driven off by the destroyers' gunfire. Vast columns of smoke were drifting westwards from the burning oil tanks ashore, and houses on the sea front were bursting into

---

6 Report by the *Wolfhound.*

flames from time to time.[7]

The destroyers *Codrington*, *Jaguar* and *Javelin*, diverted from patrol, arrived off Dunkirk at 1315. They had picked up 33 survivors that morning from the S.S. *Abukir*, which had been torpedoed by an E-boat while returning with about 200 evacuees from Ostend to the United Kingdom; these survivors were transferred to the destroyer *Grenade* which subsequently went on to Dunkirk. The *Codrington* went into Dunkirk harbour, while the *Jaguar* and *Javelin* using their own boats, embarked troops from Bray beach. At 1730 the *Grenade* left Dunkirk with 1,000 troops on board.

Between 1230 and 1815 the *Vivacious*, making her second trip, embarked 359 troops from Zuydcoote, assisted by ships' boats, the M.T.B.16, and the skoot *Lena*. The *Vimy* also made a second trip, embarking 591 troops from Dunkirk harbour.

More ships were on the way. From 1230 onwards 19 minesweepers were sailed from Harwich, from Dover and the Downs, for Dunkirk and the beaches. By 2130 five of them had arrived off Bray beach,[8] and four off La Panne;[9] three reached Dunkirk by 2140.[10]

Four other minesweepers arrived off the beaches late on the night of 28th and 29th May[11], and two more reached the beaches at 0600/29.[12]

Early on the 28th May the eight ships of the 7th and 8th minesweeping flotillas had been ordered from Rosyth to Harwich, to work under the orders of the Vice-Admiral, Dover;[13] they could not, however, reach the beaches until about 72 hours later.

During the forenoon and afternoon of the 28th May the call went out for more and more destroyers, and seven reached the evacuation area next day.[14] In the signals from the Admiralty and the Vice-Admiral, Dover, summoning them there sounds the same note of extreme urgency, traceable to S.N.O. Dunkirk's

---

7 Report by the *Montrose*.

8 The *Albury, Gossamer, Leda, Kellett* and *Sutton*.

9 The *Salamander, Halcyon, Skipjack* and *Waverley*.

10 The *Ross, Pangbourne* and *Lydd*.

11 The *Hebe, Sharpshooter, Duchess of Fife* and *Emperor of India*.

12 The *Oriole* and *Marmion*.

13 A.M.0163/28.

14 The *Verity, Harvester, Esk, Malcolm, Express, Shikari* and *Scimitar*.

message[15] declaring that evacuation on the night of 28th and 29th May was problematical. "If the older class destroyers and other vessels cannot compete with the situation" signalled the Admiralty, "destroyers of all classes are to be used for bringing men off".[16] "Every available destroyer" in the Western Approaches and Portsmouth Commands was to be sailed to Dover.[17] Destroyers on patrol or on escort duty were to be diverted to Dunkirk or the beaches.[18]

Vulnerability of Personnel Vessels

The vulnerability of the personnel vessels, with their large troop-carrying capacity, was a cause of anxiety. On the 27th May the *Biarritz* and *Archangel*, the *Monas Queen*, *King Orry*, *Sequacity*, *Yewdale*, and the *Isle of Thanet*,[19] had all come under fire from the shore guns at Calais and Gravelines. At 0415 on the 28th May the *Queen of the Channel*, loaded with 904 troops, was attacked by one aircraft; 3 or 4 bombs were dropped, which straddled the ship abaft the mainmast and broke her back, the starboard propeller shaft and the rudder. By good fortune the *Dorrien Rose*, *en route* for Dunkirk, was in the vicinity and rescued the troops: the *Queen of the Channel* sank about ¼ hour later. The *St. Seiriol*, which left Dunkirk at about 0415 with 494 troops, reached Folkestone in safety.

Civilian Crews Feel the Strain

Some 45 personnel vessels were used during Operation "Dynamo".[20] Of these eight were sunk, at least six were so damaged by bombing or gunfire as to render them unfit for further use during the operation, and two were damaged in collision. Nine of the largest of these personnel vessels had been engaged prior to "Dynamo" in operations at Dunkirk, Calais and Boulogne, and their Captains and crews were beginning to feel the strain when Operation "Dynamo" started.

Thus it was that the Master of the *Canterbury*, which had already completed

---

15 Appendix M.4.

16 A.M.0754/28.

17 A.M.1229/28.

18 Appendices D.4, D.5 and D.7.

19 At 0254, on 28th May, shortly after leaving Dover for Newhaven, the *Isle of Thanet* collided with the Examination Service Vessel *Ocean Reward*, which sank immediately. Assisted by the tug *Lady Brassey*, a search was made for survivors, but none was found.

20 This number includes 3 store ships, 3 motor vessels and a few freighters, coasters and tramps.

2 round trips to Dunkirk in Operation "Dynamo", reported, on the 28th May, that he was too worn out to make a third trip. The P.S.T.O. went on board and explained the gravity of the situation to the Master, and the *Canterbury* sailed at 0930 the next day. On her return voyage from Dunkirk she was bombed and damaged, and after landing her 1960 troops went into dock for repairs. In the 3 trips she made the *Canterbury* brought back 4,416 troops; her Master, Captain C. A. Hancock, was awarded the D.S.C.

Personnel Vessels not to be Employed During Full Daylight

On the 28th May, however, it had become apparent that development of the German air threat over the evacuation area, and the increasing artillery fire from shore batteries covering the sea approaches to Dunkirk, prohibited the employment of personnel and similar vessels during daylight, until the position was restored, and that evacuation from Dunkirk by day must for the moment be confined to warships and small vessels.[21]

It was not, therefore, until later in the day, that the P/V *Royal Daffodil* sailed for Dunkirk, and eight other personnel vessels and a hospital carrier[22] received their sailing orders during the afternoon and evening.

The northern Route Y was by this time in general use,[23] but ships proceeding from Dover to Dunkirk were ordered to use the southern and shorter Route Z, if the passage from Calais Bell buoy to Dunkirk could be made in darkness.

N.O.I.C. Ramsgate Responsible for Servicing Skoots

In these circumstances some 20 skoots reached Dunkirk, or arrived off the beaches during the day and evening of the 28th May; others were on the way. Their speed varied, but most of them were very slow. Eight of them went into Dunkirk harbour,[24] and four to Bray beach.[25] The *Abel Tasman*, loaded with ammunition, the *Alice* and *Kaap Falga*, loaded with food, and three others[26] were off La Panne beach. The *Alice* which arrived in the early morning, was put

---

21 D.R. p. 4, para. 13.

22 The *Scotia, Malines, Prague, Manxman, Royal Sovereign, Tynwald, Lochgarry, Killarney* and the H.C. *Paris.*

23 Appendix K. 1.

24 The *Caribia, Fredanja, Friso, Jutland, Tilly, Patria, Sursum-Corda,* and *Twente.*

25 The *Amazone, Doggersbank, Hilda,* and *Oranje.*

26 The *Reiger, Pacific* and *Pascholl.*

aground to facilitate unloading; a few hours later, however, after she had been refloated, her engines seized up as a result of damage during an air attack, and she was abandoned.

At this stage began the running of a continuous service of skoots between Margate and Ramsgate and the beaches, whose servicing was performed by N.O.I.C. Ramsgate.

Evacuation Plan for the Night 28th and 29th May

The full significance of this rapidly growing armada of ships became apparent in the numbers of troops lifted the following day. By midday on the 28th May, approximately 12,000 troops had been transported since the commencement of Operation "Dynamo"; about 1,000 were *en route* to the U.K., and about 5,000 were embarking in 5 destroyers. Nine more destroyers were on the way to Dunkirk, and a total force of 16 destroyers would be maintaining a continuous ferry service during the day.

The plan for the night of 28th and 29th May, was to sail all available ships, small craft and boats, so as to develop the maximum effort at 2200. The details of the plan were signalled by V. A. Dover to S.N.O. Dunkirk at 1555. Briefly, 2 hospital carriers, 7 personnel vessels and 2 destroyers were to embark troops at the east pier Dunkirk; while some 20 destroyers, 19 paddle and fleet sweepers, 17 drifters, 20 to 40 skoots, 5 coasters, 12 motor boats, 2 tugs, 28 pulling cutters and lifeboats, were to work along the 10 mile stretch of beach from Dunkirk to La Panne.

Fighter Command Patrols Strengthened

Meanwhile, at Dunkirk, conditions had proved easier during the day; enemy air activity over the port was restricted, probably by the heavy pall of smoke from the burning town, and increased fighter activity was keeping the enemy in check.[27] Fighter Command patrols were strengthened from an average of one squadron to an average of 2 squadrons, and Coastal Command maintained a continuous daylight patrol (usually of 3 aircraft at a time) on the line North Goodwins – Gravelines – Ostend. About 320 sorties were flown on Continental patrols during the day, and severe losses were inflicted on the enemy. Nineteen Me.109's and 4 bombers were definitely destroyed for a loss of 13 British fighters.[28]

---

27 Appendix L.3.

28 R.A.F. Narrative, p. 323.

Windsor Damaged

At 1000 some 40 Me.109's were engaged by our fighters, and at 1040 they encountered a German force of nearly 150 bombers and fighters[3]. At 1125, the destroyer *Anthony* observed 40 to 50 planes in aerial combat over Dunkirk. At 1145 the destroyer *Windsor*, which was on patrol, was attacked near the South Goodwin Light Vessel by 15 dive-bombers supported by 10 fighters; she suffered considerable damage from near misses and m.g. fire and had 30 casualties.

Boy Roy and *Paxton* Damaged and Beached

At 1215 German fighters in strength were encountered by our fighter patrols; during the rest of the day there was no further air fighting,[29] but the minesweeper *Sandown* was bombed off the Gull Light buoy at 1230, and Bray beach was bombed at 1420.[30] In an air raid off Dunkirk channel at about 1800, the drifters *Boy Roy* and *Paxton* were damaged by near misses and had to be beached; there were, however, no casualties.

Difficulty of synchronising arrival of ships with flow of troops

Meanwhile, at 0935, 2,000 troops were on Malo beach and 7,000 more were on the sand dunes, waiting anxiously for ships to come.[31] An hour after midday, 6,000 troops were reported to be on Bray beach, 7 miles east of Dunkirk pier, and 4 minesweepers were sailed from the Downs to embark them. When they arrived at 2130, however, conditions had changed, and three of them, the *Salamander*, *Fitzroy* and *Skipjack*, went to La Panne; the fourth, the *Sutton*, went to the beach at Zuydcoote 4 miles east of Dunkirk.[32] Throughout the whole operation it was never found possible to adjust the arrival of ships, either at Dunkirk or opposite the beaches, to synchronise with the ebb and flow of troop concentrations.

---

29 R.A.F. Narrative, p. 323.

30 Report by S.N.O. Dunkirk, (R.O. Ill p. 346).

31 Appendix N.2.

32 It is not always possible to record precisely the beaches off which ships were lying. The 10-miles stretch of beach had arbitrarily been divided up into 3 *sections,* Malo, Bray and La Panne. In the confusion of the times, and particularly in the darkness of the night, it is not surprising that ships in company sometimes gave different names to the particular section of beach off which they were lying.

Shortage of Drinking Water

At this time the troops were sorely in need of drinking water; joint naval[33] and military measures were taken to provide it in tanks and cans, and ships off the beaches were directed to do what they could from their own resources. There was, however, inevitably some delay before all requirements could be met, and as late as the 30th May no water or food had yet reached Malo beach.[34]

Brighton Belle Sunk

Meanwhile, at 1230, the *Brighton Belle*, returning to Ramsgate with the 350 troops she had picked up from the beach at Zuydcoote, struck a submerged wreck off the Gull Light buoy during an air attack and sank. All the crew and troops were transferred to the *Sandown*, *Medway Queen*, and *Yser*. Paymaster Sub.-Lieut. W. J. Butler, R.N.V.R., of the *Sandown* was killed and 2 ratings were wounded.

Shortage of Boats

At 1420, when Bray beach was bombed, S.N.O., Dunkirk, ordered some of the troops there to march to Dunkirk in spite of the congestion in the port. By 1830, however, there were still several thousand troops at Bray and more were arriving. At this time the *Grafton* reported that she was off Bray beach with the *Calcutta*,[35] the *Gallant*, *Wakeful*, *Verity*, two skoots the (*Doggersbank* and *Hilda*), two power boats and a tow of pulling boats; at 2115 this force was joined by the minesweepers *Kellett* and *Leda*, but there were insufficient boats and motor launches to cope with the number of troops on the beach.

Off La Panne, at 2157, the *Calcutta*, assisted by the skoot *Reiger*, embarked 70 wounded (cot cases); heavy surf made embarkation difficult and the *Calcutta* had already lost one of her two whalers.[36]

By the 28th May beach evacuation had become a vitally essential part of Operation "Dynamo". It was, however, severely restricted by the almost

---

33 The *Maid of Orleans* had landed 6,000 two-gallon cans of water at Dunkirk on the 26th May. The motor boat *Glitter II* went over with water for the beaches on the 29th May and the lighter *Seine* took 5,000 cans of it; the *Friso* and the *Monas Queen* also went over on the 29th with water, but the latter was mined and sunk before she could unload it.

34 Appendix P.I.

35 The *Calcutta* reported she was off La Panne.

36 Appendix H.2.

complete lack of small beaching craft, other than ships' boats - aftermath of the wish, already noticed, to prevent early information of the operation becoming known to the enemy; and an urgent and persistent cry for boats arose from the ships off the beaches.[37]

Beach Craft are Sailed for Dunkirk

Steps had already been taken, however, to begin the provision of small boats. At 0800 on the 28th May, 8 motor boats were sailed from the Thames for the South Downs. At noon the tug *Sun V* with 8 cutters and 2 whalers in tow, and the tug *St. Clears* with 11 cutters in tow, left Sheerness for Ramsgate, and both tugs sailed for Dunkirk late in the evening. Of these two tows, however, only 7 cutters reached the beaches, the remainder being lost *en route*.[38]

At 1500 the tug *Java* left Ramsgate for Dunkirk, in company with four drifters[39] and 5 motor launches.[40] They arrived off Bray beach at 0100 on 29th May, and were the first arrivals of small motor craft off the beaches. With them, at 1500 on the 28th May, 5 drifters of the 1st Mine Recovery Flotilla left Ramsgate for Dunkirk,[41] and at 1845, 18 motor boats with 17 whalers left Sheerness for Dover.[42]

Supply of Small Craft is Accelerated

These supplied only a portion of what was required. There was still a lack of small craft, and at 2002 V.A. Dover asked that every available shallow draft power boat should be sent to the beaches.[43] The Admiralty's vigorous reaction to this request became fully evident on the following day, the 29th May, when the Portsmouth and Nore Commands, the Thames estuary and the Port of London Authority were combed for motor boats, lighters and barges.[44] To accelerate the journey

---

37 Appendices H.l and H.2.

38 The *Sun V's* tow line was lost early next morning in a collision with the destroyer *Montrose*. Five of the *St. Clear's* cutters were lost *en route* to Dunkirk the next day, as a result of the enemy gunfire from Gravelines and Nieuport; one of the 5 was, however, subsequently picked up by the Sp. Serv./V. *Crested Eagle*.

39 The *Lord Rodney, Lord Keith, Lord Collingwood* and *Lord St. Vincent*.

40 The *Walker I, Walker II, New Britannic, Nayland,* and *Angler II*.

41 The *Lord Cavan, Fidget, Jacketa, Silver Dawn* and *Fisher Boy* (Appendix G.5).

42 Appendix G.6.

43 Appendix G.7.

44 Appendices G.13 to G.18.

arrangements were made to route them direct to the beaches, provided they had charts, food, fuel etc.,[45] though some difficulty was experienced in providing the large number of charts required. Indeed, on the 31st May the Master of the coaster *Hythe* states that he was given an "army road map" to navigate on.

In spite, however, of every effort as more and more ships were drawn into Operation "Dynamo", the pressing demand for beaching craft grew, almost hourly, more insistent. A climax was reached on 1st June,[46] when, in spite of the number sent over, the "inshore flotilla" – crippled by weather, accidents, mechanical breakdowns, exhaustion of crews and enemy action – was still unable to meet requirements, and the minesweeper *Gossamer's* urgent request for boats received the curt reply "It is now impracticable to send more boats. You must do your utmost with yours".[47] A perusal of the "Dynamo" signals brings sharply to notice the great driving force of the Vice-Admiral, Dover; the clamorous signals for "more boats" were an indication of the great strain to which he was being subjected.

Beach and Harbour Evacuation Compared

There can be little doubt that had not valid reasons prevented more beach ferrying craft from being made available for the first 5 days of the evacuation, a greater number of troops could have been evacuated. "The initial problem", says the Vice-Admiral, Dover, "called for a maximum effort over a limited period, regardless of the future, and accordingly all resources in the way of small boats were thrown on the beaches, before adequate provision had been made for their maintenance off the coast in such matters as relief of the personnel and the provision of large beach parties".

It was only due to the foresight of the Admiralty in making arrangements for a continued flow in ever increasing numbers of small power boats and beach craft, which became available on the fifth day onwards, that the continued evacuation from the beaches remained a reasonable proposition after the initial crisis had passed.

A perusal of the signals that passed between Dover and the French coast here reveals the many occasions on which the responsible officers stationed on the coast considered so little had been achieved from the beaches that they

---

45 Appendix G.9.

46 Appendices H.17 to H.25.

47 Appendix H.22.

advocated restriction of evacuation to Dunkirk harbour. Many complaints of 'no boats', 'no ships' might lead a detached observer to the conclusion that the great effort that was being made was proving abortive.

"At Dover, where the whole operation could be viewed in truer perspective because the number and origin of the troops being landed in England was always to hand, it was clear that the evacuation from the beaches required by the military situation was, in fact, achieving a considerable success."[48] Admiral Ramsay's view is borne out by these recorded figures: Of the 251,000 troops landed in the United Kingdom between May 28th and June 1st inclusive – the period during which Dunkirk and the beaches eastward were available day and night except for enemy interference – 90,000 were lifted from the beaches, while 55,000 were lifted by personnel ships and hospital carriers, and 106,000 by other vessels, direct from Dunkirk harbour.

Anti-submarine Patrols are Maintained

While the lifting of troops from Dunkirk and the beaches was progressing with ever-increasing speed, anti-submarine patrols had been maintained from the North Goodwin to Kwint Bank; but on the 28th May all destroyers except the *Vega* and the Polish *Blyskawica* were diverted from them to the beaches.[49] On patrol this day with these two destroyers were the corvettes *Mallard*, *Widgeon*, *Sheldrake*, *Shearwater* and eleven A/S trawlers.[50] Of the latter, the A/S trawler *Thuringia* was sunk by a mine early in the day, and her Captain, Chief Skipper D. W. L. Simpson, D.S.C., D.S.M., R.N.R., was not among the 3 survivors.

Owing to a misunderstanding the LL trawlers *Our Bairns*, *Inver Forth* and *Thomas Bartlett*, which were in company, carried out a sweep in Dunkirk roads instead of sweeping the war channel. These vessels were shelled off Calais; and the *Thomas Bartlett*, while endeavouring to get out of range of the guns, ran on to a British minefield, and, striking a mine at 1017, sank with the loss of 8 of her crew.[51]

During the night of 28th and 29th May, to strengthen this patrol, all available M.T.B/s of the Nore and Dover Commands were ordered to patrol north-east of

---

48 Letter from V. A. Dover (A. 14/0/876/40 of 18/6/40) covering his Report on Operation "Dynamo". Italics not in original.

49 The *Windsor* had returned to Dover after being damaged in an air attack at 1145.

50 The *Cayton Wyke, Kingston Alalite, Kingston Andalusite, Kingston Galena, Saon, Spurs, Stella Dorado, Westella, Blackburn Rovers, Lady Philomena* and *Thuringia*.

51 Report by C.M.S., Dover (R.O. II, p.498). See also Appx. J.12

the line Wandelaar L/V and Whistle Buoy.

Summary of Troops Landed in England

The figures for May 28th gave grounds for hope. 17,804 troops were transported to England[52] (of which 11,835 were transported by destroyers). Of these, 11,874 were lifted from Dunkirk east pier, and 5,930 from the beaches.

Ships Lost or Damaged on 28th May

Lost
The A/S trawler *Thuringia*
The drifter *Ocean Reward*
The M/S *Brighton Belle*
The trawler *Thomas Bartlett*
P/V *Queen of the Channel*
The skoot *Alice*
The H/C *Isle of Thanet*.

Damaged
The destroyer *Windsor*.

52 D.R. gives 14,409, but this figure is not confirmed by the recorded numbers of troops disembarked by the various ships, as shown in Tables 2 and 3.

Wednesday 29th May

First Heavy Enemy Air Effort – German Bridgehead in Nieuport

Throughout the 29th May, the enemy attempted to cross the canal between the Franco-Belgian frontier and Nieuport – and, indeed, succeeded in establishing a bridgehead in the town of Nieuport, although everywhere else he was driven back. Some of the enemy attempted to cross in rubber boats; others, disguised as civilians, with the refugees, horses and cattle. The few vital hours gained made it possible, against all expectation, to embark practically the whole British force.[1]

Two-day Traffic Block in Perimeter

Large numbers of French troops arriving in the perimeter brought a mass of transport which caused such traffic congestion that for two days the main road between La Panne and Dunkirk became totally blocked with vehicles three deep.[2]

French Evacuation not yet Ordered

Admiral Abrial (whose headquarters were at Bastion No. 32, near Dunkirk Mole) had apparently received no orders from his Government that the whole of the British troops were to be embarked, and he professed great surprise when he heard of Lord Gort's intentions. He imagined that British troops would stay and defend the perimeter to the last, side by side with the French.[2]

Meanwhile, the French troops were expecting to embark along with their British comrades, notwithstanding that only two French ships had so far been provided;[3] the beaches were becoming crowded with French soldiers,

1 Lord Gort's Second Despatch para. 53.

2 Lord Gort's Second Despatch, para. 55.

3 So far, the French torpedo boat *Cyclone* had brought back 460 troops, and the minesweeper *Commandant Delage* 520 - both on 29th May, from Dunkirk harbour.

and difficulties might have occurred at any time.[2] Later in the day, however, three French torpedo boats and one minesweeper sailed to Dunkirk harbour to evacuate troops. [4]

Dunkirk Perimeter Established

On the evening of the 29th May the organisation of the perimeter was complete, and General Sir Ronald Adam, his task accomplished, embarked for England that night. [5]

Mackay and *Montrose* out of Action

The story of the 29th May is largely one of ships sunk or damaged. Our losses were very heavy and began very early. At 0005, the destroyer *Mackay* (*en route* to Bray beach with the destroyer *Harvester*) ran aground at the western end of Zuydcoote Pass. Eight minutes later, about 1 mile W.S.W. of No. 2 Buoy, the destroyer *Montrose*, *en route* to Dunkirk, ran into a patch of fog and collided with the tug *Sun V*, which was towing 11 naval cutters. The *Sun V* put her helm hard to starboard, but she received a severe glancing blow, and narrowly escaped sinking; the 11 cutters were lost in the darkness. The *Montrose* had to be towed, stern-first, to Dover by the tug *Lady Brassey*. Neither the *Mackay*, the *Montrose* nor the tug were able to take any further part in the evacuation.

The *Harvester* reached Bray beach at 0050, and sent in her motor boat in charge of Sub-Lieut. E. C. Croswell, R.N., who found about 4,000 soldiers awaiting embarkation … There was a strong cross sea and sand bars made the launching of boats difficult. During the course of the night the *Harvester* managed to evacuate about 700 which included some 100 wounded. At 0400, however, the supply of boats for embarkation ceased. There had been considerable wastage of boats through overcrowding, which was difficult to control as the embarkation beach extended for over one mile. At 0500, the *Harvester* moved to La Panne.[6]

---

4 The torpedo boats *Cyclone, Mistral* and *Sirocco* and the minesweeper *Commandant Delage*.

5 Lord Gort's Second Despatch, para. 57.

6 Sub-Lieut. Croswell, who remained at La Panne until 1st June, says in his report, "Except during the first day of evacuation, the bearing of the B.E.F. at La Panne was magnificent." (C.W. 23187/40).

Wakeful Sunk

In the meantime, at 0045, there occurred the only two E-boat successes against British destroyers. The destroyer *Wakeful*, returning from Bray beach with about 650 troops on board, was ¼ mile west of Kwint Whistle buoy when 2 parallel torpedo tracks about 30 yards apart were seen approaching, 150 yards away on the starboard bow.

Avoiding action was taken, and one torpedo missed ahead, but the other hit the *Wakeful* in the forward boiler room. The *Wakeful* broke in half and the two portions sank within about 15 seconds, each portion remaining upright with the bow and stern standing about 60 feet above the water.

Most of the guns' crew floated clear, 30 men and an officer remaining on the stern portion. All the troops were asleep below, and all except one went down with the ship. All the *Wakeful*'s engine room department, except one or two, were lost. The Captain, Cdr. R. L. Fisher, R.N., floated clear of the bridge.

After about half an hour, the danlayers[7] *Nautilus* and *Comfort*, which were *en route* to La Panne, arrived and began to pick up those still swimming. The *Nautilus* picked up 6 and the *Comfort* 16, including Cdr. Fisher. Then the minesweeper *Gossamer*, returning from Dunkirk harbour with 420 troops, arrived, lowered her boats, and picked up a further 15 survivors.

Cdr. Fisher directed the *Comfort* to go alongside the wreck and take off the men clinging to the stern. The *Nautilus* continued on her way to La Panne, where she was lost during the afternoon in an air attack.

Grafton Torpedoed

It was now 0220, and the minesweeper *Lydd* arrived on the scene bringing 300 troops from Dunkirk harbour. By the light of an Aldis lamp, she sighted the bow and stern portions of the *Wakeful* with men clinging to them. The *Lydd* lowered her boats, but was ordered by the *Gossamer* to put out her Aldis lamp and drop a depth charge; the latter order could not, however, be carried out because of the men in the water. By the time the *Lydd* had picked up 10 survivors, the destroyer *Grafton*, loaded with about 800 troops from Bray beach, also arrived and ordered the *Lydd* to circle round her.

---

7 Isles-class naval trawlers used for laying and retrieving dan buoys during minesweeping operations.

The *Gossamer* went on to Dover

In the meantime, the *Comfort* had reached the stern portion of the wreck of the *Wakeful*, and finding that it had fallen over,[8] went alongside the *Grafton* to warn her of the danger of torpedoes. It was then about 0240, and the *Grafton* having first sighted a small darkened vessel about 3 cables on the port quarter, signaled it to pick up survivors. Almost at once a torpedo hit the *Grafton*'s port side and exploded; a second explosion followed, thought to be a shell or grenade hit, which wrecked the *Grafton*'s bridge killing her Captain, Cdr. C. E. C. Robinson, R.N., and 3 others. The torpedo blew off the *Grafton*'s stern, abaft the after magazine bulkhead, and broke her back, but she still floated on an even keel. A German submarine, U.69 had fired the torpedo.

The torpedo explosion almost swamped the *Comfort*; she rose, and Cdr. Fisher was washed overboard. He seized a rope's end, but with the *Comfort* going full speed ahead soon had to let go. The *Comfort* came round in a wide circle until within about 50 yards of the stricken *Grafton*, whereupon the *Grafton* and *Lydd*, mistaking her in the darkness for an E-boat, opened a heavy raking fire with 4-inch and Lewis guns.[9]

Comfort cut in Half

When the firing ceased Cdr. Fisher, who had reached the bow of the *Comfort*, endeavoured to get aboard; but the *Lydd*, having circled round to finish off the supposed E-boat, bore down at full speed and, ramming the *Comfort* amidships (it was then about 0307), cut her in half. Some of the *Comfort*'s crew attempted to spring aboard the *Lydd*, but the *Lydd*, mistaking them for boarders, opened up with rifle fire. Two men were, however, taken off the rammed vessel and it was then discovered that she was the *Comfort*. Altogether, the number saved from this most tragic occurrence, shrouded in the darkness of the night, were only 5, of which 4 were survivors from the *Wakeful*. As the *Grafton* then appeared able to look after herself, the *Lydd* set course for Ramsgate.

When the *Comfort* went down Cdr. Fisher again sank, but he came to the surface and, after swimming about until 0515, was picked up by a boat lowered

---

8 On the 30th May the corvette *Sheldrake* was ordered to destroy the *Wakeful*'s asdic apparatus. She found the *Wakeful* completely capsized with her stern resting on the bottom. As, by then, information was received that the area had been mined, the *Sheldrake,* to minimise the risk, sank the wreck by gunfire and a pattern of depth charges.

9 Later the *Grafton*'s fire was shifted to another vessel further away on the port quarter, which was observed to blow up with a bright flash. This may well have been the E-boat.

from the Norwegian S.S. *Hird*, which was *en route* from Dunkirk to England with about 3,500 troops and refugees on board.

Grafton Sunk

In the meantime, at 0400, the personnel ship *Malines*, which was returning empty from Dunkirk, heard SOS signals; she placed herself alongside the torpedoed *Grafton* and transferred the destroyer s 800 troops. "The Master ... handled his ship with extreme skill", reported the acting Captain of the *Grafton*, Lieut. H. C. J. McRea, R.N.

It was now 0430, just before sunrise, and the destroyers *Javelin, Icarus, Vanquisher, Intrepid* and *Ivanhoe, en route* from Dover to Dunkirk, sighted the sinking *Grafton*. The *Ivanhoe* went to her assistance and embarked the seriously wounded. The *Grafton* was by then listing heavily, and had her after end awash; the *Ivanhoe* fired 3 shells into her at 500 yards range and then proceeded to Dunkirk, where she berthed alongside the east pier and embarked troops.

Following the loss of the *Grafton*, destroyers were ordered not to stop to assist ships in distress.[10]

Mona's Queen Sunk by Mine

In the meantime the *Javelin* and *Icarus* had entered Dunkirk harbour, and the *Vanquisher* had anchored off Malo beach. The *Intrepid*, waiting for a berth, anchored off the harbour, ahead of the personnel vessel *Mona's Queen*, which was loaded with fresh water for the troops. Then, at about 0530, the *Mona's Queen* blew up on a magnetic mine and sank in two minutes. The *Vanquisher*'s whaler and the *Intrepid*'s motor boat picked up the Master, Captain A. Holkham and 31 of the crew.

The German Minelaying Effort

Minelaying by the enemy during the dark hours probably took place during the night 28th/29th May, and was maintained with great intensity during the following two nights. Not only was the Dunkirk road mined, including the Zuydcoote Pass, but also Route X and the area round the Kwint buoy. Folkestone and Dover Harbour entrances were also mined. In spite of the large number of mines laid, only one British ship other than the *Mona's Queen* was known for certain to have been sunk by magnetic mines – the Fleet Air Arm yacht *Grive*

---

10 Appendix 0.6.

which was sunk on 1st June. On that date, also, the hospital carrier *St. David* was damaged at anchor off Dover when a mine was exploded by a LL. trawler sweeping close at hand. The A/S trawlers *Thuringia*, *Westella* and *Blackburn Rovers* were believed at the time to have been sunk by moored mines laid by a U-boat, although at first it was thought that the last two at any rate had been torpedoed. If the enemy had been able to lay moored contact mines by aircraft, instead of magnetic mines, the results would have been very different.[11]

Allied Air Cover, 29th May

The remainder of the long list of naval losses on this day was caused by hostile bombers. The odds which our fighters had encountered on the 27th and 28th May, led on the 29th to a further strengthening of the fighter patrols up to 4 squadrons; actually the largest number of fighters on any one patrol was 44, the smallest 25. All fighter patrols were concentrated within a radius of 10 miles of Dunkirk, except for a Hurricane patrol at midday covering a line Dunkirk – Furnes – Cassel.[12]

The Dunkirk area was covered during the day by fighter patrols at approximately the following times: 0440 – 0610, 0720 – 0925, 1030 – 1200, 1300 – 1400, 1450 – 1620, 1700 – 1800, 1930 – 2030, 2000 – 2110.[13] Coastal Command patrols covered the line North Goodwins – Gravelines – Ostend throughout the day; all three aircraft of one of the Coastal Command patrols were shot down by Me.109's at about 1130[3].

Gallant put out of Action

The destroyers *Jaguar*, *Gallant* and *Grenade*, *en route* for Dunkirk by the new middle Route X with instructions to test it for opposition by shore batteries, were attacked at 1155 off Snouw Bank by about 17 dive-bombers. The attack was concentrated on the *Gallant* which was damaged by a near miss and had to retire; she was unable to take any further part in Operation "Dynamo". "One dive-bomber, was seen to be hit by pom-pom, and while losing height" observes the *Jaguar*, "was despatched by a fighter". This attack appears to have taken place "just when one of our main [fighter] patrols had turned for home".[13]

On arrival at Dunkirk, the *Grenade* reported that there had been no

---

11 V. A. Dover's letter, No. A. 14/0/876/40, p.3, paras. 7(a) and 7 (c).

12 R.A.F. Narrative, p.326.

13 R.A.F. Narrative, p.326.

interference from shore batteries. Shipping was thus able to make use of the route directly it had been swept. The minesweepers completed this work late on the same afternoon, and the route was taken into use within a few hours of both the other routes, Y and Z, being rendered unsafe for use by day owing to the German shore gunfire.

Bombing of Dunkirk and Beaches Commences

At 1358 the S.N.O., Dunkirk reported to V.A. Dover that the bombing of the beaches and of Dunkirk pier had commenced without fighter opposition. This attack occurred while Hurricanes were sweeping inland to Cassel.[1]

At 1250 the *Grenade* berthed alongside the east pier in Dunkirk outer harbour (the Nouvel Avant-Port), the *Jaguar* securing alongside her. The *Grenade* was ordered by S.N.O., Dunkirk, to remain at his disposal and not to embark troops. Between 1400 and 1525, the *Jaguar* embarked about 1,000; level bombers were being held off by fighters and A/A fire during this period, and two patterns of heavy bombs which were dropped close to the pier did no damage to ships.[14]

Fourteen Ships Lying at Dunkirk

In the meantime, at 1330, six Oropesa trawlers of the Dover M/S Command, viz.: the *Fyldea* (Lieut. R. Bill, R.N., S.O.), the *Arley, Brock, Calvi, John Cattling* and *Polly Johnson*, arrived off Dunkirk harbour and the *Fyldea* and *Arley* were ordered inside to pull the personnel vessel *Lochgarry*, which had embarked over 1,000 troops, away from the east pier.[15] By 1420 when they had done this, the six trawlers, triple-banked, occupied the *Lochgarry*'s berth. Ahead of the six trawlers were the *Grenade* and *Jaguar*; astern of the trawlers was the personnel vessel *Canterbury*, and astern of her, at the Quai Felix Faure in Dunkirk inner harbour (the Avant-Port), was the French destroyer *Cyclone*.

On the opposite side of the outer harbour, at the west Quay, lay the French destroyers *Mistral* and *Siroco*. Outside the harbour, on the seaward side of the east pier opposite the *Grenade*, was the P/V *Fenella*, and at 1430 the Special Service Vessel *Crested Eagle* berthed astern of her (see Diagram p.40). Off Malo, Bray and La Panne beaches were numbers of destroyers, minesweepers, skoots, personnel vessels, trawlers, tugs and small craft.

14 *Jaguar*'s report.

15 See *Fyldea*'s report.

This was the first occasion on which a massed target of ships had been presented in Dunkirk harbour, and the scene was thus set for one of the most disastrous air onslaughts of the operation; indeed, it was only by good fortune that the vital Dunkirk harbour channel was not blocked by sinking ships at this early date. The air onslaught, which took place between 1530 and 2000, appears to have comprised 4 separate air attacks; the manner of it was as follows:

Air Onslaught Begins

The first air attack over Dunkirk commenced at 1530, and was made by 12 bombers.[16] The 20 or 30 bombs which were dropped on the harbour fell mostly wide, but the *Polly Johnson* was severely damaged by a near miss (see p.44). One bomber was shot down by fighters.[17]

Mistral Damaged

At 1555 a bomb struck the west quay and damaged the *Mistral*, killing 3 and seriously wounding 4, including her captain.

Jaguar Severely Damaged

Meanwhile, at 1550, the *Jaguar* was ordered out of Dunkirk harbour, to act as escort to the *Lochgarry* then waiting outside. While taking station ahead of the *Lochgarry* at about 1630 the second air attack over Dunkirk took place.[18] Dive-bombers attacked with salvoes of 4 bombs. About 14 salvoes were aimed at the *Jaguar* and one at the *Lochgarry*. A near miss severely damaged the *Jaguar*, holing her near the waterline and putting her engines and steering gear out of action; a list to port developed. The destroyer drifted helplessly until, at 1645, she was in danger of drifting on to a wreck 50 yards away. The destroyer *Express* then sighted her and taking her in tow alongside transferred some of her troops. The skoot *Rika*, *en route* for La Panne beach, although she had been severely shaken by bombs off Middelkerke buoy, closed the *Jaguar* and took off 295 troops. The *Jaguar* eventually reached Dover at 2350 (in spite of further high level bombing attacks at 2014 and 2026), making the last part of the passage under her own power. She was unable to take any further part in "Dynamo".

---

16 See *Mistral*'s report.

17 *Fyldea*'s report.

18 "At 1630 hours, a renewed spell of Luftwaffe activity began, ... when none of our fighters was on the line ... (*R.A.F. Narrative*, p.327).

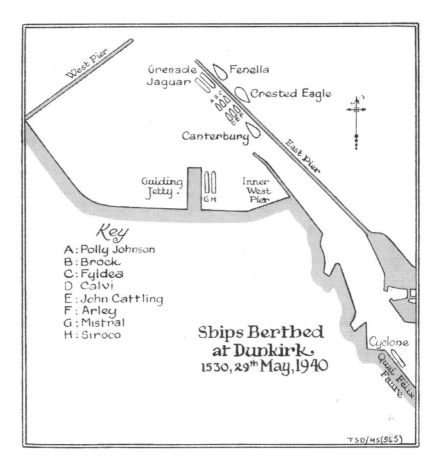

Key
A : Polly Johnson
B : Brock
C : Fyldea
D : Calvi
E : John Cattling
F : Arley
G : Mistral
H : Siroco

Ships Berthed
at Dunkirk.
1530, 29ᵗʰ May, 1940

TSO/HS(565)

Clan Macalister Sunk

In the attack which damaged the *Jaguar*, the *Lochgarry* was also damaged by a near miss; she was, however, able to proceed, and did so unescorted. Near 6 W buoy, she passed the S.S. *Clan Macalister* which, after having hoisted out 6 motor landing craft earlier in the day and subsequently embarked troops, had just been bombed and was on fire and sinking. The destroyer *Malcolm* had already taken off the wounded members of the *Clan Macalister*'s crew and some of her troops, and the minesweeper *Pangbourne* had embarked the remainder. The *Clan Macalister* settled on the sea bed on an even keel with her upper works above water, and remained on fire for days. For days also, she acted as a target for enemy airmen, who thought she was still afloat.

Gracie Fields Abandoned

Continuing on her way near Kwint Bank buoy, the *Lochgarry* saw the paddle-minesweeper *Gracie Fields* (which was carrying about 750 troops from La Panne beach) hit amidships by a bomb. The *Gracie Fields*, unable to stop her engines, and with her upper deck enveloped in clouds of steam, continued underway at 6 knots with her helm jammed with 15° starboard wheel on. Nevertheless, the skoot *Twente*, which was on her way to La Panne beach, secured alongside the circling *Gracie Fields* and transferred as many injured and others as she could. The skoot *Jutland*, returning from La Panne beach with 275 French troops, also secured alongside the *Gracie Fields* disengaged side and took off some more of her troops.

Later, at about 1830, the minesweeper *Pangbourne* (which had just been holed on both sides above and below the waterline and had had 13 killed and 11 wounded by near misses off Bray beach) went alongside the *Gracie Fields*, transferred about 80 British troops, and took her in tow. The M/S *Kellett*, carrying 550 troops from Bray beach, led the *Pangbourne*, whose compasses had been put out of action by bomb blast. At 0130 next morning the *Gracie Fields* (in approx. position 51° 20' N., 02° 05' E) reported that she was sinking. The *Pangbourne* slipped the tow, took off the *Gracie Fields* ship's company and abandoned her.

Grenade Damaged

Meanwhile, at about the time that the *Jaguar* had left Dunkirk harbour, the *Express* (with 500 troops she had picked up from Bray beach) entered it to berth alongside the *Grenade* and embark more troops. Before she could do so, however, the previously mentioned second air attack took place, and the *Express* was near-missed ahead and astern. Only splinters came on board the *Express*, but the *Grenade* was damaged and had some casualties. The *Express* thereupon cleared out of the harbour.

Greyhound Severely Damaged, *Nautilus* Sunk

The bombing between 1530 and 1600 was widespread.[19] The destroyer *Anthony*, which left La Panne for Dover at 1525 with 550 troops, was bombed at 1555

---

19 "From the vessels off-shore there came a series of signals, between 1545 and 1555 hours, to the effect that the anchorages at Bray and La Panne were being bombed. These attacks seem to have begun at about 1430 ... when none of our aircraft were on the line ..." (*R.A.F. Narrative*, p.327).

(and 1645), but the bombs fell wide. Off La Panne, at about 1600, a high level bombing attack was made on the destroyer *Greyhound*, on the minesweepers *Sutton* and *Salamander*, and on the paddle-minesweeper *Sandown*. The *Sutton* was straddled but no damage was done. In the dive-bomb attack which followed, however, the *Greyhound* was severely damaged by 2 near misses, and had 90 casualties, 20 of which were fatal. The Sp. S/V *Royal Eagle*, which was assisting in rescue work, escaped damage, but the trawler *Nautilus*, which had already ferried some 600 troops from the beach, was straddled by bombs and had her engines and steering gear put out of action. Making water rapidly, she managed to get alongside the *Greyhound* and transfer to her the 150 troops she was carrying. The *Nautilus*, already 6 feet down in the water and sinking, was then abandoned and set on fire.

The *Greyhound* limped back to Dover carrying 506 troops, but for 4 hours of the passage she was in tow of the Polish destroyer *Blyskawica* which had been on patrol with the destroyer *Vega* in the vicinity of the West Hinder buoy. The *Greyhound* took no further part in "Dynamo".

Waverley Sunk

Meanwhile, at about 1630, the *Cyclone* left the harbour with 500 troops on board *en route* for Dover. Near Kwint Bank buoy she saw the minesweeper *Waverley* sinking; a bomb had struck her on the port quarter and passed right through her bottom, leaving a hole about 6 feet in diameter. Four of the 600 troops she had embarked from La Panne beach were killed and a number wounded. When the *Waverley* sank, many of her troops were left swimming or trying to keep afloat, but the numbers thinned out considerably within 15/20 minutes.[20] The *Cyclone* picked up 158. About an hour later the Sp. S/V *Golden Eagle* picked up 285 and, guided by a plane, the tug Java and 2 drifters picked up a few more.

Canterbury Damaged

While these air attacks had been going on the *Canterbury* had embarked 1,960 troops from the east pier. During a brief lull in the bombing, at about 1650, she left the harbour, but soon after was damaged by a near miss. She was able to reach Dover, but took no further part in "Dynamo". At 1720 the berth vacated by the *Canterbury* in Dunkirk harbour was taken by the destroyer Verity.

---

20 Report by the Captain of the *Waverley.*

Intrepid Severely Damaged

Meanwhile, at 1700, the Intrepid, hurrying back to Dunkirk from Dover (where she had disembarked 661 troops), was bombed between Middelkerke Bank and La Panne. A near miss caused severe damage, started fires, and killed 2 and wounded 19. The *Intrepid* had to return to Dover, and took no further part in Operation "Dynamo".

Hospital Ship Deliberately Bombed

At 1700 also, the H/C *St. Julien, en route* for Dunkirk harbour, was deliberately bombed "for a considerable period" in the vicinity of Nieuport Bank buoy;[21] she was slightly damaged by near misses. The *St. Julien* lay off Dunkirk harbour for about ½ an hour waiting for an opportunity to enter; when air attacks recommenced, however, she sailed for Dover without having entered the harbour.

At 1730 the *Siroco* sailed from Dunkirk harbour with 500 troops and a little later was joined outside by the *Mistral* which had only embarked 4 troops. Both the French destroyers proceeded to Dover. The *Mistral* took no further part in "Dynamo".

Grenade Hit, *Calvi* and *Fenella* Sunk

At about 1750 the third air attack was made over Dunkirk harbour by waves of bombers; some 100 bombs were dropped. Allied fighters, being engaged by enemy fighters, were unable to interfere with the bombing.[22] A near miss blew a hole in the *Grenade*'s side; the trawler *Calvi*, lying outside the *John Cattling*, received a direct hit and sank immediately. Her masts and funnel were above water, and her ensign remained flying from the foremast. The personnel vessel *Fenella*, which by then had 650 troops on board, was hit on the promenade deck; a second bomb hit the pier, and blew some concrete through the *Fenella*'s side below the waterline; a third bomb, falling between the pier and the *Fenella*'s side, wrecked the engine room. The *Fenella*'s troops were disembarked on to the pier and re-embarked in the *Crested Eagle*. The *Fenella* was abandoned while

---

21 Reports by *Pangbourne* and *Lydd*.

22 According to the *R.A.F. Narrative*, p.327, two Hurricane squadrons which arrived at 1710 were attacked by large numbers of Me. 109's ; one Spitfire squadron was attacked from above and behind at 1715, and another was in combat with enemy fighters at 1740. "None of our squadrons encountered enemy bombers, and the attacks on our shipping between 1630 and 1745 hours (resulting, amongst other casualties, in the *Crested Eagle* being hit and beached off Bray) can thus not have been interfered with by our patrols *R.A.F. Narrative*, p.327).

sinking. The P/V *St. Seiriol*, which shortly before had secured alongside the outer east pier, astern of the *Crested Eagle*, cast off and shifted eastward to the beaches.

Grenade Hit, set on Fire, and Abandoned

Then five minutes after the third air attack had begun the *Grenade* received two direct hits; her engines were put out of action and she caught fire. As she swung round, some of her ships company were able to step on board the damaged trawler *Polly Johnson*. The *Verity* (which had been continuously straddled by bombs for 35 minutes), seeing that traffic all along the east pier had ceased, cast off, and skirting the burning *Grenade* and the sunken *Calvi*, proceeded out of harbour, grounding slightly on a sunk drifter in the entrance.

The troops now began climbing out of one ship into another; but, acting on the instructions of the Piermaster Cdr. J. C. Clouston, R.N., Lieut. Bill (Fyldea) restored order.

At 1815 the *Grenade* was abandoned and her Captain, Cdr. R. C. Boyle, R.N., having made arrangements with the Piermaster to tow her clear of the fairway, embarked with some of his ship's company in the *Crested Eagle*.

Polly Johnson Sunk

The burning wreck of the *Grenade* did, in fact, commence to drift down on to the five remaining Oropesa trawlers. The *John Cattling* was instructed to attempt to pull her clear, and the remaining 4 trawlers, with troops and survivors on board, proceeded out of the harbour towards the beaches. A little later, near Nieuport Bank buoy, the *Polly Johnson*, leaking badly as a result of the damage caused by a near miss in the first air attack, and with damaged engine, was abandoned; the *Arley* embarked her crew and troops and sank her by gunfire.

Grenade Blown Up

The *Grenade* was guided into a pocket to the westward of the main channel. She burned fiercely for some hours and then blew up.

Crested Eagle Blazing, is Beached

Meanwhile, when the Verity left the harbour at 1755, the *Crested Eagle* swung clear of the east pier and proceeded on an easterly course. Shortly afterwards, however, she was hit by 4 bombs and caught fire; out of control, she continued under way. The *Verity* instructed the *Crested Eagle* to stop so that she might transfer her troops; but the *Crested Eagle* could not stop. At about 1830, blazing fiercely fore and aft (she was a wooden ship) the *Crested Eagle* ran aground west of Bray beach. The 200 survivors, who could be seen in the water, were heavily machine-gunned from the air, and the ships that came to the rescue were bombed. Some of the survivors, several with severe burns, were picked up by the minesweepers *Hebe* and *Lydd*; others, including the Captain and other survivors of the *Grenade*, by the minesweeper *Albury*. Among those picked up by the *Sabre* was the Second Engineer of the *Crested Eagle* and a stoker from the *Grenade*.

Normania Sunk

In the course of this third air attack the personnel vessel *Normania* was hit by a bomb off 11 W buoy. She was towed clear of Dunkirk channel by the gunboat *Mosquito*, but then began to sink. The *Mosquito* and the minesweeper *Ross* took off the crew and the few troops that were on board. The *Normania* sank off 11 W buoy at about 0245 the following day.

Saladin Severely Damaged. *Lorina* Sunk

The fourth air attack, which was widespread, took place between about 1830 and 2000. Ships returning to England were bombed. There were continuous attacks off Bray beach and its vicinity; the destroyers *Sabre*, *Verity* and *Saladin* in company there were attacked; the *Saladin*, attacked 10 times, was so severely damaged in the engine room by a near miss that she had to return to Dover at 15 knots, and could take no further part in "Dynamo". The personnel vessel *Lorina* was bombed and sunk at about this period, but no details are forthcoming.

Icarus Damaged

The destroyer *Icarus*, which had been embarking troops off Zuydcoote, and in addition had embarked about 470 from the skoot *Doggersbank*, was attacked by 10 dive-bombers at 1830. She received only slight damage from near misses but had 1 killed and 25 wounded.

King Orry Sunk

The armed boarding vessel *King Orry* arrived at Dunkirk harbour at about 1900, to find it apparently occupied only by burning and sinking ships. She herself was immediately subjected to a bombing attack which put her steering gear out of action and shattered all her instruments. Further air attacks, and damage by near misses ensued. Realising the risk of the ship blocking the channel, S.N.O. Dunkirk instructed her Captain, shortly after midnight, to take her out of harbour. She struggled out at 0230/30, but when clear of the harbour entrance the *King Orry* foundered. Several ships, including the drifter *Vivacious*, the trawler *Lord Grey*, and a D.C./M.B., picked up survivors.

Isle of Guernsey Deliberately Bombed

At about the same time that the *King Orry* was being bombed, the M/S *Halcyon* witnessed the deliberate bombing of the hospital carrier *Isle of Guernsey*. She was bombed by 10 planes off Dunkirk harbour while attempting to pick up an airman. The airman was subsequently picked up by the *Halcyon*. Although damaged by near misses, the *Isle of Guernsey* entered the harbour after dark and embarked 490 wounded in the early hours of 30th May. She then proceeded to Newhaven, but was not repaired in time to make another trip to Dunkirk.

Bideford's Stern Blown Off

The air onslaught had not yet, however, come to an end. The sloop *Bideford* had arrived off Bray beach at 1730. At 1750 the first boat loads of troops (mostly French) came alongside. "The boats/' says her Captain, Lt. Cdr. J. H. Lewes, R.N.," were dangerously overcrowded and several swamped on the way off from the shore. On arrival alongside, the men would all jump on board and let their boats drift off on the tide. Paddles were lost overboard, rendering the boats useless. *Bideford*'s M/B was lowered and ordered to collect and tow inshore any empty boats. The whaler was lowered and 2 officers and a signalman were sent in to endeavour to take charge on the beach ... this was next to impossible. The men rushed the boats and capsized them in shallow water, and then left the boats without making any attempt to right them and use them again. There were only 2 motor landing craft in the vicinity. One [A.L.C. 17] had one engine out of action; the other [A.L.C. 16] was blown up subsequently when lying alongside the ship".

Dive-bombing attacks commenced on the *Bideford* at about 1915. She was then machine-gunned by low flying aircraft. At 2007 four bombs were dropped; one landed 30 yards away; one hit the quarter deck; and one hit or near missed the stern, detonating a depth charge. About 40 feet of the *Bideford*'s stern was blown away completely; a further 40 feet was reduced to a tangled mass of metal; the mainmast fell in 3 pieces on the searchlight and machine gun platforms, wrecking them both; the bridge superstructure was severely shaken, a bulkhead was dished, and several frames cracked. Of the ship's company, 3 officers and 13 men were killed, 1 officer and 18 men wounded; of the passengers, 2 officers and 10 men were killed and 2 officers wounded. Then a fire broke out, and orders were given to flood the magazine and burn the signal books. A further dive-bomb attack took place, but the bombs fell wide. The *Bideford* anchored.

The M/S *Kellett* came alongside the *Bideford*, and took off about 300 troops, and the tug *St. Clear*'s endeavoured to take the *Bideford* in tow; she was, however, fast aground, and the tow parted. The dr. *Havant* then tried to take her in tow, but again the tow parted.

Bideford Towed to Dover

During the night of 29th-30th May, 350 French and 50 British troops embarked in the *Bideford*. Near dawn, the gunboat *Locust*, carrying 620 British and French troops from La Panne beach, passed a tow to the *Bideford*, and at daylight she floated – in tow. At less than 2½ knots course was set for Dover; *en route*, during the first 3 miles, the tow parted 3 times. Throughout the 30th May the *Locust* struggled on with her burden. During the night a French soldier jumped overboard, fully equipped. The tow was stopped, a buoy was dropped and a boat lowered; but, in spite of good visibility and a calm sea, the unknown soldier was not recovered although a search was made for 30 minutes. In spite of the tow again parting, the *Bideford* reached Dover at 1130 on the 31st May and disembarked 436 troops.

The momentous issues at stake in Operation "Dynamo" were not to be attained without grievous losses, but the *Bideford*'s heroic voyage to safety marked a momentary respite from the rapidly mounting toll of lives and ships.

Twelve Hundred Troops Wade out to a Skoot

At about 2300 on the 29th May the skoot Patria arrived off Bray from Ramsgate and, in the glow of the still burning *Crested Eagle*, saw troops on the beach. The Captain of the *Patria*, who decided to ground his ship, records that "The troops, holding hands, waded out and clambered on board by nets, ladders and ropes' ends. The sight of two solid phalanxes of men, delineated by phosphorescence in the water and steadily advancing to the ship, will be memorable ... Over 1,000 men were embarked in just over two hours. Among them were naval ratings – casualties with severe burns from the *Grenade*, the *Crested Eagle* and the *Fenella*.

Dover Unaware of Losses

Little information of the disastrous losses of the afternoon and early evening filtered through to Dover, except that it was known that Dunkirk was under heavy bombardment and that destroyers there were being hit soon after 1600.[1]

Lord Gort and 3rd Corps at La Panne

Earlier in the day other important information had, however, come through to Dover, and at 0127 the Vice-Admiral, Dover, informed the *Calcutta* that Lord Gort and the 3rd Corps of the B.E.F. were at La Panne, and that every effort was to be made to concentrate destroyers and light craft at that end of the beach and embark the force.

Calcutta Contacts Lord Gort

On receipt of this signal at 0345 the *Calcutta*, which had already been embarking troops from La Panne beach, sent her boats in again, in charge of Mr. F. J. March, Gunner. Mr. March made personal contact with Lord Gort about 8 miles inland, and placed the *Calcutta* at his disposal for his or his staff's evacuation. Lord Gort, however, "courteously refused" to be evacuated at this stage.[23]

La Panne Beach Cleared of Troops

Meanwhile the *Calcutta* was proceeding with the embarkation, having enlisted the assistance of the minesweepers *Sutton* and *Salamander*, the tug *Java*, five drifters,[24] and three motor launches.[25] By 1357 the *Calcutta* had embarked 1200 troops, with whom she proceeded to Sheerness.

In addition to the ships assisting the *Calcutta*, 7 minesweepers,[26] 4 skoots,[27] and 5 destroyers[28] also embarked troops from La Panne beach. Of the destroyers, the *Greyhound* was bombed and severely damaged (see p.42). The minesweepers embarked, in all, 3415 troops, the skoots 1137 and the destroyers 2100. The tramp *Yewdale* and the motor vessels *Beal* and *Bullfinch* between them brought off 1,854. The assault landing craft A.L.C.15 ferried about 750 troops from the beaches to off-lying ships, and finally transported 25 to Dover; the A.L.C.5 also

---

23 *Calcutta's* report.

24 The *Golden Sunbeam, Lord Rodney, Lord Keith, Lord St. Vincent,* and *Lord Collingwood.*

25 The *Emperor of India, Gracie Fields, Halcyon, Hebe, Oriole, Princess Elizabeth* and *Waverley.*

26 The *Emperor of India, Gracie Fields, Halcyon, Hebe, Oriole, Princess Elizabeth* and *Waverley.*

27 The *Reiger, Doggersbank, Jutland* and *Oranje.*

28 The *Shikari, Harvester, Anthony, Sabre* and *Greyhound.*

ferried troops throughout the day.

The paddle-minesweeper *Oriole* had beached herself at La Panne at about 0600, thus permitting about 2,500 troops to pass over her decks to be embarked by other ships before she refloated at about 1800. In this connection, Sub-Lieut. Croswell, who had been landed at La Panne at about 0600 with a small beach party in the *Harvester*'s motor skiff, says: "On the beach we found 14 boats which we launched. A line ferry was established from a paddle-steamer [the *Oriole*] which was aground close inshore, and this steamer served as a pier alongside which other boats were able to come. ... Throughout the day embarkation continued".

Later in his report, Sub-Lieut. Croswell says:

"About 1400 ... bombing commenced – there were no casualties though 8 heavy bombs fell within 100 yards of the place of embarkation. A supply ship [the danlayer *Nautilus*] to the right of the beach was fired and destroyed by a near miss, and a destroyer [the *Greyhound*] was hit by an incendiary bomb [in fact she was severely damaged by a near miss] but continued in action. I joined up with the Army Staff controlling evacuation – there were no other naval officers at La Panne.[29] About 2300 ... I requested that piers should be built but was told nothing could be done that night ... Lord Gort arrived on the beach on Thursday morning [30th May] and asked what could be done to assist. I again suggested erection of piers, and under Colonel Porter's direction this was begun, the pier at La Panne being ready and in use by 1400".

More Personnel Ships Feel the Strain

In the early hours of 29th May information was received at Dover that the personnel vessels (manned by Mercantile Marine crews) were having difficulty in making the entrance to Dunkirk harbour in the face of the navigational difficulties caused by the heavy pall of smoke over the entrance, and the bombing and shelling encountered *en route* to, and off, Dunkirk. After completing one round trip during the previous 24 hours, the Captain of the *St. Seiriol* felt unable

---

29 Sub. Lt. Croswell was not given orders by his commanding officer to remain ashore. He says "as at La Panne there was no liaison between Army and Navy, I realised I could do a much more useful job by remaining there," and he stayed there until 1st June. Commenting on this, Lt. Cdr. M. Thornton, R.N., Captain of the *Harvester* says: "This young officer wisely accepted responsibility of missing his ship and then took charge of the beaches and embarkation. ..." (C.W.23187/40.)

to sail and an officer, (Lt. A. R. MacKewn, R.N.R.) took the ship over and sailed at 1100. On her return voyage the ship was bombed and damaged,[30] and did not sail again.

Parties to supplement ships' crews were lent to three personnel vessels and a hospital carrier[31] and to various drifters and motor boats.[32]

Commodore E. G. de S. Jukes-Hughes, R.N., who was Principal Sea Transport Officer at Dover during "Dynamo", says that on two occasions Sea Transport Officers took the place of Officers in personnel ships and proceeded to sea in them. "The effect of the personality of the Master", he says, "was very noticeable. A strong Master carried his crew with him and imbued them with his spirit. A weak Master only succeeded in disturbing his crew".[33]

Surf. More Ships sent to Dunkirk

S.N.O., Dunkirk, and other Senior Officers on the French coast reported during the early hours of 29th May that surf on the beaches was retarding boat-work.[34] At 0709 S.N.O., Dunkirk, reported that embarkation from Dunkirk was going on at the rate of 2,000 an hour and asked for all ships to go to Dunkirk harbour.[35] An increased number of H.M. ships was therefore sent to the harbour, in spite of the danger that an accumulation of ships alongside the east pier at Dunkirk by day might well invite an intensive air attack – and, as has been seen, it actually did so. In view, however, of the military situation the limitations of Dunkirk harbour (with its narrow gangway along the east pier), and the probability of the surf reducing as the tide rose, the Vice-Admiral, Dover, continued to send a proportion of ships to the beaches.[36]

Route Y Under Gunfire

Meanwhile, at 1100, enemy troops were reported north-east of Nieuport, and shortly after noon enemy shore batteries near Nieuport brought the Zuydcoote

---

30 Authority for this is V. A. Dover's *Report on Personnel Vessels,* M011882/40. No report by the officers or owners of the *St. Seiriol* mentions that she was damaged. She apparently did not sail again because her crew were in an overwrought state. (R.O.III, p.213, -219).

31 The *Canterbury, Lady of Mann, Princess Maud* and the H/C *St.Julien.*

32 Report by officer in charge of No. 3 Party (R.O.III, p.416).

33 [32] R.O.III, p.564.

34 See Appendix 0.1.

35 [34] Appendix 0.2.

36 D.R., p.6, para. 24.

Pass (on Route Y) under spasmodic gunfire. The southern Route Z was already under fire from the guns at Calais and Gravelines, so that Route X would soon be the only practicable daylight approach to Dunkirk and the beaches. By 1606 Route X was fully swept, and all ships were ordered to use it; ships from Dover, however, were instructed to use Route Z, provided the passage between Calais Bell Buoy and Dunkirk could be made in darkness.

Route X passed some 26 miles to the south-west of the extreme north-east point of Route Y, the locality in which E-boat attack threatened, and the route was shielded by the French minefields in the Ruytingen and Dyck channels. The E-boat Command apparently failed to appreciate this withdrawal of traffic to the south-west, and did not follow up.[37]

Barge Piers Impracticable

The considerable alarm as to the immediate safety of the B.E.F. felt during the night of 27th/28th and the forenoon of 28th May, which caused all available resources to be immediately concentrated on the French coast, eased during the 29th. But emergency measures taken late on the 28th had an adverse effect on the orderly organisation for evacuation so necessary if effective measures were to be devised and put in force.[38] On the 29th, for instance, the practicability was considered of building piers on the beaches to facilitate embarkation, using lines of barges;[39] but reports from ships that worked off the beaches showed that the very gradual shoaling of the water at all states of the tide would necessitate such piers being inordinately long, and beyond the resources available. A much needed Medical Party was shipped in the *Verity* for use on the beaches, and a Naval Medical Party was sent to Dunkirk.

Captain Howson Sails for Dunkirk

As the result of a report of an Army Officer recently evacuated it was decided that a party of Naval officers was required on the beaches between La Panne and Dunkirk. Accordingly, Captain J. M. Howson R.N., with Commanders H. G. Gorton and R. J. O. Otway-Ruthven, R.N., Lt. Cdrs. Cockburn, R.N. and R. G. Wardrop, R.D., R.N.R., and Lieuts. Whalley, Nettle and Jones sailed at

---

37 D.R. p.9, para. 29.

38 D.R. p.7, para. 27.

39 Appendix G.

1600 in the *Sabre* for Dunkirk.[40] Captain Howson arrived at Dunkirk at 1815 to find that S.N.O., Dunkirk, had been away at La Panne since noon on a visit to Lord Gort. Captain Tennant returned to Dunkirk at about 2140, and at 2300 Captain Howson was able to have a consultation with him. Captain Howson then divided the beach party into two; 3 officers under Cdr. Gorton proceeded to the beach east of Bray, and two officers under Cdr. Otway-Ruthven to the beach at Bray. Captain Howson went with the latter party. These appointments appear to have had good results, for embarkations at the beaches reached peak next day.

Rear-Admiral, Dover Sails for Dunkirk

Captain E. W. Bush, D.S.C., R.N., had also taken passage in the *Sabre* at 1600, to act as "S.N.O. afloat off the beaches" in the *Hebe*;[41] but an hour and a half later, the Admiralty appointed Rear-Admiral W. F. Wake-Walker, O.B.E. as Rear-Admiral, Dover, "for command of sea-going ships and vessels off the Belgian coast", and left it to the Vice-Admiral, Dover, to decide in which ship the R.A., Dover, should fly his flag.[42] Rear-Admiral Wake-Walker, who was to take over from Captain Bush,[43] sailed in the destroyer *Esk* at 2000 for Dunkirk. With him on board were Vice-Admiral (acting Commodore) G. O. Stephenson, C.B., C.M.G., and Vice-Admiral (acting Commodore) T. J. Hallett, C.B., C.B.E. Also on board were 12 officers and 60 ratings to act as beach parties. On the way over he arranged that Commodore Stephenson should take charge off La Panne and Commodore Hallett off Bray. It was then thought, says Rear-Admiral Wake-Walker, that the embarkation could hardly go on for more than a day or two, and each day was expected to be the last. At this time, he says, he had very little idea of what it was going to be possible to do, or how to set about it.[4]

As early as 1321 V.A. Dover had informed "Ships and Authorities, Nore and Dover Forces", and S.N.O., Dunkirk, that all vessels arriving at Dunkirk were to report for orders to Captain Bush, S.N.O.(A), in *Hebe*. Following the Admiralty's appointment of Rear-Admiral Wake-Walker, however, V.A. Dover sent a further signal, at 1943, informing S.N.O., Dunkirk and *Hebe* that R. A. Wake-Walker was proceeding to the *Hebe* to carry out the duties of S.N.O.,

---

40 Captain Howson's report. (R.O.III, p.394).

41 [40] D.R. p.9, para. 30, and R.O.III, p.394.

42 Appendix O.4.

43 D.R. p. 11, para. 36.

Dunkirk, in charge of all embarkation arrangements.[2] On the next day, the 30th May, presumably to clarify the situation, the Vice-Admiral Dover sent the following signal[3] to all authorities concerned:

"… Authority for Operation "Dynamo" under V.A. Dover is as follows:
R.A. Wake-Walker has been appointed as R.A. Dover, for command of seagoing ships and vessels off the Belgian coast.
R.A. Dover has hoisted his flag in *Hebe*. Captain Tennant has been appointed as S.N.O. Dunkirk, and is responsible under R.A. Dover for all shore organisation. T.O.O. 1328/30".

Plan for the Night 29th/30th May

Meanwhile, at 1906, the Vice-Admiral, Dover promulgated the plan for the night by signal[4] as follows:

"Evacuation of British troops to continue at maximum speed during the night. If adequate supply of personnel vessels cannot be maintained to Dunkirk east pier destroyers will be sent there as well. All other craft except hospital carriers to embark from beach which is extended from one mile east of Dunkirk to one mile east of La Panne. Whole length is divided into 3 equal parts referred to as La Panne, Bray, Malo, from east to west with a mile gap between each part. La Panne and Bray have troop concentration points each end and in middle; Malo at each end. These points should be tended by inshore craft. Pass this message by V/S to ships not equipped W/T as opportunity offers. 1906".

Dunkirk Harbour Reported Blocked

Almost at the same time he received (through the War Office and the Admiralty) a telephone message from La Panne military headquarters to the effect that Dunkirk harbour was blocked by damaged ships, and that all evacuation must therefore be effected from the beaches.[5]

"Pier undamaged", but "impossible … embark … troops"

About the same time as this telephone message came through a corrupt message from S.N.O., Dunkirk, was received, stating: "continuous bombing, one destroyer sinking, one transport with troops on board damaged and impossible at present to embark more troops, though pier undamaged".[6]

No Contact with S.N.O. Dunkirk

At 2057 the Vice-Admiral, Dover, asked the Verity and the S.N.O., Dunkirk, whether the harbour was blocked.[44] At 2120 the Verity replied that the eastern halt of the channel was blocked, and that on leaving the harbour she had grounded slightly on a sunken drifter in the entrance. S.N.O. Dunkirk replied at 2150 that the harbour was not blocked, but that it was doubtful whether much more could be done during daylight hours. [45] It is not known if or when this reply was received, because as late as 2357 V.A. Dover signalled Admiral Abrial, "I cannot get in touch with Captain Tennant. Can you inform me whether it is still possible for transports to enter harbour and berth alongside".

It is noteworthy that reception on the Naval W/T set at Dunkirk was not established until 2300 on the 30th May, and full communication with Dover was not established on the set until daylight on the 31st May.

Vice-Admiral, Dover, Diverts all Ships to the Beaches

Indeed, already at 2128, the situation, as it could be seen by the staff at Dover, was confused, and it seemed probable that the use of Dunkirk harbour would be denied to us except possibly for small ships.[46] Consequently, the Vice-Admiral, Dover, ordered all ships approaching Dunkirk not to close the harbour, but to remain off the eastern beach and collect troops from the shore;[47] drifters and minesweepers which were about to be despatched to Dunkirk harbour were also diverted to the beach.[48]

A Good Opportunity at Dunkirk Missed

In the event, only 4 drifters and a yacht[49] entered Dunkirk during the hours of darkness, and as only 2 bombing attacks were made a good opportunity was missed. It is probable that about 10,000 troops could have been lifted from the harbour during the night with little reduction of the numbers embarked from

---

44 S.N.O. Dunkirk's report. (R.O.III, p.350).

45 Appendix 0.12.

46 D.R. p. 10, para. 34.

47 D.R. p. 10, para. 34.

48 D.R. p. 10, para. 34.

49 The 4 drifters of the 1st M/R Flotilla - the *Fidget, Fisher Boy, Jacketa* and *Silver Dawn* - and the yacht *Bystander*.

the beaches.[50] Nevertheless, it was only by good fortune that the vital Dunkirk channel was not blocked by sinking ships at this early date.[51]

Admiralty's Urgent Call for Small Craft

Meanwhile, during the forenoon of the 29th May, in response to the insistent call for beaching craft, the Admiralty called on the C's in C. Portsmouth and the Nore "to investigate as a matter of urgency" the provision of additional small motor craft and X and other self-propelled lighters, which could be made available within 48 hours from all ports in their Commands.[52] Thereafter, the supply of beaching craft increased rapidly.

The A.L.C.'s Arrive Off the Beaches

On this day, however, only the first trickle of the anxiously awaited small motor craft began to arrive off the beaches. The most important arrivals were the 8 assault landing craft (A.L.C.'s), under the command of Cdr. R. A. Cassidi, R.N., which had been loaded into, and brought over by, the S.S. *Clan Macalister*. They were A.L.C.'s 3, 4, 5, 8, 15, 16, 17 and 18. While A.L.C.4 was being hoisted out, off No. 6 W buoy, at about 1030, the dr. *Vanquisher* passed at speed, causing the *Clan Macalister* to roll heavily; A.L.C.4 crashed down on A.L.C.18 and both craft were rendered unfit for service. The remaining six A.L.C.s however, did valuable work ferrying some thousands of troops from the beaches.

French Troops Rush A.L.C.S.

Cdr. Cassidi, who was in A.L.C.5 proceeded some way up the coast and then carried on inshore; his craft was "immediately rushed on all sides by French soldiers, so many of them got on board that the boat was grounded".[53] Some of the troops had to be forced off the boat before she could be got off the beach. The second attempt to embark French troops failed, so A.L.C.5 proceeded to La Panne beach.[1] Thence, British troops were ferried to off-lying ships at the rate of about 3 trips an hour, 50 men per trip, throughout the day, except for interruptions by frequent air attacks. The A.L.C.5 made 15 trips.

---

50 D.R. p. 10, para. 35.

51 [51] V.A. Dover's letter No. A 14/0/876/40 of 10th June 1940 (covering his report on Operation "Dynamo"), para. 7(b).

52 Appendix G.14.

53 Report by *A.L.C.5*.

A.L.C.16 is Sunk

The A.L.C.16 (S/Lt. R. O. Wilcoxon, R.N.V.R.) made 7 trips, after which "she was boarded by French soldiers, who overwhelmed the boat to such an extent that she became partially swamped, the starboard battery was flooded and both engines failed. Eventually sufficient French were evicted to enable A.L.C.16 to be floated off and the port engine started".[54] In going astern, however, the port stern tube was damaged and water poured into the boat; nevertheless, continually pumping and bailing, A.L.C.16 continued ferrying for a further 1½ hours. She then went alongside the sloop *Bideford* to transfer a load of troops. S/Lt. Wilcoxon went on board the *Bideford* to arrange for a tow back to England. Then came the dive-bomb attack in which the Bideford's stern was blown off. S/Lt. Wilcoxon was mortally wounded. A.L.C.16 was heavily damaged, and sank in a few minutes; she had ferried about 600 troops.

French Troops Rush A.L.C.17

A.L.C.17 followed A.L.C.5 up the coast towards Bray beach. "On approaching the beach she was promptly boarded by a crowd of French troops who so overloaded the boat that she grounded".[3] With a falling tide she remained stranded for 3 hours. As the tide rose, "the French … again attempted to rush the boat [but] the cox'n of A.L.C.17 procured the assistance of some British troops, who, drove off the French".[55] Ferrying was continued all day and throughout the night from La Panne, until the A.L.C.17's engines broke down; she was towed by a drifter to England next day for repairs.

A.L.C.'s 3, and 8 also ferried troops, and transported 20 and 10 troops respectively to Dover, where they arrived at 0400 next day.

M/B *Minikoi* Sunk

One of the earliest of the privately owned M/B's to start for the beaches was the *Minikoi*. Unfortunately, at 0015/29, while still in the Downs, she was rammed and sunk by the M.A./S.B.6, which picked up her crew of three.

M/B *Sceneshifter* Swamped andL

The M/B *Silver Moon*, from Ramsgate, arrived off the beaches at 0800 and ferried troops to ships at anchor. Without charts or compass she returned to

---

54 Report by *A.L.C.16*.

55 Report by *A.L.C.17*.

Ramsgate that night. The M/B *Sceneshifter*, on arrival, was rushed by French troops, swamped, and became a total loss.

M/B *Viewfinder* Dragged Aground and Lost

The six motor yachts, *Advance*, *Bobeli*, *Elizabeth Green*, *Hanora*, *Reda* and *Viewfinder* sailed from Dover for La Panne beach and were machine-gunned from the air off Gravelines. They arrived off La Panne beach at about 1500/29, and at once began towing whalers full of troops to off-lying ships. At 1830, the *Viewfinder* was dragged aground by Belgian soldiers and became a total loss.

M/B's *Hanora* and *Bobeli* Abandoned

At 1900, the *Hanora* fouled her propeller and was abandoned; her crew transferred to the *Elizabeth Green* and thence to the minesweeper *Lydd*. At 1900 also, the dr. *Sabre* requisitioned the *Advance* and embarked in her a W/T transmitter and 2 operators for transportation to G.H.Q. at La Panne. The *Reda*, having ferried troops, sailed for Ramsgate at 2200 with 21 troops on board. The *Bobeli* having received some damage while alongside a destroyer which suddenly went full ahead on account of an air attack, subsequently fouled her screw and rudder; she made fast to the minesweeper *Albury*, but was abandoned when the *Albury* departed and became stranded on the beach. The *Elizabeth Green* and *Advance* sailed in company that night for Ramsgate.

M/B *Glitter II* Brings Drinking Water

The *Glitter II* arrived off Bray beach at 1600 on the 29th May, loaded with tins of fresh water. She then ferried troops. Next day she lost her rudder and was towed to Dover by a drifter.

M/B *Queen of England* Sunk

A number of other small motor craft left Southend, Sheerness or Dover for the beaches on the 29th May, but did not arrive until 30th May. Among them was the *Shamrock*, and in company with her were the *Princess Maud*, *Canvey Queen* and *Queen of England*. On the way over on the night of the 29th/30th May the *Queen of England* was rammed amidships by the skoot *Tilly* and sank immediately; her crew were picked up by the *Shamrock* and transferred to the *Tilly*.[56] The remaining three motor boats were all abandoned and lost next

---

56 *Shamrock's* report, unconfirmed. The name of the vessel is in doubt; the matter is not referred to in *Tilly's* report.

day after ferrying troops to various destroyers, among them the *Anthony*; the *Canvey Queen* and *Shamrock* fouled their propellers, and the *Princess Maud* went aground.

The *Mirasol*,[57] alongside Dunkirk mole, was damaged by a near miss. She was taken in tow by a trawler, but later sank.

Other M/B's that Sailed for the Beaches on 29th May

The *Triton* and *Silver Queen*, with 6 motor launches in company, sailed for La Panne at 2200. Three of the motor launches broke down on the way over and returned to harbour; the remainder reached La Panne at 0500/30. The Dutch eel-boats *Johanna* and *Chantecler* and the M.B. *Golden Lily* also left Ramsgate at 2200/29. The *Chantecler* was only capable of 4 knots, and her "compass which was situated over the engine … revolved slowly round and and round".[58] She reached the beaches, however, at 0900 on the 30th May, and brought back 30 troops. The *Johanna* did not get over on this trip; she had no charts, lost her way in the Downs in the darkness, and returned to Ramsgate on the morning of the 30th May. Later on that day she was towed to the beaches by the skoot *Jutland*.

Troops Transported on 29th May

The 29th May closed with a formidable list of ships lost or damaged, a marked reduction in the number of destroyers available and with failure to achieve the high rate of evacuation hoped for. The effect of the day's occurrences was even more marked next day, when instead of the 50,000 to 60,000 British troops which had been calculated as the probable achievement, only 48,000 odd were in fact transported.[59]

Nevertheless, 47,310 troops (including some 2,000 casualties) were landed in England on the 29th May (see Table 2), 13,752 having been lifted from the beaches and 33,558 from the harbour. Only about 1½ per cent of these were French troops,[60] whose organised evacuation had not yet begun. (See Appendices Y.2 to Y.s).

During the morning and forenoon of the 29th May, when there was no

---

57 Commonly, but erroneously referred to in reports as the "*Marasole*".

58 Report by *Chantecler*.

59 D.R. p.11, para. 38.

60 D.R., which incidentally puts the total of troops and casualties landed on 29th May as 40,724. This figure probably does not include troops carried by foreign ships.

bombing of Dunkirk harbour, 10 personnel vessels[61] lifted 14,760 troops from the east pier; during the afternoon, in spite of the bombing, the *Canterbury* lifted a further 1,960.

The development of beach evacuation is indicated by the fact that nearly 2½ times the number of troops were lifted from the beaches on 29th May as compared with the number lifted on the previous day. Seventeen destroyers[62] each made one round trip during the 24 hours of the 29th May and an eighteenth destroyer, the *Icarus*, made two such trips. On these trips the 18 destroyers embarked and transported to England 10,694 troops of which 6,198 were lifted from the beaches and 4,506 from Dunkirk harbour. Nine minesweepers[63] together lifted 2,426 troops from the beaches although one of them, the *Albury* did not land her troops in England until the next day. Among other ships which brought back troops from the beaches was the cruiser *Calcutta* with 1,200.

The record of troops landed in England now stood as follows:
From the beaches 26th May 0, Harbour 0, Total 0
From the beaches 27th May Nil, Harbour 7,669, Total 7,669
From the beaches 28th May 5,930, Harbour 11,874, Total 17,804
From the beaches 29th May 13,752, Harbour 33,558, Total 47,310

Ships Lost or Damaged on 29th May

H.M. Ships Sunk The destroyers *Wakeful*, *Grafton* and *Grenade*.
The armed boarding vessel *King Orrry*.[64]
The Special Service Vessel *Crested Eagle*.
The Paddle Minesweepers *Waverley* and *Gracie Fields*.[1]
The Personnel Vessels *Normania*,[1] *Lorina*, *Fenella* and *Mona's Queen*.
The trawlers *Polly Johnson* and *Calvi*.
The danlayers *Comfort* and *Nautilus*.
The drifter *Girl Pamela*.[65]

---

61 The *Cote d'Argent*, *Killarney*, *King George V*, *Maid of Orleans*, *Manxman*, *Prague*, *Royal Daffodil*, *Royal Sovereign*, *Scotia*, and *Tynwald*.

62 The *Anthony*, *Codrington*, *Esk*, *Express*, *Greyhound*, *Harvester*, *Intrepid*, *Ivanhoe*, *Javelin*, *Malcolm*, *Sabre*, *Scimitar*, *Shikari*, *Vanquisher*, *Verity*, *Wolsey* and *Worcester*.

63 The *Albury*, *Duchess of Fife*, *Emperor of India*, *Fitzroy*, *Halcyon*, *Hebe*, *Leda*, *Marmion* and *Sharpshooter*.

64　Actually sank on 30th May, as a result of damage received on 29th May.

65　In collision with the *Lydd* off Dunkirk harbour on the night of 28th/29th May.

H.M. Ships Damaged and put out of Action

The destroyers *Saladin, Greyhound, Intrepid, Montrose, Mackay, Gallant* and *Jaguar*.

The sloop *Bideford*.

The minesweeper *Pangbourne* (required dockyard repairs).

The personnel vessel *Canterbury*.

The hospital carrier *Isle of Guernsey*.

Other Vessels

Sunk A.L.C.16 , the S.S. *Clan Macalister* (6,900 tons), the M/B's *Minikoi, Viewfinder, Bobeli, Hanora, Sceneshifter* and *Queen of England*.

Damaged and put out of Action

The tug *Sun V*.

Destroyers of the "H", "I" and "J" Classes withdrawn

As a result of the heavy casualties and losses amongst the destroyer force, particularly the misfortunes which befell those of the larger and more modern types, a consultation was held between the Admiralty and the Vice-Admiral, Dover, on 29th May, which led to a decision to withdraw the 7 destroyers of the "H", "I" and "J" Classes from "Dynamo";[66] they were the only modern destroyers remaining with Vice-Admiral, Dover. All destroyers of the "G" class[67] were already out of action.

There remained available for "Dynamo" 15 destroyers:

Esk

Malcolm

Verity

Express

Whitehall

Vanquisher

Anthony

Winchelsea

Sabre

---

66 The *Icarus, Impulsive, Intrepid, Ivanhoe, Harvester, Havant* and *Javelin*.

67 The *Gallant, Grafton, Grenade* and *Greyhound*.

Keith
Worcester
Scimitar
Codrington
Windsor
Shikari

Excluding any casualties, this number of destroyers might be expected to maintain a flow of one destroyer per hour to the coast and would lift 17,000 troops in 24 hours.[68] It is noteworthy that in spite of their unsuitability for the work of troop carrying, the 39 destroyers so employed in "Dynamo" brought off more troops – 96,000 – than any other type of ship. The 45 personnel vessels brought off 87,000; the 36 minesweepers 46,000; the 39 skoots 22,000; and among the smaller vessels, the 51 drifters brought off 12,000.

---

68 [69] D.R. p. 11, para. 37.

Thursday, 30th May

French and British Troops to Embark in Equal Proportions

By the 30th May Lord Gort estimated the British troops remaining in the area at 80,000, and he set about completing his plans for their final withdrawal. He had received the following telegram from the Secretary of State for War:

> "Continue to defend present perimeter to the utmost in order to cover maximum evacuation now proceeding well. ... If we can still communicate with you we shall send you an order to return to England with such officers as you may choose at the moment when we deem your command so reduced that it can be handed to a Corps Commander. You should now nominate this commander. If communications are broken you are to hand over and return as specified when your effective fighting force does not exceed equivalent of three divisions. This is in accordance with correct military procedure and no personal discretion is left to you in the matter. ... The Corps Commander chosen by you should be ordered to carry on defence and evacuation with French whether from Dunkirk or beaches. ..."

The problem, as Lord Gort saw it, was to thin out the troops, while maintaining a proper defence of the perimeter, with a force which could be embarked finally in one lift.[1]

Meanwhile Lord Gort had received orders from home that French and British troops were to embark in equal proportions, and early next morning this policy of H.M. Government was also promulgated by the Admiralty to the V.A. Dover, R.A. Dover Straits (i.e. Rear-Admiral Wake-Walker), and S.N.O. Dunkirk.[2]

The adoption of this policy, desirable as it was, made Lord Gort's problem more difficult, and necessitated a prolongation of the time that the existing

---

1 Lord Gort's Second Despatch, para. 57.

2 Appendix Y.3.

perimeter, or a smaller one, must be held, to enable all the troops to embark. "Yet the enemy pressure was increasing and there was no depth in our position. A line on the dunes could only be held during the hours of darkness to cover the final phase of the withdrawal".[1]

After discussing the situation with the Commanders of the 1st and 2nd Corps, Lord Gort came to the conclusion that the eastern end of the perimeter could not be held much longer, as the enemy had already begun to shell the beach at La Panne. He therefore motored to Dunkirk to inform Admiral Abrial of his views and to assure himself that the arrangements for embarking British and French troops in equal proportions were working smoothly. Admiral Abrial assured Lord Gort of his agreement about the evacuation of the sector, and the problem of embarkation was discussed.[1]

Judging that it would be imprudent to continue to maintain the British position on the perimeter, outside the permanent defences of Dunkirk, for more than another 24 hours, Lord Gort decided to withdraw the 2nd Corps on the night of 31st May/1st June, and the necessary moves began to take place on the morning of the 31st May.[1]

Naval Situation

So far as the Navy was concerned it was not easy to appreciate the situation at Dunkirk and off the beaches. As an example of the difficulty of doing so, Admiral Ramsay records that, at 0030/30,[3] the S.N.O. on the French coast (Rear-Admiral Wake-Walker) reported that he had no destroyers, though in fact, at that time, all available destroyers (namely ten) in the Dover Command were either on the coast, or on passage, while the remaining 5 were at Dover discharging troops embarking ammunition, fuelling, etc., and were to sail within the next 4 hours. Simultaneously, says Admiral Ramsay, "the V.C.I.G.S. reported[4] that the beaches were well organised, the troops in good heart, and there had been no bombing since dark, but that there was still a great shortage of small craft which were urgently required. "This last fact", says Admiral Ramsay, "was well known to the Vice-Admiral, Dover".[5]

In fact, on practically every occasion when officers on and off the coast complained of the lack of ships, investigation of ship's reports goes to show that

---

3 Error for 0039/30. (See Appendix H.7.)

4 Appendix H.8.

5 D.R. p. 13, para. 40.

all ships were working to their utmost capacity and that the only reason for their absence in any one place was that they could not be in two places at once. The sharp rise in the numbers of troops landed in England on consecutive days – e.g., from 17,000 troops on the 28th May, to 47,000 on the 29th, 53,000 on the 30th, and 68,000 on the 31st May – indicates the remarkably effective effort which was being made in spite of the occasional shortage of ships at Dunkirk or off the beaches.

It was the constantly changing situation which invariably made abortive any attempt – by the authorities either in England or in the evacuation area – to centralise the conduct of the operation except in its broadest aspects. Rear-Admiral Wake-Walker (Rear-Admiral, Dover), states that La Panne was in telephonic communication with England and sometimes he received messages by W/T from Dover about the situation there [i.e. at La Panne] – as for instance one timed 1749 saying that ships were urgently wanted off La Panne though actually at 1900 there were 4 destroyers and one minesweeper there and the situation was constantly changing.

Further, he pointed out that G.H.Q. was in touch with the Admiralty and Vice-Admiral, Dover, and were constantly presenting their own views and criticisms of what was happening which probably accounts for a signal from the First Sea Lord on the 30th May, asking if boats were distributed along the beaches to the best advantage.[6] Actually at the time whalers were the only boats that could get inshore, (except the pontoons and a few local craft), and their distribution was entirely dependent on the position of their parent ship.[7]

Rear–Admiral, Dover, takes over his Command

Rear-Admiral Wake-Walker points out that where incidents are so crowded it is difficult not to give a confused picture. "The picture was, however, confused, and so far as operations off the beaches were concerned organisation was not possible. The most that could be done was to exercise some control and direction".[8]

This is a just appreciation of the situation, and it provides an explanation of the not infrequent occasions when officers – both senior and junior and whether on or off the beaches – considered that, from their own particular view point, things were going awry. "Dynamo", though termed an operation, was

---

6 Appendix G.21.

7 R.A. Dover's report (M.017978/41).

8 R.A. Dover's report of Proceedings. (R.O.III, p.373).

in the nature of a desperate improvisation; but it was carried out with such courage, energy and single-mindedness, and in the face of such incredible and unpredictable difficulties, that it has since come to be spoken of as a miracle.

By 0100 Rear-Admiral Wake-Walker found the *Hebe* off Bray, and, transferring to her from the *Esk*, he took over the duties of S.N.O. (Afloat) from Captain Bush. From him, Rear-Admiral Wake-Walker heard more of the situation, and "of the ghastly sight of the shore, black with men standing in the water up to their waists." He had had "to watch the terribly slow progress of embarkation", says Rear-Admiral Wake-Walker, "which I had not then seen, but I did not feel that I could accept the note of despair which I seemed to detect in his voice".[9]

Commodores Stephenson and Hallett were transferred to drifters, the former proceeding to take charge off-shore at La Panne, and the latter off-shore at Bray.

By dawn the *Hebe* was off La Panne, and in the growing light Rear-Admiral Wake-Walker was able to glimpse for the first time the environment in which he had to work. He saw a dark line of men at the water's edge, and large groups of men all over the beaches. Off Bray the *Bideford* was ashore with her stern completely blown off and the *Locust* was trying to take her in tow. Nearer Dunkirk the *Crested Eagle* was high and dry on the beach – burnt out. Lying off the beaches were destroyers, sloops, drifters and other craft, while men were making their way off in whalers, motor boats and pontoon craft. There was a slight swell which made landing difficult, and many boats were lying broached-to and stranded by the tide.

As daylight illumined the scene Rear-Admiral Wake-Walker saw that the beaches were packed with troops, who were orderly and under proper control. To anyone with an appreciation of the practical difficulties of embarking in small boats with a long pull to seaward, the sight of that beach black with troops was indeed almost dismaying. The numbers increased steadily as more men filed down the sand dunes, and "at the back of our minds all the time", says Rear-Admiral Wake-Walker, "was the question of how long the defence line could hold and the weather remain fair." The crux of the matter was boats.[10]

Twice during the day Rear-Admiral Wake-Walker went to Dunkirk in unsuccessful efforts to contact Captain Tennant. With his staff he transferred from the *Hebe* to the *Windsor* and thence to the *Worcester*, as these ships in turn

---

9 M.017978/41, p.4.

10 [10] R.A. Dover's report (M.017978/41).

filled up with troops. Captain Bush took passage home in the *Hebe* "to stress the vital necessity for boats and crews if any large numbers were to come off the benches".[11]

There was great difficulty in exercising control off the beaches. The Rear-Admiral was hampered "by lack of means of getting about quickly". Ships would arrive at beaches and start loading; and a redistribution, though desirable, would be impracticable. The urgency of the moment governed everything.[12]

At 2000 on the 30th May Rear-Admiral Wake-Walker landed at La Panne where he met Lord Gort and Captain Tennant. The situation was discussed and arrangements were made for Lord Gort's embarkation from La Panne at 1800 next day, and Commodore Stephenson was put in charge of it.

On this evening a method of identifying the beaches from seaward was established – two lights being shown at La Panne and one at Bray – and Dover was informed accordingly.[13]

Later that night Rear-Admiral Wake-Walker transferred from the *Worcester*, by that time full of troops, to the Express – his fourth transfer in twenty-four hours.

Captain Howson, N.O.I.C., Beaches

On the beaches the progress was better than appeared at the time. Captain Howson, Naval-Officer-in-Charge of beaches, making his first acquaintance with conditions there, says that on the 30th May, off Bray, "in the lightening dawn, a number of destroyers, sloops and skoots were seen to be lying off, and embarkation was proceeding in such boats as were available. Several boats were aground, others were holed, and some had no oars. ... By about 0600, all destroyers, sloops, etc., had cleared for England and there were no further ships available

Before leaving Dover he had understood that there would be 24 signal ratings along the beaches adequately supplied with Aldis lamps, but he never saw any of them.[14] "Communication along so many miles of flat beaches was very difficult, if not impossible, with so many troops on the shore ... there was no communication until Thursday afternoon [30th May] between La Panne and

---

11 R.A. Dover's *Report of Proceedings*. (R.O.III, p.374).

12 R.A. Dover's Report (M.017978/41).

13 Report by S/Lt. E. C. Croswell, R.N. (C.W.23187/40).

14 Report by S/Lt. E. C. Croswell, R.N. (C.W.23187/40).

Bray,[15] and never any between Bray and Dunkirk".[16]

At about 0600 Captain Howson went to Corps Headquarters in a house at Bray, where he met one of his party, Commander Gorton, and also some naval officers "who had apparently been working on the beaches for some time before our arrival".

"About 0800", continues Captain Howson, "I proceeded on a motor bicycle to La Panne where I met Commander J. S. Dove, R.N., who ... took me to see Q.M.G. [Lieut. General Laidsell] with whom I discussed the position ... off La Panne " there were 2 or 3 destroyers and sloops, and embarkation appeared to be proceeding satisfactorily. ... On the return to Bray an hour later the sky was ... overcast and a Scotch mist prevailed which was a Godsend, for throughout the forenoon vast masses of French troops, quite apart from British troops, were proceeding along the beaches, and had aircraft attacked the carnage would have been dreadful. No further ships arrived during the forenoon off Bfay or La Panne and a great opportunity was missed for embarking troops undisturbed. ..."

"During the forenoon ... on my way to Dunkirk I found the water lighter *Claude*[17] high and dry, but with ample supplies of water, and on my return ... arranged with the military authorities for lorries and cans to collect and distribute this sorely needed requirement".

Meanwhile, during the forenoon also, the sappers and troops of the First Division had built a long pier of lorries off Bray into the sea[18] with plank decking. This was an excellent piece of work, and though not strong enough for use by heavy craft, nor even by small craft in a lop, it was invaluable later for embarking troops into small boats. A similar pier was commenced on the morning of the 30th May at La Panne, and was completed and in use by 1400 the same day.

---

15 S/Lt. E. C. Croswell, R.N., on shore at La Panne, says, "Lt. Cdr. McCullough [?L. Cdr. J.W. McClelland R.N.] and signal staff " arrived at La Panne on the evening of 30th May. (C.W.23817/40). The *Gossamer* reports that she embarked a party of signalmen for La Panne on 30th May, and arrived there at 1930.

16 1st Corps had a H.Q. at Bray.

17 [17] She had been towed over to Dunkirk on 25th May by the tug *Fairplay I*.

18 This was done at the suggestion of Cdr. H. du P. Richardson R.N., who was in charge of a section of Bray beach. (R.O.III, p.369).

Captain Howson goes on to say that in the afternoon one or two skoots and 2 or 3 motor yachts and paddlers arrived and anchored to the westward of Bray; none proceeded east of the Bray pier, where the First Division had waited many hours patiently. One or two destroyers or sloops passed from the westward to La Panne, and he tried without success with a lamp to tell them to anchor off the pier. Eventually he managed to get a signal to Rear-Admiral Wake-Walker asking him to arrange for this. Captain Howson also sent an officer to Dunkirk to represent the urgent need for destroyers off Bray. It was not until 2 days later that he learned that all the destroyers, etc., had been given specific instructions as to which, beach they were to anchor off. Later a certain number of destroyers, sloops and skoots anchored off Bray and the embarkation proceeded satisfactorily. Unfortunately, time after time, owing to a lack of naval ratings, he saw a procession of boats going off loaded with troops, only to be cast adrift and left floating empty out to seaward.[19]

Later that evening Captain Howson got in touch with Rear-Admiral Wake-Walker, then in the *Worcester*, and obtained permission to embark the following day in a motor boat off the beaches so as to prevent a recurrence of this waste of beaching craft.[20]

In spite of the difficulties and shortcomings emphasised in the above reports great progress was being made. In fact, beach evacuation reached its peak on this day; 29,500 troops were lifted from the beaches (as against 24,300 from the harbour); and some 50 ships, including destroyers, minesweepers, skoots, trawlers, drifters, personnel and special service vessels, were engaged continuously in the arduous work.

The Armada Grows, but Service of Ships to Dunkirk is Slowed Up

Meanwhile the build-up of ships continued, and some 31 additional craft reached Dunkirk and the beaches this day. They included two minesweepers of the 8th M.S.F. 3, the Fleet Air Arm training vessel *Grive*, 4 yachts and a drifter of the Dover M/S Command,[21] the corvette *Kingfisher*, (with the ex-Belgian canal boat *Sambre* in tow), the Yarmouth Examination Service yacht *Laroc*, the M/V

---

19 R.O.III, p.396.

20 [20] R.O.III, p.397.

21 The danlaying yachts *Gulzar* and *Sargasso,* the echo sounding yachts *Chico* and *Conidaw* and the danlaying drifter *Starlight Rays.*

Scottish Co-operator, the S/M tender *Dwarf*, the drifters *Fair Breeze* and *Ocean Breeze*, the ex-Belgian canal boats *Ambleve* and *Escaut* (in tow of the minesweeper *Skipjack*), the motor coasters *Seine* and *Lady Sheila*, the coasting barge *Viking*, the ex-Dutch eel-boat *Johanna* (in tow of the skoot *Jutland*), the oyster dredging smacks *Seasalter* and *Vanguard*, the steam hopper *W.24*, the sailing barge *Beatrice Maud*, and the dumb barges *Sark* and *Shetland*. The *Ramsgate* (R.N.L.I.) lifeboat *Prudential* (towing 7 wherries loaded with fresh water, and the punt *Carama*), and the *Margate* (R.N.L.I.) lifeboat *Lord Southborough*, were manned by their own crews, but naval ratings manned the wherries. The trawler *Olvina*, which should have been on A/S patrol, went to Bray beach in error and picked up 244 troops. Another important contingent appeared on the scene. At long last a dozen of the long awaited motor boats[22] reached the beaches, and by retrieving the abandoned and drifting pulling boats they were able to do much to increase the rate of lifting.[23]

Many more were on the way. The destroyers *Basilisk* and *Venomous* from the Western Approaches Command were making for Dover, and the mine sweepers *Niger* and *Dundalk* were coming down from the Humber. The attempt to maintain an adequate rate of lift with only the older destroyers soon proved unavailing, and all the modern destroyers of the H, I and J classes which had been withdrawn on the 29th May were ordered back to Dunkirk on the 30th.[24]

Small craft were hastening up from Portsmouth, Newhaven and Sheerness; six tugs were plodding along from Tilbury (towing 23 motor and 46 rowing lifeboats), and five others had left Gravesend (towing barges). Yachts, drifters and trawlers; launches, lighters and steam hopper barges; car ferries, coasters and cockle boats; train ferries, speed boats and picket boats; seaplane tenders, fishing craft and pleasure craft; steam pinnaces, sailing craft and a Thames fire float – a host of vessels – were heading in ever-increasing numbers,[25] for Dover, the Downs, or Dunkirk direct, while the cry "more ships, more boats", still went up off the French coast.[26]

Set-backs were inevitable, but this concourse of ships, big and little, fast

---

22 The *Constant Nymph, Bonny Heather, Adventuress, Black Arrow, Sunshine, Reda, Triton, Silver Queen, Cordelia, Golden Lily, Pauleter* and *Ma Joie.*

23 D.R. p.15, para. 49.

24 Appendices D.9, D.10. Except the *Intrepid* and *Jaguar* (in need of repairs) and the *Javelin.*

25 Appendices G.20, G.27, G.28.

26 Appendices H.7 to H.10.

and slow, manned by willing and eager crews fired by one purpose of saving the British Expeditionary Force, continued to grow until it assumed the proportions of an armada.

Late on the previous evening the *Bideford* had sent a call for large quantities of rope for towing to be sent, and within a few hours 9 coils (1080 fathoms) of 4-inch grass hawser were speeding by lorry from Chatham dockyard to Ramsgate to help the skoots to haul boats off the beaches, thus speeding up the boat work and compensating for the shortage of boats, "which would continue", says Vice-Admiral, Dover "for at least another 24 hours".[27]

Undoubtedly as a result of the messages and signals received on the 29th May by V.A. Dover with regard to the harbour at Dunkirk, the number of ships sent there on the 30th May was curtailed, with a corresponding reduction in the volume of embarkation. After V.A. Dover's signal to Admiral Abrial late on the 29th May, asking whether it was possible for transports to berth alongside, further signals to the same effect were sent to the Vanquisher and the Codrington and to Rear-Admiral Wake-Walker. Finally, at 1020, the *Wolsey* was called upon for a detailed report of conditions alongside the east pier; and by 1524 V.A. Dover was able to inform destroyers that "a good berth with bollards exists 400 yards from end of east ... pier".

In the meantime signals were coming in from Rear-Admiral Wake-Walker and from the *Vivacious* stating that the beaches were filling up rapidly and more ships and boats were urgently required there.[28] Although it was known that the destroyers could use Dunkirk, it appeared, says V.A. Dover, that the best division of transport was to send the great majority of destroyers to the beaches, where urgent demands could not be ignored, and the personnel vessels to Dunkirk harbour, only an occasional destroyer being sent to Dunkirk from the reduced number available.[29]

In pursuance of this decision, during the forenoon and early afternoon only seven destroyers went to Dunkirk,[30] although later in the afternoon four of them, the *Vanquisher, Malcolm, Vimy* and *Wolsey* made a second trip to the east pier.

There was delay in the sailing of personnel vessels, while enquiries about the harbour were being made, and this resulted in only one of them – the *Royal*

---

27 D.R. p.13, para. 41.

28 Appendices H.7, H.9 and G.22.

29 D.R. p.13, para. 43.

30 The *Vanquisher, Vimy, Malcolm, Wolsey, Sabre, Express* and *Scimitar*.

Daffodil – reaching Dunkirk during the forenoon. The store ship *Dorrien Rose* arrived there at 0650, and unloaded part of the provisions she was carrying; then, in view of the number of troops awaiting transport, she was filled up with 590 and sailed. The *Dorrien Rose* had not brought any of the much needed fresh water, but some was obtained from the destroyers.

The only other ships arriving at Dunkirk harbour during the forenoon were the drifters *Girl Gladys*, *Golden Sunbeam* and *Yorkshire Lass*.[31]

It was this restricted service of ships during a day of quiet (because of mist and low visibility) and a night of little enemy activity during which only 4 drifters and a yacht had entered Dunkirk,[32] that called forth the reproachful comment from the harassed Naval Staff, in their dug-out at the shore end of the east pier,[33] "a great opportunity ... again lost".[34]

At 1257 the P/V *Princess Maud, en route* for Dunkirk, was fired on when 3 miles west of Gravelines, by a shore battery and received 3 hits, one being six inches above the water line. Three of the crew were killed and three wounded, and the ship had to return to Dover for repairs.

French Ships Arrive in Larger Numbers. *Bourrasque* Sunk

The contribution of French ships had so far been negligible. On Friday (May 30th), however, some 15 ships went to Dunkirk harbour, including 2 destroyers and 3 torpedo boats,[35] the minesweepers *Arras* and *L'Impetueuse*, 4 trawlers[36] the tug *Lutteur*, and 3 motor fishing vessels.[37]

The participation in "Dynamo" of one of these French reinforcements was unfortunately very short-lived, for an enemy battery at Nieuport was instrumental in sinking the torpedo boat *Bourrasque*. She had sailed from Dunkirk at 1530 loaded with over 600 French troops of all descriptions – officers without troops, a mixture of artillerymen, Moroccan troops, air force personnel, sailors from barracks, fleet air arm personnel, naval recruiting officers, crews of sunken ships, etc. ... even one woman ("I did not notice her presence

---

31 Reports by Captain A/P, Dover, and S.N.O., Dunkirk.

32 See Section 139, footnote [8].

33 M.017978/40, p.7.

34 S.N.O. Dunkirk's report.

35 *Foudroyant, Branlebas, Bourrasque, Bouclier* and *Siroco*.

36 *Louise Marie, Chasse-Maree, Angele Marie* and *Jeune France*.

37 *Louise Marie, Chasse-Maree, Angele Marie* and *Jeune France*.

until at sea," says Capitaine de Fregate R. Fouque, "or she would have been one of the first to be saved"). The troops had few arms; on the other hand the decks were encumbered with baggage and there were even some bicycles. An attempt to make an approximate count of the passengers had to be given up, because of the congestion in the gangways and spaces.

At about 1600, after passing Nieuport buoy, the *Bourrasque* came under the fire of a battery at Nieuport, the salvoes falling regularly at about 3½ minute intervals. To open the range more rapidly and so avoid this bombardment, course was set closely to the edge of an adjacent French minefield and speed was increased. The crowded decks made it dangerous to return the fire of theGerman battery. When the *Bourrasque* was about 5 miles north of Nieuport buoy a shock was felt, followed by one more violent; smoke rose from the torpedo firing platform and there was a big escape of steam. The ship stopped and the electricity failed. It was difficult to say if the ship was seriously damaged; there was a breach in the deck and water was entering some compartments, but it was not possible to get to the engine room to assess the damage there. During this time, not unnaturally, a certain degree of panic, which had to be controlled, reigned among this mixed crowd of passengers; some of them threw themselves into the water, while others lowered the boats and threw themselves into them in such numbers that they sank, even the rafts. Order was, however, restored. The *Branlebas* was approaching. It soon became evident, however, that the *Bourrasque* was doomed, and "abandon ship" was ordered.[38]

At 1625 the French torpedo boat *Branlebas*, which had been 4 cables astern of the *Bourrasque*, saw a heavy explosion take place in the *Bourrasque* which disappeared from view in a column of smoke and water. When the column subsided the *Bourrasque* appeared to have broken in two and was sinking rapidly. She had apparently struck a French mine. The *Branlebas*, which had already embarked 300 troops from Dunkirk picked up 100 survivors, the drifter *Ut Prosim* 250, and the drifter *Yorkshire Lass* (assisted by an English motor launch) 194. At 0530 next morning the motor vessel *Bat*, *en route* for Dunkirk, took off 15 naked and oil-covered survivors from the capsized wreck of the *Bourrasque*.

It is officially considered by the French Admiralty that the *Bourrasque* was sunk by a mine, but her Captain was of the opinion that her sinking was the result of one or more shell hits.

---

38 Report by Capitaine de Fregate R. Fouque (French Admiralty Record, Folio 4).

Troops Embark at the Double

Following the disastrous air attacks on massed shipping on the 29th May S.N.O., Dunkirk, decided on the 30th May that only one destroyer at a time should enter Dunkirk and secure alongside the east pier. This policy was adhered to throughout the forenoon and early afternoon.

At about 1700 Captain Tennant turned over the duties of S.N.O., Dunkirk, to Commander G.O. Maund, R.N., and went by car to G.H.Q. at La Panne to confer with Lord Gort.

Cdr. Maund says: "Towards the close of the day [i.e. the 30th] a great number of ships had arrived, and I accordingly decided to accept the risk of further losses, and ordered the vessels waiting in the roads to proceed alongside and embark troops. Strong air attacks were launched by the enemy, but fortunately they were mostly concentrated against wrecks in the roads. Time and again they sent waves of bombers and directed their attack, not against our ships loading troops, but only against these wrecks in the roads. We got a great deal of amusement and satisfaction from this, for loading was proceeding apace with no casualties. At the same time, I decided that the rate of embarkation must in some way be speeded up as the capacity of the ships now alongside was more than adequate for the rate of the flow of troops. This laid our vessels open to attack from the air. ... I therefore went down to the Eastern Arm and rigged up a loud speaker[39] and addressed the troops in the following terms: 'Remember your pals, boys. The quicker you get on board, the more of them will be saved'. "This", continues Cdr. Maund, "worked like a miracle. The thousands of troops, tired, depressed, and without food or water for days, broke into a double and kept it up for the whole length of the Eastern Arm for more than two hours. During that period I estimate that more-than 15,000 troops were embarked. The Army certainly responded splendidly".[40]

Cdr. Maund's estimate was triumphantly confirmed: between 1802 and about 2100, eight destroyers[41] embarked from the east pier an aggregate of 8,528 troops; four personnel vessels[42] embarked an aggregate of 5,694 troops; and other vessels, including the skoots *Reiger* and *Doggersbank*, also embarked

---

39 A portable loud speaker equipment had been brought to Dunkirk on 30th May.

40 Cdr. Maund's report (R.O.III, p.443).

41 The *Anthony* (1137), *Codrington* (1100), *Esk* (1041), *Vimy* (948), *Impulsive* (1112), *Keith* (1200), *Winchelsea* (925) and *Wolsey* (1065).

42 The *Prague* (1039), *Royal Sovereign* (1502), *St. Helier* (2000) and *Tynwald* (1153).

troops, while the hospital carrier *Dinard*, well down the pier, embarked a number of wounded.

Anthony and *Sabre* Damaged

Of the eight destroyers referred to above, one, the *Anthony*, when returning to Dover was attacked by a single aircraft which dropped 5 bombs, which extinguished her lights, stopped her engines, and put her compasses and W/T out of action. She was subsequently able to proceed, steering by her engines, and the *Keith* escorted her into Dover.

Earlier in the day another destroyer, the *Sabre*, when near No. 6 Calais buoy, on her way to Dunkirk by Route Z, came under fire from shore batteries and received several hits on the bridge and upper works. A shell went through the gyro-compass, an oil fuel tank was pierced, the magnetic compass put out of action, and she had to return to Dover for repairs.

The destroyer crews, who had hardly slept since the operation began, were beginning to show signs of exhaustion, and at 2341 (May 30th) the Admiralty ordered a spare destroyer's crew to be sent to Dover to provide temporary reliefs.

Air Patrols

In the air low visibility checked the enemy's activity, but as on the previous day patrols were again carried out by Fighter Command at three – or four – squadron strength, the largest number of aircraft on the line at any one time being 44, and the smallest 26. Sixteen squadrons again operated, the total number of sorties amounting to 265. Small Coastal Command patrols operated as before throughout the day along the line North Goodwins – Gravelines – Ostend, and at night the patrol over Dunkirk by single Blenheims continued; but the governing factor cf the air operations over Dunkirk on the 30th May was the low visibility, which restricted the enemy's activities.[43]

Summary of Troops Landed in England

Thus the day was one of reviving hope. It ended with the numbers going up, and a record number were embarked from the beaches.

Arrangements for Evacuation of B.E.F. Rearguard

Meanwhile, during the forenoon, representatives of the Commander-in-Chief of

---

43 R.A.F. Narrative, p. 331.

the B.E.F. had attended a conference with the Vice-Admiral, Dover.

The Commander-in-Chief's plan was explained; it gave daylight on Saturday, 1st June, as the latest reasonable date up to which the B.E.F. might be expected to hold the eastern perimeter with an available force of about 4,000.

Thursday, 30th May

Summary of Troops Landed in England

From the beaches 26th May 0, Harbour 0, Total 0

From the beaches 27th May 0, Harbour 7,699, Total 7,669

From the beaches 28th May 5,930, Harbour 11,874, Total 17,804

From the beaches 29th May 13,752, Harbour 33,558, Total 47,310

From the beaches 30th May 29,512, Harbour 24,311, Total 53,823

By that date and time the Vice-Admiral knew that he would have available ocean-going tugs, ships' lifeboats and ships' power lifeboats which he could specially reserve for the climax of this critical operation.

The conference made the following decisions:

(a) That evacuation should proceed with the utmost vigour to ensure that by 0130 on 1st June the British forces ashore should have been reduced to the rearguard of 4,000.

(b) That special boats and tugs should be accumulated and held aside to ensure them being available in the early hours of 1st June.

(c) That the plan should provide for lifting the rearguard of 4,000, plus R.N. beach parties, in one or more flights between 0130 and 0300 on 1st June.

(d) Final decision, based on the progress of the evacuation of the main body to be made by the Vice-Admiral at 1400 on Friday, 31st May, as to the possibility of adhering to the plan.

Other technical details were settled at the meeting, and the Military staff were assured that the ever increasing rate of lifting made it probable that an affirmative decision would be reached at the critical hour of 1400 on the 31st May. In the event, the Military plan was changed on the 31st May, as it was found to be impossible to hold the original covering position with 4,000 troops and then withdraw them to the beaches for embarkation by boat.

Friday, 31st May – Evacuation Reaches its Zenith

Lord Gort Hands Over his Command to Major–General Alexander

Orders had been issued on the 30th May for the 3rd, 4th and 5th Divisions (2nd Corps) to withdraw to the beaches and Dunkirk. The 50th Division was to fall back to the French defences on the Belgian frontier and, together with the British Base staff at Dunkirk, to come under the 1st Corps. These moves began to take place on the morning of 31st May.[1]

This meant that the remnant of the B.E.F., on being withdrawn inside the area of the French defences, came under the orders of Admiral Abrial; the time had therefore arrived for Lord Gort to hand over his command in accordance with the instructions he had received.[2] He selected Major-General the Hon. H. R. L. G. Alexander to remain in France in command of the 1st Corps, now numbering less than 20,000 men in all; and, on taking over command of the 1st Corps, Major-General Alexander handed over command of the 1st Division to Brigadier M. B. Beckwith-Smith.

Lord Gort agreed with Major-General Alexander that a provisional date for evacuating his force was to be the night of 2nd/3rd June.

On the 31st May therefore, Lord Gort's headquarters closed at 1800, and, after handing over command to Major-General Alexander, Lord Gort embarked with his A.D.C. in the *Hebe*'s whaler, which had been towed in by the motor yacht *Lahloo* to a point a little west of La Panne beach. He proceeded to the *Lahloo* and thence to the *Hebe*. During the embarkation an enemy attack was made by about 40 aircraft and considerable shelling was directed on to La Panne beach itself. With Lord Gort on board, the *Hebe* proceeded to La Panne beach and continued to embark troops.

It was not, however, till about midnight, that the motor yacht *Bounty* with

---

1 Lord Gort's Second Despatch, para.57.
2 Lord Gort's Second Despatch, para. 58.

Cdre. Stephenson on board proceeded to transfer Lord Gort from the *Hebe* to the *Keith*. At about the same time, however, the *M.A/S.B.6*, having embarked Lord Gort's chief staff officer General Leese from the *Keith*, was sent to the *Hebe* with orders from Rear-Admiral Wake-Walker to embark Lord Gort. On finding that he had left the *Hebe*, the M.A /S.B.6 returned to the *Keith*, embarked Lord Gort, and sailed at 0304 on the 1st of June for Dover which she reached at 0547 the same evening.

It had been the intention of the Admiralty that Lord Gort and his staff should be embarked in M.T.B.'s and at 1522 V.A. Dover had informed Rear-Admiral Wake-Walker by signal that 4 of these vessels would be available for this purpose.[3] Unfortunately, V.A. Dover's signal did not reach R.A. Dover, and the 4 M.T.B.'s were put to other uses; and indeed were all four back at Dover by 2315. Speaking of the non-receipt of V.A. Dover's signal, Rear-Admiral Wake-Walker says, "The signal informing me of this, like many others, never reached me". At 1543/30 Rear-Admiral Wake-Walker had asked that he be embarked in a ship capable of keeping 2 wireless lines for communication purposes, and at 0645/31 he embarked in such a ship, viz. the flotilla leader *Keith*, and thereafter (until she was sunk 24 hours later) kept her free from troops so that his movements should be unrestricted.[4]

One of the four M.T.B.'s, viz: *M.T.B.67*, had been ferrying troops to the gunboat *Mosquito* at 1915 from La Panne beach, and her commanding Officer, Lieut. C. C. Anderson, R.N., says, "It is desired to express appreciation of an unknown soldier, who, although severely wounded about the face and head and on the point of collapse, remained quietly in the water watching *M.T.B.67* draw away because he thought we looked full up and might not want him. This man was of course taken on board".

Meanwhile anxiety was felt at Dover at the non-appearance of Lord Gort and at 2336, the Admiralty sent a peremptory signal to Rear-Admiral Wake-Walker demanding an explanation. Rear-Admiral Wake-Walker says, "About 2300 I received an urgent signal from Admiralty asking where Lord Gort was and why I had detailed the M.T.B.'s sent for him to other work. As the *M.A./S.B.* [i.e. *M.A/S.B.6*] had just returned with [Lt. Cdr.] C. J. Wynne-Edwards,[5] I sent it off at once to *Hebe* to collect Lord Gort ... it came back almost at once to say

---

3 M.T.B's. *67, 107, 68* and *102*. (See Appendix G.30).

4 R.A. Dover - Report of Proceedings (R.O.III, p.374, para. 19).

5 He had been engaged in directing the then arriving tows of boats to the beaches.

that Lord Gort had just left *Hebe* in a motor launch. It was very dark and *Hebe* could not be seen though we knew where she was, and I waited anxiously for the boat to arrive. Presently out of the dark a boat appeared and came alongside, still not the right one, and I had a bad moment thinking of the boat getting lost. However, to my relief, after what appeared about half an hour, the right boat, in charge of [Commodore] Stephenson once more, found us at last. Apologising to Lord Gort for keeping him waiting so long, I transferred him to the *M.A/S.B.* and sent him off to Dover with General Leese".[6]

In the meantime, a little before 1800, Lord Gort's staff had been embarked during an air attack by the *Keith*'s boats at a point 2 miles west of La Panne.

Signal Communication Established Between Dunkirk and Dover[7]

At daylight on the 31st full signal communication was at length established between Dunkirk and Dover.

On the 26th May the destroyer *Wolsey* had been despatched to Dunkirk to act as W/T link. The S.N.O., Dunkirk, on arrival next day, decided, however, that conditions in the port made it impossible for a destroyer to lie there. On the morning of the 27th May Commander M.O.D. Ellwood, R.N., who had been placed in charge of communications in Operation "Dynamo", proceeded to Dunkirk in the *Wolfhound* that afternoon with a signal party consisting of one yeoman of signals and 24 signalmen, who were distributed between Naval headquarters at Dunkirk (one yeoman and 8 signalmen) and the beach parties (2 signalmen each). The only equipment available other than hand flags was one Aldis lamp, which was taken over from the British Naval Liaison Officer and made to function with the help of a battery acquired from a French motor car.

A Headquarters signal station was established at the shore end of the East Pier for communication with ships arriving, but until 30th May, when one Naval wireless set arrived, there was no means of communication between Headquarters and the various parties, nor between one party and another, except by despatch riders, for the distances were too great for the effective employment of semaphore. Beach parties improvised signalling arrangements as best they could with the help of lamps of commandeered motor cars. Messages for transmission to Dover by W/T were either sent through the French station at the

---

6 M.017978/41, page 21.

7 R.O. Case 5468, Vol. III, p.417.

Bastion or, for the sake of greater secrecy as well as convenience, taken by hand down the pier for transmission by destroyers. This was done because the coding of messages sent through the French Station was a laborious business which first necessitated the translation of the message into French, and decoding the type of code (the Anglo French) in use at that date was a very slow business.

Reception on the naval W/T set which arrived on the 30th May was established by 2300 on that day, but owing to a defective transmitter full communication was not established with Dover until daylight on the 31st. Transmission broke down altogether on the evening of 1st June, probably on account of sand in the generator.

On the 1st June the Royal Corps of Signals established a W/T station in a lorry by the Bastion, as well as telephone communication between the Bastion and the Headquarters Signal Station. The intense bombing and shelling by the Germans that day severed the line more than once.

In view of the possibility of the arrival of enemy forces on the 2nd June all signal forms and records were destroyed on that day.

British Sector to be Held Till Midnight 1st–2nd June

Meanwhile, on taking over command of the 1st Corps, Major General Alexander proceeded to Dunkirk to interview Admiral Abrial who informed him that he intended to hold the perimeter till all the troops were embarked. A French Corps on the right was to hold the sector from Gravelines to Bergues (though Gravelines had not apparently been in French hands for some days) and a mixed French and British Corps under command of Major General Alexander was to hold a line from Bergues to Les Moeres and thence to the sea.[8]

Major General Alexander at once told the Admiral and General Fagalde that in his view this plan did not take account of the true naval and military situation which was serious and deteriorating rapidly. The fighting condition of the troops was now such that prolonged resistance was out of the question, and the present front could not in his opinion be maintained after the night of 1st/2nd June; furthermore, the line to be held was so close to the beach and to Dunkirk that the enemy might soon stop all further evacuation by short range artillery fire.[1]

Major General Alexander gave the same opinion to the Secretary of State for War, and received a reply that the British force should be withdrawn as rapidly as possible on a basis of British and French troops being embarked in equal

---

8 Appendix to Lord Gort's Second Despatch.

numbers from that time onward. This he showed to Admiral Abrial and General Fagalde, stating that he would hold the sector allotted to him till midnight lst/2nd June, and then withdraw under cover of darkness, which they agreed was the only plan feasible.[1]

Cyclone Damaged by Torpedo

Day and night our patrols were maintaining their vigil northward, but on this day two French destroyers were subjected to E-boat attacks. One, the *Cyclone*, was on her way to Dunkirk when, apparently between T buoy and the West Hinder, the track of a torpedo was seen at 0121 crossing from port to starboard 10 yards ahead; a minute later another track was seen to port, and although avoiding action was taken the torpedo struck forward and considerably damaged her, but the *Cyclone* was still able to steam and she proceeded back to Dover at 4 knots escorted by an English vessel; later, the French torpedo boat *Bouclier* and then the French minesweeper *Arras* took over the duty of escort. The *Cyclone* reached Dover at 1600, having transferred two serious casualties to an English M/B while on passage. She took no further part in "Dynamo".

Siroco Sunk

At 0145, some 20 minutes after this attack, the French destroyer *Siroco*, on her way to Dover with 770 troops from Dunkirk, was hit near T buoy by 2 torpedoes fired by an E-boat which had stopped and was unseen in the darkness; the destroyer *Vega*, on patrol 4 miles to the south-east, saw a column of flame 200 feet high. The *Siroco* capsized shortly after. Survivors to the number of 252 were picked up, 50 by the trawler *Wolves*, 21 by the trawler *Stella Dorado*, 166 by the corvette *Widgeon* and 15 by the Polish destroyer *Blyskawica*.[9]

---

9 Appendix J.2. The pleasure launches Enterprise and Wave Queen), the Foremost 101, Lady Southborough, Queen's Channel, Gallion's Reach; and the hopper barge *W.26*. The M/B's. *Minotaur, White Heather, Westerley, Naiad Errant, Lansdowne, Balquhain, Tigris I, Rapid I, Marsayru,* and *Mermaiden.* The *Excellent's* A/A M/B, the *Dolphin's* power boat, the *Nelson's* picket boat and the motor coaster *Hythe.*

The X lighters *95, 149, 209* (towing a boat), *213,* and *217.* The motor barge *Sherfield,* the motor launch *Nanette II* the lighter *Y.C.63.* The War Department's seven 30 knot motor launches *Grouse, Haig, Kestrel, Marlborough, Swallow, Wolfe* and *Vulture;* an eighth, the *Pigeon,* went over on 1st June.

The skoot *Hilda* towed over the motor boats *Moss Rose, Rose Marie, Lady Haig, Britannic, Gipsy King, Golden Spray II* and two *life-boats.*

Three more of Pickford & Co. Ltd.'s motor vessels went over, viz: the *Chamois, Hound* and the *M.F.H.*

At 0700, the *Vega*, which had been on patrol since noon 28th May, was relieved by the destroyer *Jackal*.

It was on this morning that clear evidence of the presence of enemy submarines was obtained, for the *Vimy*, *en route* to Dunkirk, sighted the periscope and conning tower of one between the North Goodwin buoy and the North-West Goodwin buoy. A depth charge was dropped, and a hunt began in which the trawlers *Westella* and *Spurs*, the corvette *Sheldrake*, and the *Jackal* joined, but without success.

Conditions on the Beaches

Meanwhile, conditions on the beaches were by no means favourable. Already at 0400 a lop had started. At about 0600 the R.N.L.I. life boat *Lord Southborough* was ferrying troops to the destroyer *Icarus* off Bray. "There was a nasty surf," said the coxswain of the life boat. "Troops were rushing out to us from all directions and were being drowned close to us and we could not get to them. ... it seemed to me we were doing more harm [than good] by drawing the men off the shore, as with their heavy clothing, the surf was knocking them over and they were unable to get up. ... The whaler from the destroyer ... was swamped, so was the motor pinnace that was working with the whaler, and so it was all along the sands as far as I could see, both sides of us, and there was not a boat left afloat". At 0600 also, Lt. Col. R. L. Hutchins, M.C., Grenadier Guards, in command of the War Department motor launch *Swallow*, arrived off Dunkirk, and described the situation as follows: "Dunkirk was under a pall of smoke from fires which appeared to be mainly to the south and west of the port. There were numerous wrecks outside the harbour, and along the beaches. There were large numbers of troops on the shore as far as it was possible to see to the eastward, and the beach was strewn with all forms of motor transport. Along the foreshore were a very large number of pulling boats, aground, capsized or damaged, and abandoned. There were also a considerable number of motor boats, motor launches and yachts aground and, in most cases, abandoned, and several wrecks close inshore. About one mile out in the Dunkirk roads were numerous destroyers and other vessels waiting to embark troops, but scarcely any boats were running between the shore and these ships ... the beaches were quiet except for occasional shelling and intermittent bombing. ..." Nevertheless between 0800 and 1315 Lt. Col. Hutchins ferried about 450 troops to the *Impulsive* off Malo, and thereafter, about 250 troops to the *Winchelsea* off Bray. The Swallow sailed for Ramsgate at about 1800 with 30 troops on board.

At 1035 Rear-Admiral Wake-Walker informed V.A. Dover that the majority of pulling boats were broached-to and had no crews; that conditions on the beaches were very bad owing to a freshening on-shore wind; that only small numbers were being embarked even in daylight; that motor boats could not get close in, and that under present conditions any large scale embarkation from the beaches was quite impracticable. He considered that the only hope of embarking any number was at Dunkirk, but that he would attempt to beach a ship to form a lee and so improve conditions.[10]

Sailing of Personnel Vessels Suspended

Simultaneously with this bad news came a signal from S.N.O., Dunkirk, to the effect that Dunkirk was being continuously and heavily bomarded; that the enemy artillery were gradually finding the range of the loading berths; and that only ships necessary for the flow of troops should enter.[11] This signal confirmed the V.A. Dover in a decision he had made to suspend the sailing of personnel vessels to Dunkirk until the number of those *en route* had been reduced. There were at this time no less than 9 personnel vessels and 3 hospital carriers known to be on the round trip U.K. – Dunkirk and back, and one other personnel vessel had been ordered to sail during the night but her whereabouts was unknown. In addition, 3 other personnel vessels were under orders to sail between 0900 and 1030.

Military Plan Changed

The plan, arranged between V.A. Dover and representatives of the C.-in-C., B.E.F. on the 30th May, was to lift the B.E.F. rearguard of 4,000, plus R.N. beach parties, on the night of 31st May/1st June; and naval arrangements had been made.[12] The minesweepers had received their orders;[13] instructions had been issued for the special tows to leave Ramsgate at 1300/31 for Dunkirk via Route X; and C.-in-C. Nore, and F.O.I.C. Harwich, were requested to provide all available M.T.B.'s to escort this convoy for as much of the outward passage as possible.[14] Speed of advance 6 knots. A party of Naval Officers assembled at

---

10 Appendix Q. 6.

11 Appendix Q. 7.

12 Appendices Q.1, G.29.

13 Appendix Q. 1.

14 Appendix G.29.

Dover to embark in these tows were given detailed instructions on the plan. At 1000 the *Hebe* arrived off La Panne beach carrying the plans for this evacuation. In the afternoon of the 31st May, however, Dover was informed that the Military plan had been changed, as it was no longer possible for the original covering position to be held by 4,000 troops who were finally to withdraw to the beaches for embarkation. Instead, the easternmost Division was to be withdrawn westward from La Panne area, and the special flight of boats was to lift this force from the beaches. At the same time the troops in the Bray and Malo sectors were being thinned out by movements westwards towards Dunkirk itself. This change of plan involved concentrating the special tows and minesweepers to which they were to transfer the troops, into the stretch opposite the beach between Zuydcoote Sanatorium and the one mile east of La Penne,[15] and also advancing the commencement of the operation by one hour.[16]

A risk was involved in this change of plan as the boat tows were not in communication with the Vice-Admiral, and it would therefore be necessay for minesweepers to see that the escorting M.A./S.B.'s shepherded the tows to the new positions. It had been explained to the Naval Officers in each tow that the minesweepers would be anchored so as to serve as guiding marks.[17]

> "It was always impossible for me to do more than deal with the situation of the moment", says Rear-Admiral Wake-Walker. "I did not know what ships were coming or when – except for the pre-arranged plan of the sloops. Nor was it possible for Dover to give me much information. Ships got back there, unloaded, and were off again, the steam was constant but irregular and it was not possible to see any way ahead. My policy was always to keep only sufficient ships off the beaches and send all the others into Dunkirk, but the situation changed continually".[18]

Small Craft Arrive in Hundreds

It was in such circumstances that, at about 1900, Rear-Admiral Wake-Walker had proceeded to Dunkirk in the *Keith* to see how the boat situation was getting

---

15 See Appendix Q. 18, observing that D.R. p.20, para. 61 says "the beach between Bray and 1 mile east of La Panne".

16 Appendix Q.19.

17 D.R. p.20, para. 61.

18 M.017978/41, p.17.

on. There he saw for the first time that strange procession of craft of all kinds the story of which was to become famous – tugs, towing dinghies, life-boats and all manner of pulling boats[19] – small motor yachts, motor launches, drifters, Dutch skoots, Thames barges, fishing boatd, pleasure steamers.[20] This was indeed the first time that the small craft had come over in hundreds.[21] Since noon Lt. Cdr. J. Wynne-Edwards, R.N. (of R.-A. Dunkirk's staff), embarked in *M.T.B.68*, had been directing the tows to various beaches.

---

19 The following 14 tugs (their tows are shown in brackets) reached Dunkirk that evening: The *Racia* (12 life-boatd), *Sun VIII* (12 life-boats), *Sun XV* (6 life-boats), *Vincia* (3 life-boats), *Sun IV* (9 boats), *Tanga* (6 boats), *Ocean Cock* (6 M/B's), *Sun II* (seaplane tenders *243, 254, 276, 291* and *A.M.C.3*), *Foremost 87* (two sailing barges), *Fairplay I* (sailing barge *Barbara Jean*), *Empire Henchman* (sailing barge *Aidie*), *Crested Cock* (a lighter), *Sun XI* (a lighter), and the *Sun XII* (sailing barges *Tolllesbury* and *Ethel Everard*).

In the early hours of 1st June other tugs arrived. The *St. Fagan* (auxiliary barges *Pudge* and *Lady Rosebery*, and the sailing barge *Doris*), *St. Abbs* (auxiliary barge *Thyra* and sailing barges *H.A.C.* and *Duchess*), *Cervia* (sailing barge *Royalty*), and the *Persia* (sailing barge *Glenway* and *Lark*).

20 M.017978/41, p.19.

21 New arrivals off Dunkirk and the beaches on 31st May included the following:

The yachts *Amulree, Aronia, Glagla, Caleta, Christobel II* and *Llanthony*, the nine yachts of the Portsmouth Inner Patrol, viz: the *Ahola, Ankh, Bounty, Caryandra, Eilla II, Lahloo, Noneta, Seriola* and *Thele*; and from R.N. Air Station, Ford, the yacht *Andora*.

The drifters *Ben* and *Lucy* (towing 4 boats), *Dorienta* (towing boats), *Monarda, Renascent* and the 13 drifters of the Yarmouth Base, viz: *Alcmaria, Feasible, Genius, Gula, Jeannie MacIntosh, John and Norah, Lord Barham, Lord Hood, Overfalls, Reed, Rewga, Swift Wing* and *Taransay*. The drifters *Fair Breeze* and *Ocean Breeze* were again over, the former towing a motor life-boat and 3 life-boats.

The steam hopper barges *Foremost 102* (towing the *Excellent's* 35 ft. motor boat and the pleasure launches *Enterprise* and *Wave Queen*), the *Foremost 101, Lady Southborough, Queen's Channel, Gallion's Reach*; and the hopper barge *W.26*. The M/B's *Minotaur, White Heather, Westerley, Naiad Errant, Lansdowne, Ballquhain, Tigris I, Rapid I, Marayru* and *Mermaiden*. The *Excellent's* A/A M/B, the *Dolphin's* power boat, the *Nelson's* picket boat and the motor coaster *Hythe*.

The X lighters *95, 149, 209* (towing a boat), *213* and *217*. The motor barge *Sherfield*, the motor launch *Nanette II* and the Lighter *Y.C.63*. The War Department's seven 30 knot motor launches *Grouse, Haig, Kestrel, Marlborough, Swallow, Wolfe* and *Vulture*; an eighth, the *Pigeon*, went over on 1st June.

The skoot *Hilda* towed over the motor boats *Moss Rose, Rose Marie, Lady Haig, Britannic, Gipsy King, Golden Spray II* and two life-boats.

Three more of Pickford & Co. Ltd.'s motor vessels went over, viz: the *Chamois, Hound* and the *M.F.H.*

Typical of the urge which characterised this movement of small craft was the trawler *Strathelliot*, which sailed from Ramsgate at 0205 on the 31st May escorting motor boats, 8 of which were disabled and in tow of various vessels; the M/B *Skylark*, disabled, was in tow of *Strathelliot*. At 0640 the *Skylark's* towing bollard tore away and she was taken in tow stern first. Then the M/B *Mary Rose*, which had been in tow of the M/B *Rapid I*, was damaged. Her crew were transferred to the *Strathelliot* and the *Mary Rose* was sunk. Later, the *Skylark* also became damaged, and she was sunk after her crew had been embarked in the *Strathelliot*. Shortly after this the M/B *Malden Annie IV* had to be taken in tow – and later taken in tow stern first – and she arrived off Dunkirk beaches with her pumps choked, bilge full of rubbish and making water fast, and drifting on to the beach she was abandoned. She fulfilled some useful purpose, however, by being used as a pier.

It is impossible to give the story of every ship, although each ship has its story. Here, for instance, is the unvarnished history of the M/B *Marsayru* which went over on the 31st May in company with the lighters *X.217* (S/Lt. R. A. W. Pool, R.N.) *X.213* and *X.149*. They arrived off Malo beach at about 1600. During an air attack X. *213* and X. *149* were sunk. The Z. *217* was beached and, assisted by the dinghy, embarked 95 troops which were transferred to the yacht *Llanthony*. The *X.217* continued to embark troops using the *Marsayru* and a cutter. At about 2100 that evening, with the *Marsayru's* skipper and crew and about 200 British and French troops on board, the *X.217* left for home towing the *Marsayru* and a cutter.

Shortly after sailing the *Marsayru* broke adrift, and in darkness could not be found. Next day, the 1st June, however, at 1400, S/Lt. T. E. Godman, R.N.V.R. in a Naval steam pinnace, off La Panne, sighted the *Marsayru* drifting with the tide and unoccupied. She was found to be in working order; the engine was started up and Sub-Lieut. Godman took an A.B. and a soldier as crew. He left Petty Officer Morrison in charge of the steam pinnace with orders to lay off and wait for the return of the *Marsayru*.

With the dinghy in tow the *Marsayru* proceeded to the western end of the beach and anchored; the dinghy ferried 19 troops to her, which filled her to capacity.

In the meantime the crew of the steam pinnace had embarked in the skoot *Doggershank* and had left the steam pinnace anchored near Dunkirk harbour. Sub-Lieut. Godman decided to leave her there and sailed in the *Marsayru* for England; he overtook the *Doggershank* on the way and obtained some fuel from her.

At 2330 on the 1st June the *Marsayru* made fast to a conical flashing buoy and waited for daylight. At 0430 on the 2nd June a trawler took the *Marsayru* in tow to Ramsgate, which was reached at 0800, and the 19 troops were disembarked. Later on 2nd June, on instructions from the N.O.I.C., the original crew took charge of the *Marsayru*, but she did not, apparently, make a second trip to Dunkirk.[22] Her skipper (G. D. Olivier) received the D.S.M. for his services, and her engineer (C. Coggins) a mention in despatches.

The Cockle Bawley Boats

Of the small craft that went over on this day, Admiral Ramsay speaks in the following terms of the Cockle Bawley boats:[23]

"The conduct of the crews of these cockle boats was exemplary. They were all volunteers who were rushed over to Dunkirk in one day, probably none of them had been under gunfire before and certainly none of them under Naval discipline. These boats were Thames estuary fishing boats which never left the estuary, and only one of their crews had been further afield than Ramsgate before. In spite of this fact perfect formation was maintained throughout the day and night under the control of a Sub-Lieutenant R.N.V.R.[3] in command of the Unit, and all orders were carried out with great diligence even under actual shell fire and aircraft attack".

One of these cockle boats, the *Renown*, was blown up by a mine while returning to England disabled and in tow of the drifter *Ben* and *Lucy*. Her skipper, W. H. Noakes, and his crew[24] were killed. The *Ben* and *Lucy* had been towing the drifter *Feasible* (disabled by a shell hit), 3 life-boats and the cockle boat *Letitia*. At 0115 on the 1st June the *Renown*, by then disabled, attached herself to this tow, but an hour later she was blown to pieces and a hail of wood and splinters came down on the *Letitia*'s deck. The *Letitia*'s skipper (A. J. Dench) says, "In the pitch dark we could see nothing, and after the explosion we hard nothing and we could do nothing, except pull in the tow rope, which was just as we passed it

---

22 The *Marsayru*'s skipper says that throughout 31st May, "and the days and nights that followed (its all a complete jumble in my mind) we were ... under constant fire ... but the ship was not hit by anything." It seems, however, that Mr. Olivier was only in the evacuation for 5 hours, i.e. from 1600 to 2100, 31st May.

23 *Defender, Endeavour, Letitia, Reliance, Renown* and *Resolute*.

24 L. V. Osborne, Mate, and F. W. Osborne, Engineer.

to the *Renown* about ¾ hour before.

French and Belgian Ships Arrive

Early on the 31st it became known that the Belgian Government were anxious that several small Belgian fishing craft lying at Brixham should take part in the evacuation and steps were taken to arrange this.

At 1335 the French destroyer *Leopard* routed from the Downs to Dunkirk two French trawlers,[25] three French motor fishing vessels,[26] and ten Belgian trawlers.[27]

The Belgian trawlers were under the orders of Pilote Malet; the remainder of the ships under Lieutenant de vaisseau Drogou.

Other Allied ships that sailed for Dunkirk on this day were the French cargo ships *Ingenieur Cachin* and *Margaux*, the trawlers *Pierre et Marie*, *Emma* and *Duperre*, and the patrol vessel *Diligente*; the Belgian trawlers *Lydie Suzanne* and *Yvonne*, and the drifters *Gerard-Leon* (H.64), *Anne Marie* and *Therese Compas*. On her return journey the *Pierre et Marie* picked up 3 English sailors from a drifting motor boat. The French trawlers *Marie* and *Pierre* carrying munitions, and the Ste. *Isabelle* carrying food, also went to Dunkirk. While unloading under shell fire the *Pierre*'s munitions were hit and exploded and the ship caught fire. She was still on fire when her consorts left Dunkirk at 1100.

Captain Howson Returns to Dover

Meanwhile the enemy made the last of his three major air attacks of the day; the other two having been made at 1415-1500 and 1700-1715.[28] Off Bray at about 1930 some 30 bombers escorted by fighters appeared overhead. Most went on to bomb Dunkirk, others bombed the *Mosquito*, destroyers, sloops and small craft.[29]

The yacht *Ankh*, which Captain Howson was using as his headquarters, received some damage from a near miss and started making water forward and also through the stern glands. Being of opinion that the *Ankh* would be unlikely to stand up to further "rough treatment", Captain Howson decided to return

---

25 *Chasse-Maree* and *Angele Marie*.

26 *Margaux* (D.692), *Jeune France* (Di.1213) and *Du Guesclin* (D.G.910).

27 *Independence* (0.308), *Victor-Erna* (H.63), *Louise-Irene* (H.80), *Pharailde* (H.42) *Raphael-Raymonde* (H.43), O.L.V. *Van Vlaanderen* (N.49), *John* (0.210) *Anna Marguerite* (Z.2), *Buffalo Bill* (Z.4) and the *MAI*.

28 R.A.F. Narrative, p.336.

29 Captain Howson's Report (R.O.IV, p. 119).

to Dover, ordering the yacht *Amulree* to keep company. Being then some 2 to 3 miles to seaward, in the failing light Captain Howson was unable to signal to Rear-Admiral Wake-Walker in the *Keith*. The yachts *Eilla II* and *Caryandra* closed the *Ankh*; the former reported that she was short of fuel and the latter that she was damaged and short of lubricating oil, so they returned in company with the *Ankh* to Dover.

It was at about this time, 2000, that the yacht *Glagla* (which was standing by to tow the boats of the *Vivacious* from the beach) found that her tiller wire was reduced to a single strand. Her Commanding Officer said, "The bombing and shelling which had been going on continuously, became intense. A Captain R.N. in yacht No. 1 of the Solent Patrol [i.e. Captain Howson in the *Ankh*], ordered us to make for the open sea, and all the smaller craft followed him out."

It was in the above circumstances that a number of power boats started a withdrawal to Dover, and that at 0611 on the 1st June Rear-Admiral Wake-Walker found it necessary to report to V.A. Dover that all craft used for towing boats had left during the night, and to urge that they be sent back.[30]

At about 0145 on the 1st June the yacht *Amulree*, which was escorting the *Ankh*, was rammed and sunk by the *Vimy* in the vicinity of the *Gull*. Her crew were picked up. The Commodore-in-Charge, Sheerness, Captain H. R. Marrack, R.N., D.S.C., in a report to V.A., Dover, says that it was "a matter for regret that this vessel [the *Amulree*] was diverted from the very valuable work which she was performing in towing out pontoons from the beaches, to carry out a seemingly minor administrative duty which indirectly resulted in her being rammed and sunk by a British destroyer in the Downs".[31]

The *Ankh* arrived at Dover at 0815 on the 1st June.

Casualties to Towing craft

Of the motor boats lost this day, 2 were lost by enemy action. The M/B *Commodore* ferried troops to the *Worcester* off Malo. She was eventually machine gunned, holed and abandoned. Her crew embarked in the M/B *Eastbourne Queen*. The M/B *New Prince of Wales* was damaged by a shell from a shore battery. Two able-seamen were killed, and S/Lt. P. H. E. Bennett, R.N. and 2 of the crew were wounded. The vessel was abandoned and the crew embarked in the M/B *Triton*.

---

30 Appendix H.26.

31 R.O.III, p.551.

At least fourteen other motor boats[32] were lost by misadventure, e.g. engine failure, grounding, swamping, damaging rudders and/or propellers on floating or submerged wreckage, or breaking adrift and being lost when on tow. The seaplane tender *No. 291* managed to get back to England in spite of the damage she had sustained, but was unable to take any further part in "Dynamo".

Conflicting News of La Panne

Meanwhile, as the tows of boats (which Rear-Admiral Wake-Walker now saw for the first time at 1900 on the 31st May), arrived off Dunkirk they were directed to the beaches by Lt. Cdr. Wynne-Edwards, first from *M.T.B.68* and later at about 2100, from *M.A /S.B.6*. It was found, however, that in the growing darkness, and with no lights to help them, there was a tendency for the boats to stop at the first place they came to where other craft were assembled. At about 1930 the *Codrington*, then off Bray, was warned by Rear-Admiral Wake-Walker to send on the boats detailed for La Panne, but the bulk of them did not get further than Bray.

The night was dark, and Rear-Admiral Wake-Walker stayed off La Panne, "wondering how things were going. Everything was black, ships and boats and shore showed no lights", although arrangements had been made for a light to be shown to seaward to guide boats inshore. Shelling was continuous and seemed to be falling among the ships at the anchorage. News was conflicting; a message from the shore said that thousands of men were waiting but there were no boats, while messages came from ships that their boats could find no one on the beach ... the ships and the boats were there, and the troops ashore, and one could do no more. ... I do not know to this day", says Rear-Admiral Wake-Walker, "what really took place there".[33]

La Panne Beach 31st May–1st June

It is not easy to discover what happened at La Panne, but the following account, based on a report by Lt. Cdr. J. W. McClelland, R.N., who with a party of signalmen reached La Panne in the minesweeper *Gossamer* at 1930 on the 30th May, gives the main course of events. He was S.N.O., La Panne, for the seven hours prior to its abandonment as a place of embarkation at about 0200 on the 1st June.

---

32 A.L.C. 8, A.L.C.15, *Enterprise, Excellent's* 35 ft. M/B, *Excellent's* A/A M/B, *Golden Spray II, Princess Lily, St. Patrick,* and the Seaplane tender 243 and A.M.C.3; the *Sea Falcon, Sunshine, Triton* and the *Two Rivers.*

33 M.017978/41, p.21.

About 1600 on May 31st Captain Tennant, who had been visiting Lord Gort at La Panne, decided to return to Dunkirk, but he first instructed Lt. Cdr. McClelland to arrange for the evacuation of Lord Gort and his staff, to carry out the duties of S.N.O., La Panne,[34] and to join Major General B. L. Montgomery, then in command of 2nd Corps.

At that time, says Lt. Cdr. McClelland, an enemy battery near Nieuport, assisted by 2 kite balloons, had found the range of the beach and the off lying-ships, which had accordingly withdrawn to the westward. Rear-Admiral Wake-Walker asked for the balloons to be shot down, and aircraft came over for that purpose; at times the balloons were hauled down – but they always re-appeared.[35]

Work was commenced on a second lorry pier at La Panne by Lieut. Great-wood R.N.[36] and the 12th Lancers who had been marshalling the beaches for the past 24 hours.[37] Parties were organised to collect all the oars and boats that could be found, the intention at the time – about 1600 – being to recommence the embarkation of troops from La Panne at 2030 with two ships, when it was hoped the fire of the Nieuport battery would be less effective.[3]

At about 1630, arrangements were made from La Panne direct with V.A. Dover for the embarkation of Lord Gort at about 1800 from a point 2 miles westward of La Panne, which Lt. Cdr. McClelland considered would be out of range of the Nieuport battery. In the event, however, Lord Gort embarked in the *Hebe*'s whaler nearer to La Panne.

At 2030 two ships arrived off La Panne,[38] and the beaching craft there which were already filled put off. No additional boats arrived, however, and the rate of embarkation was no more than 300 an hour; indeed, as darkness set in, the rate fell to about 150 an hour. With about 7,000 men awaiting embarkation before 0400 the next morning (when the beach would be exposed to gunfire, and might even be in the hands of the enemy) a rate of at least 1,000 an hour was necessary. Urgent representations were made to V.A., Dover, and to ships in the vicinity for more boats, but none came, although at 2130 V.A., Dover, informed Rear-

---

34 Lt. Cdr. McClelland speaks of the final evacuation of A, B and C beaches La Panne, but this is evidently an error as the beaches were lettered from West to East (See Plan 3) and must therefore have been M, N and O Beaches.

35 M.017978/41, p.16.

36 Lt. Cdr. McClelland's report. The name "Greatwood" is not in the May 1940 Navy List.

37 S/Lt. E. C. Croswell R.N. (C.W.23187/40).

38 [26] Probably the *Worcester* and *Hebe*.

Admiral Wake-Walker that La Panne had reported 6,000 troops to clear urgently and that they lacked ships and boats.[39] It was probably, however, in response to this signal that at 2223 the *Keith* asked V.A., Dover, to tell S.N.O., Dunkirk, that troops must be moved down to Bray, as tows of boats got intercepted at Bray in the dark, with a resulting shortage of boats at La Panne.

During darkness hostile low-flying aircraft were patrolling continually overhead and bombing promptly all lights shown, which no doubt explains why Rear-Admiral Wake-Walker in the *Keith* did not see the pre-arranged shore lights.

By 2200 the situation at La Panne had become serious; only about 600 troops had been embarked and the few boats available, which had to be handled and pulled in the darkness by troops inexperienced in this work, had dwindled to three. At this time, as the telephone to Dover was still working, Lt. Cdr. McClelland destroyed the W/T set.

At about 2300 the situation was becoming critical, as troops for whom there were no boats were piling up on the beach, and the military withdrawal which would leave La Panne in no-man's-land by 0400 the following morning was in full swing. To make matters worse the Nieuport battery opened a slow fire on the crowded beach, causing casualties with almost every shell.

Lt. Cdr. McClelland discussed the situation with the G.O.C., Major-General D. G. Johnson, V.C., D.S.O., M.C., Commanding the 4th Division, who in turn conferred with the Duty Captain at Dover, and it was finally decided to march the 6,000 men remaining at La Panne to Dunkirk, via Bray-Dunes, the decision being reached after Lt. Cdr. McClelland had made a personal reconnaissance right along the beaches, without finding any more ships or boats, and after he had informed the G.O.C. in reply to a direct question that he thought they would not arrive.[5]

Thereupon, at about 0050 on the 1st June Lt. Cdr. McClelland informed Dover that he was closing down the telephone line as the headquarters were now being abandoned.

While this decision was being arrived at further batteries had come into action on the town of La Panne, and by 0100 the rate of fire on the beach was increased. Lt. Cdr. McClelland says that he had by that time lost touch with Major-General Montgomery, who had left earlier and subsequently embarked in the *Codrington* at Dunkirk at 0525 on the 1st June.

---

39 [27] Appendix H.16.

By 0130 it was low water, and about half a mile walk to the end of the piers which were now highland dry. While walking there with the intention of assisting in the embarkation of the few men who had not been ordered to march to Dunkirk, Lt. Cdr. McClelland was twice knocked down by shell bursts; a splinter smashed the box signalling lantern he was carrying, and another slightly injured his ankle. Several houses on the front were now blazing fiercely.

On reaching the embarkation point Lt. Cdr. McClelland was told that no boats had been in for over half an hour, and that the naval beach party had left – apparently in accordance with his orders that they were to leave in the last boat.[40] As will be seen later, the beach parties at Bray also embarked early on the 31st May.

There being neither ships nor boats now at the beaches, Lt. Cdr. McClelland ordered a general retirement westward of all the groups on the beaches with the object of getting them inside the defended perimeter outside Bray-Dunes before 0400.

At 0200, two or three miles down the beach towards Bray, three ships[41] at anchor and some troops had been trying unsuccessfully to attract their attention by firing their rifles. Further on, as other large groups were waiting for boats, Lt. Cdr. McClelland decided to swim off and report on the situation. He managed to get close enough to the *Gossamer*, which was anchored 4 cables from the shore, to pick up a lifebelt on a line brought to him by one of the ship's company.

He was just able to gasp out his message to the Captain of the *Gossamer* before collapsing, but he had told of the 4th Division's change of plan and of the state of the beaches and had asked that Rear-Admiral Wake-Walker and Vice-Admiral Dover be informed. The former was evidently informed at 0215,[42] and at 0235, the *Gossamer* signalled V.A. Dover that 6,000 British were marching from La Panne through Bray on Dunkirk.[43]

Being very exhausted and no longer able to walk because of the pain from the wound in his ankle, Lt. Cdr. McClelland remained in the *Gossamer*.[44]

Sub.-Lieut. E. C. Croswell's report on La Panne confirms that of Lt. Cdr. McClelland. He says: "On Friday [31st May] embarkation at La Panne was

---

40 Lt. Cdr. McClelland's report (R.O.III, p.392).

41 The *Codrington, Ivanhoe* and *Gossamer*.

42 M.017978/41, p.21.

43 Appendix H.20.

44 [32] Lt. Cdr. McClelland received a mention in despatches.

slowed up as shelling caused some ships to move westward to Bray-Dunes. The rest camp in the rear of La Panne beach and a small arms ammunition hut were hit during bombing attacks which continued throughout Friday, and ships also suffered shell fire. ... On Friday evening German gunners found the range of the beach and were aided by 2 observation balloons which we did not manage to destroy. At 0200 Saturday [1st June] La Panne was abandoned as a place of embarkation".[45]

The following extract from War Diary General Staff 4 Division, dated the 1st June 1940,[46] confirms the above accounts:

"[At La Panne] by 0100 hrs. not more than three to four hundred men of the Division out of eight thousand to be embarked had been put on transports. A conference was called at Divisional H.Q. which had now opened in a house by the side of the beach where it was decided that it was useless to continue the embarkation from La Panne. Motor Contact officers were sent out to inform Brigades that they were to proceed direct to Bray Dunes and Dunkerque Mole. Whilst this conference was going on the beach was heavily shelled by 5.9's and a few casualties were sustained. A Staff Officer was sent to warn the French Guards at the Frontier that 4 Division would be passing through them. Another Staff Officer was sent to order the men on the beach to make their way along the beach either to Bray or Dunkerque. From this moment H.Q. ceased to operate until it arrived at Dunkerque Mole. Certain officers arrived at Dunkerque Mole as follows GSO II, GSO III, and Camp Commandant at 0500 hrs. 1 June. GOC, GSO I, AA and QMG, I.O., ADC, Motor Contact Officer at about 0700 hrs."

Captain R. Pim, R.N.V.R., Beach Master

In view of the foregoing outline of events at La Panne, it is necessary, in order to avoid confusion, to refer briefly to a report by Captain Pim who was sent over from the Admiralty to assist in speeding up the embarkation.

After visiting as many of the beaches as possible he assumed the duties of Beach Master (at Bray beach) and arranged to continue the organisation of ferrying boats until "all the troops on the beaches" were on board. "I told

---

45 C.W.23187/40.

46 Provided by Lt. Col. H. F. Joslen, (Historical Section, War Cabinet).

them", he said, "that if anything went wrong during the night we would return at dawn".[47]

Later, Captain Pim stated: "All the troops that I could find were embarked by midnight and placed in ships which sailed for England. Just before midnight I went along certain beaches to look for stragglers. A Staff Officer informed me that no more troops would embark from these beaches[48] but that they would march to Dunkirk, as it was anticipated these beaches would be shelled and would probably be in German hands the following day".[49] Captain Pim estimated that from pontoon bridges and beaches, approximately 5,000 troops were probably embarked.

Although his report is entitled "Final evacuation of troops from the beaches of La Panne and Bray", Captain Pim does not say that these 5,000 troops were embarked from La Panne, and it is evident from Rear-Admiral Wake-Walker's report, and particularly from Lt. Cdr. McClelland's report, and the War Diary of the 4th Division, that they were not embarked from La Panne. Vice-Admiral Dover,[6] however, assumes from Captain Pim's report that he worked at La Panne, the weight of evidence shows that he worked at Bray and immediately to the east and west of it.

During the night, Captain Pim found it necessary to shift his anchorage to the west, as shells meant for the beaches were ricocheting over the *Hilda*. Then, at 0315 on the 1st June, in accordance with his undertaking to the troops, Captain Pim "sent off all [his] boats ... to search the beaches, starting from the western end of Bray-Dunes". During the next 3 hours, he says, only about 250 men were taken from the beach, apparently stragglers. A large rearguard party (probably troops of the 4th Division) marching along the beach decided to continue to Dunkirk.[50]

Bray Beach Parties Return to England

It was on this day that the majority of the beach parties returned to England. Captain Howson records that on the evening of the 30th May he had "learnt that the enemy were closing in and that it might be expected that the final evacuation would take place during the following day (31st May) or night at latest". As

---

47 Capt. Pim's report (R.O. IV, p.52).

48 Evidently the La Panne beaches.

49 D.R., p.20, para.61.

50 Capt. Pim's report (R.O. IV, p.52), Italics not in original.

he had received orders that beach parties were not to be taken prisoner,[51] and anticipated that very many troops would be left ashore, he deemed it undesirable for all naval personnel to embark "in the final rush". Accordingly he arranged that half the naval personnel should embark during the early hours of Friday (31st May).[52]

This arrangement to some extent accounts for V.A. Dover's 1229/31 to Rear-Admiral Wake-Walker saying that officers and men of beach parties had returned to Dover on instructions from Dunkirk, and that they must be retained to the last;[53] and his further signals notifying that more beach parties were being sent out with all despatch in the destroyer *Worcester*.[54]

An account of the activities of the beach parties at Bray has been given by Lieutenants G. W. Vavasour and J. G. Wells, R.N. They were among the 12 officers and 60 ratings, who sailed from Dover in the Esk with Rear-Admiral Wake-Walker and Commodores Stephenson and Hallett on the 29th May (Page 49).

On the way over the 12 officers were divided into 3 groups of 4 officers, and to each of the 12 officers was allocated a party of 1 P.O., 1 Leading Seaman, 2 Able Seamen and a Signalman. Rear-Admiral Wake-Walker told the officers that on no account were their parties to be captured, and that with this in mind, they were to re-embark when they thought fit.

On arrival off the various beaches at about 2330 on May 29th the *Esk* stopped off each and the 3 beach parties were landed in whalers; one party went to La Panne where Cdre. Stephenson was to be S.N.O., Afloat, off the beach,[55] one went west of Bray, and the third went to Bray where Commodore Hallett was to be S.N.O., Afloat, off the beach. There is no report available of the activities of the first two parties.

---

51 Rear-Admiral Wake-Walker says that the V.A. Dover had stressed that Naval ratings (in beach parties) were not to risk being taken prisoner (M.017978/41, p.3).

52 Capt. Howson's Report (R.O. IV, p. 117).

53 Appendix Q.12.

54 Appendices Q.13 and Q.14.

55 Lt. Vavasour's report, R.O.III, p.422. Lt. Vavasour says that Cdre Stephenson was S.N.O., A.B.C.D. Sections. But the beaches had been lettered A to O, from west to east and so the La Panne beach was L.M.N.O. It was probably because of the almost invariable confusion about the lettering of the beaches that this method of designating beaches was changed by signal at 1906/29 (Appendix O.ll), and the whole length was divided into 3 equal parts, referred to as Malo, Bray and La Panne, from west to east with a mile gap between each part.

The 4 officers in Cdre. Hallett's section were Lieuts. Vavasour, Wells, Tibbits and Cameron, R.N., all of H.M.S. *Excellent*. Cdre. Hallett had previously explained to these officers that he himself would be afloat approximately in front of his sections (E, F, G and H) of the beach, and repeated the warning that the officers were to be the sole judges of when to evacuate the naval parties. Moreover, if one party had to leave, it was to communicate along the whole beach so that all would have the warning.[56]

On landing, the 4 section Lieutenants of the Bray party decided that all 4 sections, being small, should remain close together, and they took up a position covering a frontage, in all, of about 400 yards; they at once proceeded to organize 3 embarkation points. There were at first no signs of any soldiers but, within 2 minutes of landing, about 5,000 troops left their cover in the sand dunes and approached the boats. The troops were on the whole easy to control and implicitly obeyed orders about boats given by the naval officers and ratings, except the orders to bring back the boats from ships to shore.

Evacuation in Commodore Hallett's section was very slow and Lieut. Vavasour says that by 0500 on the 30th May it is doubtful if 80 men were got off. A few boats appeared, were loaded and sent off; but when the troops reached a ship, they let the boats go adrift, as there were no boat-keepers.

At dawn Lieut. Vavasour contacted a headquarters[57] in one of the houses along the front at Bray. There he saw a Captain R.N. and 2 Commanders.[58] No suggestions or orders were issued from headquarters, says Lieut. Vavasour. One of the commanders, "who had come from Dunkirk", told him that the port was out of action, and the moles were in ruins.

Shortly after 0500 on the 30th May there was a destroyer and a minesweeper off Bray beach, but the boat situation had become acute and there were now about 15,000 troops on the beach. With the assistance of some senior Army Officers who by then had arrived, the troops were moved away from the water's edge and settled in the sands.

By 0600, a considerable number of collapsible boats had been collected from the Royal Engineers and these were loaded with 10 soldiers apiece and sent off. In the majority of cases, however, on arrival at the ships the boats were

---

56 Report by Lt. Vavasour (R.O.III, p.423).

57 Probably the Corps Headquarters referred to by Capt. Howson (Section 158).

58 Captain Howson R.N. and probably Cdrs. Otway-Ruthven and Gorton, or Richardson.

abandoned and, drifting to the east, came ashore abreast the French, who used them to go off to British ships. By 0700, there were no power boats at all, and whaler trips were very infrequent. The rate of evacuation continued to be very slow.

Meanwhile the "Captain R.N." (Captain Howson) had gone to La Panne and Lieut. Vavasour did not see him again.

By 0730 more ships had arrived and evacuation proceeded more quickly, as the beach parties had organised their own boat keepers. It was still, however, far from satisfactory. The troops found it difficult to get into the boats in the surf, and the beach parties had to wade out shoulder-deep to keep the boats stern-on to the beach.

Lieut. Vavasour and his party then boarded the *Anthony* to get a change of clothing, and while there obtained a motor boat which they manned for 12 hours until she broke down. They first proceeded to recover the majority of their lost boats, now in use by the French, and then organised a ferry service.

At 0900 contact was made with Commodore Hallett who was then in a drifter "I informed him of what I was doing" says Lieut. Vavasour. "He approved. He informed me that he was very short of coal. At approximately 0930 the Commodore steamed away to seaward. I did not see the Commodore again".

Lieut. Wells said: "We never saw him [the Commodore] at all as I believe his boat broke down, and he had to be towed clear of the danger area." As to the method of embarking the troops, Lieut. Wells found that the best way to organise them into a long queue at each of the 3 embarkation points. The queues were 3 deep and were spaced out in groups of 10, this number being most suitable for the type of boat available. The following group could be used for shoving off a loaded boat, which took a good deal of moving at half tide owing to a bar running parallel to the sea. The Army pontoon boats proved most suitable, because of their draught, double-ended construction and general handiness.

The main difficulty, according to Lieut. Wells, lay in the insufficiency of naval boat keepers. As a rule the soldiers detailed to return the boats did not carry out orders and the beach parties had to swim or wade out for drifting boats, which continually delayed and slowed up the operation. Lieut. Wells considered that the troops could hardly be blamed as it was clearly a naval responsibility. More ratings were asked for from outlying ships, but none could be sent.

At 0930 on May 30th there was only one other motor boat working within 4 miles either side of Lieut. Vavasour's beach, i.e. G section. It was a destroyer's motor boat which, being aground when the destroyer sailed, had been left behind.

By about noon, all ships within sight from G beach had departed fully loaded. About an hour later a destroyer [the *Windsor*] anchored east of Bray, and as many boats as possible were towed out to her. Lieut. M. A. Hemans R.N., says Lieut. Vavasour closed the destroyer. On board her were two officers, Lieuts. Stubbs and Fletcher from the beach party which had gone to La Panne (under Cdre. Stephenson) who said they had been told to leave by their Commodore. Rear-Admiral Wake-Walker was on board the destroyer and he told Lieuts. Hemans and Vavasour to carry on with the boats.

At about 1300 some 10 trawlers, drifters and minesweepers began to arrive, and evacuation proceeded apace until 2000, in spite of there being only 3 motor boats for towing and ferrying. By 2000 all ships had left except the Special Service vessel *Royal Eagle*. By 2100, however, just after dark, many destroyers and minesweepers commenced to arrive.

Lieut. Vavasour went on board the *Royal Eagle* at about 2000 in response to a signal. While his motor boat was away collecting boat loads of troops for the *Royal Eagle* the former broke down and was picked up by a destroyer which was on the way to La Panne. That was the last Lieut. Vavasour saw of his party. He later got on board a minesweeper at 0100/31 and sailed for Harwich. Subsequently, on arrival at H.M.S. *Excellent* he found the remainder of Cdre. Hallett's lieutenants were back. They had been told, he says, to abandon the evacuation about midnight "by the S.N.O. of the beach – a Commander".

"I felt most limited in my activities," says Lieut. Vavasour, "by the very definite orders that I had received that on no account was the naval party to be left behind. No accurate information was available. ... I was unable to obtain any information at all from any single one of the large number of ships to which I towed boats during the day and night". This is not surprising because in the circumstances, with the situation continually and rapidly changing, no one either ashore or afloat had any accurate information. Thus, for instance, the *Gossamer* which anchored one mile west of La Panne at 2207, had sent in the motor boat *Handy Billie* in charge of S/Lt. M. Phipps R.N. to search for troops. He found none, and received no answer to his hails. "Inside an hour, however, the situation had changed, and thousands were massing abreast the ship".[59]

Lieut. Wells says that at 0100/31 he was informed that naval personnel

---

59 Report by *Gossamer* (R.O.I, p.264).

would have to evacuate at dawn if the shelling continued. Some officers not in his original party had already left, and at 0300/31 he swam out to fetch a boat for the "Brigadier" [Major General W. G. Holmes] in command of the 42nd Division, who was embarked at about 0330.

The shelling of the beach continued, and (says Lieut. Wells) "the order was passed from Headquarters that as the embarkation would probably be over at dawn the following day [1st June], all naval personnel were to embark forthwith". Lieut. Wells accordingly remained in the *Halcyon*, where he had taken the "Brigadier". The *Halcyon* arrived at Dover at 0845/31.

There is clearly some connection between the above "order from Headquarters" and Captain Howson's arrangement for embarking naval personnel during the early hours of the 31st May.

The only other account of the activities of the beach parties comes from Cdr. H. du P. Richardson, R.N., who worked with Lt. Cdr. D. B. Dowling, R.N., and a naval platoon at Malo beach from 2000 on May the 27th until the beach was cleared of troops at about noon on the 28th May.[60]

S.N.O. Dunkirk then ordered him to Bray beach to embark 5,000 troops, and he arrived there at about 1700 on the 28th May, with Cdr. Ken[61] [? Kerr] and 16 men. They found about 30,000 troops, stretching from Bray to the eastward, awaiting embarkation. Cdr. Richardson's beach party, as will be seen, also returned on the 31st May.

At 0130 on the 29th May a high wind got up which made beach embarkation almost impossible. Cdr. Richardson therefore sent off about 20,000 troops to Dunkirk in batches of 1000.

During the night of 29th/30th May another naval embarkation party arrived on the beach to the eastward,[62] and this reduced the limits of Cdr. Richardson's beach.

Early on the morning of the 30th May Cdr. Richardson went to Brigade HQ.[63] at Bray and suggested that piers be built by running lorries into the sea. This, he says, was quickly done and proved successful.

Between 1800 and 2000 on the 30th May the enemy directed accurate

---

60 Cdr. Richardson's report (R.O.III, p.367).

61 There is no officer of this name in the May 1940 Navy List.

62 Evidently the party landed at E.F.G.H., Cdre. Hallett's sections of the beach.

63 These were probably the same H.Q. as those referred to by Capt. Howson as "Corps headquarters" (p. 59).

artillery fire on to the beach, and continued firing throughout the night. Cdr. Richardson's beach was completely evacuated by allied soldiers. "No boats", he says, "had now been in for 16 hours on our beach".

During the night of the 30th/31st May, the weather became bad once more, and a heavy surf was running. By about 0300 on the 31st May it was impossible to carry out embarkation from the beaches.

Cdr. Richardson's men were by now showing signs of extreme exhaustion, and as it was impossible to communicate with the S.N.O. he decided to take over a whaler they had saved and go to the nearest destroyer to report to the S.N.O.

They waited for high water, and at about 0730 put to sea. There was a very heavy surf running, and they had an uneven set of oars, rope crutches and only an oar to steer by. They approached 2 destroyers, but both got underway. Two other destroyers passed at about 7 cables, but paid no attention.

After about an hour the Margate life-boat, the *Lord Southborough*, appeared. All destroyers were now under way, and as the life-boat was returning to Margate the party went back in her.[64] She reached Margate at 1450 on May 31st.

Thus, by about 0830 on the 31st May all the beach parties of which there are any records had returned or were on their way to England.

Devonia is Beached

At 1035 Rear-Admiral Wake-Walker had informed V.A. Dover that he would beach a ship in the hope of improving conditions for boat work, which was then being made difficult by a lop and he instructed Cdre. Stephenson accordingly. Cdre. Stephenson, then in the yacht *Bounty* off La Panne, boarded the minesweeper *Devonia* at 1600 and gave orders to beach the ship. The *Devonia*, already much damaged by near misses at 1230, was beached at full speed off La Panne, and at 1930, on account of the shelling and bombing, she was abandoned. Fortunately by 1700 the weather off the beaches had much improved.

Casualties to H.M. Ships

With the exception of the *Devonia* none of H.M. ships was lost on this day, but the following were slightly damaged: the *Vivacious* was damaged by a shell hit and had 3 dead and 12 wounded; the *Hebe* received slight damage from a near miss; the *Wolsey* was in collision with the P/V *Roebuck*; the *Impulsive* damaged

---

64 Cdr. Richardson's report (R.O.III, p.370).

a propeller on uncharted wreckage; the *Malcolm* was in collision with Dunkirk pier; and the *Scimitar* was in collision with the *Icarus* and later with a drifter.[65]

Air Patrols

During the 31st May Fighter Command carried out patrols, as on the 30th May, at an average strength of three to four squadrons. Eight patrols in all were flown, involving 289 sorties. The periods in the day when the Dunkirk area was not covered were 0620-0800, 0830-1110, 1510-1615, and 1745-1915.[66]

Coastal Command patrolled the line North Goodwins – Gravelines – Ostend throughout the day, patrols being of one section strength, involving in all 37 sorties.[67]

Shortly before 0930 the Air Ministry intercepted a message indicating that the enemy air force had been ordered not to attack the town or harbour of Dunkirk but to concentrate attacks on shipping at sea, or leaving the coast.[3]

It was at about 1230 that, off La Panne, the *Devonia* received extensive damage to her hull from 4 near misses, but the first major attack on our ships occurred about 1415-1430 when one of our squadrons estimated the enemy strength as about 100 aircraft (bombers and fighters). Rear-Admiral Wake-Walker says, "a terrific air battle took place overhead and it seemed to go against us."[68] Actually, we lost 9 aircraft and claimed 7 enemy shot down.[69]

Air attacks then followed at half-hourly intervals between 1530 and 1730, and at about 1717 the *Ivanhoe*, *Whitehall* and *Express* off Dunkirk harbour were attacked by about 50 bombers. The *Whitehall* received some damage and the *Express* slight damage from near misses. At this time also the *Hebe* was attacked off La Panne by 4 bombers and was damaged by near misses; she shot down one Heinkel in flames. Between 1630 and 1745 our air patrols encountered many enemy aircraft in mixed formations, the largest being a group of about thirty. In this series of combats we lost 5 aircraft for 12 enemy definitely destroyed.[70] It was during this latter period that a squadron detailed to shoot down the enemy

---

65 Probably either the *Gervais Rentoul* or the *Eileen Emma* which both returned damaged as the result of collisions.

66 R.A.F. Narrative, p.334.

67 R.A.F. Narrative, p.336.

68 M.017978/41, p.17.

69 R.A.F. Narrative, p.335.

70 R.A.F. Narrative, p.335.

observation balloon failed to find it. It was, said Rear-Admiral Wake-Walker, "at times hauled down but always re-appeared."

At 1800, when Lord Gort was due to embark, there were further air attacks which continued until 1930.

At 1920, off Dunkirk, the *Whitehall*'s after group shot down a bomber. Between 1920 and 1930 our patrols were engaged with a formation of about 70 H.E.Ill's and M.E.109's. In the encounter, Fighter Command lost 3 aircraft and claimed 10 bombers and 6 fighters definitely destroyed. Some of the Hurricane pilots complained on their return that they had been shot at by the Spitfires.[1]

At 2010 six Hurricanes trying to locate the observation balloon at Nieuport engaged about thirty M.E.109's, but no bombers were intercepted.[1]

Final Evacution of B.E.F. Expected on Night 1st–2nd June

Meanwhile, at 1920, all ships in the Nore and Dover Commands were informed by the V.A., Dover, that the final evacuation of the B.E.F. was expected on the night 1st/2nd June, and that the evacuation of the French from Dunkirk and Malo beach would continue from the 1st June by both British and French ships.[71] At 2309 General Lloyd informed the D.M.O. of the new plan and stated that General Alexander had been placed in command of the final phase of the evacuation, that the composition of his force was not known, and that it was impossible now to state how long the French evacuation would take but that the Alexander force would remain till the last.[72]

Meanwhile, no firm information could be obtained from the French on the following matters:[73]

(1) the number of French troops to be evacuated;

(2) the nature and extent of French seaborne transport;

(3) the French military plan for the defence of the perimeter and the final withdrawal of French troops.

Embarkation Reaches its Zenith

The main features of the day had been:

(a) the increased enemy artillery activity on Dunkirk, La Panne beach and the approach channels;

---

71 Appendix Q.19.

72 Appendix Q.22.

73 D.R. p.21, para. 63.

(b) the change in the military plan as regards the locality and time of lifting the final contingents of the B.E.F.;

(c) the set-back to beach evacuation that occurred during the choppy weather of the forenoon, followed by an excellent recovery in the afternoon and evening, when large numbers were lifted from the western beaches.

The rate of embarkation had, however, come up to expectations. A total of 22,942 were lifted from the beaches and 45,072 from the harbour. The grand total of 68,014 proved to be the highest daily total of the whole operation.

Saturday 1st June – Germans Renew their Heavy Air Effort

E-Boat Activity: Sinking of the *Stella Dorado* and *Argyllshire*

During the night of 31st May – 1st June there was a recrudescence of enemy E-boat activity. After the torpedoing of the destroyers *Grafton* and *Wakeful* off Nieuport in the early hours of the 29th May M.T.B. patrols had been established during the dark hours to prevent enemy E-boats from using the inshore channels. It was, however, in the less confined waters along Route Y that the enemy obtained their successes, despite intensive air and surface patrols. Route Y was patrolled that night by 2 corvettes and 6 trawlers, while Coastal Command provided 6 aircraft with bombs and parachute flares; and owing to magnetic mines ships evacuating troops were given permission in the early hours of 1st June to use that route as well as Route X.

At 0230 on the 1st June the A/S trawler *Stella Dorado*, which 24 hours earlier had picked up 55 survivors from the *Siroco*, torpedoed by an E-boat near T buoy, was herself torpedoed in the same position and sunk whilst on patrol. About a quarter of an hour later the A/S trawler *Argyllshire*, on patrol in company with the *Lord Melchett* and *Stella Rigel* about 2 miles east of S buoy, commenced an attack on what appeared to be a submarine. Within 5 minutes she was struck by a torpedo fired by an E-Boat and sank immediately. Five survivors, including her Captain, Sub-Lieutenant J. S. Weddle, R.N.R., S.O. 11th A/S Striking Force, were picked up by the trawler *Malabar*.

At the time there were many trawlers and other small craft in the neighbourhood, and one of the two E-Boats responsible for these sinkings was reported to have been disguised as a sailing boat.

Final Evacuation Postponed

Already on the afternoon of the 31st May ships in Dunkirk road had come under fire from guns on shore at Mardyck, and early on 1st June it became evident that

Major General Alexander's force could not be evacuated completely on the night of 1st/2nd June. At 0800, therefore, he agreed on a modified plan with Admiral Abrial and General Fagalde which involved holding his present line till midnight 1st/2nd June, so as to cover Dunkirk and to enable the French to evacuate as many of their troops as possible. Subsequently Major General Alexander was to withdraw to a bridgehead round Dunkirk with all available A/A and anti-tank guns and such troops as had not yet embarked.

Embarkations Over Bray Beaches

It was not only in Dunkirk roads that the ships had been under fire on the previous day; off Bray they had the same experience. Troops were moving westward, and embarkation at La Panne was no longer possible. It was clear to Rear-Admiral Wake-Walker that beach work at Bray would be costly, and he so informed Vice-Admiral, Dover (0235/1), who concurred, whilst pointing out the necessity of using the beaches up to the last possible moment.

The Rear-Admiral, in the *Keith*, with the *Basilisk* for supporting fire against enemy tanks or lorries along the beach, was investigating the position to the east of Dunkirk. As the light grew, at 0330, it was seen that the beach by La Panne was deserted. The sea too, was empty, small boats had vanished under instructions to move westward to Dunkirk whilst those which were full were going back to England as intended. However, ships were still loading off Bray and to the westward, though men were moving westward along the beaches.

The minesweeper *Speedwell* was anchored a little west of La Panne, using her motor boat and two whalers to ferry troops to the ship as the pontoon pier had been hit by shell fire. She closed the shore at daylight, and at about 0500, shortly after low water, she grounded aft and continued thus to embark troops under machine-gun fire by enemy aircraft of the troops on shore, the boats, and the ship, until the minesweeper *Albury* towed her off. She sailed at 0730 for Dunkirk. On the way she took off 100 troops from the *Ivanhoe* which was damaged by a bomb as the *Speedwell* was steaming past her. At Dunkirk she made up her number of troops to 972 and left for Dover at 0950 after being repeatedly but unsuccessfully bombed. The minesweeper *Salamander* was anchored a mile east of Bray Dunes, similarly engaged in embarking troops with her boats, and she sailed for Dunkirk astern of the *Keith* and *Skipjack* soon after 0600. At Dunkirk she came in for two air attacks in one of which, at about 0820, she was damaged by a near miss, but she reached Dover on one boiler at 1530 and disembarked 479 troops. It was her last trip. A mile east of Bray, too, the minesweeper Sutton embarked 453 troops from the beaches before sailing at 0600 for Dover. She was bombed and machine-gunned, but the only man hit was one wounded soldier. The minesweeper *Dundalk* was anchored nearer to La Panne, also embarking troops. Having no motor boat, the *Speedwell* and *Salamander* both lent a hand to tow her whalers. From 0500 onwards she was subjected to air attacks at regular intervals, and about 0800 she "decided to proceed to Margate," where she arrived at 1215 with 280 troops. Still further east, the minesweeper *Halcyon* was anchored off La Panne embarking troops swimming off to the ship, paddling in rubber boats, and in her whalers, during which she had one officer (Lieut. N. Thurston, R.N.) mortally wounded and suffered some casualties amongst the crew from machine gunning by enemy aircraft.

Off Bray, the destroyer *Sabre* was embarking 451 troops and the minesweeper *Niger* 310, pressing into service carley floats and lifebelts with which men swam from the beach. Daylight showed a minesweeper and a paddle minesweeper ashore, and the Rear-Admiral hailed a tug which was on its way homeward with soldiers on board, and told him to go in and try to tow off the minesweepers. However, the tugs had been sent over from England with pulling boats in tow and told to load up, and they regarded themselves as transports only, whereas Rear-Admiral Wake-Walker, who knew nothing of these instructions, naturally regarded them as tugs. It was not until a gun was trained on the tug and an R.N.V.R. Sub.-Lieutenant put on board to take charge, that the master's anxiety to get away was overcome.

A welcome addition to the evacuation craft consisted of the first of a dozen Belgian fishing boats which now appeared on the scene from seaward down the Zyuidcoote Pass.[1]

Early Liftings from Dunkirk

At 0241 Rear-Admiral Wake-Walker had given orders for all small craft to move westward with boats in tow in the direction of Dunkirk, towards which the troops were now marching from La Panne.

The first loaded ship to leave Dunkirk seems to have been the *Whippingham*, in time of peace an Isle of Wight paddle ferry boat belonging to the Southern Railway. She had been embarking troops alongside the mole since 2200 on the previous day, and when she cast off at 0130 on 1st with 2,700 troops on board she was overladen and her sponsons were only about a foot above water. Disaster

---

1 Probably the 10 Belgian trawlers from Brixham, referred to in Section 176.

nearly overwhelmed her at the start, when she was straddled by shell fire and the troops rushed over to the port side, causing the ship to list 20°. Fortunately, the sea was calm. The chief mechanician (Ch. Mech. 2nd Cl. F. A. Ford) checked the rush, moved the troops back to starboard, and thereby probably saved the ship.

Another early sailer was the personnel vessel *Lady of Mann*, who proceeded at 0430 for Dover, with 1500 casualties. The hospital carriers *St. Andrew* and *St. Julien* disembarked in England this day 130 and 287 wounded, respectively, after which no more hospital ships brought wounded from Dunkirk. Space alongside the large-ship berths was too valuable to be occupied by hospital ships, and walking wounded went with the troops, whilst those that could not walk had to be left behind.

The personnel ship *Maid of Orleans* berthed at the East Mole at about 0330 and for 6 hours, most of the time under air attack, she acted as a floating stage for the embarkation of troops on board the destroyers *Icarus*, *Vanquisher* and *Windsor*, whose upper decks were far below the top of the mole. The pier was crowded and as many troops as possible were embarked over mess tables rigged across the "B" gun decks of inside ships to the outside vessel. The *Vanquisher* was the first of the three to leave, at 0630 with 1200 troops. An hour later the *Icarus* and *Windsor* sailed in company, with 1,114 and 493 troops respectively. Finally, at about 0900 the *Maid of Orleans* herself proceeded, during an air attack, with 1,856 troops, which, like the destroyers, she disembarked at Dover. In six trips, once being diverted without completing the trip and once returning on account of collision, the *Maid of Orleans* had transported in all 5,461 men; but this was her last crossing, for when leaving Dover again for Dunkirk at 2030 that day she was rammed amidships by the destroyer *Worcester* returning from Dunkirk with manoeuvrability impaired through damage to propellers and rudder, caused by air attack at 1630 in which she had 6 men killed and 40 wounded, and shot down two enemy aircraft. No lives were lost in the collision, but the *Maid of Orleans* was too badly damaged to continue her voyage. For the *Worcester*, too, this was the final crossing: she had evacuated 4,545 troops in 6 trips.

Other destroyers were embarking troops at the same time alongside Dunkirk pier. The *Vivacious*, after being dive-bombed whilst waiting to enter harbour, went alongside at 0630, embarked 475 troops in a quarter of an hour, and sailed again for Dover at 0645. The *Winchelsea* was bombed at 0745 and again at 0830, but was not damaged, and she sailed at 0830 with 1150 troops on board.

Despite vicious air attacks, the embarkation of troops continued. The gunboat *Locust*, after embarking troops for four hours from Malo beach in her whalers, having no power boat, moved to Dunkirk at 0415 and took on board a further 500 at the east pier under air attack before sailing for Dover at 0610. The corvette *Kingfisher* left the east pier at 1130 with 210 troops and some wounded, embarked under almost continuous high level bombing.

There were times, however, during the day when the harbour was deserted. When Rear-Admiral Wake-Walker left about 0930 to make contact with Vice-Admiral, Dover, all the ships which had not been sunk had gone. "At about 1800" he wrote, "the harbour was full of destroyers, sloops and minesweepers, many with the signs of their strenuous times upon them – bent bows, holes and the evidence of bumps and collisions. Some were out of action altogether and all were enjoying the first few hours at rest in harbour that many of them had had for many days."[2]

Air Patrols

Consequent on the bombing of the day before, Rear-Admiral Wake-Walker had asked for fighter protection at dawn. As the morning mists and clouds dispersed many aircraft appeared on the scene, and fighters constantly came low over the ships. More often than not they were Spitfires, but the ships were not taking chances and nearly always opened fire indiscriminately on them. In order to stop the firing Rear-Admiral Wake-Walker hoisted 6 Flag – "Cease fire", and blew the siren to draw attention, in spite of which, however, the after machine gun of his own ship the *Keith* continued to fire regardless of the "cease fire" gong; once firing started they could hear nothing.[3]

Route X to Dunkirk was patrolled during the early hours of daylight by the A.A. cruiser *Calcutta*, which sailed from Margate at 0315 with the corvettes *Mallow* and *Shearwater* and carried out a patrol between W and V buoys. The *Calcutta* was recalled to Sheerness at 0938 in readiness to perform the same service next night, and at 1015 she shot down a Heinkel which had bombed and damaged the *Mosquito* by a near miss 15 miles from Dover.

Fighter Command provided 8 patrols during the 1st June of an average strength of 3 to 4 squadrons. The main periods when no fighter protection was afforded were approximately 0730-0850, 1020-1120, 1120-1145, 1545-1615 and 1715-1845. Coastal Command continued to fly patrols of 3 aircraft over the North Goodwins – Gravelines – Ostend line throughout the day.

---

2 *Report,* M.017978/41 p.29.

3 M.017978/41, p.23.

Enemy Air Attacks Begin: *St. Fagan* Sunk 0355

Sporadic enemy air attacks began at early light. Ships alongside the mole reported being attacked at 0415 and 0500. This was before the first main R.A.F. air patrol appeared on the scene, for the R.A.F. had been asked to provide maximum protection from 0500 onwards.[4]

Before the first patrol appeared enemy aircraft claimed what was to prove the first of a long series of victims that day. The tug *St. Fagan* had towed over from Dover during the night three Thames barges. At about 0355, in the Dunkirk Channel, abreast the town the ship was hit by a bomb and practically disintegrated. Only two officers, including her Captain, Lieut.-Commander H. Warren, M.B.E., R.N., and 6 ratings, were saved out of a total complement of 25. They were picked up by the tug *Tanga* which had come over from Ramsgate with 6 boats in tow and had "hung off " outside Dunkirk most of the night waiting for troops to be brought out to her, and was then on her way home with 160 men on board and a motor-boat in tow.

Almost simultaneously with the withdrawal of our aircraft at 0730 a heavy dive bombing attack developed by a compact formation of some 30 or 40 Ju.75s, causing the loss of the destroyers *Keith* and *Basilisk*, the minesweeper *Skipjack*, and the tug *St. Abbs*. The second series of attacks, which began at about 0906 and caused the loss of the *Havant*, coincided with the arrival of the third main R.A.F. patrol of the day. Coastal Command patrols were also over the ships, and at about 1015 one drove off a He.Ill which was about to attack two destroyers.

The third, a particularly heavy and prolonged enemy air attack, took place from about 1009 to 1120, at which latter time a patrol of 28 Hurricanes appeared and within ten minutes was engaged with an enemy force of 50 or 60 M.E.109s and 110s. The presence of enemy bombers was also reported, but they were not engaged. They were responsible for sinking the French destroyer *Foudroyant*, the minesweeper *Brighton Queen*, personnel vessel *Scotia*, and damaging a second personnel vessel the *Prague*. A fourth air attack developed, at about 1230, during the Hurricanes' patrol. In this raid the corvette *Kingfisher* received damage from a near miss which rendered her unseaworthy in heavy weather, and the gunboat *Mosquito* was sunk.

There was a lull after this and the next air attacks fortunately occurred at a time when the fifth R.A.F. patrol was operating, at 1500 and 1530, and a Coastal

---

4 R.A.F. narrative.

Command patrol was also on the spot; and no ship was damaged. Renewed attacks occurred at 1600-1630 in the very short interval before the sixth R.A.F. patrol came up, and it was in this raid that the paddle minesweeper *Westward-Ho*, sailing from Dunkirk with 900 French troops, and the destroyer *Worcester* were damaged, over 100 bombs being dropped near the latter ship When this was over, visibility had so far declined that at 1750 the paddle minesweeper *Princess Elizabeth*, trying to approach Bray beach, ran into fog and was compelled to return to Dover. The seventh R.A.F. patrol was troubled by poor visibility, and the eighth and last encountered no enemy at all. No bombing attacks were reported after 1840.

Five destroyers, a gunboat, two minesweepers, two personnel vessels, and two tugs were sunk or put out of action by the German bombers on this 1st June.

The weight of the enemy attacks may be gauged from the fact that over 1000 German bombing sorties were reported over the Dunkirk area during the day. Forty-three enemy aircraft were destroyed.

The First Heavy Air Attack, 0730. *Keith*, *Skipjack* and *St. Abbs* Sunk

The *Keith* and *Salamander* moved westward from the deserted eastern beaches. At 0737, off Bray, a large number of enemy bombers accompanied by fighters was seen approaching, and a dive-bombing attack was made on the *Keith*. The latter's manoeuvrability was restricted by shoals, magnetic mines and wrecks, but she was not hit. But a delay action bomb from a dive-bomber exploded just astern of the ship and caused the steering wheel on the bridge to jam. Tiller flat steering was connected up and the ship was conned by telephone from the bridge. By this time all the *Keith*'s 3-inch ammunition had been expended, and the only defence which the ship could put up was the passive one of continuing to turn in small circles at high speed in the restricted waters

At about 0800 numerous dive-bombing attacks took place, and the *Keith* was hit or near missed on the starboard side. A large hole was blown in the side at the forward end of the starboard engine room below the water line, and the bulkhead between the engine room and the after boiler room was ruptured, flooding both spaces and killing Lieut. (E) W. H. Kenward, R.N. and several men. The boiler room shortly afterwards caught fire, possibly as the result of a further bomb hit. It seems probable that serious damage was now caused to the port side by two further hits, for the ship took a heavy list to port, which increased until the upper deck was within a few inches of the water. Steam was gradually lost and the ship stopped, with one anchor down. Torpedoes were fired with no range on and all depth charges were set to safe and jettisoned.

As the ship was now settling, Rear-Admiral Wake-Walker transferred from the *Keith* to *M.T.B.102*; the order to abandon ship was given, and most of the men left her. At this moment a further series of dive-bombing attacks shook the ship with near misses which landed amongst the men in the water.

About 0830 the tug *St. Abbs* came alongside and assisted by the tug *Vincia* took off survivors and picked up men in the water. The skoot *Hilda* rescued Lt. Gen. Laidsell, 2 officers, and 20 ratings. The minesweeper *Salamander* rescued 7 ratings. An unidentified grey yacht which was picking up survivors was bombed and sunk. As late as 1100 men were still struggling in the oil slick, and the motor barge *Sherfield*, which had arrived off the coast with a small convoy of 2 X lighters and a motor launch, rescued 15.

At about 0940 aircraft again appeared, and the *Keith* was sunk in a salvo of bombs from about 50 of the enemy. Three officers and 33 men were reported lost.

Ten minutes later the *St. Abbs*, by this time off Dunkirk, was hit by bombs and sank in 45 seconds. Of the 135 officers, ratings and troops on board, 30 were left swimming in the water, including the Captain of the *Keith*, Capt. E. L. Berthon, D.S.C., R.N., who was saved.

Meanwhile the *Skipjack*, which had been busy off Malo embarking troops and fighting off continuous air attacks from 0530 which had reduced her ammunition supply to about 12 rounds a gun, was dive-bombed at 0845 by 10 aircraft and hit by 2 bombs. A minute later 3 more bombs hit her. She turned turtle and floated bottom upwards for about 2 minutes before finally sinking. A few survivors were picked up by the *Hilda* and the *St. Abbs*. Nearly all the 275 troops on board were below decks and had no chance to escape. Enemy aircraft machine-gunned men in the water.

Ivanhoe Damaged, *Basilisk* Sunk

Already, by this time, another destroyer had been put out of action. At 0800 off Dunkirk harbour, the *Ivanhoe*, with 1,000 troops on board which she had embarked from La Panne, was dive-bombed and hit amidships. Damage was severe and she had 26 killed and 30 wounded. The troops and wounded were transferred to the *Havant*, the *Speedwell* and the yacht *Grive*; and the *Ivanhoe*, assisted by the tug *Persia* and escorted by the War Dept. M. L. Haig, proceeded to Sheerness. While within a radius of 1 mile of No. 6 W buoy, 3 waves (each of

21 bombers) attacked the *Ivanhoe* and other vessels in that area for half an hour, but the *Ivanhoe* received no further damage.

At about the time that the *Keith* and *Ivanhoe* were under attack off Bray and Dunkirk, the Basilisk was also being bombed off La Panne. Three attacks were made. In the first attack one bomb exploded in No. 3 boiler room, cutting the main and auxiliary steam lines and putting all machinery out of action; six other bombs exploded underneath the ship, causing the upper deck and the ship's sides to buckle.

Torpedoes and depth charges were jettisoned and at 0845 the ship was floating on an even keel.

An hour later, while efforts were being made by the French trawler *Jolie Mascotte* to tow the *Basilisk*, the enemy returned to the attack but made no hits. The French trawler slipped the tow and moved off to a safer distance.

At noon bombers returned for a third time, diving to about 400 feet. Smothered by hits and near misses the *Basilisk* shuddered and heeled to starboard, righted herself momentarily, but sank in about 3 minutes, settling on the bottom on an even keel in some 4 fathoms. As soon as she was abandoned the *Whitehall* completed her destruction by gunfire and torpedoes.

The *Jolie Mascotte* picked up 6 officers and 71 ratings, the *Whitehall* 2 officers and 52 ratings. Other survivors got away in the motor boat and a whaler.

Second Air Attack, 0906: Sinking of the *Havant*

Meanwhile the Havant, after transferring 500 troops from the damaged Ivanhoe, proceeded down Dunkirk Channel. At 0906, at the western end of the channel, she was hit by 2 bombs which entered the starboard side of the engine room killing everyone in it. A third bomb dropped 50 yards ahead and exploded as the *Havant* passed over it. Out of control and listing to port, the ship continued to steam ahead towards the sandbanks opposite Dunkirk. The engine room and No. 2 boiler room were on fire, there was a heavy escape of steam and all auxiliary machinery was out of action, resulting in a failure of the electric supply. It was impossible to enter the engine room, but Chief Stoker M. Gallon, in spite of the fire, let the steam out of the boilers and the ship was brought up in 4 fathoms by the starboard anchor.

The *Saltash* and *Grive* came alongside and the *Havant*'s troops were transferred during almost continuous bombing. The *Saltash* took the *Havant* in tow, but further concussion from near misses increased considerably the destroyer's list to port, so the majority of her ship's company were transferred to the skoot *Aegir*. A bomb fell between the *Havant* and the *Saltash* followed by another close to the *Havant*'s port quarter. By 1000 the list had increased and the decks were almost awash. "Abandon ship" was ordered, the tow was slipped and the remainder of the ship's company were transferred to the *Aegir*. At 1015 the *Havant* rolled over and sank. 1 officer and 7 men were killed, 25 wounded.

Third Air Attack, 1009. *Prague* Damaged

The enemy air attacks had not been confined to ships off the beaches. At 1009 the personnel vessel *Prague*, which had embarked about 3000 French troops from Dunkirk harbour, was attacked by dive-bombers between W and V buoys and suffered severe damage astern from 3 near misses which put the starboard engine out of action.

The majority of the troops were transferred, whilst the ship continued to go ahead on the port engine, to the *Scimitar*, the minesweeper *Halcyon* and the paddle minesweeper *Queen of Thanet*, the later taking on board no less than 500 and the *Scimitar* 376; and at 1331 the tug *Lady Brassey* took the *Prague* in tow to the Downs, where the remaining troops were transferred to the trawlers *Olvina* and *Lady Philomena*. The *Prague* had ended her service in Operation "Dynamo", for to save her from sinking she was beached off Sandown Castle, Deal, at 1730 that day. In three trips, she had taken out from Dunkirk over 6,000 men.

Sinking of the *Foudroyant*

Before the morning was out yet a fourth destroyer, the French *Foudroyant*, was sunk by air attack. The ship had sailed from England at 0800. She reached the Dunkirk Channel, at the beginning of Route X, about 1030, during the third heavy air attack of the day, when she was hit by two consecutive salvos of bombs, blew up, and sank in 2½ minutes. A French trawler, herself damaged, picked up 137 of the Foudroyant's crew and transferred them to the trawler *Gara*; and the motor yacht *Naiad Errant* rescued about a score and put them on board a nearby French tug. Some were also picked up by the French minesweeping trawler *Bernadette*.

Brighton Queen and Scotia Sunk

The paddle minesweeper *Brighton Queen* arrived at Dunkirk at 1035 on the 1st June, having for the last hour been under continuous enemy air attack which she successfully fought off with 12 pounder and Lewis gun. In little more than half an hour she took on board 700 French Moroccan troops and sailed for Margate.

The ship had barely rounded No. 5 buoy, off Mardyck, and entered the channel (Route X) when a formation of enemy dive-bombers came out of a cloud and peeled off to attack. One bomb, estimated at 200 pounds, exploded very close on the starboard quarter, causing severe damage and a number of casualties. The ship began to settle at once, took a heavy list, and in five minutes filled and sank on an even keel in about 5 fathoms of water. The crew worked quickly and intelligently in getting life rafts and floating material over the side, and the French troops, despite the language difficulty, behaved steadily and intelligently though nearly half of them were killed by the explosion or drowned. The minesweeper *Saltash* was quickly alongside, rescued some 400 survivors, and landed them safely at Margate.

The main attack of the enemy formation was directed against the personnel ship *Scotia* (3,500 tons) which had left Dunkirk carrying 2,000 French troops very shortly after the *Brighton Queen*, and was now only 2 cables distant on her port bow. The enemy attacked in sections of 4 aircraft, two each with machine guns and bombs of small size. At least 4 of the latter hit the ship, which began to sink by the stern, and the order to abandon her was given. The *Scotia* heeled over until her forward funnel and mast were in the water. The enemy now made another attack on the sinking vessel, dropping 4 more bombs and machine gunning the men swimming and clinging to the wreckage. By this time, however, the destroyer *Esk* had come out from Dunkirk and drove off the enemy aircraft when they returned yet again. The destroyer put herself alongside the sinking *Scotia* and transferred nearly 1,000 of the troops, a fine feat, and the destroyer *Worcester* and other craft picked up several; but 28 of the *Scotia*'s crew and an estimated 200 to 300 of the French troops were unfortunately lost.

Fourth Air Attack, 1230. Sinking of the *Mosquito*

Among the vessels which went to the assistance of the *Scotia* was the gunboat *Mosquito*, though she never reached her.

The *Mosquito* arrived off Dunkirk from the Downs at about 1230; she was attacked on the way over by a single dive-bomber and was damaged by a near miss, but was able to continue on her course. Off Dunkirk she embarked some 30 French and Belgian troops from the motor boat *Rapid I*. Hearing that the *Scotia* was reported to be sinking at the west end of the channel, she proceeded towards the scene, followed by the *Rapid I*.

Almost immediately (about 1330) six or more of a flight of 20 Ju.87s attacked her from different directions, obtaining a direct hit and a near miss. With boiler and engine rooms badly holed, the steering gear jammed with the rudder hard over, the ship took a heavy list to port. The crew of the pom-pom were all killed or knocked out except Acting Leading Seaman Ronald Thirlwall, who, although shockingly badly wounded in at least four places, kept the one undamaged barrel firing until ammunition was exhausted. The 0.5" gun aft was also kept in action by Able Seaman C. A. L. Hirschfield, who went aft and brought the gun into action single handed after all the crew were wounded. With water pouring into the ship, the *Mosquito* was abandoned, the survivors being picked up by the *Rapid* and two drifters. Among the killed was the executive officer Lieutenant A. H. Mainwaring, R.N.

Fifth and Sixth Air Attacks, 1500 and 1610

Between 1230 and about 1500 there was a lull in the air attacks on shipping, and when attacks were renewed at the latter hour R.A.F. and Coastal Command patrols were operating and no damage occurred.

About 1600 the French minesweeping trawlers *President Briand*, *Denis Papin*, *Moussaillon* and *Venus*, were approaching Dunkirk after landing troops in England, when gunfire from a shore battery opposite 6 W buoy caused the two former, who were ahead, to turn back. Ten minutes later, a formation of enemy aircraft dived on them, directing their bombs on the *Venus* and the *Denis Papin*. The latter apparently sank immediately with total loss of her crew, and the *Venus* in four minutes, after a direct hit. Whilst the other two trawlers were engaged in rescuing the survivors of the *Venus*, the *Moussaillon* was hit and sank within a minute.

Losses from Mines

On this black day mines were also taking their toll of shipping. Enemy aircraft had been mining the inshore channels during the night 31st May-1st June, and at 0313 Vice-Admiral Dover informed the Admiralty that he was allowing ships evacuating troops to use Route Y as well as Route X. In the early hours the corvette *Sheldrake* "after a night spent in dodging M.T.B. torpedoes", was skilfully directed by aircraft to a position between the West Hinder and Kwint buoys, where she found wreckage with men clinging to it. This was the remains of the trawler *St. Achilleus* which had been mined on patrol. The *Sheldrake* rescued 11 men, but 4 of them died before they could be got to harbour. About the same time, i.e. at 0330, the little Thames Estuary cockle bawley boat *Renown* was blown to pieces with her crew of 3, on the way back from Dunkirk.

The third ship to be sunk on this day was the F.A.A. training yacht *Grive* a vessel which, on account of her untiring activity, could ill be spared. Having disembarked 374 troops at Dover at 0100 on the 1st June the *Grive* sailed again two hours later for Dunkirk without waiting to replenish ammunition, of which she had only 5 rounds per gun remaining. On the way in to the harbour she lent assistance to the *Ivanhoe* after the latter was bombed and damaged, went alongside the jetty and embarked troops under heavy bombing. At 0800 she left again. On the way out, she passed the sinking destroyer *Havant* with the *Ivanhoe's* troops and survivors of the crew on board; these she transferred, and arrived at Dover with 785 persons about 1300. Three hours later, her indefatigable Captain (Capt. the Hon. L. J. O. Lambart, D.S.O., R.N. (Retired)) sailed once more for Dunkirk. But he never arrived, for at about 2230, when a mile or so outside the harbour, the *Grive* was blown to pieces by a mine. Nineteen survivors were picked up, but her Captain was not among them.

Loadings at Dunkirk During the Day

In the space of a few hours the enemy had caused almost as much damage to shipping as during the whole of the previous 7 days. C.-in-C. Nore, concerned at the losses of destroyers, a type of vessel which was in all too short supply at any time, asked the Admiralty to give orders that they should be used only in positions where they could manoeuvre at high speed under bombing attack. In the short view, however, the effect on the evacuation of the loss of personnel vessels was perhaps equally serious. These ships possessed great carrying power; no other vessels could compare with them. Up to date the services of no less than 15 of them had been lost to the operation, 9 by sinking and 6 through serious damage.

Nevertheless, and despite the increasing difficulty of threading a way into Dunkirk through the growing number of wrecks, the supply of personnel vessels was maintained throughout the day, though not without a series of setbacks.

The *Cote d'Argent*, a French mail boat transferred to the orders of Vice-Admiral Dover, disembarked 1,000 troops from Dunkirk harbour on the 1st June, the *King George V* 700, the French vessel *Rouen* 800. The *St. Helier* disembarked 1,250 troops at Dover in the morning and left again about 0930 At 1530 she entered Dunkirk harbour to embark wounded and troops, and was twice hit by shore batteries before sailing for Dover once more at 2230 with 1,334 troops.

The Controlling Organisation

The organisation which controlled the supply of shipping functioned in a room below Dover Castle, known as the "Dynamo Room" from the codeword of the Dunkirk operation. In charge was Captain M. M. Denny, R.N. With him there were 20 or more officers, soldiers, naval officers and Board of Trade and Sea Transport officials, and the work they did was marvellous. They were controlling, organizing, fuelling and supplying, not only men-of-war, but a variety of merchant vessels. Sometimes a merchant vessel would need a new crew to take her over to Dunkirk again, but within a few hours the Sea Transport Officer would get one and the ship would sail. At Ramsgate, the Nore, and various other places besides Dover, ships and boats were collected and organised, but the head and control of the whole was in this room, where they worked continuously and tirelessly against time day and night.[5]

Crews for the numerous small craft, working parties, and beach parties were provided by the Chatham Depot. The great majority of the small craft of the inshore flotillas were serviced and controlled by N.O.I.C. Ramsgate. At Harwich, an exceptional Naval and Military system was organised to assist those ships which called there to make a quick turn round by relieving the tired ships' companies of the work of cleaning and clearing their vessels.

Naval Losses of the Day

Sunk by Air Attack
Destroyers – *Basilisk, Havant, Keith, French Foudroyant*
Gunboat – *Mosquito*
Minesweepers – *Brighton Queen, Skipjack*
French Minesweeping Trawlers – *Denis Papin, Moussaillon, Venus*
Personnel vessel – *Scotia*
Tugs – *St. Abbs, St. Fagan*
Barges – *Lady Robinson, Doris*

Sunk by E-Boat Torprdoes
Trawlers – *Argyllshire, Stella Dorado*

---

5 Report of R. A. Wake-Walker, M 017978/41, p.27.

Sunk by Mines
Trawler – *St. Achilleus*
Small craft – *Renown*

Sunk by Gunfire
Drifter – *Lord Cavan*

Sunk by Collision or other Misadventure
Drifters – *Eileen Emma, Fair Breeze, Gervais Rentoul*
Yachts – *Amulree, Pellag II*
Barges – *Aidie, Barbara Jean, Duchess, Ethel Everard, Lark, Royalty*
Small craft – *number unknown*

Damaged by Air Attack
Destroyers – *Ivanhoe, Worcester*
Minesweepers – *Ross, Salamander, Westward-Ho*
Corvette – *Kingfisher*
Personnel vessel – *Prague*

Damaged by Mine
Hospital carrier – *St. David*

Damaged by Gunfire
One trawler – *name uncertain*

Damaged by Collision or Grounding
Destroyer – *Vimy*
Personnel vessel – *Maid of Orleans*

The Evacuation Figures for the Day

Little ships added their quotas to those of the big ships, though not without casualties: they suffered heavy losses from collision or other misadventure, although in the circumstances it was not always possible to obtain details (See App. B.I.)

On this day there were lifted from the beaches and from Dunkirk harbour: by motor boats and the like 2334 persons, by hopper barges 1470, by tugs 736, by yachts 1,831, by skoots 3,170, of which almost all were from the beaches, by special service vessels 1,250, by drifters 2,968, and by trawlers 1,876 practically all of whom were lifted from Dunkirk harbour. French ships lifted 3,967, Belgian trawlers 402, and a Dutch yacht 114; all troops evacuated by foreign ships were embarked in Dunkirk harbour, none coming from the beaches.

Though losses of ships had been highest this day the total of troops lifted was the second highest of the operation, no less than 64,429 being landed in England. Of these, 47,081 had been embarked in Dunkirk harbour and 17,348 from the beaches.

The Night of the 1st– 2nd June Daylight to Dusk on 2nd

Situation Ashore on Evening of 1st (Plan 3, pages 274–275)

During the 1st June heavy enemy attacks developed on the British sector of the line, and our forces had to give some ground. By nightfall, however, the enemy advance had been checked on a line Bergues – Uxem – Ghyvelde, thence due east of the frontier and along the frontier defences to the sea.

French troops were holding a line in rear of ours, and the British rearguard was to withdraw through this line which the French would continue to hold.

Two divisions of French Territorial troops reduced in strength, in addition to part of the British 1st Corps and rearguard of 4,000 men, still remained to be evacuated on the evening of the 1st. The War Office, aware that they were not in a position to judge the local situation, did not set a period to the evacuation but ordered Major-General Alexander to hold on as long as possible in order that the maximum number of French and British might be embarked. It was left to the General, in close co-operation with Admiral Abrial, to decide the moment when evacuation must come to an end.[1]

Plan for the Night lst–2nd June (See Plan 4)

Early in the afternoon of the 1st June the only remaining Route X came under the fire of German guns, and it was judged impossible to carry out any further evacuation by day. There was hope both at Dover and at the War Office that it would be possible to complete the evacuation of the B.E.F. during the dark hours of the night 1st/2nd June, by using both sides of Dunkirk harbour, pier and eastern beach. The War Office asked General Weygand to urge Admiral Abrial to co-operate in completing the evacuation of the French this night.

Evacuation was to be confined to the period between 2100 and 0330. It was estimated that British vessels could lift about 17,000 men, probably in the

---

1 Report of Captain W. Tennant, S.N.O. Dunkirk, Record Office Case 5458 Vol. 3, p.357.

PLAN 4

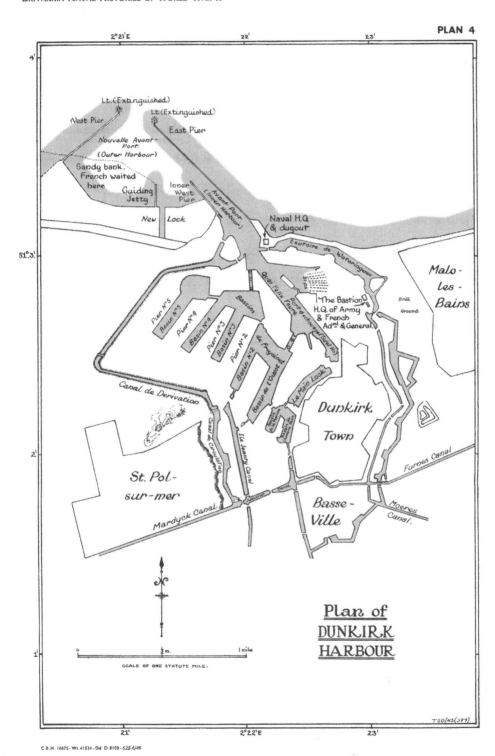

Plan of
DUNKIRK
HARBOUR

SCALE OF ONE STATUTE MILE.

proportion 50 per cent British and 50 per cent French, during these hours, as follows: (Appendix R8):

(a) From the beach between Dunkirk and 1½ miles to the eastward between 2100/1 and 0300/2, 9,000 men.
(b) At the East Pier between 2100/1 and 0330/1,[2] 7,000 men. This time might be extended.
(c) On the east side inside the harbour, between 2200/1 and 0300/2, 1,000 men.

It was Intended to Withdraw all Naval Personnel this Night.[3]

All minesweepers, both fleet and paddle, and skoots and all small craft except certain flotillas specially organised, were to lift from the beach stretching eastward 1½ miles from Dunkirk, and it was hoped to employ here also about 100 French small beach fishing craft and drifters. Personnel ships up to 7 in number and 8 destroyers were to enter Dunkirk harbour and go alongside the East Pier, where British troops were. Only by using this pier would it be possible to evacuate large numbers, and there was considerable apprehension lest the Germans should shell it heavily and damage it or render it impossible for ships to lie alongside. The pier had already been damaged by the armed boarding vessel *King Orry* when she secured alongside at 1730 on 29th May with her steering gear out of order and all instruments shattered by air attack, but the gap had been bridged. Drifters and other small craft were to be sent into the inner harbour at Dunkirk, to lift troops from the Quay Felix Faure, in the Tidal Harbour, the North Quay, in the shipyard, and the quay in the new outer harbour.

The French troops assembled on the west side of the harbour, and it was intended that French vessels, including torpedo boats, should serve the West Quay in the new outer harbour, whilst private small boats used the Quay Felix Faure.

---

2 The originator's copy of this signal is (rather exceptionally) typed instead of being written by hand, and the time has been altered by the typewriter, either from 0300 to read 0330 or from 0330 to read 0300, though it is not possible to say with certainty which figure was intended to be sent. The time was received at the Admiralty at 0330, and Rear Admiral Wake-Walker in his *Report*, M.017978/41 p.32 says 0330 was intended.

3 S.N.O. Dunkirk reported, however (Appendix R.24) that he did not receive the message giving details of the plan until 0430/2.

Assembly of Shipping

Early in the afternoon of the 1st June Vice-Admiral Dover recalled all destroyers to harbour: and minesweepers of the 1st, 4th, 5th and 6th M/S Flotillas were warned for duty: only ships having degaussing equipment were to sail. Five vessels, the *Sharpshooter*, *Albury*, *Kellett*, *Ross*, and *Leda* were unable to comply; the compasses of another the *Pangbourne*, were unreliable, though her D.G. gear was functioning; and in the event, she sailed, led by a Dutch skoot, though she was too late to go to the beaches, and accordingly proceeded along Route Y as far as T buoy, looking for any ships in need of assistance.

The destroyers designated Force K, were to proceed in pairs at hourly intervals to berth at the East Pier in Dunkirk harbour, returning to Dover when loaded. If there was no vacant berth at the pier when a pair of destroyers arrived, they were to assist at the beach instead. Four pairs were detailed, viz. the *Windsor* and *Icarus*, *Codrington* and *Sabre*, *Shikari* and *Esk*, *Winchelsea* and *Whitshed*. The *Esk*, however, which had been running almost continuously since 27th May, was unable to sail and was given 24 hours stand off.

Preparations to assemble the requisite small craft for working off the beach commenced early in the forenoon of 1st June, when a number of Senior Officers were despatched from Dover in fast motor boats to round up all stray motor boats in the Downs and along the routes, and direct them back in the evening to the beach 1½ miles east of Dunkirk. A flight of 30 motor boats and 34 lifeboats with 3 tugs, the last three large tugs left in London, was sent during the early hours of 1st June from London to Ramsgate where they were prepared for beach work, naval crews being placed in the lifeboats that lacked crews and extra towage provided. Motor boats were also sent from Harwich and Sheerness. A number of flotillas under Commodore A. H. Taylor and Captain the Hon. G. Frazer were re-organised for the night's effort.

Abandonment of Daylight Evacuations
(Appendix R, page 399)

It was decided to abandon daylight evacuation after 1st June, because the scale of enemy air attack experienced on that day, and the fact that the Germans could by now command the newly swept central route at its point of junction with Dunkirk Roads by gunfire from the shore, rendered it too costly. Vice-Admiral Ramsay, when drawing up the plan for the night, intended sailings to cease at 0300 or 0330; and Captain Tennant at Dunkirk, who did not yet know of the plan arranged for the night, independently gave orders, in the late afternoon of the 1st June with General Alexander's concurrence, that no ships were to sail during daylight and that evacuation by transports was consequently to cease at 0300 on 2nd. If the perimeter held, evacuation by the B.E.F. would be completed on the following night, by which time most of the French troops would also have been lifted.

The Admiralty, however, decided that, should it be possible to use any of the three channels during daylight hours, evacuation was to continue until 0700 and, if necessary also from 1730 on the 2nd June until dark provided daylight evacuation was then still possible. Only between 0700 and 1730 on the 2nd there would be no sailings. They intended to be the arbiters as to whether evacuation was possible in daylight as late as 0700.

At 2114, an hour and a half after the receipt of these instructions, Vice-Admiral Ramsay informed the Admiralty and all concerned at Dunkirk that, owing to casualties now being caused to shipping by heavy artillery, all ships had been ordered to withdraw before daylight on the 2nd. The Vice-Admiral followed up this signal at 2329 by a message to the Admiralty giving in some detail the shipping situation as he knew it. All three channels to Dunkirk, X, Y and Z were now under fire of German batteries, for traffic on the last remaining daylight route X, had had to be suspended on account of a new enemy battery which came into action that evening and was maintaining a heavy barrage.[4] Vice-Admiral Ramsay's information (not altogether correct) was that a total of 16 transports (personnel vessels invaluable in the work of evacuation) were now out of action, 8 being lost and 8 disabled, and that two of the sinkings had been caused by enemy shell fire on Route X. It was now difficult to compel the crews of the remainder to face the conditions which existed.

This had been a day of very heavy naval sinkings coupled with losses of troops from drowning. It is obvious that at some point losses incurred in continuing daylight evacuation would more than counterbalance the gains; it seems clear that Vice-Admiral Ramsay considered that this point had now been reached, and, in accordance with the Admiralty's own direction sent to him earlier in the evening, he now informed them that any attempt to continue the evacuation in daylight was unwise and he asked permission to withdraw all his forces at 0300 until the following night. In this, he told the admiralty, Major General Alexander concurred.

The Admiralty, however, were unwilling that evacuation should cease

4 The War Office 1330/1 reported: "Only remaining channel now coming under fire of German guns."

altogether at daylight and directed that it was to continue up to 0700, but only by destroyers unless further experience showed that enemy gunfire was rendering the channel prohibitively dangerous.

Danger to Personnel Ships

It is impossible to resist the conclusion that in the difficulty of obtaining accurate reports of conditions on the routes and estimating the true causes of the mounting losses of ships the danger from enemy shell fire was magnified in the minds of those at Dover. By some means the planners had been informed that two personnel ships had already been sunk by shell fire in the fairway near No. 5 buoy. Not only was this incorrect, but in point of fact no ship of any kind was lost from gunfire on the routes during the 1st June; the only sinking by shell fire on that day was the drifter *Lord Cavan*, depot ship of S.N.O. Dunkirk hit as she quitted the pier at Dunkirk, whilst the only other ship to be hit was the personnel vessel *St. Helier*. This ship arrived at Dunkirk and entered harbour at 1530 on 1st June. Whilst there, she was twice hit by shore batteries, though damage was slight and there was only one light casualty. The ship lay alongside for 7 hours, embarking stretcher cases and troops and finally proceeded at 2230.

Amongst the various classes of ships none had suffered proportionately heavier losses than the personnel vessels to which Vice-Admiral Dover referred in his message to the Admiralty. Their crews had been doing magnificent work in the face of nerve-racking experiences. Up to date 8 of these ships had been sunk and 4 disabled. It was arranged that during this night's evacuation personnel ships in addition to destroyers were to berth at the East Pier in Dunkirk where they were to be given priority.

The danger of sending these valuable ships in to Dunkirk in daylight was too great, and after the 1st of June they were sent in only under cover of darkness, with a naval Lieutenant-Commander or Commander on board each ship as adviser to the Master and with crews stiffened by 10 seamen for handling the wires and going alongside under fire. It was hoped by these means not only to get the ships to sail to time but also to ensure that they would enter Dunkirk harbour and not linger outside awaiting a quiet interval, or return empty. To their credit it must be recorded that not all the personnel ships needed the moral support of naval ratings.

Air Operations, Morning of 2nd June

The batteries which had brought Route X under fire were between Le Clipont, near Pointe de Gravelines (see Plan 3, pages 274-275), and Les Huttes, about a mile north east of Gravelines; they were attacked by the R.A.F. in 24 Blenheim sorties between first light and 0745 on the 2nd, the object of spreading the attack in this manner being to neutralise the batteries during the period of daylight evacuation. The Blenheims encountered much anti-aircraft fire, and though no aircraft were lost some were damaged and afterwards crash-landed on their airfields.

The Air Ministry were asked to provide strong continuous patrols over Dunkirk and the beaches from 0430 to 0830 on the 2nd June, with night fighter patrols during the hours of darkness. It was arranged that the fighter patrols should go out over the routes in use by our ships, and on the return journey fly low on the routes to give maximum protection to ships against low flying bomb and machine gun attacks. The concentration of fighter patrols in the dawn and dusk periods resulted in a great decrease in the total number of flying hours on the 2nd June (See Appendix C.)

The early morning was hazy, and the first two main R.A.F. patrols, both at four squadron strength, encountered no enemy aircraft and no ships reported being attacked during this period. The third patrol, the strongest yet flown, consisting of five full squadrons, which was over the Dunkirk area from 0745-0845, encountered very considerable enemy forces, and claimed to have shot down 18 enemy bombers and 10 fighters, themselves losing 7 Spitfires. Again, no reports of attacks came from the ships; and as far as can be ascertained no attacks occurred until the *Calcutta*, patrolling near W buoy with the *Mallard* and *Shearwater*, was attacked at 1035 by 3 Ju.88 which dived out of the sun and bombed her, causing slight damage from near misses. A Coastal patrol witnessed the incident and drove off the enemy. The French light cruiser *Epervier* and destroyer *Leopard* were also on the patrol line, but they apparently left the patrol when bombing began at 1035 and up to 1442 when the *Calcutta* returned to Sheerness by orders of Vice-Admiral Dover, nothing more was seen of them (Appendix J.7). Air protection by Coastal Command had been arranged from 0830 until 1100 on 2nd June, and Fighter Command patrols of three aircraft of Nos. 206, 235, 801 and 806 Squadrons operated under Coastal Command during these hours, to cover Route X.

Fifth Column Activities (Appendix H27–32, page 382)

On the 1st June there came to notice, for the first time during Operation "Dynamo", fifth column activities of the type of which the Germans made such effective use during the war.

At 2150 on the 1st the Minesweeper *Niger, en route* to Dunkirk with the Sutton in company, met a number of power boats and small boats returning empty, and orders were sent out from Dover to the destroyers of Force K and the minesweepers, to keep a look out and turn such boats back to their duty. Apparently it was at first believed at Dover that small boats were daunted by the severe conditions and enormous wastage on the French and Belgian coasts; but a report came in from the S.N.T.O. Ramsgate during the evening that a fifth column skoot was going about the beaches at Dunkirk giving false information and orders to return. The first example to come to notice was at 1300 on the 1st when the skoot *Oranje*, off Dunkirk Channel, was informed by another skoot that evacuation from the beaches was complete, that there were already sufficient ships in Dunkirk Harbour, and that the *Oranje's* boats were not required. The *Oranje* remained where she was, however, in case the four boats she had towed over were needed, and until all ships in her neighbourhood turned for home about 1515, subsequent to air attack.

Although on the night of the 1st-2nd June the services of a number of small craft were lost to the coast, there actually were a sufficient number off the beaches to cope with the troops available.

Embarkation from the Beaches

The first ships of the night flight to arrive off the beaches were minesweepers, which began to anchor off Malo about 2000 on 1st. Here there were already some 3 or 4 Thames barges, besides the paddle minesweeper *Medway Queen* which had arrived some four hours earlier and had been engaged in filling up with troops ever since. The skoot *Lena* had been there since 1300 on the 1st embarking 340 B.E.F. and 6 French troops; she was slightly damaged by air attack during the day, and sailed at 2145 for Ramsgate. By midnight on the 1st-3nd June there were anchored off the beaches the minesweepers *Marmion, Snaefell, Niger, Glen Avon, Emperor of India, Glen Gower* and *Lydd*, besides the personnel ship *Portsdown* and the special service vessel *Royal Eagle*. Loading was a slow process, for there were more ships lying off the beaches than could be loaded by the boats available. Only one ship finished in 3 hours, most of them taking nearly twice that length of time.

The *Emperor of India* was apparently the first ship to sail from Malo, at 0238, with 213 troops. She left behind her, abandoned on the beach, the R.N.L.I. motor lifeboat *Mary Scott* which had ferried troops and towed the *Emperor of*

India's whalers from the shore until she broke down. The *Medway Queen* left at 0245, after nearly 11 hours at anchor during which the ship claimed to have shot down an enemy aircraft on the beach west of Dunkirk. She took 426 troops and some details, including 10 Spanish refugees rescued from an open boat, and the crews of two motor boats, one, the *Aura*, whose engines broke down after some hours of ferrying troops and towing, and another, with name unrecorded, like so many small craft which came to grief in the course of rendering valuable service in the operation. The *Glen Avon*, which sailed a quarter of an hour after the *Medway Queen*, also picked up 24 Spaniards, from the Dutch S.S. *Alphacca*; it is not known how they came to be afloat, for the *Alphacca* was not sunk until 4 April 1942. The *Lydd* left at the same time as the *Medway Queen*, with 200 troops, but defective degaussing then necessitated putting an end to her service in Operation "Dynamo". The *Niger*, *Snaefell*, and *Royal Eagle* all sailed within half an hour of one another. The last ship to leave Malo beach was, by her own account, the *Glen Gower* at 0320, as day was breaking, by which time it was low water. Her Captain, Acting Commander M. A. O. Biddulph, R.N., S.O. 8th M.S.F., reported that the embarkation had been very trying, for the enemy's gunfire during the night had been mainly directed at the beaches, which had been very heavily shelled,[5] and the *Glen Gower* was continually under fire from guns and howitzers on shore from the time she anchored at 2355. "Sight and hearing were almost overwhelmed by the ruddy glow of flames, the flashes of gunfire, the shrieking of shells all around, and the noise of their explosion as they burst". When the *Glen Gower* sailed, with 435 troops, she had lost two of the boats (one from shrapnel hits) which she had brought from England to ferry troops from the beach to the ships, whilst a third was left aground.

Of all the minesweepers that left the beach this night only the *Snaefell* was filled to capacity.

Embarkations at Dunkirk

Although there were more ships than were required off the beaches there was plenty of room at the East Pier, and during the night Rear-Admiral Wake-Walker, who had come over from Dover and was afloat in *M.A/S.B.10*, diverted some of the redundant ships from Malo. He met the minesweeper *Sutton* at 2121 and sent her to load at the East Pier, where she embarked in about 1½ hours

---

5 Report of R. A. Wake-Walker, M.017978/41, p.31.

725 troops, about a third of whom were French. The *Duchess of Fife* arrived off Malo at 2310, found no troops and was sent on to Dunkirk Pier where she embarked 550 men. The destroyer *Venomous* had come over to Malo with a beach party of 10 officers and 90 men; no boats came off from the shore, and at 0200 Rear-Admiral Wake-Walker sent her to Dunkirk, where she took on board 632 troops and sailed for Dover about 0230. The paddle minesweeper *Marmion* was ordered into Dunkirk Harbour at 0200 on 2nd, after waiting in the roads for four hours, and embarked 225 French troops. Ships were led into harbour and allocated to their berths by Commander Maund in a motor boat.

French troops, to the number of 285, were also embarked by the trawler (danlayer) *Strathelliot* alongside the inner jetty: amongst them was General Nicolle and his staff. The *Straihelliot* grounded outside the harbour on sailing at 0130 but got off undamaged, by her own efforts. Another small ship to get away early with French troops only on board was the skoot *Reiger* which left the jetty in the Nouvel Avant Port at 2215 on 1st after lifting 330 men in 45 minutes.

The first pair of destroyers to berth alongside the East Pier were the *Codrington* at 2300 and the *Sabre* a quarter of an hour later. The former embarked 878 troops, the latter 756 both ships taking only 45 minutes. The *Icarus* which left Dover with the *Windsor*, also berthed at 2300 and took on board 677 troops. On the way home, she was in collision with a trawler in Dunkirk Channel, and her further service in Operation "Dynamo" was cancelled.

The *Windsor* did some quick turns round. From the present night's work she returned to Dover with 493 troops, sailed again for Dunkirk and lifted a further 624 men which she disembarked at Dover, leaving about 1900. Before the day was out, she was once more alongside Dunkirk East Pier embarking troops, and she sailed at 0100 on 3rd June, loaded with 1,022 men.

As the *Esk* was unable to sail owing to exhaustion of her crew the *Shikari* proceeded alone. She berthed at Dunkirk at 0125 and left again at 0200 with 470 troops. When the first vessel of the last pair of destroyers, the *Whitshed* and *Winchelsea*, arrived at Dunkirk the East Pier was bare of troops; but by using a loud hailer and making a search a total of 512 were collected. The *Winchelsea* disembarked 1,100 men at Dover.

On this night personnel vessels were not much in evidence at Dunkirk. The *Cote d'Argent* disembarked 1,250 troops in England on 2nd June, the *Newhaven* 716 at Dover at 1030. The *Royal Daffodil*, after bring turned back earlier in the day by a French destroyer, left Margate again at 2200 on the 1st and was back at 0600 on the 2nd with 1,500 troops. The *Manxman* did not arrive at Dunkirk until 0506 on the 2nd, long after daylight; she brought back 177 troops and disembarked them at Dover at 1043. The only other considerable lift from Dunkirk pier by a British ship on this night was by the 220 ton coaster *Seine*, which arrived at Dunkirk about 2000 and, after an air attack lasting about an hour, went alongside the pier and embarked 250 troops. After landing these at Ramsgate the crew, who had worked continuously for four days and nights, had their first night's sleep.

In addition to the large ships, tugs, skoots, drifters and all manner of small craft evacuated troops on this night. Some lay off and were loaded by smaller boats ferrying troops out to them, others went up harbour, past the large ship berths. Over 4,000 men were brought to England on the 2nd June in this way. Of these the skoot *Hondsrvg* took 421 French and the skoot *Reiger* 330 French.

French Embarkations

During the early part of the night 1st-2nd June French troops embarked as arranged at the West Pier, though none of the French torpedo boats which it was intended to employ disembarked troops in England.[6] Looking shoreward from the sea, the characteristic helmets of the endless line of French troops on the West Pier showed up against the glare of fires inland. The town and harbour lay under a pall of smoke. The minesweeping trawler *Chasse-Maree* lifted from the harbour 391 troops, the patrol vessel *Reine des Flots* 350, the cargo ship *Cap d'Antifer* 291, and trawlers and motor fishing vessels a further 548; all these were landed in England.

Four Belgian trawlers brought over 313 troops from Dunkirk on the 2nd June.

British Naval Base Party Embarks, 0245/2

At 0200 on the 2nd Rear-Admiral Wake-Walker in *M.A/S.B.10* went up to the shore end of the East Pier at Dunkirk, to embark the base party as arranged. The party arrived and the M. A/S.B. sailed at 0245.

By this time it was beginning to get light, and although at one time there had been haze which had prevented some ships from arriving the morning was now very clear and the Rear-Admiral decided to get the ships away at 0300 instead of 0330 as originally planned. The Admiralty orders that evacuation by personnel ships from Dunkirk Pier was to continue until 0700 did not

---

6 Rear-Admiral Wake-Walker in his *Report* M.017978/41 p.32 says, however, French T.B's. loaded on this night alongside the West quay.

apparently reach S.N.O. Dunkirk (Appendix R.20, 23); and it is to be presumed that Rear-Admiral Wake-Walker did not receive the orders which went out from the Admiralty at 0115/2, that destroyers were to continue the evacuation until 0700 (Appendix R.21). Although men were still coming down the pier, the Rear-Admiral was unwilling to run the risk of having ships sunk alongside and blocking the pier and harbour. Accordingly he told the ships to leave and himself followed out of harbour the last of them, apparently the destroyers *Winchelsea* and *Whitshed* about 0300.

British Rearguard Held Up

Meanwhile, a most disquieting message had been received at Dover. At 0040 on the 2nd the *Lydd*, while embarking troops off Malo beach, was requested by the Brigadier of the brigade then embarking to transmit to Rear-Admiral Wake-Walker a message from Major General Alexander reporting that on account of French congestion on the mole at Dunkirk a considerable number of British troops were held up and further arrivals were still expected. It was essential that the rearguard of the B.E.F. should embark from the beaches east of the mole, where they were expected to arrive by 0230.

What had happened was, that French troops had cut into the flow of British making their way along the road to the East Pier, by a converging route; and both British and French troops were now being embarked at the pier.

Rear-Admiral Wake-Walker apparently never received the message and knew nothing of the state of affairs at the East Pier until he arrived there at 0200.

Vice-Admiral Dover, who received the message at 0200 at once sent orders to all destroyers of Force K still on the coast, the minesweepers, and the gunboat *Locust* which was off Bray supporting the evacuation by covering fire, to endeavour to embark the British rearguard from the beach, remaining after 0300 if necessary. The coding and transmission of the message took some time, and the orders apparently went out too late; all ships had sailed, and the rearguard could not get away that night. Only the personnel vessel *Portsdown* was left on the coast. This was an undegaussed ship manned by a naval crew, which had anchored off Malo at 2205/1. After running to death her own two dinghies ferrying troops she got hold of a large motor boat, and she sailed about 0400. On the way home the ship collected further troops from a French vessel aground off Dunkirk, and from two further vessels encountered, and she eventually disembarked at Dover 168 British and 450 French.

Bombing of the Hospital Ships *Worthing* and *Paris*
(Appendix S, page 403)

There was a large number of wounded in Dunkirk because no hospital ships had sailed for 24 hours, orders having been given to evacuate fit men in preference, since, other considerations apart, embarking wounded would have taken up too much valuable time. The cessation of daylight sailings rendered it possible for hospital ships to occupy berths alongside, without detriment to the operation, and it was decided to get some of the wounded away in daytime in hospital ships, in the hope that the Germans would respect them.

In order to afford the enemy no excuse to attack a warning signal was sent *en clair* asking for hospital ships to be sent across and stating that for our part we should scrupulously observe the Geneva Convention. Two hospital carriers were despatched from Dover, the *Worthing* at 1255 and the *Paris* at 1648, both clearly marked as hospital ships. Neither of the two ever reached Dunkirk.

At 1433 the A/S trawler *Grimsby Town*, on patrol on Route X, reported that 12 aircraft bearing 90° South Foreland 27 miles (between V and W buoys) had bombed a hospital ship. This was the *Worthing*. Visibility was good. Nine bombs were dropped and the ship was machine gunned, she was slightly damaged by near misses and the *Calcutta* sent the corvette *Mallard* to stand by her. The *Worthing* returned to harbour.

The *Paris*, after running into thick fog, was in clear visibility at about 1900, near W buoy, when two aircraft attacked her, near misses putting out of action her engines and extinguishing all lights. About an hour later the ship was attacked again by 3 aircraft, and received further damage. She was abandoned by all but the Captain and some of the officers, who were shortly afterwards taken off by a fast motor boat which also rescued men from some of the *Paris*'s lifeboats that had been wrecked by bombing. Three tugs, the *Sun XV, Sun IV* and *Lady Brassey* attempted to tow the ship; but at 0400 on 3rd June, after a further air attack, the *Paris* sank ¾ mile east of W. buoy.

Evacuation Figures, 2nd June

A total of 26,256 men were landed in England on 2nd June, 19,561 from Dunkirk harbour and 6,695 from the beaches. Of these totals, French ships working only from the harbour carried 1634, and Belgian trawlers carried 313. The accumulated total of men evacuated to this date was 285,305.

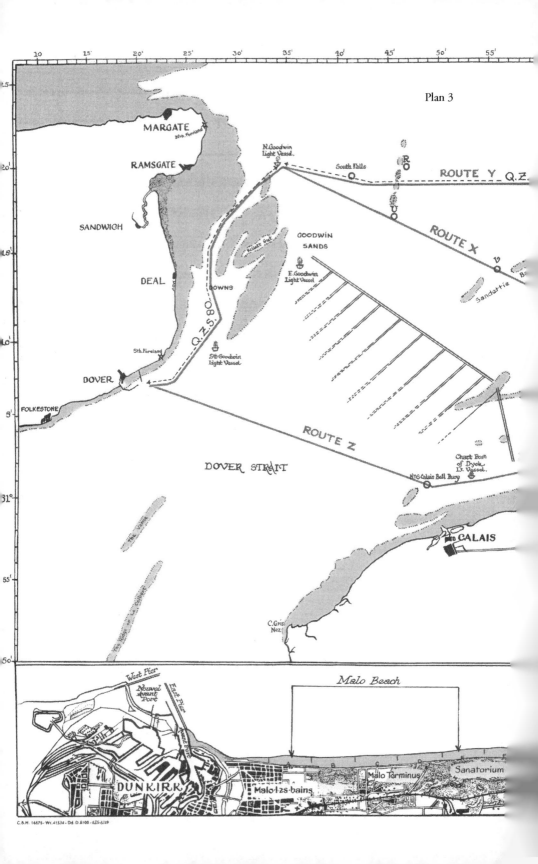

Plan 3

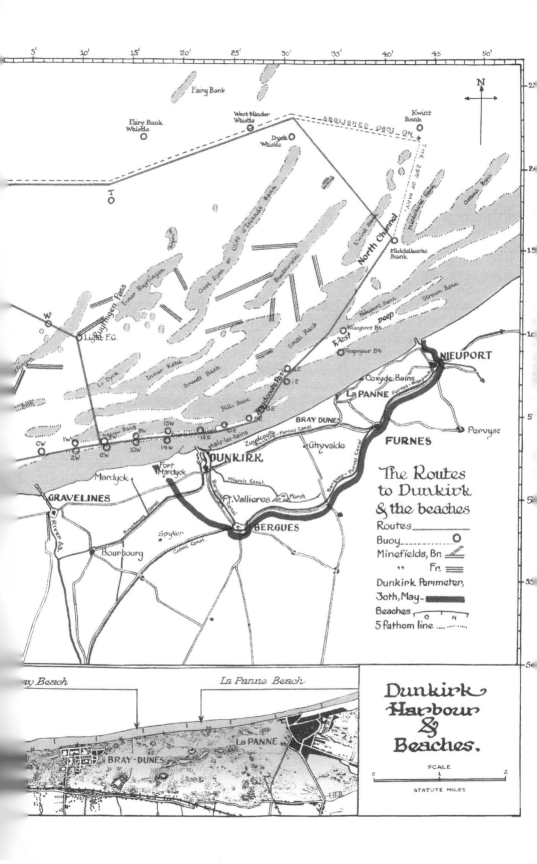

The Routes to Dunkirk & the beaches

Routes ———————
Buoy ————————— ○
Minefields, Br. ⌿
  " Fr. ☰
Dunkirk Perimeter, 30th, May. ▬▬▬
Beaches ╶○──H─
5 fathom line ······

Dunkirk Harbour & Beaches.

SCALE
0   1   2
STATUTE MILES

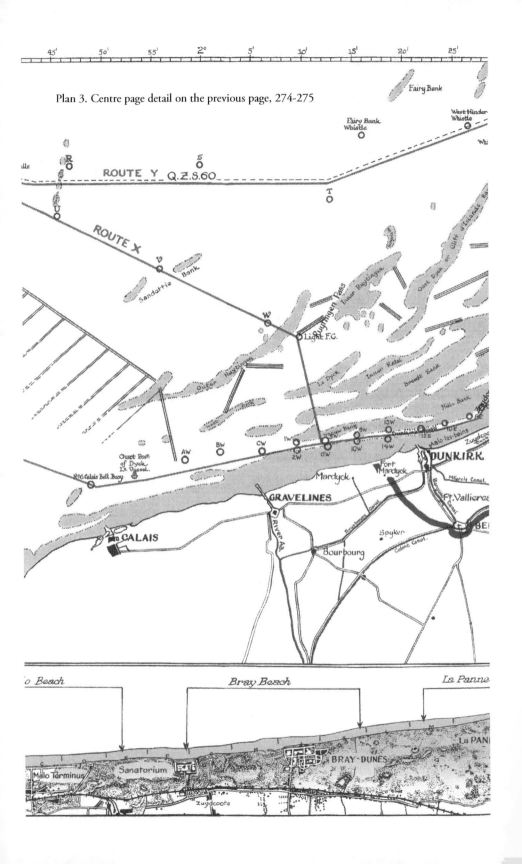

Plan 3. Centre page detail on the previous page, 274-275

The Night 2nd–3rd June – B.E.F. Evacuated 2330/2

Plan for the Night 2nd–3rd June

During the forenoon of the 2nd June considerable doubt existed at Dover as to the numbers remaining to be evacuated from Dunkirk. Captain Tennant thought that about 5,000 British and 30,000 French remained, but it was estimated at Dover, that in addition to the rearguard of 4,000, (who had been withdrawn according to plan, from the front line), a further 2,000 British troops might be found in Dunkirk; while the estimated number of French troops remaining increased during the forenoon from 25,000 quoted on the previous evening to figures in the region of 50,000 to 60,000. Admiral Nord himself estimated the French remaining to number 65,000 of which he hoped that 30,000 might be evacuated on the night 2nd-3rd and the remaining 35,000, who were holding the bridgeheads, on the following night.

Major-General Alexander intended that all British troops should be evacuated by 2400 on 2nd, and Captain Tennant asked for the maximum number of transports to be sent over. During the forenoon of the 2nd a joint Naval and Military conference was held at Dover, attended by Rear-Admiral Wake-Walker who came over from Dunkirk in the early hours, and by Commander J. C. Clouston, Pier Master at the East Pier, to devise a plan to accomplish this. The French Admiralty wished daylight evacuation to be resumed, but Vice-Admiral Ramsay refused to countenance it. The suspension of traffic in daylight hours had the advantage of enabling all transport resources to accumulate during the day and to be held available for a "massed descent" upon Dunkirk harbour during the night. By making provision for increased pier and berthing parties and control of traffic in the harbour channels by motor boats, it was hoped to berth all craft that were available between the hours of 2100 on 2nd and 0300 on 3rd.

At 1052 Vice-Admiral Dover made a signal to the destroyers and minesweepers, which practically amounted to a call for volunteers for the night's work (Appendix T.3):

"The final evacuation is staged for tonight, and the Nation looks to the Navy to see this through. I want every ship to report as soon as possible whether she is fit to meet the call which has been made on our courage and endurance".

The replies showed that there was no lack of willing spirit. Ships were "fit and ready", "ready and anxious to carry out your orders", "ship unfit but ... officers and ship's company are willing to serve in any capacity:" so the replies came in. Only the paddle minesweeper *Medway Queen*, which had returned to Ramsgate three hours earlier on her fifth evacuation trip, was unable to sail owing to the exhaustion of her crew, and was sent on to Dover where additional officers and crew were lent from the *Sandown*, which, like the destroyer *Javelin*, was not degaussed and was consequently forbidden to sail.

It was hoped to avoid on this night the situation which occurred on the previous night, when more ships could have used the pier had they been available, by working out a programme whereby personnel ships, destroyers, fleet minesweepers and paddle minesweepers were to come in at intervals of half an hour to different berths so that three or four ships should be alongside the East Pier continuously. Five inside berths were established, three large, A. B, and C at the outer end of the pier for destroyers and personnel vessels, and two smaller, D and E, at the inner end for minesweepers, all of which were to be kept constantly filled. If all inside berths were occupied a berth might be used on the east side of the pier, though this would not normally be filled.

A pier master (Commander E. R. Lewis, R.N. (Retd.)) was to direct the berthing, and ships were to be guided to their berths by motor boat, two of which were sent over in the afternoon. However, one of the two motor boats was sunk by air attack on the way across with Commander Clouston, and the other disabled.

Special brows and ladders were prepared at Dover, for even at high water the decks of all but the larger personnel ships were below the level of the footway of the pier; and ships were told to have boxes ready to form steps.

Thirteen destroyers were detailed to sail to arrive at Dunkirk at intervals of half an hour from 2100. Groups of minesweepers were to sail at intervals of an hour and a half from Margate, Sheerness, Dover, and Harwich respectively, commencing with the Margate contingent at 2100, and ships in each group were to stagger their time of arrival at Dunkirk.

In addition to the large ships, tugs, scoots, drifters and various small craft were to go over for the night's work, some to lie oft and be loaded by smaller boats, and others to go right up the harbour, past the larger ships' berths.

Demolitions at Dunkirk (Operation X.D.(E))
(See Plan 4)

Now that the operation was drawing to a close it was time to carry out demolitions in the port. The Royal Naval demolition party, which arrived at Dunkirk on the 23rd May, had carried out the placing of demolition charges at the New Lock, the Trystram Lock, and the Guillain Lock in Dunkirk harbour, demolition of which had been agreed upon at an Anglo-French conference as a British responsibility. The French undertook to destroy Le Main Lock and all the pumping stations and the bridges over the locks and canals.

On the 2nd June Admiral Abrial decided to carry out the following modified programme of demolitions:

New Lock – gates and bridge to be demolished;
Trystram Lock – the two gates at the outer and inner ends to be demolished;
Guillian Lock – the two northern gates to be demolished.

All bridges had to be left intact as large numbers of French troops were still withdrawing across them.

By now, however, two of the charges which were not under water and four primers had been exploded by bomb or shell fire; they had been replaced and refuzed, but supplies of demolition stores were running short.

Demolitions were completed by 1400 on the 2nd June, except one depth charge at Guillain Lock which misfired. A second charge which was placed and primed also misfired; and there remained now no further primers or fuzes.

Situation Ashore

Although during the forenoon the military position had seemed critical, on the afternoon of the 2nd the S.N.O. Dunkirk hoped to get the troops away that night. The French were still maintaining the front line except for an area east of Bergues where the Germans had penetrated to a depth of two miles, to Teteghem, on a front of two miles. The French intended to counter-attack at 1500 but in the event this was postponed until 2000 and when it took place some ground was regained. There was no movement in the port. Later Admiral

Nord reported that Bergues was in the hands of the enemy, but they had not advanced beyond. Further attacks were expected by the French this day, when the situation regarding munitions might become critical.

Sailing of the Night Flight from England

The movement from England towards Dunkirk commenced at 1700. The armada consisted of 13 personnel vessels, 2 large store carriers, 11 destroyers, 5 paddle minesweepers, 9 fleet sweepers, 1 special service vessel, 9 drifters, 6 skoots, 2 armed yachts, 1 gunboat, a large number of tugs, lifeboats, etc., formed either in organised tows or proceeding individually. For various reasons, however, not all of these ships evacuated troops.[1]

The composition of the French contingent was not known at Dover. Actually, 3 French torpedo boats, two minesweeping trawlers, two patrol vessels, and 17 trawlers and motor fishing vessels landed troops in England on the 3rd June. One Belgian patrol boat and 16 or 17 trawlers brought troops.

B.E.F. Evacuated, 2330/2

The first destroyers to reach Dunkirk were the *Sabre* and *Shikari*, which sailed together from Dover at 1845. As the latter ship rounded No. 6 W buoy enemy shore batteries opened fire, but caused no damage. Berthing was carried out by an officer with a loud speaker at the pier head. Both destroyers sailed again at 2200, the *Sabre* with 500 and the *Shikari* with 700 troops. The *Venomous*, which arrived at 2150, had difficulty in going alongside the East Pier. This was not a solid jetty, but was built of concrete piles through which the west-going tide set. This, coupled with a fresh easterly wind, made it very difficult for ships to get alongside until the tide turned, about 2300. Rear-Admiral Wake-Walker, who was afloat in *M.A /S.B.10* used the latter to push the *Venomous* in and tried to get other small craft to do likewise. The narrow harbour was now filled with numbers of small French craft of every sort, size and description. At this moment a defect developed in the *M.A/S.B's* clutch, apparently as the result of pushing the *Venomous* alongside, which prevented her from going astern and made turning a most hazardous adventure with boats of all sorts bearing down on her from both directions. The *Venomous* was away again in half an hour, with 1,500 troops, including Major-General Alexander and his staff who had been taken on board *M.A/S.B.10* by Rear-Admiral Wake-Walker and transferred to

---

1 The following ships (other than those on patrol which picked up survivors and landed them) landed troops in England on 3rd June, (numbers in brackets)

the destroyer. The *Windsor*, too had difficulty in getting alongside but managed to clear the harbour with 1,022 troops, one minute before the next destroyer was due to enter. The stream of British troops was evidently diminishing in volume now, for the *Winchelsea*, which arrived at the pier at 2300, embarked only 152. The gunboat *Locust*, however, which sailed two minutes later, carried 800 troops, a proportion of whom were French.

Eight drifters disembarked 1,004 men in England, the *Starlight Rays* bringing 319 of these. The yacht *Sargasso* brought 252. Only two personnel vessels lifted British troops from the East Pier; *the King George V* embarked 1,460 in 27 minutes and sailed at 2225; and the *St. Helier* embarked 2,000 and sailed at 2330 for England.

This completed the evacuation of the British rearguard.

At 2330 Captain Tennant made the welcome signal: "B.E.F. evacuated." He embarked in *M.T.B.102*, together with the demolition party and left for Dover.

A Pause in the Embarkation

After the last of the B.E.F. were clear there was a long pause. French troops should have followed the British rearguard on the East Pier, but they did not appear. The West Quay, however, was crowded with French in their distinctive helmets, though there seemed a scarcity of ships on that side of the harbour. The personnel ship *Royal Sovereign*, which had been joined that afternoon by Commander L. P. Skipwith as adviser to the Master, Captain T. Aldis, went alongside the West Quay at 2130, "handled magnificently, turning and going alongside bows out", as Rear-Admiral Wake-Walker reported. She embarked 1,500 French troops and sailed at 2205 for Margate. The Rear-Admiral also sent the personnel ship *Rouen*, a French cross-channel steamer, to the West Quay. In getting away she got broadside on to the wind and grounded just to the westward of the quay, where she lay, on a falling tide, showing up clearly against an oil fuel fire behind her. A tug was sent to help her but drew too much water and could not get near. However, the ship remained unhit throughout the shelling, and she floated off with the next tide in daylight and reached England safely with 1,286 men.

Rear-Admiral Wake-Walker was unable to discover the reason for the cessation of the flow of French troops to the East Pier; it was apparently caused by the necessity either of repelling a German attack or holding them up to make a counter-attack, for the counter-attack which was to have been made at 1500 to restore the line east of Bergues was postponed until 2000. With destroyers waiting to be filled the situation was most exasperating. Five destroyers had to be sent back to England for lack of troops to fill them. The *Vanquisher* was ordered to return to Dover to 0230, taking only 37 troops which she embarked from a small boat while lying off the harbour. The *Codrington* was also stopped off the harbour by orders at 0050 and had only 44 troops when she sailed at 0250. The *Express* entered the harbour at 0200, found the pier devoid of troops and was ordered by Rear-Admiral Wake-Walker to return to Dover with the *Codrington*. The *Whitshed* found no berth on arrival at 0030 and lay outside with orders to hail and stop other ships from entering. She sailed at 0245 with 82 men collected from small craft. Finally, the *Malcolm* was ordered back at 0248, empty. Thus five destroyer trips were wasted.

Only the minesweepers which berthed at the inner end of the East Pier after the British rearguard had embarked, managed to collect normal quotas from the trickle of French troops.

Dunkirk was the headquarters of a French Naval Command and there was always a considerable number of French marines in evidence. But after the British naval ratings left at 2300 there was difficulty in getting ships berthed, as the French did not replace them.

The *Albury* embarked 200 French troops, the *Duchess of Fife* 300, the *Dundalk* 399, the *Gossamer* 490, the *Halcyon* 416, the *Kellett* 350 French and 14 British, the *Marmion* 198, the *Medway Queen* 481, and the *Speedwell* 300. The *Niger* slipped at 0120 with 430 French troops. While turning an unknown French craft crossed her bows and was rammed, though apparently no damage was done to her. A few minutes later the Frenchman returned and rammed the *Niger*.

Personnel ships did well. The *Royal Sovereign* sailed at 2205 with 1500 troops, the *King George V* at 2225 with 1460, the *St. Helier* at 2330 with 2,000. The *Cote d'Argent* took 955 men, the *Newhaven* 396 French, the *Tynwald* 1,200, the *Rouen* 1,286; but the *Lady of Mann* was ordered back for lack of troops and took only 18 French embarked from a small boat.

Amongst the French ships the torpedo-boat *Bouclier* embarked 340 men and the *La Flore* 410. The patrol vessel *Reine des Flots* "embarked 500 troops during a violent bombardment" and also reported air attacks (from German strays returning no doubt), *en route* to England, for which she sailed from Dunkirk at 2300 on the 2nd. Seventeen French trawlers and motor fishing vessels brought off 1,662 troops and a Belgian patrol boat 229.

Summary of Troops Evacuated, Night 2nd–3rd June

To Rear-Admiral Wake-Walker, who had worked out a programme by which 37,000 men could have been lifted, in addition to those that would get off in small craft, this had been a most disappointing night's work, owing to the long pause when the flow of men to the East Pier ceased for some hours after the British rearguard completed its embarkation, and the difficulty of getting ships berthed owing to the failure of the French to replace the British naval parties after these left Dunkirk. Between midnight on 2nd-3rd and 0300 on the 3rd a lifting capacity of about 10,000 men was left empty.

There were disembarked in England on 3rd June 26,700 troops. Of these, British ships lifted 21,671, French ships 3,216 and Belgian ships 1,812. The great majority of these, namely 24,830, were embarked in Dunkirk harbour, principally by ships berthed alongside, though a few were ferried to ships waiting outside the port. Most of the remainder were taken out of small craft by ships which were likely to reach England with greater expedition and certainty: many of these found in small craft had no doubt come off from the beaches. At noon on the 3rd June the total of troops evacuated had reached 305,078. Of these 211,137 were British fit and 13,004 casualties. Allied fit numbered 79, 808 and casualties 1,129.

Naval Losses 2nd June

The brightest feature of the night was that embarkation in the crowded harbour at Dunkirk had been carried out without disturbance by enemy action, and apart from one motor boat sunk off Malo, and losses off small craft from collision or other misadventure, sinkings were confined to the routes.

In marked contradistinction from the heavy losses of the 1st June only one ship was sunk by air attack on the 2nd. This was the fast motor boat Seaplane Tender *243*, from Calshot R.A.F. station, which sailed from Dover for Dunkirk at 1500 with Commander J. C. Clouston, R.N., pier master of the mole, who was returning from discussing the situation with the staff at Dover, and a naval embarkation party; she was in company with *S. T.276*, the intention being that the two boats should be used as "runners" for Rear-Admiral Wake-Walker during the night's work. At 1855, about 6 miles from Gravelines, 4 enemy aircraft attacked *S. T.243*, which received severe damage from a near miss and was abandoned in a sinking condition. Commander Clouston ordered *S. T.276* to proceed as the enemy aircraft were still continuing to attack, and she subsequently arrived at Dunkirk though too badly damaged to be of service. Commander Clouston was seen later, drowned, and only one officer and one rating from *S. T.243* were picked up and saved.

The transport *Royal Daffodil* nearing Dunkirk from England was attacked by aircraft about an hour after *S. T.243*. The ship was holed but by shifting all movable gear to port and filling boats with water she was listed to bring the damage above water. The engineers, J. W. Coulthard and W. L. Evans kept the motors running although the water had risen in the engine room, and the ship returned to Margate under her own steam. Another personnel ship, the *Ben-My-Chree*, was in collision on the evening of the 2nd shortly after leaving Folkestone for Dunkirk, and took no further part in the operation.

Two further ships were sunk by mines on Route Y on the 2nd June, although it was at first thought they had been torpedoed. At about 1600 the trawlers *Blackburn Rovers* and *Westella* were on patrol near T buoy, when the former blew up on a mine and sank instantly. As the *Westella* closed the position, explosions from the *Blackburn Rovers* depth charges lifted the ship out of the water and put her asdic installation and pumps out of action. About 40 minutes later the *Westella* was herself blown up by a mine between S and T buoys, and commenced to sink. Her depth charges were set to 'safe', and the trawlers *Saon* and *Grimsby Town* sank her and picked up her survivors and those of the *Blackburn Rovers*, some badly injured. (Appendix J.9, J.10).

Two other trawlers met with misadventure on the 2nd, but neither was sunk. Details are lacking but it is known that the *Spurs* and another trawler, probably either the *Kingston Alalite* or *Kingston Olivine*, were both damaged by gunfire. The *Spurs* was on the patrol line, and it is not known how she came close enough to the coast to be damaged by shore gunfire. Gunfire also sank the *Gallant*'s motor boat off Malo at 0210.

Three Belgian trawlers were lost on the 2nd June, though no details are known. These were the *Getuigt Vor Christus*, the O.L.V. *van Vlaandaren*, and the *Sunny Isle*.

Air Co-operation, Night 2nd–3rd June

The R.A.F. flew a patrol over the approaches to Dunkirk from about 2010 to 2120 on the 2nd June, to clear the air for the night's work. No enemy aircraft were seen and no ships reported being attacked. Blenheims of No. 604 Squadron then continued to patrol singly over Dunkirk throughout the night.

Only on three occasions during the 2nd June were enemy aircraft formations reported, and R.A.F. fighters intercepted successfully on all three.

During the early morning hours of the 3rd June the R.A.F. carried out a series of attacks on the batteries near Pointe de Gravelines, to coincide with the evacuation effort. Eighteen Blenheims bombed from a low level (1,000-3,000 feet), but were unable to observe results.

By night, the policy was continued of directing a small proportion of our air effort to targets near the battlefront and the main weight against Germany; and in conformity with this policy twelve Wellingtons attacked Bergues.

Blocking of Dunkirk Inner Harbour (Operation G.K.)
(See Plan 4 and Appendix Z)

The blocking of the inner harbour at Dunkirk was under the command of Captain E. Dangerfield, R.N., and was carried out on two successive nights. The operation was first timed to be carried out on the night 1st-2nd June, but at 1808 on the 31st the Admiralty ordered its postponement.

On each night three blockships, escorted by a destroyer, an MA/S.B. and an M.T.B., were employed. The blockships assembled in the Downs, and (as usual) they were such crocks that one, the French built *Emerald Wings* (Government Yard, Cherbourg, 1920) broke down soon after leaving Portsmouth for the Downs and had to be towed back to harbour; a second could not keep up with the convoy; and a third, the *Moyle*, developed defects which, however, by dint of working on her all night, were remedied in time.

The ships finally employed on the night 2nd-3rd June were as follows:
Vivacious (destroyer)
M.A/S.B.7
M.T.B.107
Blockships *Westcove* 2734 tons, built 1912
Edvard Nissen[2] 2062 tons, built 1921.
Holland Dutch M.V. 895 tons, built 1923.

Early on the 2nd of June Admiral Nord asked that the blockships might be sent over to arrive at the entrance to Dunkirk harbour at 0300 on the 3rd, the latest hour at which they could enter on that night, by which time it was hoped the evacuation would have been completed. During the afternoon of the 2nd however, the Admiralty received a message from the Admiral postponing the

2 This is her correct name

operation because the evacuation would not be completed that night. However, the Admiralty still hoped to complete the evacuation and ordered the blockships to sail.

At 2030 on the 2nd the *Vivacious*, with Captain Dangerfield on board and with *M.T.B.107* in tow and *M.A/S.B.7* in company, sailed from the Downs, leading the three blockships, and proceeded to Dunkirk by Route Z. The *Holland*, unable to maintain the 7½ knots speed of the convoy, was soon lost to sight astern. Nearing Dunkirk a tug (either the *Sun X, Sun XI* or *Foremost 87*), towing a very long line of boats, crossed her bows and still further delayed her, but she eventually made contact with *M.A/S.B.7* and asked to be led into the harbour. The other two blockships had anchored at 0230, and aquarter of an hour later they all three proceeded, with the *Holland* last in the line, to carry out their part in blocking the port. As they neared Dunkirk a "long line of destroyers came out" of the harbour. "Astern of them", stated the *Holland*, "there was a gap of over a mile and then a large and fast transport". *M.A/S.B.7* led the *Holland* through the gap between the destroyer line and the transport. When the latter was 6 cables away, and steaming very fast with the first streaks of dawn behind her, the danger of collision became apparent, so the *Holland* sounded one blast and put her wheel hard astarboard. Lieutenant-Commander E. C. Coats, R.N., captain of the blockship, reported that the transport "had then only to alter course 5° to starboard to pass well clear. ... However, she appeared to alter to port", with the result that she struck the *Holland* hard on the bridge and just before the boiler room bulkhead. The transport, which did not appear to have sustained much damage, backed out and carried on her way. The *Holland* had no buoyancy in hand, and, a few seconds before she was struck, her captain ordered "abandon ship", seeing that it was inevitable she would be rammed. The bows sank at once and rested on the bottom, there being apparently only 8 feet of water under her keel; the stern remained above water. Two seamen were crushed and seriously injured in the collision. *M.A/S.B.7* took off the crew and transferred them to the *Vivacious*. The wreck of the *Holland* came within an ace of being rammed a second time, for two more ships, reported to be destroyers, passed and missed the *Holland*'s stern by no more than a few feet.[3]

---

3 No transport reported being in collision at this time and it has not been possible to identify any of the vessels concerned. The following destroyers and transports sailed from Dunkirk at the times given: destroyers – *Vanquisher* 0230, *Whitshed* 2045, *Malcolm* 0248, *Codrington* 0250 and *Express* 0250; transports *Newhaven* (French 1,888 tons) 0245, *Tywald* (British 2,376 tons) 0300, *Rouen* (French 1,882 tons time not known but ship was in Dunkirk in the early hours of 3rd June), and *Côte d'Argent*

At 0300 the blockship *Westcove* entered Dunkirk, followed ten minutes later by the *Edvard Nissen*. Both ships proceeded into the channel leading to the inner harbour. When in her allotted position the *Westcove* put her wheel hard astarboard to ram the Inner Western Jetty, but her bows struck mud about 50 feet from the pier, with the ship at an angle of about 30° across the channel. By going full speed ahead on the engines, the athwartship's angle was increased to 50°.

As the *Edvard Nissen* came in with the intention of ramming the East Pier she endeavoured to strike the *Westcove*'s stern a glancing blow in order to increase her angle to the channel before scuttling herself; but underestimating the strength of the ebb stream she passed close under the *Westcoves* stern, and rammed the East Pier abreast of the latter. Letting go an anchor, she applied full port helm with all engine power to increase the blocking angle. The *Westcove* now fired her scuttling charges, which probably owing to coal gas in the bunkers, caused a large column of flame and smoke to envelop the ship's stern. When this had dissipated, the crew, who had pulled clear in their boat, saw that the *Westcove* had slid off the sloping bank of the channel and was lying on an even keel in the line of the piers, almost in mid stream, thus causing a minimum of obstruction. Between the sterns of the two ships there was now a gap of 80 feet which was reduced to 50 feet by heaving on a hawser run by the *Edvard Nissen*'s motor boat from the ship's stern to the *Westcove*. No more could be done and the *Edvard Nissen* abandoned ship and fired her scuttling charges from the boat. *M.A/S.B.7* took out both ship's crews to the *Vivacious*.

(French 3,047 tons, time not known but ship landed troops at Dover on 3rd June).

The Final Night, 3rd–4th June

Decision to Terminate Evacuation after Night 3rd–4th June
(Appendix V, page 407)

After the last ship quitted Dunkirk at daylight on 3rd June a large number of French troops still remained behind, and it was decided at Dover that the evacuation must continue.

There was no certainty that the coming night would see the end of the operation. Admiral Nord stated in a situation report timed 0403 June 3rd, that as enemy attacks were probable during the day the situation concerning munitions might become critical; but the message was much mutilated, and the possibility that exhaustion of ammunition might prevent the continuance of resistance after the night 3rd-4th June was apparently not taken into account at Dover.

Vice-Admiral Ramsay, who had no reliable information of the number of French troops still to be evacuated but was aware that the figure was considerable and conscious that it was his duty to our Allies to continue evacuation as long as any French troops offered themselves for embarkation, was faced with a situation with which the forces remaining at his disposal might, with the best will in the world, be unable to cope.

The operation which had been in progress for the past nine days was of a nature unprecedented in naval warfare, and imposed on the crews of ships engaged an unprecedented strain. Officers and men had not only to cope with the ordinary hazards of the war – such as bombing on an unparalleled scale, frequent shelling, constant working in mined waters, and rescue work under most unpleasant conditions – but were also exposed to the exhaustion produced through having their mess decks and every other available space in their ships constantly crowded with troops. This precluded rest for the watch below, the preparation and enjoyment of proper meals, and such meagre amenities as a small ship operating in face of the enemy could offer. Stokers suffered equally with the seamen because, owing to the physical exhaustion of boats' crews after hours of work, relief crews of stokers were frequently provided from amongst the many who volunteered.

Even as early as the 28th May the strain was beginning to tell. Lieutenant P. F. S. Gould, R.N. of M.T.B. 16, working off Bray Beach, reported: "Comparatively fresh appearance of troops ... contrasted increasingly as the evacuation progressed with the evidence of strain shown by ship's companies of H.M. ships."[1] Exhaustion was particularly marked in the destroyer force, the remnants of which had been executing a series of round trips without intermission for several days. Some of the ships had been working off the coasts of France and the Low Countries for the two weeks preceding the beginning of Operation "Dynamo", engaged on various duties such as evacuating refugees and giving supporting fire to the army and evacuating Boulogne, work which had imposed an intense strain and resulted in heavy losses of ships and men. Vice-Admiral Ramsay consequently represented to the Admiralty that continuance after the night of 3rd-4th June of the demands made by the evacuation would subject a number of officers and men to a test that might be beyond the limit of human endurance, and he requested that fresh forces should be employed if evacuation continued after the coming night, any consequent delay being accepted. The Admiralty had already (2312/2) undertaken that ships would be provided and air protection continued for the evacuation of French troops on the night 3rd to 4th June, and they now urged the French Admiralty to complete the evacuation on this night. To this the French agreed.

Plan for the Night

For this last night it was decided to cut down by one hour the time for embarkation, and the maximum effort was to be made, with such ships as remained available, between the hours of 2230/3 and 0230/4. From the East Pier, liftings were to be made by personnel vessels, destroyers, and paddle minesweepers; ships were to be sent to the entire length of the pier as fast as they could be received, and it was estimated that accommodation would thus be provided for 14,000 men. Drifters and small craft were to go right up to the quays and docks of the inner harbour. French ships, for which no numbers could be estimated, were to be responsible for evacuation from Malo beach, the Quai Felix Faure, and the New Avant Pert (West Pier); from the latter pier the remaining British ships

1 M.011S83/40, p.38.

(minesweepers other than paddle, corvettes and skoots) would also lift troops, to the number of 5,000. The gunboat Locust was to remain outside and receive loads ferried out to her by small boats.

It was intended to employ on the work a force of 9 personnel vessels, 9 destroyers (all that were available), 4 paddle minesweepers, 7 fleet minesweepers, 9 drifters, the Locust, 2 corvettes, 4 French torpedo boats, and a number of organised motor boats flotillas including lifeboats from Ramsgate and Dover, together with a large number of French and Belgian fishing vessels. Eleven small French ships and 3 small tugs left Cherbourg for Dover on the night 2nd-3rd June; Le Havre was scheduled to send 8 trawlers, 2 minesweepers, 1 tug, and 20 small dinghies; and Fecamp sent 14 trawlers.[2]

During the afternoon of the 3rd the French authorities transmitted the figure of French troops still remaining in Dunkirk. This was about 30,000, a proportion of whom belonged to other than combatant units. The total capacity of the lifting force, if used to the full, was 30,000, but this was about 5,000 more than the facilities within the port would permit of being embarked in 4 hours, even if the French troops moved with the greatest rapidity at all points of embarkation. On previous occasions there had been some instances of difficulty in persuading French troops to embark otherwise than as complete units. Vice-Admiral Ramsay consequently impressed on the French liaison officers the necessity of speed, and he added a number of French officers and ratings to the augmented pier parties which were despatched to Dunkirk at 2200, in advance of the evacuation force. Captain de Revoir, the French Naval Attache, also crossed over to assist.

There were still many British wounded in Dunkirk, and Admiral Nord was asked to make special arrangements to evacuate as many as possible in return for the effort the British were making on behalf of the French Army.

---

2 The following ships landed troops in England on 4th June (numbers landed in brackets): British - destroyers *Express* (611), *Malcolm* (736), *Sabre* (592), *Shikari* (383), *Vanquisher* (414), *Venomous* (1200), *Whitshed* (444); Corvettes *Guillemot* (460), *Kingfisher* (200, transferred to trawler off Dunkirk on account of collision damage); Gunboat *Locust* (196); Minesweepers *Albnry* (400), *Halcyon* (501), *Kellett* (30), *Leda* (500), *Medway Queen* (266), *Princess Elizabeth* (329), *Queen of Thanet* (150), *Speedwell* (396); Trawler *Saturn* (418); Drifters *Forecast* (123), *"L.H.W.D."* (90); Skoots *Bornrif* (96), *Hondsrug* (308), *Pascholl* (255), *Ruja* (300); Yacht *Gulzar* (140); Personnel vessels *Autocarrier* (712), *Canterbury* (659), *Cote d'Argent* (1349), *King George V* (817), *Lady of Mann* (1244), *Newhaven* (729), *Princess Maud* (1270), *Royal Sovereign* (took the place of *Manxman* which refused to sail).

Air Protection

Coastal Command were to provide protection for shipping between Dover and Dunkirk during the period from 1930 on the 3rd until dark.

Fighter Command was to maintain a continuous patrol by one Blenheim over the Dunkirk area during the dark hours. Fighter protection over the Dunkirk area and shipping in the Channel was arranged for first light, the intention being that Fighter Command should patrol from 0345 to 0600 on June 4th, and Coastal Command from 0600 to 0800. The execution of the first part of this programme was hindered, and that of the second part prohibited by fog which, however, no doubt supplied an even more thorough form of protection for the ships.

From 0430 to 0615 four Spitfire squadrons were on the line, but encountered no enemy aircraft. Fog rendered their landing in England difficult on their return. Hurricane squadrons continued the patrol, reaching the Dunkirk area about 0530: again no enemy aircraft were encountered, and again great difficulty was experienced in landing, one squadron losing 4 aircraft. With this unfortunate anti-climax, the fighter patrols over Dunkirk came to an end.

The Scene at Dunkirk 2200, 3rd June

Movements from England of the 50 or so ships and numerous small craft for the night's evacuation commenced according to plan. Rear-Admiral Wake-Walker, who had come over to Dover earlier in the day for consultation, returned to Dunkirk, arriving at 2200 in *M.T.B.102* "to find the harbour swarming with French fishing craft and vessels of all sorts. They were yelling and crowding alongside the East Pier which was already thick with French troops. At one time it looked as if they would get in the way of the transports and destroyers which were on their way, but I managed to get them to go on up the inner harbour and out of the way in time."[3]

"The congestion," said Lieutenant J. N. Wise, R.N.V.R., one of the officers of the skoot *Pascholl* which arrived at Dunkirk at 2300, "was chaotic, ships going astern into others coming ahead. French destroyers shrieking on their sirens, small craft nipping here and there, rendering the exit most dangerous."

The numerous wrecks in the harbour and its approaches increased the difficulty and danger of entering. In addition to old wrecks marked on the charts there were now a dozen or more new ones, 3 to the west, and 9 to the east, half

3 M.017978/41 Report of R. A. Wake-Walker, p.37.

of them in the fairway; and more wrecks lay in the harbour. One lay alongside the East Pier; there was a wrecked trawler off the end of the piling on the west side of the Channel leading up harbour and blockships in the Channel, though luckily the tide was high.

Off the Thanet Coast and in mid-Channel there was thick fog (the *Royal Sovereign*, 40 minutes out from Margate, reported visibility nil), though the ships were spared this added difficulty at Dunkirk where a fresh easterly wind was blowing and there was a choppy sea at the entrance.

Casualties from Collison and Grounding

It was under conditions such as these that the corvette *Kingfisher*, which had embarked 200 French troops at the West Pier between 2255 and 2319, was rammed when just clear of the harbour entrance by the French trawler *Edmond Rene*; her port bow, 20 feet from the stern, was opened up to the water line, cutting her degaussing circuits. The collision caused the two ships to swing alongside one another, and the troops trans-shipped to the trawler, which was undamaged. The *Kingfisher*, making a little water, proceeded towards England at 7 knots, eventually joining company with the minesweeper *Leda*, another collision casualty.

The *Leda*, having embarked 484 French troops, had pushed off from the West Pier about an hour after the *Kingfisher*. At 0300, on the way back to Margate, the ship ran into the prevailing fog, and off the Goodwin Light Buoy she ran down the Belgian trawler *Marechal Foch*. The *Ledas* bows were damaged, and for a while the minesweeper *Albury*, which had sailed from the West Pier at about the same time as the *Leda*, with 400 troops, stood by her; but the *Ledas* forward bulkhead held, so the ship continued on her way to Margate, escorted for a while by the *Kellett* until the latter had to break off to assist a ship in greater trouble and left her with the *Kingfisher* as companion in misfortune. The fog was thick at Margate, and in the roads the *Kingfisher* was rammed once more, the personnel vessel *King George V* hitting her on the starboard bow, though only minor damage was caused.

Meanwhile, the *Marechal Foch* had sunk. In economy of operation this Belgian trawler seems to have been unequalled, for despite the fact that her entire complement consisted only of the Master, Captain P. Lusyne, and one man, (F. Decoster), she had embarked no less than 300 troops. To accomplish this, the ship had lain alongside the quay at Dunkirk since the 2nd of June, for she had grounded on the falling tide and did not get away until the night of the

3rd-4th. It is satisfactory to know that the Captain and his crew were picked up and landed at Dover; but half of the 300 troops she was carrying were drowned. The French M.T.B. *V.T.B.25* which was bringing Admiral Abrial from Dunkirk picked up some but was hampered by a propeller disabled by wreckage, and some were rescued by the destroyer *Malcolm*, which left Dunkirk at 0245 and reported picking up, in fog near the North Goodwin, survivors of an unknown "schuyt" which had been sunk in collision with a minesweeper.

Another ship that grounded in Dunkirk and was lost in consequence, was the Skoot *Lena*. This vessel had sailed from England at 1530 on the 3rd June, in company with four other skoots, the *Pascholl* (S.O.), *Hondsrug*, *Bornrif*, and *Reiger*. The latter ran aground on the Ouern Sand soon after leaving Ramsgate, and was left behind. Going alongside the "middle pier of Avant Port" at Dunkirk (probably the West Quay or Guiding Jetty, or possibly the Inner Western Pier) the *Lena* grounded at about 2300. A tug was asked for, but none was available and attempts made to tow her off by the *Bornrif* and a British drifter were unsuccessful. At 1045 on the 4th June, two hours after high water, orders having been given that no further embarkation was to take place after daylight, it was decided to abandon ship. Part of the crew embarked in a British drifter, part in a French drifter, and the remainder, including the officers, were ferried to the *Locust* outside the harbour.

It was presumably owing to difficulty of communication that no tug was forthcoming to tow off the *Lena*, for within a few minutes of her grounding a considerable convoy of tugs arrived off the entrance to the harbour. At 1700 on the 3rd the tugs *Sun IV*, *Tanga*, *Sun XV*, and *Racia*, towing between them 14 motor boats, sailed from Ramsgate to Dunkirk. Two of the motor boats, were abandoned on the way across: the *Thark* with foul propeller and rudder, the *Santosy* on account of water in the petrol; while the *Diana Mary* was abandoned at Dunkirk with engine trouble (though she eventually returned to Dover with 28 troops), and the barge of the Admiral Superintendent, Portsmouth, piled up on some submerged masonry in Dunkirk harbour and was abandoned. After waiting off Dunkirk since 2300 on the 3rd, the four tugs were ordered at about 0200 on the 4th to go alongside the (East) Pier and embark as many troops as possible, and by the time they were "ordered to clear out" they had collected 203 between them. Of the 14 motor boats which started from Ramsgate with the tugs only 5 or 6 found their way back; all the remainder were abandoned for one reason or another.

Embarkations at the West Pier (see Plan 4, page 262)

Owing to confusion of nomenclature it is impossible in every case to specify definitely at which of the west piers or jetties the ships (other than destroyers and personnel vessels which berthed at the east pier) embarked their troops. In the western part of the port, reading from west to east, were (1) the West Pier (termed western jetty in the Sailing Directions), (2) the West Quay or Guiding Jetty, and (3) the Inner Western Pier (the inner or old western jetty of the Sailing Directions). Of the other three skoots that came over with the *Lena*, the *Bornrif* stated that she embarked 96 troops at the "West Mole" between 2230 on the 3rd and 0100 on the 4th, and the *Hondsrug* 308 at the "West Pier" between 2245 and 0000; while the *Pascholl*, which had been commanded by four different captains in 8 days, does not specify from which part of the port she lifted the 255 troops with which she sailed at 0030. Another skoot, the *Rina*, which had spent 24 hours at Dunkirk, sailed about this time with 300 troops.

The corvette *Guillemot*, which had come over with the *Kingfisher*, went to the "Western mole" and secured ahead of the minesweeper *Speedwell* at 2355, leaving again at 0154 with French troops "embarked to capacity" (460). This was her first and only trip, her previous service having been as base ship at Margate. The *Speedwell* which had berthed nearly an hour earlier than the *Guillemot*, took off 396 French troops, and the *Halcyon*, which had sailed from Dover in her company, 501.

The minesweeper *Kellett* grounded forward against the western breakwater on a falling tide when she attempted to go alongside at 0100. It was an anxious moment, for almost simultaneously there same a report that 6 enemy T.B.Ds. were proceeding south-westward from off Ostend; but the motor lifeboat *Greater London* towed the *Kellett*'s stern away from the wall and enabled her to back away. She embarked a few troops from motor boats and sailed for Margate at 0220 by orders of Rear-Admiral Wake-Walker, for the West Pier was occupied and it would be some time before she could be loaded, and the Rear-Admiral feared that so slow a ship might not be able to reach England while our fighter patrols were operating. Two of the personnel ships were sent by Rear-Admiral Wake-Walker to the West Pier instead of to the East Pier, since the former was continuously crowded with French troops, whereas at the East Pier there were gaps in the flow of men. One of the two, the *Royal Sovereign*, embarked 1,350 men and sailed "overladen", half an hour after she should have been clear.

Among the many ships and craft of which few or no details are recorded were the trawler *Saturn* which brought 418 troops to England, and the yacht *Gulzar* which brought 140. An unknown drifter brought 90, and 260 troops boarded the sailing barge *Beatrice Maud*, while she was lying at Dunkirk abandoned by her crew, and were picked up in mid-Channel and towed to Dover by a destroyer on the 5th June.

The *Leda* paid tribute in her report to the excellent arrangements at West Pier for the embarkation on this night. Commander H. R. Troup R.N., on the staff of Rear-Admiral A. H. Taylor, "Dynamo" Maintenance Officer, assumed charge at the Centre Pier at 2230, making ships fast, finding out the number of men they could take and then getting the French officers to assist him to embark the troops quickly. Commander Troup estimated that he embarked at least 10,000 troops.

Embarkations at the East Pier

Meanwhile, there had been some heavy liftings of troops from the East Pier despite a hold up which threw out the programme of ships entering the harbour and caused great congestion in the entrance. The flow of French troops to the East Pier was better than on the preceding night, though there were some bad pauses.

The first ship to arrive off the pier was the destroyer *Whitshed* at 2215, with Commander H. J. Buchanan, R.A.N. and pier party on board. In consequence of the fresh easterly wind and the west going tide the ship could not get alongside the East Pier, where there was nobody who could be persuaded to take a line. However, after disembarking part of her pier party into Rear-Admiral Wake-Walker's M.T.B. for transfer to the pier, she got her bows alongside the personnel ship *Autocarrier* and her stern alongside the *Sabre* and commenced embarking troops. The *Sabre* had been working since 30th May with a compass damaged and rendered unreliable by a shell splinter, and had been led across by the *Venomous*. She got away from the East Pier at 0025 with 592 troops and followed other ships towards England until they were lost to sight near U buoy at the south end of the South Falls. This was within hearing of the North Goodwin Light Vessel, which the *Sabre* located by sound, subsequently proceeding from buoy to buoy until she reached Dover at 0500.

When the *Autocarrier* left in her turn at 0035 she carried 712 French troops. The *Canterbury* left ten minutes later with 659, while the *Cote d'Argent* had shoved off from the pier five minutes earlier with 1,349 troops. After these three practically simultaneous sailings of personnel ships some time elapsed before another bunch got away. The *Princess Maud* had berthed at the extreme end of the pier, and sailed at 0150 with 1,270 troops and "dogs of all kinds" that managed to get aboard. The *Lady of Mann* which berthed about the time when the first three personnel vessels left, took 1,244 troops at 0200. The *Tynwald* seems to have been the last to leave the East Pier. She sailed at 0305 with the record lift, only equalled by the *Scotia* on 29th May, of 3,000 French troops: in 4 trips she had evacuated 8,953 men. With a single exception all destroyers had now gone; the *Malcolm* went at 0245 with 736 troops, *Vanquisher* at 0240 with 414, and the *Venomous*, which had arrived at 0245 to find the harbour very congested and was ordered to wait outside until 0130, took out no less than 1,200 troops. In four days the *Venomous* had made 5 trips, evacuating 4,410 men in all.

The British pier party was taken off by the destroyer *Express* which, owing to fog, did not arrive at Dunkirk until 0230 on the 4th. She left half an hour later, having embarked 611 troops. The *Locust* also, after embarking troops ferried out to her from 2300, came alongside the East Pier at 0225, and when she sailed ten minutes later had on board 196 troops.

Mining of the *Emile Deschamps*

The personnel vessel *King George V* which left the East Pier about 0300 with 817 troops, ran into thick fog off the English coast. About 0615, near the Elbow Buoy 2½ miles east of the North Foreland, she passed a "small French naval vessel." Suddenly there was a heavy explosion astern of her, and within a minute the vessel had sunk.

The small French ship was the Fleet Auxiliary *Emile Deschamps* which had sailed from Dunkirk for England at about 2100 on 3rd June, crowded with troops and refugees. About 0558 the minesweeper *Albury*, 5 cables ahead of her, gave her a course for the North Goodwin Light Vessel, which the French ship had missed. A quarter of an hour later the *Emile Deschamps* struck the magnetic mine which sank her.

Several vessels were near and hastened to rescue the survivors. The firefloat *Massey Shaw*, on passage from Ramsgate to London, was only 200 yards away at the time and picked up 40, reported to be all sailors, which she transferred to the *Albury*. The *King George V* lowered four boats and picked up 67. The minesweeper *Kellett*, called up by signal from the *Albury*, rescued some very badly injured people as did also H.M.S. *Nelson*'s motor boat, whose log contains the apparently, but no doubt unintentionally, casual entry: "2400. L/Sea. Eggington lost overboard with candle-lantern." Fog came down again as the rescue operations were completed. Among the survivors landed at Margate were 7 French women and a boy.

Blocking Operation Repeated Night 3rd–4th June

Owing to the failure of the blocking operation of the previous night to close the port, the Admiralty, during the forenoon of the 3rd June, ordered it to be repeated on this night with Admiral Abrial's concurrence. Captain E. Danger-held, R.N. was again in charge.

The ships employed were as follows:
destroyer: *Shikari*
coastal craft: *M.A./S.B.10, M.T.B.107*
blockships: *Gourko*, 1975 tons, built 1911, *Moyle*, 1761 tons, built 1907, *Pacifico*, 687 tons, built 1905

The force sailed from the Downs at 2030 on the 3rd by Route Z, *M.T.B.107* being in tow of the *Shikari*, and anchored at 0130 on the 4th between No. 14 W and 16 W buoys, near the entrance to Dunkirk harbour.

At 0230 Captain Dangerfield, who had transferred to *M.A/S. B.10* ordered the ships to weigh and the *Shikari* proceeded to lead them to the entrance. The *Gourko*'s anchor was barely aweigh when a violent explosion occurred aft, caused, it is reported, by a magnetic mine, although the ship was degaussed and had been wiped in Chatham Dockyard as recently as the 31st May. The *Gourko* began to sink rapidly and was ordered to be abandoned. She sank stern first in 3 minutes. *M.A/S.B.10* took off 9 survivors and transferred them to the Shikari. M.T.B. 107 rescued 7 others, some of them from the water. One of the crew was missing, and 8 were wounded.

Meanwhile, the other two blockships carried on with the operation. The *Moyle* rammed the Inner Western Pier abreast the wreck of the *Westcove* and scuttled herself. As she sank, she slid off the bank towards the centre of the channel, as the *Westcove* had done, and finally settled at a slight angle to the line of the channel, her after part being against the *Westcove*.

The *Pacifico* decided to scuttle in the position allotted to the *Gourko*. Her intention was to proceed between and beyond the wrecks of the *Edvard Nissen* and *Westcove* and then drift down between them broadside on. However, the strong current defeated this manoeuvre, so the *Pacifico* rammed the *Westcove* abreast her after hold, dropped anchor into her and secured the cable. The stern then swung over to port towards the *Edvard Nissen*, but, after a certain point, would not turn further owing to the tide race between the two ships. Orders were then given for the scuttling of the *Pacifico*; As in the case of the *Westcove*, this was accompanied by a considerable sheet of flame, probably due in this instance to oil fuel vapour.

The time now was about 0330 and at this juncture shelling recommenced. One shell hit the pier, causing many casualties, for there were still some 200 French troops on the East Pier. General Bathelemy, Commander of the Flanders Garrison, who was taken off by the *Shikari*, stated that 12,000 French troops still remained in Dunkirk. The *Shikari* carried 383 when she sailed from Dunkirk at 0340 by orders of Captain Dangerfield she was the last ship to leave. Apart from an air attack, which caused no damage, her passage home was uneventful.

An M.T.B. had been detailed to evacuate Admiral Abrial but the latter could not be found, and as a matter of fact he was brought out from Dunkirk in a French M.T.B. *V.T.B.25*. Near the North Goodwin Light Vessel the vessel's propeller became disabled by wreckage, and the *Malcolm* towed her to Dover about 0600.

On the conclusion of the blocking operation there remained a gap of about 100 to 120 feet unobstructed on the west side of the channel. Part of this gap was, however, shoal water, because of the shelving bank.

Disembarkation Figures, 4th June

There were landed in England on 4th June 26,175 persons, of which British ships had evacuated 21,600, French 3,838, and Belgian 737. These figures included a number of survivors, both troops and ships' crews, from sunken ships and some refugees. It was recorded that 622 of the total were evacuated from the beaches, but it is doubtful whether any of these were actually evacuated from the beaches, for the figure includes many such as the 43 French troops landed by the *Pangbourne*, who were taken from a French vessel (probably the mail packet *Rouen*) which had run aground on a sand bank: the 260 brought over by the *Beatrice Maud*: a number (apparently 210) recorded as evacuated from the beaches and landed in England but actually ferried from Dunkirk pier to various transports, by the motor launch *Bonny Heather*.

Operation "Dynamo" Completed, 1423/4th June

When the *Shikari* sailed, the enemy were reported to be only 3 miles away. Ammunition in Dunkirk was exhausted, and the troops remaining consisted principally of non-combatant units. Accordingly, Admiral Nord agreed that the operation should be considered as terminated. The fleet of rescue ships was dispersed at 1030.

The decision to terminate the operation was agreed to by the French Admiralty, and at 1423 on the 4th June a message went out from the Admiralty: "Operation Dynamo now completed."

Vice-Admiral Ramsay was aware that the aftermath of the operation would probably be a number of open boats, barges and so forth drifting about in the Channel with troops on board. Air reconnaissances were accordingly carried out on the 4th and 5th. On the 4th a transport was reported lying on its side between Dunkirk and Gravelines and a barge was sighted east of the Goodwins with survivors on board. Two M.T.B.s. despatched by C.-in-C. Nore searched for the transport without success.

Air reconnaissance was carried out on the morning of the 5th but nothing was reported. However, an R.A.F. speedboat carried out a sweep south of a line Goodwins – Boulogne and recovered 33 French troops and two naval ratings. During the day, patrols picked up French troops and brought them in to Dover, Margate and Ramsgate; and troops also arrived in French and Belgian trawlers. It is reported that in all about 1,100 men were brought in during the 5th June.

Analysis of the Operation

Inadequate Planning

Operation "Dynamo" was an improvisation, in which the initiative of those taking part largely took the place of planning. Events on the Continent developed so swiftly and unexpectedly that lack of time prevented any but the most meagre preparation for what proved to be a far more extensive operation than was anticipated.

The problem of evacuating large numbers of British troops from the Continent was not mooted until the 19th May, seven days before the operation commenced; and even at that date it was considered unlikely that it would actually be undertaken. As late as the 24th May it was still uncertain whether the British Expeditionary Force would be evacuated.

Two days later, when the Admiralty ordered the operation to commence, the military situation was thought to have deteriorated so rapidly that a lift of no more than 45,000 troops within a period of 48 hours was considered possible, after which the evacuation would have to be terminated on account of enemy action.

In the event, seven times as many men were evacuated, and the operation continued for 9 days.

The organisation was built up as the evacuation proceeded. A Maintenance Officer to take charge of the small craft was appointed on the 27th May, the day after the beginning of the operation. S.N.O. Dunkirk assumed duty at 1900 on the same day, and S.N.O. Afloat off the beaches two days later. It was not, however, until the 30th May that an S.N.O. arrived to take charge off the French-Belgian coast, together with an N.O.I.C. Beaches and two Commodores to take charge off shore. How great was the Effect of these appointments, will be shown in due course in the analysis of the evacuation figures.

The arrival of beaching craft at the beaches was unnecessarily delayed on the 28th and 29th May, owing to the Admiralty (and the majority of the Naval Authorities who provided craft), directing them to Dover instead of the Downs, as had been requested by Vice-Admiral Ramsay.

Lack of Signal Communications

Difficulties and confusion were caused throughout the operation owing to the absence of efficient signalling arrangements, both locally between Dunkirk and the beaches and between Dunkirk and Dover. The equipment taken by the signal party which proceeded from England to Dunkirk on 27th was inadequate either for inter-communication between the beaches or from the beaches to Dunkirk.

The naval beach parties, as might have been expected, used their ingenuity to improvise local inter-communication arrangements but it was not until the 30th May that a naval wireless set capable of communicating with

England was sent to Dunkirk; until then messages had either to be sent through the French station in an unsuitable code, or fortuitously via any destroyer which might be lying alongside, necessitating a messenger forcing his way along the narrow crowded footway of the pier.

In the absence of efficient communication it was impossible to distribute ships to the best advantage off the beaches or between Dunkirk harbour and the beaches; whilst the uncertainty as to whether the harbour was blocked on the 29th May was responsible for a reduction of 10,000 men in the possible lift during the night 29th-30th.

Air Co-operation

There is no doubt that the R.A.F. carried out, as far as their available resources permitted, all the tasks which they were asked by the Navy to undertake. The odds at which our airmen fought were very long, four or five to one. Formations of single squadron strength or less would boldly attack German groups of forty or fifty machines, usually with success out of all proportion to the odds against them. It was a direct test of British against German quality.

Numbers did not, however, permit of a continuous patrol being maintained over the scene, though 'the whole Metropolitan Air Force, our last sacred reserve, was used. Sometimes the fighter pilots made four sorties a day'. Unfortunately, the troops on the beaches and on Dunkirk piers saw but little of the fighting in the air, for much of the weight of the effort of the Royal Air Force was directed against objectives far inland, to prevent or breakup enemy raids before these reached the beaches and ships. It was the ships that took the brunt of the German attack. Galling though it was to our troops to be bombed and machine gunned with little or no opportunity to defend themselves their losses, grievous enough, were yet never of such severity as to jeopardise the entire operation, as did the losses of ships. However, the system of co-operation in force at that early date, which did not permit of direct contact with R.A.F. operational units allocated for duty with the Naval Command, rendered difficult complete coordination of effort with naval requirements on the spot.

Evacuation Figures Analysed

In analysing the evacuation figures it is necessary to consider separately the rates of lift from day to day and the daily total figures of troops lifted. The former naturally affected the latter; but the days which showed the best rates of lift were not necessarily those giving the highest evacuation total, since circumstances affected the two sets of figures differently and factors which affected one set often had no effect whatever on the other.

The following table shows the number of men from the beaches and the harbour landed daily in England by British ships, and the number of round trips undertaken. Evacuations of wounded by hospital carriers have been omitted, as have also the liftings from the beaches on 3rd and 4th of June, which were largely fortuitous.

1. Landings in England by British Ships

From Beaches

Trips average lift of men

May 27 Large Vessels[1] nil. Small Craft nil

May 28 Large Vessels 13, 318. Small Craft 12, 95. 5,930 men

May 29 Large Vessels 34, 391. Small Craft 3, no data. 13,746 men

May 30 Large Vessels 55, 491. Small Craft 19, 40. 29,512 men

May 31 Large Vessels 50, 376. Small Craft 44, 73. 22,942 men

June 1 Large Vessels 47, 260. Small Craft 44, 53. 17,314 men

June 2 Large Vessels 19, 276. Small Craft 20, 73. 6,695 men

June 3 Large Vessels nil. Small Craft nil

June 4 Large Vessels nil. Small Craft nil

Total 96,139 men

---

1 For the purposes of this Table 'Large vessels' are those whose average lift was over 200 men.

From Harbour

Trips average lift of men

May 27 Large Vessels 7,[2] 1,001. Small Craft nil. 7,011 men

May 28 Large Vessels 17, 698. Small Craft nil. 11,874 men

May 29 Large Vessels 37, 763. Small Craft nil. 28,225 men

May 30 Large Vessels 21, 614. Small Craft 28, 129. 19,491 men

May 31 Large Vessels 46, 652. Small Craft 21, 46. 40,281 men

June 1 Large Vessels 48, 484. Small Craft 37, 116. 42,181 men

June 2 Large Vessels 24, 688. Small Craft19, 93. 17,614 men

June 3 Large Vessels 28, 656. Small Craft 19, 103. 19,530 men

June 4 Large Vessels31, 689. Small Craft 13, 57. 20,518

Total 206,725 men

Note: 1-3 giving the figures of embarkation from Dunkirk.

It will be seen that the average lift per trip from the harbour was nearly double that from the beaches: 396 vessels evacuated 206,725 men from the harbour while 360 vessels evacuated 96,139 from the beaches, i.e., 10 per cent more vessels evacuated $2\,^1/_8$ times as many troops. Against this must be set the fact that the number of large ships engaged in lifting from the harbour was slightly greater than the number that embarked troops from the beaches, viz. 259 against 218; the number of small vessels was approximately equal in each case.

2. Lift per Ship

Type of Ship

Personnel vessels - Beaches 488, Harbour 1,054

Destroyers – Beaches 504, Harbour 751

Minesweepers – Beaches 358, Harbour 432

Skoots – Beaches 280, Harbour 290

Drifters – Beaches 140, Harbour 156

Small Craft (excluding drifters) – Beaches 90, Harbour 116

It will be seen that the average lift of ail vessels was larger from the harbour than from the beaches, and that the difference decreased with the size of vessel.

---

2 5 personnel vessels and 2 armed boarding vessels capable of very high lifts.

The difference was most marked in the case of personnel vessels, which were civilian manned and consequently less efficient in boat work.

The average lift of all types of ship and the time spent in collecting the load at beaches and in harbour respectively was as follows:

Average Lift per Trip
from beaches 344
from harbour 529

Average Number of Minutes Spent
at beaches 345
in harbour 117

One man per minute was lifted from the beaches as against 4.5 men per minute from the harbour.

The average lifts and number of minutes required by large ships to load at beaches and harbour, respectively, from day to day are shown in the following table. Data of waiting times for small craft are incomplete and consequently reliable figures cannot be given; much time was occupied by small craft in ferrying troops to larger ships.

3. Figures for Large Ships

Beaches
Arrival of Ships not Planned
May 28 Rate of lift 1 men, 1 minute. Average Lift waiting time 318 men, 312 minutes
May 29 Rate of lift 1.1 men, 1 minute. Average Lift waiting time 391 men, 358 minutes
May 30 Rate of lift 1.4 men, 1 minute. Average Lift waiting time 491 men, 356 minutes
May 31 Rate of lift 1.2 men, 1 minute. Average Lift waiting time 376 men, 315 minutes
June 1 Rate of lift 0.6 men, 1 minute. Average Lift waiting time 260 men, 447 minutes

Arrival of Ships Planned

June 2 Rate of lift 1 men, 1 minute. Average Lift waiting time 276 men, 284 minutes

June 3 nil

June 4 nil

Average RoL 1:1, Estimated norm RoL 1.1:1.

Average LWT 352 men, LWT 345 minutes. Estimated norm LWT 345 men, LWT 315 minutes.

Harbour

Arrival of ships not planned

May 28 Rate of lift 5.2 men, 1 minute. Average Lift waiting time 698 men, 133 minutes

May 29 Rate of lift 5.7 men, 1 minute. Average Lift waiting time 763 men, 133 minutes

May 30 Rate of lift 5.2 men, 1 minute. Average Lift waiting time 614 men, 118 minutes

May 31 Rate of lift 5.0 men, 1 minute. Average Lift waiting time 652 men, 129 minutes

June 1 Rate of lift 3.4 men, 1 minute. Average Lift waiting time 484 men, 140 minutes

Arrival of ships planned

June 2 Rate of lift 10.3 men, 1 minute. Average Lift waiting time 688 men, 67 minutes

June 3 Rate of lift 7.0 men, 1 minute. Average Lift waiting time 656 men, 94 minutes

June 4 Rate of lift 5.2 men, 1 minute. Average Lift waiting time 630 men, 122 minutes

Average RoL 5.2:1, Estimated norm RoL 1.1:1.

Average LWT 648 men, LWT 117 minutes. Estimated norm LWT 650 men, LWT 125 minutes.

The variations in the daily figures are believed to have been influenced by the factors recorded in the following paragraphs.

28th May

Beaches. Although the rate of lift was average (1:), and the average waiting time corresponded to the estimated norm, the number of men lifted per trip was below normal. This was probably due to shortage of beaching boats. Destroyers, which made 8 of the 13 trips, were new to the work and their lift per trip was only 356 as against a destroyer average of 504 over the whole operation. The *Calcutta's* lift was reduced by the large number of wounded (cot cases) which she embarked.

Harbour. Although the average lift was above normal, the long waiting time reduced the men: minutes ratio to the estimated norm for the operation. The figures of waiting time are not, however, entirely satisfactory; only 10 ships provided data, three of which waited for periods greatly in excess of the average.

Harbour. The increase in average lift without corresponding rise in waiting time is accounted for by the great increase in the number of personnel ships employed and the average lifts made by them on this day. The average lift per personnel ship, which on the 28th May was only 552, rose to 1,520 today.

30th May

Beaches. The increase of 25 per cent in the figure for average lift without corresponding rise in waiting time, resulting in the highest men: minutes ratio achieved at the beaches during the operation, is believed to have been due to:

(a) better organisation consequent upon the arrival of R.A. Dover as S.N.O. on the French coast and of Captain Howson as N.O.I.C. Beaches, together with the employment of two Commodores to take charge off shore at La Panne and Bray; (6) better discipline amongst the troops on the beaches; (c) employment as beaching craft of the A.L.Cs. which began to arrive on the 29th, and the arrival of 12 motor boats for retrieving abandoned pulling boats; (d) absence of enemy air attacks.

Harbour. Although the rate of lift deviated little from the average, both lift and waiting time declined. This was probably the effect of the disastrous air attacks of the previous day on shipping, which resulted in only one destroyer at a time being allowed to enter Dunkirk during the forenoon and early afternoon and perhaps engendered a feeling of insecurity and a wish to get the ships away as quickly as possible.[3]

---

3 This belief is based on the final sentence in Situation Report by S.N.O. Dunkirk

31st May

Beaches. A considerable reduction in average waiting time and a slight rise above normal in average lift gave a rate of lift slightly better than normal. This was due probably to the fact that greater numbers of beaching boats were available. Although during the forenoon conditions on the beaches were very bad they improved greatly during the afternoon and evening. On the beaches, after 1600, the piers of pontoons were largely responsible for the rapid evacuation of troops.

Harbour. Lift was average, but waiting time was high and reduced the men: minutes rate of lift. No valid reason for this can be discovered, and it should be noted that all the figures agree closely with the estimated norm.

1st June

Beaches. The climax of boat shortage occurred on this day, and "increasing enemy air attack caused continual interruptions of embarkation on the beaches and in Dunkirk" (D.R. p. 25). The disastrous figures reflect the serious situation that developed on the beaches about 2030 on the 31st May, when the rate of embarkation fell to about 150 an hour owing to shortage of boats.

Harbour. The interruptions caused by air attacks and shelling undoubtedly accounted partly for the poor rate of lift. A further factor was the berthing of destroyers two or three deep at the East Pier. It is true that some destroyers filled up in less than an hour: the *Vivacious*, for example, out of 35 minutes spent in Dunkirk, was alongside the East Pier for only 15 minutes, during which time she took on board 475 men; and the *Shikari* needed only 20 minutes to embark 623 troops. On the other hand, owing to the state of the tide, the personnel vessel *Maid of Orleans* spent 51 hours at the East Pier acting as a floating pontoon for destroyers, while the outermost destroyer, the Windsor, spent nearly 15 hours alongside.

2nd June

No daylight evacuations took place after the 1st June, all took place at night.

Beaches. The average lift and waiting time were both much below normal. There were more ships lying off the beaches than could be loaded by the boats available; consequently, scarcely a single ship left with a full load of troops. The rate of lift, however, was average.

---

timed 0943: "The moment bombing starts all must shove off and on the signal at 0950:" If this weather persists I want a ship every half hour," which would seem to imply that the single destroyer allowed to enter would remain alongside for only half an hour.

Harbour. The night of the 1st-2nd June saw the introduction of planned arrival and berthing of ships at Dunkirk. This resulted in a marked improvement in the average lift, which was almost the best of the entire operation.

3rd June

The increase in average time spent at Dunkirk during the night of the 2nd-3rd June over the previous night was probably accounted for by the difficulties experienced by ships in going alongside the East Pier. The figure was worsened by the fact that, owing to the cessation of the flow of French troops to the East Pier after the embarkation of the British rearguard at 2330 on the 2nd, five destroyers had to be sent back to England practically empty.

4th June

Owing to chaotic conditions in Dunkirk harbour time waiting to berth averaged no less than 100 minutes. Pauses in the flow of French troops to the piers, and the impossibility of inducing them to embark in quick and orderly manner (which latter factor had also operated on the previous night) sufficed to depress the rate of lift from the high averages of the two previous nights, to the norm for the operation.

Discipline

No instances of naval indiscipline came to light. But in an operation where the level of initiative was very high an unaccountably heavy wastage of small boats occurred from lack of boatkeepers. There were undoubtedly instances where small boats which were brought off from shore to ship manned only by troops, drifted away and were lost after the troops climbed out of them, owing to the omission to put boatkeepers into them.

The state of discipline of the troops had a direct bearing on the rate of embarkation. In the early stages of the operation the troops on the beaches were mainly rear units and indiscipline occurred. The arrival of combatant units soon put an end to this : meanwhile it was effectively dealt with by the British Naval officers and men of the beach parties.

In the early stages the French troops were at a disadvantage as compared with the British in being disorganised and unofficered. Due allowance must be made for the demoralising position in which they found themselves. The language difficulty and the particular system of discipline which rendered the French soldier unwilling to be separated from the remainder of his unit, together with perhaps a lack of sea sense, resulted in the embarkation of French troops being consistently slower than British.

Many reports, however, bear tribute to the discipline of the French troops when properly led; and it seems fitting to take a last look at them as seen by Commander H. R. Troup, who constituted himself piermaster at the Centre Pier on the final night:

> "I would like to put on record the wonderful discipline of the French troops when the last ship left about 0300 [on 4th June].
> About 1,000 men stood to attention four deep about half way along the pier, the General and his staff about 30 feet away; and after having faced the troops, whose faces were indiscernible in the dawn light, the flames behind them showing up their steel helmets, the officers clicked their heels, saluted and then turned about and came down to the boat with me and we left at 0320."[4]

The operation was at an end.

---

4 Commander Troup's Report, R.O. II, p.360.

Notes for following Disembarkation Records

Notes

1. There is a discrepancy of 397 between the military figure of troops disembarked in the U.K. during the period of Operation "Dynamo", 27th May-4th June, 308,491 (c), and the figure computed by H.S./T.S.D., 308,888 (f).

War Office figure (A.G. Stats.) 20 May-4 June 336,427 (a)

Subtract figure of pre- "Dynamo" disembarkations (20-26 May), to equate with naval period 27,936 (b)

Total 308,491 (c)

H.S./T.S.D. figure 27 May-4 June 338,226 (d)

Subtract figures for troops disembarked from French (22,160), Belgian (3,464), Dutch (214), and Norwegian (3,500) ships which are apparently not included in the military figure (a) 29,338 (e)

Total 308,888 (f)

2. H.S./T.S.D. figures (d) (e) are based on check of all ships' reports (British, French, Belgian, Dutch, Norwegian), but the unduly high percentage of round figures in the reports \ leads to the conclusion that some of these figures are approximate. The comparable figure to (d) in the Despatch of Vice-Admiral Dover, M.011883/40, Appendix III, is 338,682 (g), but it is there noted that the List is not necessarily complete and the numbers shown against each vessel are often approximate only.

3. The Dover Report, M.011883/40, Appendix IV and V also gives figures based on the daily disembarkations at ports in the U.K. from 27th May to 5th June as follows:

Accumulated total excluding ambulance traffic 309,682 (h)

Subtract troops disembarked on 5th June 1,096 (i)

Total 308,586 (j)

Add Hospital carriers and ambulance train totals 6,981 (k)

Add French troops disembarked in U.K. from French ships 20,525 (l)

Total 336,092 (m)

(The disembarkations from Belgian, Dutch and Norwegian vessels are presumed to be included in (l)).

4. The Admiralty in a message V.C.N.S. 251300B May, 1943, to B.A.D. Washington for 1st S.L. (War Diary) gave sets of figures as follows:

V.A. Dover's figures – British troops 193,568 (n)

Allied troops 123,095 (o)

Total 316,663 (p)

Lord Gort's figures – British troops 224,585 (q)

Allied troops 112,546 (r)

Total 337,131 (s)

(The following corrections apparently need to be applied to (p) and (5) in order to equate them with one another and with (c) and (f):

V.A. Dover's figure 316,663 (p)

Subtract hospital carrier and ambulance traffic 6,981 (i)

Total 309,682 (h)

Subtract troops disembarked on 5th June 1,096 (i)

Total 308,586 (j)

Lord Gort's figure 337,131 (s)

Subtract pre-Dynamo date figure 27,936 (b)

Total 309,195 (t)

Which compares with 308, 491 (c) and 308,888 (f)).

5. The total figure of troops disembarked from British ships in ports in the United Kingdom during the period of Operation "Dynamo", as given by the War Office (A.G. Stats.) viz. 308,491 (c) is considered the most nearly correct. It differs from the total computed by H.S./T.S.D. by 397 (=0.0013%).

Record of Troop Numbers Lifted from Dunkirk

An analysis of the Allied Ships which took part in Operation "Dynamo" and of the recorded numbers of troops lifted by them from Dunkirk Harbour and the beaches.

British Ships and Troops Landed in England

Cruiser – evacuating troops 1, patrol and other duties –, total 1, lost –, out of action –

Troops from the beach 1,856, Troops from the Harbour – *Total* 1,856

Destroyers – evacuating troops 39, patrol and other duties 2, total 41, lost 6, out of action 17

Troops from the beach 25,901, Troops from the Harbour 70,296 *Total* 96,197

Sloop – evacuating troops 1, patrol and other duties –, total 1, lost –, out of action 1

Troops from the beach 436, Troops from the Harbour – *Total* 436

Corvettes – evacuating troops 2, patrol and other duties 4, total 1, lost –, out of action 1

Troops from the beach 271, Troops from the Harbour 829 *Total* 1,100

Gunboats – evacuating troops 2, patrol and other duties –, total 2, lost 1, out of action –

Troops from the beach 2,046, Troops from the Harbour 1,466 *Total* 3,512

Minesweepers – evacuating troops 36, patrol and other duties –, total 36, lost 5, out of action 8

Troops from the beach 28,705, Troops from the Harbour 17,729 *Total* 46,434

Trawlers – evacuating troops 26, patrol and other duties 26, total 52, lost 12, out of action 3

Troops from the beach 6,271, Troops from the Harbour 3,881 *Total* 5,396

Drifters – evacuating troops 51, patrol and other duties 10, total 61, lost 5, out of action 3

Troops from the beach 1,515, Troops from the Harbour 6,099 *Total* 7,614

Special Service Vessels – evacuating troops 3, patrol and other duties –, total 3, lost 1, out of action –

Troops from the beach 3,507, Troops from the Harbour 901 *Total* 4,408

M.A./S.Bs., M.T.B. – evacuating troops 4, patrol and other duties 9, total 13, lost –, out of action –

Troops from the beach 26, Troops from the Harbour 73 *Total* 99

Armed Boarding Vessels – evacuating troops 13, patrol and other duties –, total 13, lost 1, out of action –

Troops from the beach –, Troops from the Harbour 4,848 *Total* 4,848

Skoots – evacuating troops 39, patrol and other duties 1, total 40, lost 4, out of action 4

Troops from the beach 15,414, Troops from the Harbour 17,284 *Total* 22,698

Yachts – evacuating troops 26, patrol and other duties –, total 26, lost 3, out of action –

Troops from the beach 745, Troops from the Harbour 3,936 *Total* 4,681

Personnel Vessels – evacuating troops 45, patrol and other duties –, total 45, lost 8, out of action 3

Troops from the beach 5,087, Troops from the Harbour 82,723 *Total* 87,810

Hospital Carriers – evacuating troops 8, patrol and other duties –, total 8, lost 1, out of action 2

Troops from the beach –, Troops from the Harbour 3,006 *Total* 3,006

Naval M/Bs – evacuating troops 12, patrol and other duties –, total 12, lost 6, out of action 1

Troops from the beach 2, Troops from the Harbour 94 *Total* 96

Tugs – evacuating troops 22, patrol and other duties 18, total 40, lost 3, out of action 1

Troops from the beach 1,654, Troops from the Harbour 1,510 *Total* 3,164

Landing Craft – evacuating troops 13, patrol and other duties –, total 13, lost 8, out of action 3

Troops from the beach 118, Troops from the Harbour – *Total* 118

War Dept. M/Ls – evacuating troops 8, patrol and other duties –, total 8, lost –, out of action 5

Troops from the beach 200, Troops from the Harbour 379 *Total* 579

Dockyard Lighters – evacuating troops 8, patrol and other duties –, total 8, lost 2, out of action 3

Troops from the beach 418, Troops from the Harbour – *Total* 418

Steam Hopper Barges – evacuating troops 7, patrol and other duties –, total 7, lost –, out of action –

Troops from the beach 890, Troops from the Harbour 1,276 *Total* 2,166

Auxiliary Barges – evacuating troops 8, patrol and other duties –, total 8, lost 1, out of action –

Troops from the beach 706, Troops from the Harbour 550 *Total* 1,256

Sailing Barges – evacuating troops 25, patrol and other duties –, total 25, lost 9, out of action –

Troops from the beach 866, Troops from the Harbour – *Total* 866

R.N.L.I. Lifeboats – evacuating troops 19, patrol and other duties –, total 19, lost 1, out of action 2

Troops from the beach 172, Troops from the Harbour 151 *Total* 323

M/Bs, M/Ls – evacuating troops 203, patrol and other duties –, total 203, lost 81, out of action –

Troops from the beach 1,928, Troops from the Harbour 3,103 *Total* 5,031

Blockships – evacuating troops –, patrol and other duties 6, total 6, lost 2[1], out of action –

Troops from the beach –, Troops from the Harbour – *Total* 1,856

Seaplane Tenders – evacuating troops 6, patrol and other duties –, total 6, lost 3, out of action –

Troops from the beach –, Troops from the Harbour – *Total* –

---

1 Sunk *en route*

Lifeboats – evacuating troops 56, patrol and other duties –, total 56, lost 39, out of action –

Troops from the beach –, Troops from the Harbour – *Total* –

Wherries, punts, dinghies – evacuating troops 16, patrol and other duties –, total 16, lost 16, out of action –

Troops from the beach –, Troops from the Harbour – *Total* –

British Ship Totals

Ships evacuating troops 689

Patrols and other duties 76

Total 765

Of these

Lost 218

Put out of action, by enemy action, by collision or grounding 57

Total 275

Troops landed in England by British Ships

From the Beaches 98,754

From the Harbour 210,134

Total 308,888

French Ships and Troops Landed in England

Destroyers – evacuating troops –, patrol and other duties 2, total 2, lost –, out of action –

Troops from the beach 19[2], Troops from the Harbour – *Total* 19

Torpedo Boats – evacuating troops 12, patrol and other duties –, total 12, lost 3, out of action 1

Troops from the beach –, Troops from the Harbour 6,627 *Total* 6,627

Sloops – evacuating troops 2, patrol and other duties 3, total 5, lost –, out of action –

Troops from the beach –, Troops from the Harbour 1,000 *Total* 1,000

Minsweeping Sloops – evacuating troops 2, patrol and other duties –, total 2, lost –, out of action 1

Troops from the beach –, Troops from the Harbour 2,038 *Total* 2,038

Submarine Chasers – evacuating troops 5, patrol and other duties –, total 5, lost –, out of action –

Troops from the beach 6, Troops from the Harbour 197 *Total* 203

M.T.Bs. – evacuating troops 2, patrol and other duties –, total 2, lost –, out of action 2

Troops from the beach –, Troops from the Harbour – *Total* –

Minesweeping Trawlers – evacuating troops 13, patrol and other duties –, total 13, lost 5, out of

---

2 Picked up from a damaged M/L

action –

Troops from the beach –, Troops from the Harbour 2,665 *Total* 2,665

Patrol Vessels – evacuating troops 5, patrol and other duties 2, total 7, lost –, out of action –

Troops from the beach –, Troops from the Harbour 2,504 *Total* 2,504

Cargo Ships – evacuating troops 8, patrol and other duties 4, total 12, lost 2, out of action –

Troops from the beach –, Troops from the Harbour 2,290 *Total* 2,290

Trawlers and M.F.Vs. – evacuating troops 59, patrol and other duties –, total 59, lost 3, out of action –

Troops from the beach 1, Troops from the Harbour 4,813 *Total* 4,814

French Ship Totals

Ships evacuating troops 108

Patrols and other duties 11

Total 119

Of these:

Lost 13

Put out of action, by enemy action, by collision or grounding 4

Total 17

Troops landed in England by French Ships

From the Beaches 7

From the Harbour 22,153

Total 22,160

Belgian Ships and Troops Landed in England

Patrol Boat – evacuating troops 1, patrol and other duties –, total 1, lost –, out of action –

Troops from the beach –, Troops from the Harbour 229 *Total* 229

Tug – evacuating troops 1, patrol and other duties –, total 1, lost –, out of action –

Troops from the beach –, Troops from the Harbour 183 *Total* 183

Trawlers – evacuating troops 43, patrol and other duties –, total 43, lost 4, out of action –

Troops from the beach –, Troops from the Harbour 3,052 *Total* 3,052

Belgian Ship Totals

Ships evacuating troops 45

Patrols and other duties –

Total 45

Of these:

Lost 4

Put out of action, by enemy action, by collision or grounding –

Total 4

Troops landed in England by French Ships

From the Beaches –

From the Harbour 3,464

Total 3,464

Polish Ships and Troops Landed in England

Destroyer – evacuating troops –, patrol and other duties 1, total 1, lost –, out of action –

Troops from the beach –, Troops from the Harbour – *Total* –

Dutch Ships and Troops Landed in England

Yacht – evacuating troops 1, patrol and other duties –, total 1, lost 1, out of action –

Troops from the beach –, Troops from the Harbour 214 *Total* 214

M/L – evacuating troops 1, patrol and other duties –, total 1, lost –, out of action –

Troops from the beach –, Troops from the Harbour – *Total* –

Dutch Ship Totals

Ships evacuating troops 2

Patrols and other duties –

Total 2

Of these:

Lost 1

Put out of action, by enemy action, by collision or grounding –

Total 1

Troops landed in England by Dutch Ships

From the Beaches –

From the Harbour 214

Total 214

Norwegian Ship and Troops Landed in England

Freighter – evacuating troops 1, patrol and other duties –, total 1, lost –, out of action –

Troops from the beach –, Troops from the Harbour 3,500 *Total* 3,500

Record of British Ships Lifting Troops from Dunkirk

27th may

Destroyers - Harbour 12, *Total* 12

Armed Boarding Vessels - Harbour 2,551, *Total* 2,551

Personnel Vessels - Harbour 4,460, *Total* 4,460

Hospital carriers - Harbour 646, *Total* 646

Totals for the day - Harbour 7,669, *Total* 7,669

28th May

Cruiser - Beaches 656, *Total* 656,

Destroyers - Beaches 2,849, Harbour 8,986, *Total* 11,835

Minesweepers - Beaches 1,082, *Total* 1,082

Drifters - Beaches 1,138, *Total* 1,138

Armed Boarding Vessels - Harbour 1,083, *Total* 1,083

Skoots - Beaches 5, Harbour 150, *Total* 155

Personnel Vessels - Beaches 200, Harbour 1,655, *Total* 1,855

Totals for the day - Beaches 5,930, Harbour 11,874, *Total,* 17,804

29th May

Cruiser - Beaches 1,200, *Total* 1,200

Destroyers - Beaches 6,596, Harbour 6,705, *Total* 13,301

Minesweepers - Beaches 3,099, Harbour 1,953, *Total* 5,052

Trawlers - Harbour 90, *Total* 90

Drifters - Beaches 458, *Total* 458

Skoots - Beaches 1,593, Harbour 2,757, *Total* 4,350

Personnel Vessels - Beaches 800, Harbour 16,720, *Total* 17,520

Hospital carriers - Harbour 833, *Total* 833

Totals for the day - Beaches 13,746, Harbour 29,058, *Total* 42,804

30th May

Destroyers - Beaches 7,968, Harbour 10,862, *Total* 18,830

Gunboats - Beaches 563, *Total* 563

Minesweepers - Beaches 7,455 Harbour 570, *Total* 8,025

Trawlers - Beaches 404, Harbour 674, *Total* 1,078

Drifters - Beaches 1,655, Harbour 804, *Total* 2,459

Special Service Vessels - Beaches 1,200, *Total* 1,200

M.A./S.Bs., M.T.Bs., etc. - Harbour 53, *Total* 53

Skoots - Beaches 6,651, Harbour 662, *Total* 7,313

Yachts - Harbour 1,222, *Total* 1,222

Personnel Vessels - Beaches 3,232, Harbour 3,190, *Total* 6,442

Hospital carriers - Harbour 490, *Total* 490

Tugs - Beaches 190, Harbour 207, *Total* 397

Landing Craft - Beaches 55, *Total* 55

M/Bs, M/Ls, etc. - Beaches 139, Harbour 950, *Total* 1,089

Totals for the day - Beaches 29,512, Harbour 19,684, *Total* 49,196

31st May

Destroyers - Beaches 16,613, Harbour 6,221, *Total* 22,834

Sloop - Beaches 436, *Total* 436

Corvettes - Beaches 271, *Total* 271

Gunboats - Beaches 620, *Total* 620

Minesweepers - Beaches 5,335, Harbour 2,000, *Total* 7,335

Trawlers - Beaches 399, *Total* 399

Drifters - Beaches 1,483, Harbour 1,447, *Total* 2,930

Special Service Vessels - Beaches 1,831, *Total* 1,831

M.A./S.Bs., M.T.Bs., etc. - Harbour 20, *Total* 20

Skoots - Beaches 3,940, Harbour 1,664, *Total* 5,604

Yachts - Beaches 690, Harbour 301, *Total* 991

Personnel Vessels - Beaches 74, Harbour 17,404, *Total* 17,478

Hospital carriers - Harbour 620, *Total* 620

Naval M/Bs. - Harbour 16, *Total* 16

Tugs - Beaches 187, Harbour 32, *Total* 219

War Dept. M/Ls. - Beaches 140, Harbour 180, *Total* 320

Dockyard lighters - Beaches 67, *Total* 67

Steam Hopper Barges - Harbour 696, *Total* 696

Auxiliary barges etc. - Beaches 363, Harbour 300, *Total* 663

Sailing barges - Beaches 13, *Total* 13

R.N.L.I. lifeboats - Beaches 17, *Total* 17

M/Bs, M/Ls, etc. - Beaches 463, *Total* 463

Totals for the day - Beaches 22,942, Harbour 40,901, *Total* 63,843

1st June

Destroyers - Beaches 1,244, Harbour 13,044, *Total* 14,288

Corvettes - Harbour 369, *Total* 369

Gunboats - Beaches 770, Harbour 470, *Total* 1,240

Minesweepers - Beaches 7,733, Harbour 5,086, *Total* 12,819

Trawlers - Beaches 157, Harbour 1,629, *Total* 1,786

Drifters - Beaches 1,279, Harbour 1,689, *Total* 2,968

Special Service Vessels - Beaches 350, Harbour 900, *Total* 1,250

M.A./S.Bs., M.T.Bs., etc. - Beaches 2, *Total* 2

Skoots - Beaches 2,829, Harbour 341, *Total* 3,170

Yachts - Beaches 55, Harbour 1,776, *Total* 1,831

Personnel Vessels - Beaches 145, Harbour 14,390, *Total* 14,535

Hospital carriers - Harbour 417, *Total* 417

Tugs - Beaches 541, Harbour 195, *Total* 736

War Dept. M/Ls. - Beaches 60, Harbour 84, *Total* 144

Dockyard lighters - Beaches 245, *Total* 245

Steam Hopper Barges - Beaches 890, Harbour 580, *Total* 1,470

Auxiliary barges etc. - Beaches 269, *Total* 269

Sailing barges - Beaches 200, *Total* 200

R.N.L.I. lifeboats - Beaches 17, *Total* 17

M/Bs, M/Ls, etc. - Beaches 562, Harbour 1,628, *Total* 2,190

Totals for the day - Beaches 17,348, Harbour 42,598, *Total* 59,946

2nd June

Destroyers - Beaches 512, Harbour 5,630, *Total* 6,142

Gunboats - Beaches 93, *Total* 93

Minesweepers - Beaches 3,106, Harbour 1,970, *Total* 5,076

Trawlers - Beaches 165, Harbour 1,042, *Total* 1,207

Drifters - Beaches 258, Harbour 942, *Total* 1,200

Special Service Vessels - Beaches 126, *Total* 126

M.A./S.Bs., M.T.Bs., etc. - Beaches 24, *Total* 24

Armed Boarding Vessels - Harbour 1,214, *Total* 1,214

Skoots - Beaches 346, Harbour 751, *Total* 1,097

Yachts - Harbour 245, *Total* 245

Personnel Vessels - Beaches 618, Harbour 4,977, *Total* 5,595

Naval M/Bs. - Harbour 47, *Total* 47

Tugs - Beaches 413, Harbour 502, *Total* 915

Landing Craft - Beaches 63, *Total* 63

Dockyard lighters - Beaches 106, *Total* 106

Auxiliary barges etc. - Beaches 74, Harbour 250, *Total* 324

Sailing barges - Beaches 200, *Total* 200

R.N.L.I. lifeboats - Beaches 88, *Total* 88

M/Bs, M/Ls, etc. - Beaches 503, Harbour 44, *Total* 547

Totals for the day - Beaches 6,695, Harbour 17,614, *Total* 24,309

3rd June

Destroyers - Beaches 119, Harbour 4,418, *Total* 4,537

Gunboats - Harbour 800, *Total* 800

Minesweepers - Beaches 845, Harbour 3,578, *Total* 4,423

Trawlers - Beaches 300, Harbour 118, *Total* 418

Drifters - Harbour 1,004, *Total* 1,004

Special Service Vessels - Harbour 1, *Total* 1

M.A./S.Bs., M.T.Bs., etc. –

Armed Boarding Vessels -

Skoots - Beaches 50, *Total* 50

Yachts - Harbour 252, *Total* 252

Personnel Vessels - Beaches 18, Harbour 8,797, *Total* 8,815

Naval M/Bs. - Beaches 2, Harbour 25, *Total* 27

Tugs - Beaches 311, Harbour 383, *Total* 694

War Dept. M/Ls. - Harbour 69, *Total* 69

Sailing barges - Beaches 213, *Total* 213

R.N.L.I. lifeboats - Harbour 103, *Total* 103

M/Bs, M/Ls, etc. - Beaches 11, Harbour 300, *Total* 311

Totals for the day - Beaches 1,869, Harbour 19,848, *Total* 21,717

4th June

Destroyers - Harbour 4,418, *Total* 4,418

Corvettes - Harbour 460, *Total* 460

Gunboats - Harbour 196, *Total* 196

Minesweepers - Beaches 50, Harbour 2,572, *Total* 2,622

Trawlers - Harbour 418, *Total* 418

Drifters - Harbour 213, *Total* 213

Skoots - Harbour 959, *Total* 959

Yachts - Harbour 140, *Total* 140

Personnel Vessels - Harbour 11,130, *Total* 11,130

Naval M/Bs. - Harbour 6, *Total* 6

Tugs - Beaches 12, Harbour 191, *Total* 203

War Dept. M/Ls. - Harbour 46, *Total* 46

Sailing barges - Beaches 260, *Total* 260

R.N.L.I. lifeboats - Beaches 50, Harbour 48, *Total* 98

M/Bs, M/Ls, etc. - Beaches 250, Harbour 181, *Total* 431

Totals for the day - Beaches 622, Harbour 20,978, *Total* 21,600

Grand Total for Ships

Cruiser - 1,856

Destroyers - 96,197

Sloop - 436

Corvettes - 1,100

Gunboats - 3,512

Minesweepers - 46,434

Trawlers - 5,396

Drifters- 12,370

Special Service Vessels - 4,408

M.A./S.Bs., M.T.Bs., etc. - 99

Armed Boarding Vessels - 4,848

Skoots - 22,698

Yachts - 4,681

Personnel Vessels - 87,810

Hospital carriers - 3,006

Naval M/Bs. - 96

Tugs - 3,164

Landing Craft - 118

War Dept. M/Ls. - 579

Dockyard lighters - 418

Steam Hopper Barges - 2,166

Auxiliary barges etc. - 1,256

Sailing barges - 886

R.N.L.I. lifeboats - 323

M/Bs, M/Ls, etc. - 5,031

Total - 308,888

Record of other Ships Lifting Troops from Dunkirk

French, Belgian, Dutch and Norwegian Ships

29th May – French Ships

Torpedo boats and destroyers – Harbour 460, *Total* 460

Minesweeping sloops – Harbour 520, *Total* 520

Submarine chasers – Beaches 6, Harbour 20, *Total* 26

Totals for the day – Beaches 6, Harbour 1,000, *Total* 1,006

Norwegian Ships

Freighter – Harbour 3,500, *Total* 3,500

Totals for the day – Harbour 3,500, *Total* 3,500

30th May – French Ships

Torpedo boats and destroyers – Harbour 2,043, *Total* 2,043

Sloops – Harbour 1,000, *Total* 1,000

Minesweeping sloops – Harbour 581, *Total* 581

Minesweeping trawlers – Harbour 405, *Total* 405

Patrol vessels – Harbour 15, *Total* 15

Trawlers and M.F.Vs. – Harbour 483, *Total* 483

Totals for the day – Harbour 4,527, *Total* 4,527

Belgian Ships

Trawlers – Harbour 100, *Total* 100

Totals for the day – Harbour 100, *Total* 100

31st May – French Ships

Torpedo boats and destroyers – Harbour 1,007, *Total* 1,007

Minesweeping sloops – Harbour 937, *Total* 937

Minesweeping trawlers – Harbour 612, *Total* 612

Patrol vessels – Harbour 346, *Total* 346

Cargo ships – Harbour 969, *Total* 969

Trawlers and M.F.Vs. – Harbour 100, *Total* 100

Totals for the day – Harbour 3,971, *Total* 3,971

Belgian Ships

Trawlers – Harbour 100, *Total* 100

Totals for the day – Harbour 100, *Total* 100

Dutch Ships

Yacht – Harbour 100, *Total* 100

Totals for the day – Harbour 100, *Total* 100

1st June – French Ships

Torpedo boats and destroyers – Harbour 951, *Total* 951

Minesweeping trawlers – Harbour 720, *Total* 720

Patrol vessels – Harbour 379, *Total* 379

Cargo ships – Harbour 1,001, *Total* 1,001

Trawlers and M.F.Vs. – Harbour 916, *Total* 916

Totals for the day – Harbour 3,967, *Total* 3,967

Belgian Ships

Trawlers – Harbour 402, *Total* 402

Totals for the day – Harbour 402, *Total* 402

Dutch Ships

Yacht – Harbour 114, *Total* 114

Totals for the day – Harbour 114, *Total* 114

2nd June – French Ships

Minesweeping trawlers – Harbour 416, *Total* 416

Patrol vessels – Harbour 350, *Total* 350

Cargo ships – Harbour 320, *Total* 320

Trawlers and M.F.Vs. – Harbour 548, *Total* 548

Totals for the day – Harbour 1,634, *Total* 1,634

Belgian Ships

Trawlers – Harbour 313, Total 313

Totals for the day – Harbour 313, *Total* 313

3rd June – French Ships

Torpedo boats and destroyers – Harbour 769, *Total* 769

Submarine chasers – Harbour 50, *Total* 50

Minesweeping trawlers – Harbour 157, *Total* 157

Patrol vessels – Harbour 578, Total 578

Trawlers and M.F.Vs. – Beaches 1, Harbour 1,662, *Total* 1,663

Totals for the day – Beaches 1, Harbour 3,216, *Total* 3,217

Belgian Ships

Patrol boat – Harbour 229, *Total* 229

Trawlers – Harbour 1,583, *Total* 1,583

Totals for the day – Harbour 1,812, *Total* 1,812

4th June – French Ships

Torpedo boats and destroyers – Harbour 1,416, *Total* 1,416

Submarine chasers – Harbour 127, *Total* 127

Minesweeping trawlers – Harbour 355, *Total* 355

Patrol vessels – Harbour 836, *Total* 836

Trawlers and M.F.Vs. – Harbour 1,104, *Total* 1,104

Totals for the day – Harbour 3,838, *Total* 3,838

Belgian Ships

Tug – Harbour 183, *Total* 183

Trawlers – Harbour 554, *Total* 554

Totals for the day – Harbour 737, *Total* 737

Grand Total for Ships

French Ships

Torpedo boats and destroyers – 6,646

Sloops – 1,000

Minesweeping sloops – 2,038

Submarine chasers – 203

Minesweeping trawlers – 2,665

Patrol vessels – 2,504

Cargo ships – 2,290

Trawlers and M.F.Vs. – 4,814

Total – 22,160

Belgian Ships

Patrol boat – 229

Tug – 183

Trawlers – 3,052

Total – 3,464

Dutch Ships

Yacht –214

Total – 214

Norwegian Ships

Freighter – 3,500

Total – 3,500

Summary of Operation "Dynamo"

Summary of Ships taking part

British – evacuating troops 689, on patrol 76, total 765, lost 218, out of action 57

French – evacuating troops 108, on patrol 11, total 119, lost 13, out of action 4

Belgian – evacuating troops 45, on patrol –, total 45, lost 4, out of action –

Polish – evacuating troops –, on patrol 1, total 1, lost –, out of action –

Dutch – evacuating troops 2, on patrol –, total 2, lost 1, out of action –

Norwegian – evacuating troops 1, on patrol –, total 1, lost –, out of action –

Total – evacuating troops 845, on patrol 88, total 993, lost 236, out of action 61

Allied Ships Summary of Troops Transported

British – from the beaches 98,754, from the harbour 210,134, *total* 308,888

French – from the beaches 7, from the harbour 22,153, *total* 22,160

Belgian – from the beaches –, from the harbour 3,464, *total* 3,464

Polish – from the beaches –, from the harbour –, *total* –

Dutch – from the beaches –, from the harbour 214, *total* 214

Norwegian – from the beaches –, from the harbour 3,500, *total* 3,500

Total – from the beaches 98,761, from the harbour 239,465, *total* 338,226

Disembarkation Summary

26th May – from the beaches –, from the harbour –, *total* –

Accumulated total –

27th May – from the beaches –, from the harbour 7,669, *total* 7,669

Accumulated total 7,669

28th May – from the beaches 5,930, from the harbour 11,874, *total* 17,804,

Accumulated total 25,473

29th May – from the beaches 13,752, from the harbour 33,558, *total* 47,310,

Accumulated total 72,783

30th May – from the beaches 29,512, from the harbour 24,311, *total* 53,823, *Accumulated total* 126,606

31st May – from the beaches 22,942, from the harbour 45,072, *total* 68,014, *Accumulated total* 194,620

1st June – from the beaches 17,348, from the harbour 47,081, *total* 64,429, *Accumulated total* 259,049

2nd June – from the beaches 6,695, from the harbour 19,561, *total* 26,256, *Accumulated total* 285,305

3rd June – from the beaches 1,870, from the harbour 24,876, *total* 26,746, Accumulated total 312,051

4th June – from the beaches 622, from the harbour 25,553, total 26,175, *Accumulated total* 338,226

Total – from the beaches 98,780, from the harbour 239,446, *total* 338,226

Appendix A

List of Ships which took part in Operation "Dynamo" and Numbers of Troops Transported

Note. The following list of ships which took part in Operation "Dynamo" has been compiled after critical examination of every available source of information. It differs from *The final list of British Ships*, M.020721 of 25th October 1940 accompanying V. A. Dover's *Report on Operation "Dynamo"* M.011883 of 18th June 1940, in 320 entries.

List of British Ships Part I

A.A. Cruiser

Calcutta (Capt. D. M. Lees, R.N.) *Troops Transported* 1,856

Destroyers 41, of which 6 were sunk

Anthony (Lt. Cdr. N. V. Thew, R.N.) *Flotilla* 16th, *Troops Transported* 3,107

Basilisk (sunk) (Cdr. M. Richmond, O.B.E., R.N.) *Flotilla* Nore Command, *Troops Transported* 1,115

Codrington (Capt. (D) G. F. Stevens-Guille, D.S.O., O.B.E., R.N.) *Flotilla* Capt. (D) 1, *Troops Transported* 5,677

Esk (Lt. Cdr. R. J. H. Couch, R.N.) *Flotilla* 20th, *Troops Transported* 3,904

Express (Capt. (D) J. G. Bickford, D.S.C., R.N.) *Flotilla* Capt. (D) 20, *Troops Transported* 2,795

Gallant (Lt. Cdr. C. P. F. Brown, R.N.) *Flotilla* 1st, Troops Transported 1,880

Grafton (sunk) (Cdr. C. E. C. Robinson, R.N.) (killed) (Lieut. II. C. J. Me Rea, R.N.) *Flotilla* 1st, *Troops Transported* 860

Grenade (sunk) (Cdr. R. C. Boyle, R.N.) *Flotilla* Nore Command, *Troops Transported* 1,000

Greyhound (Cdr. W. R. Marshall-A'Deane, R.N.) *Flotilla* 1st, *Troops Transported* 1,360

Harvester (Lt. Cdr. M. Thornton, R.N.) *Flotilla* 9th, *Troops Transported* 3,191

Havant (sunk) (Lt. Cdr. A. F. Burnell-Nugent, D.S.C., R.N.) *Flotilla* 9th, *Troops Transported* 2,432

Icarus (Lt. Cdr. C. D. Maud, R.N.) *Flotilla* 20th, *Troops Transported* 4,704

Impulsive (Lt. Cdr. W. S. Thomas, R.N.) *Flotilla* 20th, *Troops Transported* 2,919

Intrepid (Cdr. R. C. Gordon, R.N.) *Flotilla* 20th, *Troops Transported* 661

Ivanhoe (Cdr. P. U. Iladow, R.N.) *Flotilla* 20th, *Troops Transported* 1,904

Jackal (Cdr. T. M. Napier, R.N.) *Flotilla* 1st, *Troops Transported* —

Jaguar (Lt. Cdr. J. F. W. Hine, R.N.) *Flotilla* 1st, *Troops Transported* 700

Javelin (Cdr. A. F. Pugsley, R.N.) *Flotilla* 1st, *Troops Transported* 1,400

Keith (sunk) (Capt. (D) E. L. Berthon, D.S.C., R.N.) *Flotilla* Capt. (D) 19, *Troops Transported* 1,200

Mackay (Cdr. G. II. Stokes, R.N.) *Flotilla* 11th, *Troops Transported* 581

Malcolm (Capt. (D) T. E. Halsey, R.N.) *Flotilla* Capt. (D) 16, *Troops Transported* 5,851

Montrose (Cdr. C. R. L. Parry, R.N.) *Flotilla* 17th, *Troops Transported* 925

Sabre (Cdr. B. Dean, R.N. (Retd.)) *Flotilla* 16th, *Troops Transported* 5,765

Saladin (Lt. Cdr. L. J. Dover, R.N.) *Flotilla* 11th, *Troops Transported* —

Scimitar (Lieut. R. D. Franks, O.B.E., R.N.) *Flotilla* 16th, *Troops Transported* 2,711

Shikari (Lt. Cdr. H. N. A. Richardson, R.N.) *Flotilla* 16th, *Troops Transported* 3,589

Vanquisher (Lt. Cdr. C. B. Alers-Hankey, R.N.) (relieved sick) (Lt. Cdr. W. C. Bushell, R.N.) *Flotilla* 11th, *Troops Transported* 3,941

Vega (Cdr. C. I. Horton, R.N.) *Flotilla* Nore Command, *Troops Transported* 34

Venomous (Lt. Cdr. J. E. H. McBeath, R.N.) *Flotilla* 16th (attached Dover Command), *Troops Transported* 4,410

Verity (Lt. Cdr. A. R. M. Black, R.N.) (wounded) (Lieut. E. L. Jones, R.N.) *Flotilla* Nore Command, *Troops Transported* 504

Vimy (Lt. Cdr. R. G. K. Knowling, R.N.) (missing) (Lieut. A. P. W. Northey, R.N.) (temporarily) (Lt. Cdr. M. W. E. Wentworth, R.N.) *Flotilla* Nore Command, *Troops Transported* 2,976

Vivacious (Lt. Cdr. F. R. W. Parish, R.N.) (relieved - sick) (Cdr. E. F. V. Dechaineux, R.A.N.) *Flotilla* Nore Command, *Troops Transported* 1,999

Wakeful (sunk) (Cdr. R. L. Fisher, R.N.) *Flotilla* 17th, *Troops Transported* 639

Whitehall (Lt. Cdr. A. B. Russell, R.N.) *Flotilla* 11th, *Troops Transported* 3,453

Whitshed (Cdr. E. R. Condor, R.N.) *Flotilla* 19th, *Troops Transported* 1,038

Wild Swan (Lt. Cdr. J. L. Younghusband, R.N.) *Troops Transported* 12

Winchelsea (Lt. Cdr. W. A. F. Hawkins, R.N.) *Flotilla* 11th, *Troops Transported* 4,957

Windsor (Lt. Cdr. P. D. H. R. Pelly, R.N.) *Flotilla* Nore Command, *Troops Transported* 3,991

Wolfhound (Lt. Cdr. J. W. McCoy, D.S.C., R.N.) *Flotilla* Nore Command, *Troops Transported* 130

Wolsey (Lt. Cdr. C. H. Campbell, R.N.) *Flotilla* attached Dover Command, *Troops Transported* 3,337

Worcester (J. H. Allison, R.N.) *Flotilla* 11th, *Troops Transported* 4,545

Total 96,197

Corvettes 6

Guillemot (Lt. Cdr. FI. M. Darell-Brown, R.N.) *Troops Transported* 460

Kingfisher (Lt. Cdr. G. A. M. V. Harrison, R.N.) *Troops Transported* 640

Mallard (Cdr. The Hon. V. M. Wyndham-Quin, R.N.) —

Shearwater (Lt. Cdr. P. F. Powlett, R.N.) —

Sheldrake (Lt. Cdr. A. E. T. Christie, R.N.) —

Widgeon (Lt. Cdr. R. Frederick, R.N.) —

Total 1,100

Sloop

Bideford (Lt. Cdr. J. H. Lewes, R.N.) *Troops Transported* 436

Gunboats 2, of which 1 was sunk

Locust (Lieut. A. N. P. Costobadie, R.N.) *Troops Transported* 2,329

Mosquito (sunk) (Lieut. D. H. P. Gardiner, R.N.) *Troops Transported* 1,183

Total 3,076

Minesweepers 36, of which 5 were sunk or beached

Albury (Lt. Cdr. C. H. Corbet-Singleton, R.N.) *Flotilla* 5th, *Troops Transported* 1,536

Brighton Belle (sunk) (Lieut. L. K. Perrin, R.N.V.R.) *Flotilla* 10th, *Troops Transported* —

Brighton Queen (sunk) (Ty. Lieut. A. Stubbs, R.N.R.) *Flotilla* 7th, *Troops Transported* 160

Devonia (beached and lost) (Ty. Lt. J. Brotchie, R.N.V.R.) *Flotilla* 7th, *Troops Transported* —

Duchess of Fife (Ty. Lt. J. N. Anderson, R.N.R.) *Flotilla* 12th, *Troops Transported* 1,801

Dundalk (Lt. Cdr. F. A. 1. Kirkpatrick, R.N. (retd.)) *Flotilla* 4th, *Troops Transported* 1,129

Emperor of India (Ty. Lieut. C. Pawley, R.N.R.) *Flotilla* 10th, Troops Transported 642

Fitzroy (Lt. Cdr. R. A. Forbes, R.N.) *Flotilla* 4th, *Troops Transported* 867

Glen Avon (Ty. Lieut. B. II. Loynes, R.N.R.) *Flotilla* 8th, *Troops Transported* 888

Glen Gower (Actg. Cdr. M. A. O. Biddulph, R.N., S.O. 8th M.S.F.) *Flotilla* 8th (S.O.), *Troops Transported* 1,235

Gossamer (Cdr. R. C. V. Ross, R.N., S.O., 5th M.S.F.) *Flotilla* 5th (S.O.), *Troops Transported* 3,169

Gracie Fields (sunk) (Ty. Lt. N. Larkin, R.N.R,) (Ty. Lt. A. C. Weeks, R.N.V.R.) *Flotilla* 10th, *Troops Transported* 281

Halcyon (Lt. Cdr. J. M. S. Cox, D.S.C., R.N.) (Cdr. E. P. Hinton, M.V.O., R.N.) *Flotilla* 6th, *Troops Transported* 2,271

Hebe (Lt. Cdr. J. 15. G. Temple, R.N.) *Flotilla* 1st, *Troops Transported* 1,140

Kellett (Cdr. R. C. Haskett-Smith, R.N.) *Flotilla* 5th, *Troops Transported*,456

Leda (Lt. Cdr. II. IJnwin, R.N.) *Flotilla* 5th, *Troops Transported* 2,848

Lydd (Lt. Cdr. R. C. D. Haig, R.N.) *Flotilla* 5th, *Troops Transported* 1,502

Marmion (Ty. Lt. H. C. Gaffney, R.N.V.R.) *Flotilla* 12th, *Troops Transported* 713

Medway Queen (Lieut. A. T. Cook, R.N.R.) *Flotilla* 10th, *Troops Transported* 3,064

Niger (Cdr. St. J. Cronyn, R.N., S.O., 4th M.S.F.) *Flotilla* 4th, *Troops Transported* 1,245

Oriole (Ty. Lieut. E. L. Davies, R.N.V.R.) *Flotilla* 12th, *Troops Transported* 2,587

Pangbourne (Actg. Cdr. F. Douglas-Watson, R.N.) *Flotilla* 5th, *Troops Transported* 1,020

Plinlimmon (Lt. G. P. Baker, R.N.V.R.) *Flotilla* 7th, *Troops Transported* 900

Princess Elizabeth (Lt. C. J. Carp, R.N.V.R.) *Flotilla* 10th, Troops Transported 1,673

Queen of Thanet (Actg. Ty. Cdr. S. P. Herival, R.N.V.R.) (S.O. 7th M.S.F.) *Flotilla* 7th (S.O.), *Troops Transported* 2,500

Ross (Actg. C. O. Lt. K. A. Gadd, R.N.R. (injured) (Cdr. J. P. Apps, R.N. (Retd.)) *Flotilla* 5th, *Troops Transported* 1,096

Salamander (Lieut. Cdr. L. J. S. Ede, R.N.) *Flotilla* 4th, *Troops Transported* 1,161

Saltash (Lt. Cdr. T. R. Fowke, R.N.) *Flotilla* 5th, *Troops Transported* 800

Sandown (Actg. Cdr. K. M. Greig, R.N., S.O., 10th M.S.F.) Flotilla 10th (S.O.), *Troops Transported* 1,861

Sharpshooter (Lieut. A. E. Doran, R.N.) *Flotilla* 1st, *Troops Transported* 373

Skipjack (sunk) (Lieut. Cdr. F. B. Proudfoot, R.N. (retd.)) *Flotilla* 6th, *Troops Transported* 865

Snaefell (Ty. Lieut. F. Brett, R.N.V.R.) *Flotilla* 8th, *Troops Transported* 981

Speedwell (Lt. Cdr. F. R. G. Maunsell, R.N. (Retd.)) *Flotilla* 6th, *Troops Transported* 1668

Sutton (Actg. Cdr. G. M. Temple, R.N., S.O. 4th M.S.F.) *Flotilla* 4th (S.O.), *Troops Transported* 1,371

Waverley (sunk) (Ty. Lieut. S. F. Harmer-Elliott, R.N.V.R.) (Actg. S.O., 12th M.S.F.) *Flotilla* 12th (S.O.), *Troops Transported* —

Westward Ho (Ty. Lieut. A. L. Braithwaite, R.N.V.R.) *Flotilla* 7th, *Troops Transported* 1,686

Total 46,434

Trawlers 52, of which 12 were lost

Amethyst (Comdr. (Act.) R. C. Stokes, R.N.)[1] —

Arctic Pioneer (Lt. R. A. D. Cambridge, R.N.R.) —

---

1 Name taken from *The Navy List for June 1940.*

Argyllshire (sunk) (S/Lt. J. S. Weddle, R.N.R.) (S.O. 11th A/S Striking Force) —

Arley (Skr. Lt. G. W. Robinson, R.D., R.N.R.) *Troops Transported* 135

Blackburn Rovers (sunk) (Cdr. R. W. English, R.N.) (Skipper W. Martin, R.N.R.) —

Brock (S/Lt. K. H. G. Roberts, R.N.V.R.) (Skipper Jappy) *Troops Transported* 6

Calvi (sunk) (Skipper B. D. Spindler, R.N.R.) —

Cape Argona (Lt. K. J. Lee, R.N.V.R.) —

Cayton Wyke (Comdr. R. Ll. B. Hammond-Chambers, R.N. (Ret.)) [1] *Troops Transported* 605[2]

Clythness (Skipper E. G. Catchpole, R.N.R.) [1] *Troops Transported* 150

Comfort (sunk) (Skipper J. D. Mair, R.N.R.) —

Dhoon Troops Transported 130

Spurs (Skipper H. H. Jarvis, R.N.R.) [1] —

Edwina (Skipper P. Bedford (?)) *Troops Transported* 120

Evelyn Rose (Tempy-Skipper (F.R.) A. J. Lewis) [1] *Troops Transported* 130

Fyldea (Lieut. R. Bill, R.N., Asst. to Cdr. M/S Dover) (Lieut. J. K. M. Warde, R.N.V.R., Unit Officer) (Skipper G. Whamond) *Troops Transported* 180

Gava (Lieut. F. J. Jordan, R.N.R.) (Skipper Day, R.N.R.) *Troops Transported* 502

Grimsby Town (Lieut. W. C. Riley, R.N.V.R.) [1] —

Inverforth (Lt. Cdr. A. A. Martin, R.N.R. (Group Officer)) —

Jacinta —

Jasper (Lieut. A. Johnson, R.N.V.R.) [1] —

John Cattling (Ty. Lt. G. St. C. Rideal, R.N.V.R.) (Ty. Skipper G. W. Aldan, R.N.R.) *Troops Transported* 77

Kingston Alalite (Ch. Skipper A. H. Foster, R.N.R.) [1] —

Kingston Andalusite (Skipper J. Bruce (Act.) R.N.R.) [1] —

Kingston Galena (S/Lt. J. L. Pringle, R.N.V.R.) —

Kingston Olivine (Lieut. G. W. Gregorie, R.N.R.) [1] —

Lady Philomena (Skipper J. Hodson, R.N.R.) [1] —

Lord Grey (Ty. Lt. J. A. Simson, R.N.V.R.) (Proby. Skipper W. J. Tiller, R.N.R.) *Troops Transported* 400

Lord Inchcape (S/L S. J. Longsdon, R.N.V.R.) (Unit Officer) *Troops Transported* 240

Lord Melchett (Skipper R. C. Raylor, R.N.R.) (Group Officer Lt. W. H. Ward, R.N.V.R.) —

Malabar Troops Transported 26

Nautilus (sunk) (Lieut. W. E. Gelling, R.N.R.) (Skipper R. Maclean, R.N.R.) —

---

2 Including 300 in a barge which was picked up.

Ocean Reward (sunk) —

Olvina (S/Lt. J. II. Cooper, R.N.V.R.) (Unit Officer, 40th A/S Group) *Troops Transported* 347

Our Bairns (Skipper J. H. Miller) *Troops Transported* 200

Polly Johnson (sunk) (Skipper Lieut. L. Lake, R.D., R.N.R.) —

Relonzo (Skipper Slater) —

Restrivo (Tempy.-Skipper J. Fountain, R.N.R.) [1]

St. Achillcus (sunk) (Ty. Lt. H. A. Gellett, R.N.V.R.) (S.O. Ilth A/S Group) —

Saon (Lt. Com. A. G. G. Webb, R.N. (Ret.)) [1] *Troops Transported* 359

Sphene (Skipper C. Pennington, R.N.R.) —

Saturn (Ty. Skipper H. C. Watson, R.N.R.) *Troops Transported* 1,177

Stella Dorado (sunk) (Skipper W. H. Burgess, R.N.R.) [1] *Troops Transported* 55

Stella Rigel (Skipper L. P. Keable, R.N.R.) (Unit Officer S/Lt. J. W. Wykeham, R.N.V.R.) —

Strathelliot (S/Lt. W. E. Mercer, R.N.V.R.) *Troops Transported* 339

Tankerton Towers (Skipper J. Hannaford) *Troops Transported* 50

Thomas Bartlett (sunk) (Skipper J. J. Tomlinson, R.N.R.) —

Thuringia (sunk) (Ch. Skipper D. W. L. Simpson, D.S.C., D.S.M., R.N.R.) —

Topaze (Lt. Cdr. j. N. Hambly, M.B.E., R.N., S.O. 40th A/S Group) *Troops Transported* 118

Velia (Skipper J. Clarkson) —

Viviana (Skipper G. L. Olesen) —

Westella (sunk) (Chief Skipper A. Gove, R.N.R.) —

Wolves (Skipper J. D. Fowler, R.N.R. Skipper W. S. Flowers, R.N.R.) 3 *Troops Transported* 50

Total 5,396

Drifters 61, of which 5 were lost

Alcmaria (Skipper A. C. Offord, R.N.R.) [1] *Troops Transported* 32

Ben Lucy (Captain W. A. Watling, R.N.R., Skipper) (Actg. Lt. F. G. M. lies, R.N.V.R. Unit Officer) *Troops Transported* 100

Boy Roy (sunk) (Ty. Skipper E. F. Dettman, R.N.R.) —

Dorienta (Skipper W. F. Reynolds, R.N.R.) *Troops Transported* 65

Eileen Emma (Tempy. Skipper B. E. S. Smith, R.N.R.) [1] *Troops Transported* 114

Fair Breeze (sunk) (Lt. Cdr. A. R. W. Sayle, R.N.R.) *Troops Transported* 316

Feasible (Skipper C. C. Findlay, R.N.R.) 1 —

Fidget Troops Transported 568

Fisher Boy (Ty. Skipper G. W. Brown, R.N.R.) *Troops Transported* 777

Forecast (Lt. T. P. Graham, R.N.R., Unit Officer) *Troops Transported* 353

Genius (Skipper G. H. Green, R.N.R.)[1] *Troops Transported* 100

Gervais Rentoul (Tempy.-Skipper J. IT. Burgess, R.N.R.)[1] *Troops Transported* 57

Girl Gladys (Tempy. Skipper F. L. Strowger, R.N.R.)[1] *Troops Transported* 249

Girl Pamela (sunk) (Ty. Skipper G. Sanson, R.N.R.) *Troops Transported* 51

Golden Gift (Ty. Skipper G. S. Sampson) *Troops Transported* 273

Golden Sunbeam (Skipper W. C. F. Chaney) *Troops Transported* 397

Gula (Tempy. Skipper A. W. West, R.N.R.)[1] *Troops Transported* 110

Jacketa (Ty. Skipper D. Tause, R.N.R.) *Troops Transported* 651

Jackeve (Skipper C. E. F. Reynolds, R.N.R.) *Troops Transported* 120

Jeannie Macintosh (Skipper J. W. Nicholson, R.N.R.)[1] Not known

John & Norah (Skipper R. A. Sims, R.N.R.)[1] *Troops Transported* 61

Kindred Star (T. W. Sheridan, Tempy. Skip. R.N.R.) (G. Corney, Temp. Skipper, R.N.R.) (Lieut. A. j. Dunbar, R.N.V.R., Unit Officer) —

Lord Barham (Tempy.-Skipper J. Masterton, R.N.R.)[1] *Troops Transported* 388

Lord Cavan (sunk) (Ty. Skipper J. H. Muggridge, R.N.R.) —

Lord Collingwood Troops Transported 332

Lord Hood (Skipper J. W. Lawn, R.N.R.)[1] —

Lord Howard (Tempy. Skipper D. Davidson, R.N.R.)[1] *Troops Transported* 379

Lord Howe (Skipper W. H. Pollock) *Troops Transported* 277

Lord Keith (R. Pye, Master) *Troops Transported* 323

Lord Rodney (R. Durrant, Master) Not known

Lord St. Vincent Troops Transported 150

L.H.W.D. Troops Transported 90

Mare (Skipper A. H. W. Pendle, R.N.R.) (Group Offr. Cdr. J. W. D. Powell, D.S.C.(Bar), R.N.R.) *Troops Transported* Transported 219

Midas (Skipper H. Holden, R.N.R.) *Troops Transported* 260

Monarda (Lieut. P. T. Lovelock, R.N.V.R.) *Troops Transported* 190

Netsukis (Tempy. Skipper A. V. Muffett, R.N.V.R.)[1] *Troops Transported* 483

Ocean Breeze (Lieut. V. A. de Mauny, R.N.) (Skipper Bailey (?)) *Troops Transported* 259

Overfall (Tempy. Skipper D. Miller, R.N.R.)[1] Not known

Paxton (sunk) (Lt. Cdr. R. M. Prior, R.N.) (Skipper A. M. Lovis, R.N.R.) —

Reed (Skipper G. Hatton, R.N.R.)[1] Not known

Renascent (Skipper R. E. Hannaford, R.N.R.) *Troops Transported* 260

Rewga (Tempy. Skipper J. W. Macanley, R.N.R.)[1] *Troops Transported* 162

Rig (Skipper 1C. Beckham, R.N.R.) *Troops Transported* 60

Robert Cliff —

Sarah Hyde (Skipper H. G. Meen, R.N.R.) (Unit Officer Lt. J. I. Cruickshank, R.N.V.R.) *Troops Transported* 100

Shipmates (Ty. Skipper H. E. Ward) *Troops Transported* 196

Silver Dawn (Skipper S. A. White, R.N.R.) *Troops Transported* 694

Starlight Rays (Skipper, A. Buchan, R.N.R.) (Lt. W. R. Hutcheson, R.N.V.R.) *Troops Transported* 610

Strive (Skipper H. A. Catchpole, R.N.R.) *Troops Transported* 243

Swift Wing (Tempy. Skipper G. Frosdick, R.N.R.)[1] Not known

Taransay (Tempy. Skipper G. S. Peek, R.N.R.)[1] *Troops Transported* 162

The Boys (Skipper A. Buchan, R.N.R.) —

Thomsons (Skipper S. J. A. Drake, R.N.R.) —

Three Kings (Skipper G. W. Smith, R.N.R.) (Skipper A. V. Long, R.N.R.) *Troops Transported* 350

Thrifty (Tempy. Skipper G. Corney, R.N.R.)[1] —

Torbay II (Tempy. Skipper W. B. Jenner, R.N.R.)[1] *Troops Transported* 302

Tweenway's (Skipper E. Fawcett, R.N.R.) *Troops Transported* 126

Unicity (Skipper W. A. George, R.N.R.) *Troops Transported* 225

Ut Prosim (Skipper W. Reaich, R.N.R.)[1] *Troops Transported* 457

Yorkshire Lass (Ty. Lieut. E. H. G. Hope, R.N.V.R.) (S/Lt. M. A. A. Chodzko, R.N.V.R.) *Troops Transported* 469

Young Mon (Tempy. Skipper A. W. Lockwood, R.N.R.)[1] *Troops Transported* 120

Total 12,370

Special Service Vessels 3, of which 1 was lost

Crested Eagle (sunk) (Tempy. Lt. Cdr. B. R. Booth, R.N.R.) —

Golden Eagle (Lt. Cdr. C.O.) (Lt. W. L. Lucas, R.N.R. (navigator)) (Lt. J. C. Newman, M.B.E., R.N.V.R., in command) *Troops Transported* 1,751

Royal Eagle (Cdr. E. C. Cordeaux, M.B., M.R.C.S., L.R.C.P., R.N.) (sick) (Ty. Lr. Cdr. E. F. A. Farrow, R.N.R.) *Troops Transported* 2,657

Total 4,408

M.A./S.B.'s 7

M.A/S.B. 5 (Lieut. E. M. Thorpe, R.N.) 1 —

M.A/S.B.6 (Lieut. W. G. Everitt, R.N.) *Troops Transported* 26

M.Aj̇S.B.7 (S/Lt. A. Ecclestone, R.N.) *Troops Transported* 38

M.A/S.B.9 —

M.A/S.B.10 (Lieut. R. G. H. G. Eyre, R.N.) —

M.L.100 (Lieut. W. L. Stephens, R.N.V.R.) —

D.C./M.B. (Lieut. E. F. Hamilton-Meikle, R.N.) *Troops Transported* 15

M.T.B.'s. 6

M.T.B.U (Lieut. P. F. S. Gould, R.N.) —

M.T.B.22 —

M.T.B.67 (Lieut. C. C. Anderson, R.N.) —

M.T.B AM (Lieut. R. K. L. Walker, R.N.V.R.) —

M.T.B.102 (Lieut. C. W. S. Dreyer, R.N.) *Troops Transported* 20

M.T.B.101 (Lieut. J. Cameron, R.N.V.R.) —

Armed Boarding Vessels 3, of which I was sunk

King Orry (sunk) (Cdr. J. Elliott, R.D., R.N.R.) *Troops Transported* 1,131

Lormont (Lt. Cdr. W. S. Smithies, R.N.) *Troops Transported* 1,083

Monas Isle (Cdr. J. C. K. Dowding, R.D., R.N.R.) *Troops Transported* 2,634

Total 4,848

Skoots (ex-Dutch Schutts or coasters) 40, of which 4 were lost

Where skoots lying 22nd May (in brackets)

Abel Tasman (London) (Lt. Cdr. T. G. P. Crick, R.N.) (wounded) Lieut. C. E. S. B. St. G. Beal, R.N.) (from Kaap *Falga* 28/5/40) *Troops Transported* 220

Aegir (London) (Lieut. W. B. Whitworth, R.N.) *Troops Transported* 835

Alice (lost) (Poole) (Lieut. H. M. Slater, R.N.) —

Amazone (Poole) (Lt. Cdr. L. H. Phillips, R.N.) *Troops Transported* 549

Antje (London) (Lt. M. Buist, R.N.) *Troops Transported* 450

Atlantic (Poole) (Lt. Cdr. L. E. Fordham, R.N.R.) *Troops Transported* 590

Bart (London) (Lieut. E. G. Ball, R.N. (Retd.) —

Bornrif (London) (Lieut. A. N. Blundell, R.N.R.) *Troops Transported* 146

Brandaris (London) (Cdr. C Euman, R.N. (Retd.)) *Troops Transported* 330

Caribia (London) (Lt. M. G. Morais, R.N.R.) (Lt. G. H. Williams, R.N.R. (as from 29th May) *Troops Transported* 701

Delta (London) (Lt. Cdr. D. F. Lawrence, R.N. (retd.) *Troops Transported* 503

Dench (London) *Troops Transported* 100

Despatch II (Poole) (Lt. Cdr. F. E. Wilmot-Sitwell, R.N. (Retd.)) *Troops Transported* 428

Doggersbank (London) (Lieut. D. T. McBarnet, R.N.) *Troops Transported* 800

Fredanja (Poole) (Lt. Cdr. K. W. Stewart, R.N. (Retd.)) *Troops Transported* 850

Frisco (Poole) *Troops Transported* 1,002

Gorecht (London) (S/Lt. I). M. Edwards, R.N.R.) *Troops Transported* 47

Hebe II (Poole) (Lt. Cdr. J. B. G. Temple, R.N.) *Troops Transported* 515

Hilda (London) (Lieut. A. Gray, R.N.) *Troops Transported* 835

Hondsrug (London) (Lieut. F. T. Renny, R.N.R.) *Troops Transported* 1,453

Horst (lost) (Poole) (Lt. Cdr. G. E. Fardell, R.N.) (Lt. T. E. Sargent, R.N.R.) *Troops Transported* 1,150

Jaba (Poole) *Troops Transported* 469

Jutland (London) (Lieut. G. L. Barwell, R.N. (Retd.)) (Relieved, 30 May, re-assumed command 31st May) (Lt. Cdr. W. R. T. Clements, R.N.R.) (30th-31st May) *Troops Transported* 505

Kaap Falga (Poole) (Lieut. C. E. S. B. St. G. Beal, R.N.) (Lieut. H. F. Wykeham-Martin, R.N., 28/5/40) *Troops Transported* 5

Lena (lost) (London) (Lt. Cdr. R. P. C. Hawkins, R.N. (Retd.)) *Troops Transported* 996

Oranje (London) (Lieut. H. T. Crispin, R.N.) *Troops Transported* 605

Pacific (Poole) (Lt. Cdr. C. J. Skrine, R.N.) *Troops Transported* 945

Pascholl (Poole) (Lieut. T. Johnston, R.N.) (Relieved and appointed i/c Portsdown) (Lieut. J. N. Wise, R.N.V.R.) (Cdr. C. E. Hammond, D.S.O., D.S.C., R.N.) (Retd.) (i/c Group) *Troops Transported* 695

Patria (London) (Lt. Cdr. N. L. J. Pisani, D.S.C., R.N. (Retd.)) *Troops Transported* 1,400

Reiger (London) (Lieut. A. Tyson, R.N.) *Troops Transported* 592

Rian (Poole) (Lt. Cdr. J. I. Miller, D.S.O. R.N.) (Reported) 2 *Troops Transported* 257

Rika (London) (Lt. Cdr. J. J. Youngs, R.N.R.) *Troops Transported* 495

Ruja (Poole) (Lt. H. R. Webber, R.N.) *Troops Transported* 300

San Antonio (Poole) (Lt. Cdr. G. V. Legassick, R.N.R.) *Troops Transported* 484

Sursum-Corda (lost) (Poole) (Lieut. C. L. G. Philpotts, R.N.) *Troops Transported* 370

Tilly (London) (Lt. Cdr. W. R. T. Clements, R.N.R.) (Lt. Cdr. C. M. Ramus, R.N.R.) *Troops Transported* 602

Tiny (Poole) (Lt. Cdr. J. M. D. Hunter, R.N.) (Lt. Martin, R.N.) *Troops Transported* 261

Twente (London) (Lt. Cdr. H. G. Boys-Smith, R.N.R. to 30th May) (Lt. A. W. McMullen R.N.R.)

Troops Transported 1,139

Vrede (London) (Lt. Cdr. R. T. Lampard, R.N.) *Troops Transported* 473

Zeus (Poole) (Lt. Cdr. C. B. Hoggan, R.D., R.N.R.) *Troops Transported* 601

Yachts 26, of which 13 were lost

Ahola (Lt. J. F. Alexander, R.N.V.R.) *Troops Transported* 5

Alouettc II (S/Lt. R. E. Lee, R.N.V.R., Unit Officer) *Troops Transported* 175

Amulree (lost) (S/Lt. G. P. Probert, R.N.V.R.) —

Ankh (Lt. C. C. Bone, R.N.V.R., Senior Officer, Inner Patrol) —

Avonia (Lieut. J. S. Roe, R.N.V.R.) *Troops Transported* 42

Bounty (Lt. C. A. Lundy, R.N.V.R.) —

Bystander (S/Lt. LL J. B. Barge, R.N.V.R.) *Troops Transported* 99

Caleta Troops Transported 35

Caryanda (Lt. D. A. L. Kings, R.N.V.R.) —

Chico (S/Lt. J. Mason, R.N.V.R.) Troo *Troops Transported* 317

Christobel II (Lieut. H. E. Wigfull, R.N.V.R.) *Troops Transported* 33

Conidaw (Skipper R. G. Snelgrove) *Troops Transported* 80

Eilla II (Lt. E. H. Batt, R.N.V.R.) —

Erica —

Glagla (S/Lt. J. A. Dow, R.N.V.R.) —

Grive (lost) (Capt. the Hon. L. J. O. Lambart, D.S.O., R.N. (Retd.)[3] *Troops Transported* 1,484

Gulzar (Ty. Lt. C. V. Brammall, R.N.R.) *Troops Transported* 814

Lahloo Troops Transported 15

Laroc (Capt. G. B. Butler, (Master/Owner) *Troops Transported* 147

Llanthony (S/Lt. R. W. Timbrell, R.N.) *Troops Transported* 280

Noneta (S/Lt. A. J. Potter-Irwin, R.N.V.R.) —

Pellag II (abandoned) (Lieut. F. W. R. Martino, R.N.V.R.) —

Sargasso (Lt. C. C. L. Gaussen, R.N.V.R.) *Troops Transported* 605

Seriola (Lieut. D. A. Dawson, R.N.V.R.) —

Tarret Troops Transported 550

---

3 Ty. Lieut. C. E. West, R.N.R. is shown in the *Navy List* as Captain of the *Grive,* but the operative command seems to have been with Capt. Lambart at the time of "Dynamo". Lieut. West was not on board when the ship was sunk, Capt. Lambart having persuaded him to land at Dover at 1300 on 1st June, to recuperate.

Thele (Lt. LL M. Glassborow, R.N.V.R.) —

Total 4,681

Personnel Ships 45 (including 3 store ships and 2 motor vessels) of which 8 were sunk

Archangel —

Auto Carrier (Capt. C. M. Masters, Master) *Troops Transported* 712

Beal (M/V) (J. W. Liley, Master) *Troops Transported* 364

Ben-My-Chree (Capt. G. Woods, Master) *Troops Transported* 4,095

Biarritz (Capt. W. H. Baker, Master) —

Bullfinch (M/V) *Troops Transported* 600

Canterbury (Capt. C. Hancock, Master) *Troops Transported* 4,416

City of Christchurch (Capt. A. W. Wooster, O.B.E.) —

Clan Macalister (sunk) (Capt. R. W. Mackie, Master) *Troops Transported* 1

Côte d'Argent[4] *Troops Transported* 5,754

Dorrien Rose (store ship) (Capt. W. Thompson, Master) *Troops Transported* 1,494

Fenella (sunk) (Capt. W. Gubbon, Master) —

Foam Queen (Capt. A. T. Mastin, Master) *Troops Transported* 98

Hythe (coaster) (R. W. Morford, Master) *Troops Transported* 749

Killarney (Capt. R. Hughes, Master) *Troops Transported* 900

King George V (Capt. R. M. Maclean, Master) *Troops Transported* 4,300

Lady of Mann (Capt. T. C. Woods, Master) *Troops Transported* 4,262

Levenwood (store ship) (Capt. W. O. Young, Master) *Troops Transported* 60

Lochgarry (Capt. E. Mackinnon, Master) *Troops Transported* 1,001

Lorina (sunk) (Capt. A. Light, Master) —

Maid of Orleans (Capt. A. E. Larkins, Master) (Sick) (Capt. G. D. Walker, Master) *Troops Transported* 5,461

Malines (Capt. G. Mallory, Master) (quitted Opn. Dynamo 2 June) *Troops Transported* 1,500

Manxman (Capt. P. B. Cowley, Master) (disembarked 2 June) *Troops Transported* 2,394

Monas Queen (sunk) (Capt. R. Duggan, Master) (Capt. A. Holkham, Master) *Troops Transported* 1,200

Nephrite (store ship) (Capt. C. G. West, O.B.E., Master) *Troops Transported* 504

Newhaven[4] (Lt. Cdr. L. H. Phillips, R.N.,) (? Master) *Troops Transported* 1,841

---

4 Former French mail packet

Ngaroma (Capt. J. W. Dickinson, Master) *Troops Transported* 100

Normania (sunk) (Capt. M. C. Whiting, Master) —

Portsdown (S/Lt. R. H. Church, R.N.R.) *Troops Transported* 618

Prague (Capt. C. R. Baxter, Master) *Troops Transported* 3,039

Princess Maud (Capt. H. Clark, Master) *Troops Transported* 1,270

Queen of the Channel (sunk) (Capt. W. J. O'Dell, Master) —

Roebuck (Capt. W. Y. Larbalestier, Master) *Troops Transported* 500

Rouen[4] *Troops Transported* 2,886

Royal Daffodil (Capt. G. Johnson, Master) *Troops Transported* 7,552

Royal Sovereign (Capt. T. Aldis, Master) *Troops Transported* 6,772

St. Helier (Capt. R. R. Pitman, Master) *Troops Transported* 6,584

St. Seiriol (Capt. R. D. Dobb, Master) (Lieut. A. R. MacKewn, R.N.R.) *Troops Transported* 672

Scotia (sunk) (Capt H. W. Hughes, Master) *Troops Transported* 3,000

Scottish Co-operator (Capt. T. S. Robertson, Master) *Troops Transported* 525

Sequacity (M/V) (Capt. J. Macdonald) —

Tynwald (Capt. J. H. White way, Master) (Capt. W. A. Qualtrough, Master) (relieved 2 June) *Troops Transported* 8,953

Whippingham (Lieut. I£. Reed, R.N.R.) *Troops Transported* 2,700

Whitstable (Capt. W. Baxter, Master) *Troops Transported* 14

Yewdale (tramp) (Capt. E. Jones) *Troops Transported* 890

Total 87,810

Hospital Carriers 8, of which 1 was sunk

Dinard (Mr. J. W. A. Jones, Master) *Troops Transported* 374

Isle of Guernsey (Capt. E. L. Hill, Master) *Troops Transported* 836

Isle of Thanet (Capt. A. J. Hammond, Master) —

Paris (sunk) (Capt. E. A. Biles, Master) *Troops Transported* 630

St. Andrew (Capt. H. C. Bond, Master) *Troops Transported* 130

St. David (Capt. C. Joy, Master) (Sick) (Capt. B. H. Mendus, Master) *Troops Transported* 149

St. Julien (Capt. L. T. Richardson, Master) *Troops Transported* 287

Worthing (Capt. C. G. G. Munton, Master) *Troops Transported* 600

Total 3,006

Naval M/Bs. 12, of which 6 were sunk

Admiral Superintendent, Portsmouth's barge (sunk) —

Dolphin's power boat (S/Lt. E. J. Cornish-Bowden, R.N.) —

Excellent's (A/A) M/B1 (S/Lt. A. W. M. Matthew, R.N.) —

Excellent's 35 M/B1 (L/Sea. H. H. Dixon and a crew of four) —

40 ft. Ship's M/B (Lt. E. F. Hamilton-Meikle, R.N.) —

Gallant's M/B1 —

Naval Steam Pinnace (sunk) (S/Lt. T. E. Goodman, R.N.V.R.) —

Nelson's M/B (Lieut. H. L. Holman, R.N.V.R.) *Troops Transported* 55

Nelson's Picket boat (Actg. S/Lt. J. M. Campbell, R.N.) *Troops Transported* 16

Vernon's Pinnace (V.4) Not known

V.A. Dover's barge (sunk) (Act. S/Lt. C. E. S. Beale, R.N.) —

Vernon I, M/B (S/Lt. G. A. Gabbett-Mulhallen, R.N.) *Troops Transported* 96

Total 96

Blockships 6, of which 2 were lost *en route*

Edvard Nissen (Lt. E. J. King-Wood, R.N.R.)

Goitrko (sunk *en route*) (Cdr. A. V. Hemming, R.N.)

Holland (sunk *en route*) (Lt. Cdr. E. C. Coats, R.N.)

Moyle (Lt. Cdr. R. H. I). Lane, R.N.)

Pacifico (Lt. Cdr. G. H. F. Owles, R.N.)

West Cove (Lt. Cdr. A. M. McKillop, R.N.)

Tugs 40[5], of which 3 were sunk

C.9. (*West Acre*) (J. Treleaven, Master) *Troops Transported* 23

Cervia (W. H. Simmons, Master) *Troops Transported* 30

Challenge —

Contest (H. J. Bates, Master) —

Crested Cock (T. Hills, Master) —

Doria (A. W. Mastin, Master) *Troops Transported* 90

Dromedary (S/Lt. T. Lawrie, R.N.V.R.) —

---

5 The following tugs performed harbour duties only: *Betty, C. 11, Hibernia, Simla, Vesta* and *Water cock*.

Duke (B. P. Mansfield, Captain) *Troops Transported* 44

Empire Henchman (J. (?) E. Fishe, (?Fisher), Master) —

Fabia (F. Smith, Master) —

Fairplay I (S. Wright and G. Finch) —

Foremost 22 (C. Fieldgate, Master) (Sick) (F. M. Holden, Actg. Master) *Troops Transported* 30

Foremost 87 (J. Fryer, Master) *Troops Transported* 100

Fossa (sunk) (S/Lt. M. H. B. Solomon, R.N.V.R.) —

Gondia (C. Pratt, Master) *Troops Transported* 14

Java (W. Jones, Master) *Troops Transported* 270

Kenia (W. Hoiles, Master) —

Lady Bvassey (F. J. Hopgood, Master) *Troops Transported* —

Ocean Cock (A. V. Mastin, Master) *Troops Transported* —

Persia (H. Aldrich, Master) *Troops Transported* 27

Prima (J. B. Morran, Master) *Troops Transported* 75

Prince (J. Benson, Master) *Troops Transported* —

Princess (J. Wallis, Master) *Troops Transported* —

Racia (A. C. Addison, Master) *Troops Transported* 423

St. Abbs[6] (Lieut. T. E. Brooker, R.N) *Troops Transported* —

St. Clears (W. J. Penney, Master) *Troops Transported* 70

St. Fagan[6] (Lt. Cdr. G. H. Warren, M.B.E.) *Troops Transported* —

St. Olaves (Skipper H. Forrester, R.N.R.) *Troops Transported* 200

Sultan Troops Transported 193

Sun (Cdr. E. K. Le Mesurier, M.V.O.) *Troops Transported* 175

Sun III (F. W. Russell, Master) *Troops Transported* 148

Sun IV (Mr. C. G. Alexander, Master) *Troops Transported* 236

Sun V (W. IT. Mastin, Master) *Troops Transported* —

Sun VII (G. Cawsey, Master) *Troops Transported* —

Sun VIII (S. Smith, Master) *Troops Transported* 120

Sun X (W. A. Fothergill, Master) *Troops Transported* 211

Sun XI (J. R. Lukes, Master) *Troops Transported* 188

Sun XII (A. V. Mee, Master) *Troops Transported* —

Sun XV (J. J. Belton, Master) *Troops Transported* 106

---

6 Sunk

Tanga (H. P. Gouge, Master) *Troops Transported* 367

Vincia (A. V. Hoiles, Master) *Troops Transported* 24

Total 3,164

Landing Craft

Total 13, of which 8 were lost

A.L.C.3 Troops Transported 20

A.L.C. 4[7] Troops Transported —

A.L.C. 5 Troops Transported —

(Cdr. R. A. Cassidi, R.N. in command of 8 *A.L.Cs.* in *Clan Macalister*)

A.L.C. 8[7] Troops Transported 10

A.L.C. 10 (S/Lt. E. R. Ponsonby, R.N.V.R.) *Troops Transported* —

A.L.C. 15[7] (S/Lt. G. B. Eyre, R.N.V.R.) *Troops Transported* —

A.L.C. 16 (S/Lt. R. O. Wilcoxon, R.N.V.R.) *Troops Transported* 25

A.L.C. 17 Troops Transported —

A.L.C. 18[7] Troops Transported —

M.L.C. 12[7] (P/O Brinton, Coxswain) *Troops Transported* —

M.L.C. 17[7] (L/S A. Coleman, Coxswain) *Troops Transported* —

M.L.C. 21 (S/Lt. Towers, R.N. (PR.N.V.R.) *Troops Transported* 63

M.L.C. 22[7] (C.P.O. H. Mitten) *Troops Transported* —

Total 118

War Department M/Ls. Total 8.

Grouse (W. T. Mason, Mate i/c) *Troops Transported* 35

Haig (Lt. Cdr. N. L. J. Pisani, D.S.C., R.N., Retd.) (Cdr. H. R. Troup, R.N.) *Troops Transported* 60

Kestrel (Lt. Cdr. H. G. Boys-Smitb, R.N.R.) (transferred to Dutch M 74 1st June) (A. E. Cains, Mate) *Troops Transported* 55

Marlborough (J. Matthews, Master (1st 3 trips) (S/Lt. R. W. D. Don, D.S.C., R.N.) *Troops Transported* 146

Pigeon (S/Lt. G. A. Gabbett-Mulhallen, R.N.) *Troops Transported* 60

Swallow (Lt. Col. R. L. Hutchins, M.C., Gren. Guards) (S/Lt. W. R. Williams, R.N.) *Troops Transported* 68

Vulture (L. C. Bell, Mate i/c) *Troops Transported* 86

---

7 Lost

Wolfe (E. L. Beard, Master) *Troops Transported* 69

Total 579

R.A.F. Seaplane Tenders. Total 6, of which 3 were lost.

S.T.243[7]   (Cdr. J. C. Clouston, R.N., drowned) (Pilot Officer C. Collings, R.A.F.) *Troops Transported*, None Reported

S.T. 254[7] *Troops Transported*, None Reported

S.T. 276 (S/Lt. R. Wake, R.N.) (Corpl. Flowers, R.A.F., Coxswain) *Troops Transported*, None Reported

S.T. 201 Troops Transported, None Reported

A.M.C.3[7] *Troops Transported*, None Reported

High Speed Launch *120 Troops Transported*, None Reported

Dockyard Lighters. Total 8, of which 2 were lost.

X. 95 (Chatham. N.S. Dept.) *Troops Transported* —

X. 149[8] (Sheerness) *Troops Transported* —

X. 209 (Royal Clarence Yard, Gosport, (Victg. Dept.)) (S/Lt. W. R. Williams, R.N.) (Capt R. G. Banks, Actg. Master) *Troops Transported* 67

X. 213[8] (Chatham) *Troops Transported* —

X. 217 (Chatham. N.S. Dept.) (S/Lt. R. A. W. Pool, R.N.) *Troops Transported* 200

Y.C. 63 Troops Transported 106

Y.C. 71 (Late A.S. 28) (Chatham N.S. Dept.) *Troops Transported* Not Known

Y.C. 72 (Late A.S. 29) (Chatham N.S. Dept.) (Lieut. Mortimer, R.N.R.) (P/O G. Senior, Coxswain) *Troops Transported* 45

Total 418

Steam Hopper Barges. Total 7[9]

Foremost 101 (Mr. W. E. Llewellyn, Master) *Troops Transported* 70

Foremost 102 (Actg. S/Lt. H. Martin, R.N.) (W. C. Attwaters, Master) *Troops Transported* 206

Gallion's Reach (S/Lt. F. N. F. Johnstone, R.N.) (J. F Mason, Master) *Troops Transported* 123

Lady Southborough (Capt. A. M. Poole, Master) *Troops Transported* 350

---

8 Reported Sunk

9 Two others, the James 67 and the W.95 stood by at Ramsgate.

Queen's Channel[10] (Mr. J. L. Bunt, Master) *Troops Transported* 141

W. 24 (Capt. H. F. Boyce, Master) *Troops Transported* 980

W. 26 (Capt. W. J. Allen, Master) *Troops Transported* 296

Total 2,166

Auxiliary Barges. Total 8, of which 1 was lost.

Cabby Troops Transported —

Lady Rosebery[7] (Mr. W. F. Ellis, Master) *Troops Transported* —

Lady Sheila[11] (Mr. G. H. E. Brooks, Master) *Troops Transported* 300

Pudge (Mr. W. Watson, Master) *Troops Transported* —

Seine (Mr. C. V. Cogger, Master) *Troops Transported* 793

Sherfield (S/Lt. J. D. F. Kealey, R.N.) *Troops Transported* 74

Thyra (Mr. E. W. Filley, Master) *Troops Transported* 19

Viking (S/Lt. T. R. Rumbold, R.N.V.R.) (Mr. D. Gregory, Master) *Troops Transported* 70

Total 1,256

Sailing Barges. Total 25, of which 9 were lost.

Ada Mary Troops Transported —

Aidie[7] (Mr. H. Potter, Master) *Troops Transported* —

Barbara Jean[7] (Mr. C. Webb, Master) *Troops Transported* —

Beatrice Maud (Mr. L. Horlock, Master) *Troops Transported* 260

Burton Troops Transported —

Claud[7] (water boat) *Troops Transported* —

Doris[7] (Mr. F. Finbow, Master) *Troops Transported* —

Duchess[7] (Mr. H. J. Wildish, Master) *Troops Transported* —

Ena (Mr. A. G. Page, Master) *Troops Transported* 100

Ethel Everard[7] (Mr. T. Willis, Master) *Troops Transported* —

F.W. 23 (dumb) *Troops Transported* 13

Glenway (Mr. W. H. Easter, Master) *Troops Transported* 213

H.A.C. (Mr. R. H. Scott, Master) *Troops Transported* 100

Haste Away Troops Transported —

---

10 Erroneously referred to in official reports as the "Queensland".

11 A motor coaster.

Lark[7] (Mr. R. H. Scott, Master) *Troops Transported* —

Monarch Troops Transported —

Queen Troops Transported —

Queen Alexandria Troops Transported —

Royalty[7] (Mr. H. Miller, Master) *Troops Transported* —

Sark (dumb) *Troops Transported* —

Shannon Troops Transported —

Shetland (dumb) *Troops Transported* —

Spurgeon (Mr. — Haisman, Master) *Troops Transported* —

Tollesbury (Mr. R. Webb, Master) *Troops Transported* 200

Warrior[7] *Troops Transported* —

Total 886

Life Boats. Total 19, R.N.L.I. life boats,[12] of which 1 was lost.

Abdy Beauclerk Troops Transported —

Cecil & Lilian Philpott (A/B W. J. Morris, Coxswain) *Troops Transported* 51

Charles Cooper Henderson Troops Transported —

Charles Dibdin Troops Transported —

Cyril & Lilian Bishop (Actg. P.O. W. H. Adkin) *Troops Transported* —

Edward Z, Dresden (Lt. Cdr. R. W. Faulkner, R.N.R. (?Retd.)) *Troops Transported* 50

E.M.E.D. (Lieut. R. H. Mead, R.N.V.R., died) (P.O. Tel. W. H. Cooley) *Troops Transported* 39

Greater London (S/Lt. W. D. F. Claydon, R.N.R.) *Troops Transported* 48

Guide of Dunkirk[13] (S/Lt. R. H. C. Amos, R.N.V.R.) (S/Lt. R. H. Wallace, R.N.V.R.) *Troops Transported* —

Jane Holland (Sto. J. Strangeways) (Sto. A. H. Shaw) (S/Lt. E. R. Ponsonby, R.N.V.R.) *Troops Transported* —

Lord Southborough (E. Parker, Coxswain) *Troops Transported* 17

Louise Stephens Troops Transported 49

Lucy Lavers (S/Lt. T. W. Betts, R.N.V.R.) *Troops Transported* —

Mary Scott Troops Transported —

Michael Stephens (S/Lt. M. J. R. Yeatman, R.N.V.R.) *Troops Transported* 52

12 The reserve life boat *Agnes Cross* carried out duties at Dover. She did not go to Dunkirk.

13 At the same time of the Dunkirk evacuation, this boat had just been built and had not yet been named.

Prudential (Mr. H. P. C. Knight, Coxswain) *Troops Transported* 17

Rosa Wood & Phyllis Lunn Troops Transported —

The Viscountess Wakefield Troops Transported —

Thomas Kirk Wright (L/Sea. H. Huntington) *Troops Transported* —

Total 323

Motor Boats, Launches and Vessels. Total 202, of which 78 were lost.

Advance (Mr. C.P. Dick, Owner, Skipper) *Troops Transported* —

Adventuress Troops Transported 85

Albatross[7] *Troops Transported* —

Aljanor[7] *Troops Transported* —

Aloha-Oe[7] [14] *Troops Transported* —

Ambleve[7] (S/Lt. R. E. Blows, R.N.V.R.) *Troops Transported* —

Andora (L/Sea. H. Cook, Coxswain) (S/Lt. E. T. Garside, R.N.V.R.) *Troops Transported* 23

Angler II Troops Transported not known

Aura[7] (S/Lt. M. A. Chodzko, R.N.V.R.) *Troops Transported* —

Balquhain (S/Lt. B. D. O. MacIntyre, R.N.) *Troops Transported* 54

Bat (Mr. J. T. Butchers, Capt.) *Troops Transported* 116

Bee (Mr. W. C. Trowbridge, Capt.) *Troops Transported* 15

Belfast Troops Transported 61

Black Arrow[7] *Troops Transported* —

Blackpool Troops Transported 250

Bluebird (S/Lt. G. B. Eyre, R.N.V.R.) *Troops Transported* —

Bobeli[7] (S/Lt. W. G. PL Bonham, R.N.) *Troops Transported* —

Bonnibell[7] (Sto. 1st Cl. G. H. Rose) *Troops Transported* —

Bonny Heather (Lieut. C. W. Read, D.S.C., R.N.R.) *Troops Transported* 420

Britannia (S/Lt. S. D. Ward. R.N.V.R.) *Troops Transported* —

Brittanic Troops Transported 65

Bullpup[7] *Troops Transported* not known

Cairngorm Troops Transported not known

Canvey Queen[7] *Troops Transported* —

Chamois (Mr. A. E. Brown, Capt.) (Mr. L. Church, Engr.) *Troops Transported* —

---

14 Ex-Belgian canal boat.

Chantecler (S/Lt. T. K. Edge-Partington, R.N.) *Troops Transported* 30

Commodore[7] (S/Lt. Thompson, R.N.R.) *Troops Transported* —

Constant Nymph (Dr. B. A. Smith, Owner/Skipper) *Troops Transported* —

Cordelia (S/Lt. C. A. Thompson, R.N.V.R.) *Troops Transported* —

*Court Belle II*7 *Troops Transported* —

Cyb[7] *Troops Transported* —

Dab II (Lieut. R. W. Thomson, R.N.V.R.) *Troops Transported* —

Defender (Skpr. Mr. E. A. Turnnidge) *Troops Transported* 60

Diana Mary Troops Transported 28

Dreadnought II[7] *Troops Transported* —

Dreadnought III[7] *Troops Transported* —

Eastbourne Belle Troops Transported —

Elizabeth Green (S/Lt. E. T. Garside, R.N.V.R.) *Troops Transported* 10

Eastbourne Queen[7] Troops Transported —

Empress[7] (S/Lt. T. W. Betts, R.N.V.R.) *Troops Transported* —

Enchantress[7] *Troops Transported* —

Encore (Lt. Cdr. Wilson,) *Troops Transported* 44

Endeavour (Skipper. Mr. F. C. Halls) *Troops Transported* —

Enterprise[7] *Troops Transported* —

Escaut[7] [14] *Troops Transported* —

Eskburn Troops Transported 27

Eve[7] (L/Sea. N. Furse, R.N.R.) *Troops Transported* —

Ferry Nymph Troops Transported 44

Fervent (Lt. Cdr. W. R. T. Clements, R.N.R.) *Troops Transported* —

Fishbourne (I.O.W. Ferry) *Troops Transported* —

Forty Two (Lieut. R. Nimmo, R.N.R.) *Troops Transported* —

Frightened Lady[7] (S/Lt. S. C. Allen, R.N.V.R.) *Troops Transported* —

Gavine Troops Transported —

Gay Crusader (S/Lt. T. H. Rodgers, R.N.V.R.) *Troops Transported* —

Gipsy King (Mr. A. Betts) (Mr. H. Brown) (Mr. F. Hook, Deal boatman) *Troops Transported* —

Glitter II (Actg. S/Lt. J. W. S. Culham, R.N.) *Troops Transported* —

Golden Lily Troops Transported —

Golden Spray II[7] (Mr. J. O'Neill and Mr. N. Cohen, Deal boatmen) (Mr. A. C. Crowthall, a Lloyd's official) *Troops Transported* —

Gondolier King Troops Transported —

Godolier Queen Troops Transported —

Good Hope[7] *Troops Transported* —

Grace Darling IV7 *Troops Transported* —

Gwen Eagle[7] *Troops Transported* —

Halfway Troops Transported —

Handy Billy[7] (S/Lt. M. Phipps, R.N.) *Troops Transported* 140

Hanora[7] (S/Lt. C. Minchin, R.N.) *Troops Transported* —

Hound (Mr. H. W. Knight, Capt.) *Troops Transported* 98

Idaho Troops Transported —

Iolanthe Troops Transported 35

Iote[7] (S/Lt. R. H. C. Amos, R.N.V.R.) *Troops Transported* —

Island Queen[14] *Troops Transported* —

Johanna (S/Lt. A. Carew-Hunt, R.N.) *Troops Transported* 10

Jong (S/Lt. I. F. S. Smith, R.N.V.R.) *Troops Transported* —

Josephine I[7] *Troops Transported* —

Kayell (Mr. J. H. Crook, Skipper) *Troops Transported* 70

Kestrel (Mr. W. W. Cribbens, Skipper) *Troops Transported* 50

Kings gate Troops Transported 910

Kit Cat (S/Lt. D. C. Williams, R.N.V.R.) *Troops Transported* —

Lady Cable (Lieut. B. S. Fidler, R.N.V.R.) (Actg. S/Lt. G. A. Cadell, R.N. (Retd.)) *Troops Transported* 40

Lady Haig Troops Transported —

Lansdowne[7] (S/Lt. E. A. E. Cornish, R.N.V.R.) *Troops Transported* —

Letitia (Bawley boat) (Mr. A. J. Dench, Skipper) *Troops Transported* —

Letitia[7] (M/B) (S/Lt. B. D. O. MacIntyre, R.N.) *Troops Transported* —

Little Ann[7] (Mr. A. D. Divine) *Troops Transported* —

Luisiana Troops Transported 20

Madame Sans Gene[7] (S/Lt. K. Adderley, R.N.V.R.) *Troops Transported* —

Madame Pompadour (Lt. Cdr. Faulkner, R.N.V.R. (Retd.)) (Mr. Morley Lawson, Engr.) *Troops Transported* —

Maid of Honour[7] *Troops Transported* —

Ma Joie[7] (Mr. G. Harvey. Skipper.) *Troops Transported* —

Maldon Annie IV[7] (S/Lt. T. Lawrie, R.N.V.R.) *Troops Transported* —

Margherita[7] *Troops Transported* —

Marsayru (Mr. G. D. Olivier, Skipper, 31st May) (S/Lt. T. E. Godman, R.N.V.R., lst-2nd June) *Troops Transported* 19

Mary Rose[7] (S/Lt. H. McClelland, R.N.V.R.) *Troops Transported* —

Mary Spearing[7] (S/Lt. W. G. M. Christian, R.N.V.R.) *Troops Transported* —

Mary Spearing II (S/Lt. W. G. M. Spearing, R.N.V.R.) *Troops Transported* 15

Massey Shaw (fire float) (Sub. Officer A. J. May) *Troops Transported* 106

Matilda Troops Transported not known

May spear Troops Transported 15

Meander (Skipper Mr. G. W. Halliday, R.N.R.) *Troops Transported* —

Mermaiden (Actg. S/Lt. C. E. S. Beale, R.N.) (P/O F. J. Norton, R.F.R.) *Troops Transported* 25

Meuse[15] *Troops Transported* 50

M.F.H. (Mr. W. H. Smith, Capt.) *Troops Transported* 87

Minikoi (S/Lt. R. E. Blows, R.N.V.R.) *Troops Transported* —

Minoru II[7] *Troops Transported* —

Minotaur (Mr. T. Towndrow, Skipper) *Troops Transported* —

Minwood Troops Transported 51

Mirasol[7] *Troops Transported* —

Moss Rose[7] *Troops Transported* —

Mitrious Troops Transported —

Naiad Errant (A.B.S. Palmer, i/c) *Troops Transported* 8

Nanette II Troops Transported 30

Nayland Troops Transported 83

Nemo IV[7] *Troops Transported* —

New Britannic (Mr. W. Matthews, Coxswain) *Troops Transported* 83

New Prince of Wales[7] (S/Lt. P. H. E. Bennett, R.N.) *Troops Transported* —

New White Heather[7] *Troops Transported* —

Offemia Troops Transported 50

Patricia (T.H.V.) *Troops Transported* —

Pauleter (Sto. D. T. Banks) *Troops Transported* 400

Peggy IV[7] (S. H. Hughes, Skipper) *Troops Transported* —

---

15 Sunk of Folkestone on 14th July, by aircraft.

Pioneer[7] *Troops Transported* —

Princess Freda (S/Lt. E. S. Forman, R.N.V.R.) *Troops Transported* —

Princess Lily (Prob. Ty. S/Lt. K. E. A. Bayley) *Troops Transported* —

Princess Maud Troops Transported —

Provider (Mr. F. Hannaford, Skipper) *Troops Transported* not known

Queen Boadicea II (Lieut. J. S. Seal, R.N.R.) (Capt. J. Whittaker) *Troops Transported* —

Queen of England[7] *Troops Transported* —

Quest Troops Transported —

Quicksilver (S/Lt. D. L. Satterford. R.N.) (L/Sea. T. Phillips) *Troops Transported* 20

Quisisana (S/Lt. A. J. Weaver, R.N.V.R.) *Troops Transported* 18

Rapid I (S/Lt. J. C. Clarke, R.N.V.R.) *Troops Transported* 28

Reda (S/Lt. P. Snow, R.N.) (P.O. R. W. Rawlings, Motorman) *Troops Transported* 44

Reliance (Mr. A. Legget, Skipper) *Troops Transported* 80

Renown[7] (Mr. W. H. Noakes, Skipper) *Troops Transported* —

Resolute (Mr. H. D. Osborne, Skipper) *Troops Transported* 40

Roberta[7] *Troops Transported* —

Rocinante[7] *Troops Transported* —

Rosabelle[7] *Troops Transported* —

Rose Marie Troops Transported not known

St. Patrick[7] Troops Transported —

Sambre[14] *Troops Transported* not known

Santosy[7] (Actg. S/Lt. j. M. Chappell, R.N) *Troops Transported* —

Saviour Troops Transported —

Sea Falcon[7] (L/Sea. A. Westbrook) *Troops Transported* —

Sceneshifter[7] *Troops Transported* —

Sea Foam Troops Transported —

Seamew[7] *Troops Transported* —

Sea Roamer (Lieut. J. Bald, R.N.V.R.) *Troops Transported* 2

Seasalter (L. W. Salmon, Skipper) *Troops Transported* 70

Semois[7] [14] *Troops Transported* —

Shamrock[7] (A. Barrel 1, Owner, Skipper) *Troops Transported* —

Silicia Troops Transported 314

Silver Foam Troops Transported —

Silver Moon (Actg. S/Lt. B. D. O. MacIntyre, R.N.) *Troops Transported* —

Silver Queen[7] (S/Lt. ?) (A.B. P. T. Sullivan, C/JX 147897) *Troops Transported* 100

Silvery Breeze Troops Transported —

Singapore (S/Lt. j. W. Pratt, R.N.V.R.) *Troops Transported* 5

Singapore II (S/Lt. F. E. Greenfell, R.N.V.R.) *Troops Transported* —

Skylark I (S/Lt. E. C. B. Mares, R.N.V.R.) (S/Lt. H. McClelland, R.N.V.R.) *Troops Transported* —

Skylark II Troops Transported —

Skylark III[7] Troops Transported —

Skylark III (Sto. G. Bramhall) *Troops Transported* —

Skylark LL. III[7] Troops Transported —

Skylark III[7] (S.M. 281.11) *Troops Transported* —

Skylark 6 (Cadet Rating, G. R. Prince) *Troops Transported* —

Skylark (Southend) (P.O. R. A. Smith, R.F.R. and crew of 5) *Troops Transported* 50

Skylark (S/Lt. M. j. R. Yeatman, R.N.V.R.) *Troops Transported* —

Small Viking Troops Transported 62

Southend Britannia (Lieut. G. L. Norton, R.N.V.R.) *Troops Transported* —

Southern Queen (S/Lt. B. G. P. de Mattos, R.N.V.R.) *Troops Transported* —

Southern Queen[7] (P.L.17) *Troops Transported* —

Spinaway Troops Transported —

Stonehaven[7] Troops Transported —

Summer Maid (P.E. 42) *Troops Transported* —

Sundowner (Cdr. G. H. Lightoller, D.S.C., R.N.R., (Retd.) Owner, Skipper) *Troops Transported* 122

Sunshine[7] Troops Transported —

Surrey Troops Transported —

Tenias Troops Transported 100

Thark (S/Lt. A. Carew-Hunt, R.N) *Troops Transported* —

Thetis[7] (Mr. T. Towndrow, Scoutmaster, Mortlake Sea Scouts) *Troops Transported* —

Thomey croft M/B *Troops Transported* not known

Thyforsa Troops Transported 66

Tigris I (Mr. H. Hastings, Owner, Skipper) *Troops Transported* —

Triton[7] (Lieut. R. IL. Irving, R.N.V.R.) *Troops Transported* —

Two Rivers[7] (P.O. G. B. Thomas, R.N.R., Coxswain) *Troops Transported* —

Vanguard (Mr. A. Grimwade, Skipper) *Troops Transported* 20

Vanitee[7] *Troops Transported* —

Venture[7] *Troops Transported* —

Vera Troops Transported 30

Viewfinder[7] (S/Lt. F. N. Dann, R.N.V.R.) *Troops Transported* —

Walker I (Mr. A. Cadman, Coxswain) *Troops Transported* 29

Walker II (Mr. P. King, Coxswain) *Troops Transported* 76

Wave Queen[16] *Troops Transported* —

Westerley[7] *Troops Transported* —

White Bear (Comd. Gnr. E. Deacon, R.N.) *Troops Transported* —

White Heather (Lt. Seal ?) *Troops Transported* —

White Wing (S/Lt. A. S. Mullins, R.N.R.) *Troops Transported* 6

Willie & Alice Troops Transported —

Windsong (Mr. T. H. Falkingham, Skipper) (Mr. A. Barden, Engine man) *Troops Transported* —

Wings of the Morning (Mr. R. E. Button, Skipper) (S/Lt. T. Lawrie, R.N.V.R.) *Troops Transported* —

Yser[7] [14] (S/Lt. R. W. D. Don, D.S.C., R.N.) (P.O. W. H. Atkin) *Troops Transported* not known

Total 5,031

Life Boats. Total 56, of which 39 were lost.

Blue Star Line - life boat four, number lost 4

B.I.S.N. Co. Ltd. - life boat ten, number lost 10

Butchers - life boat two (M.L/B), number lost —

Can. Pac. S.S. Co. - life boat *Beaverdale*, number lost —

Englis & Mills - life boat four (ex-*Dumbar Castle*), number lost 4

Englis & Mills - life boat one (ex-*Lolworth*), number lost 1

Englis & Mills - life boat one (*Parales*), number lost 1

— life boat two (ex-*Flandres*), number lost 2

Houlder Bros. & Co. - life boat four (ex-*Upway Grange*), number lost 1

Orient Line life boat - *Orient IV* (M.L/B), number lost —

P. and O. S.N. Co. - life boat "G", number lost —

P. and O. S.N. Co. - life boat fifteen, number lost 10

Ropner Shipping Co. - life boat one (ex-*Hawnby*), number lost 1

— life boat four (ex-*Roslin Castle*), number lost 2

---

16 Returned to England in sinking condition.

Royal Mail Line - life boat five, number lost 3

Wherries, Punts and Boats. Total 16, all of which were lost.

Annee (wherry)

Carama (punt)

Clara Belle (wherry)

Dinky (10 ft. boat)

Doris (wherry)

Dumpling (boat)

Edina (wherry)

Lark (punt)

Medora (wherry)

Miranda No. 58 (boat)

Sarah & Emily (boat)

Viking III (dinghy)

List of French Ships Part II

Torpedo Boats and Destroyers. Total 14, of which 3 were sunk.

Bouclier (Capt. de frégate de la Fournière, Commanding 14th Div. Torpedo boats) *Troops Transported* 1,725

Bourrasque[7] (Capt. de frégate R. Fouque, Commanding 4th Div. Torpedo boats) *Troops Transported* —

Branlebas (Capt. de corvette de Cacqueray) *Troops Transported* 1,120

Cyclone[17] (Capt. de vaisseau U. de Portzamparc, Capt. (D) 2nd Flotilla) *Troops Transported* 460

Epervier (light cruiser) *Troops Transported* —

Foudroyant[7] [17] (Capt. de corvette Fontaine) *Troops Transported* 1,250

La Flore (Capt. de corvette Roussel de Courcy) *Troops Transported* 761

Léopard[17] (Capt. de fregate C. Loisel) *Troops Transported* 19

L'Incomprise (Capt. de corvette Gras) *Troops Transported* —

Mistral[17] (Capt. de corvette Lavene) (Lieut, de vaisseau Guillanton) *Troops Transported* 4

Siroco[7] [17] (Capt. de corvette de Toulouse-Lautrec-Montfa) *Troops Transported* 509

---

17 Destroyer

T.112[18] *Troops Transported* 117

T.113[18] *Troops Transported* 275

T.143[18] *Troops Transported* 406

Total 6,646

Despatch Vessels. (*Avisos*) Total 5.

Amiens (Capt. de corvette Monick) *Troops Transported* —

Amiral Mouchez Troops Transported —

Arras Troops Transported 600

Belfort (aircraft tender) (Capt. de corvette L. Viel) *Troops Transported* 400

Savorgnan de Brazza (A/A ship) *Troops Transported* —

Total 1,000

Minesweepers (*Avisos-draguers*). Total 2.

Commandant Delage (Capt. de corvette Froget) *Troops Transported* 807

L'Inipétueuse (Capt. de corvette Bachy) *Troops Transported* 1,231

Total 2,038

Submarine Chasers (*chasseurs*). Total 5.

Chasseur 5 (Lieut, de vaisseau Detroyat) *Troops Transported* 20

Chasseur 6 (Enseigne de vaisseau Desmoutis) *Troops Transported* 50

Chasseur 7 Troops Transported 39

Chasseur 11 (Enseigne de vaisseau Montillier) *Troops Transported* 88

Chasseur 42 (Premier Maitre Timonier Y. Jule) *Troops Transported* 6

Total 203

M.T.Bs. (*Vedettes torpillcurs*). Total 2.

V.T.B. 25 Troops Transported —

V.T.B. 26 Troops Transported not known

Minesweeping Trawlers. Total 13 of which 5 were sunk.

Angèle Marie Troops Transported 199

Bernadette (Maître Principal de Manoeuvre P. Stohlberger.) Tro *Troops Transported* —

---

18 Probably the pendant; the name of the ship is not known.

Chasse-Marée (Lieut, de vaisseau Y. Drogou) *Troops Transported* 974

Denis Papin[7] (A.D. 48) (Lieut, de vaisseau J. F. Raquez, S.O. 2nd Section) *Troops Transported* 405

Joseph Marie[7] (A. Le Calvez, Maltre de Manoeuvre) T *Troops Transported* —

La Majo[7] *Troops Transported* —

Louise Marie Troops Transported 57

Moussaillon[7] *Troops Transported* 309

Président Briand (L.R. 33146) (Lieut, de vaisseau (?) Le Talaer) *Troops Transported* 283

Ste. Bernadette de Lourdes Troops Transported 79

Ste, Denise (D. 618) (Pilote P. Raoult, Commanding the 102nd Section) *Troops Transported* 108

Ste. Elizabeth[19] (A.D. 385)2 (Enseigne de vaisseau Vergonzanc, S.O. 156th Section) *Troops Transported* 60

Venus[7] (A.D. 76) (Enseigne de vaisseau de R. Rosec.) *Troops Transported* 218

Total 2665

Patrol Vessels (*patrouillenrs*). Total 7.

André Louis (Lieut, de vaisseau Aubert) *Troops Transported* 549

Cerons (escort vessel) *Troops Transported* —

Diligente Troops Transported 346

La Nantaise (Lieut, de vaisseau Jaume) *Troops Transported* 15

Lucien Gougy (Lieut, de vaisseau Foignet) *Troops Transported* 282

Reine Des Flots (Enseigne de vaisseau Le Bitoux) *Troops Transported* 1,312

Sauternes (escort vessel) *Troops Transported* —

Total 2,501

Cargo Ships.[20] Total 12, of which 2 were sunk

Cap d'Antifer Troops Transported 291

Cap Tafalneh Troops Transported —

Cérès Troops Transported —

Donaisien[7] *Troops Transported* —

---

19 Reg. No. C.1478.

20 The French mail packets *Cote d'Argent, Cote d'Azure*, Newhaven and Rouen were transferred to the orders of V.A. Dover, and were employed side by side with British personnel vessels. With the exception of the Cote d'Azure which was sunk before the commencement of Op. Dynamo, they are shown in the list of British ships.

Emma Troops Transported 29

Fronsac Troops Transported 500

Francois Tixier Troops Transported —

Ingénieuv Cachin Troops Transported 601

Margaux Troops Transported 369

Monique Schiaffino Troops Transported —

Normanville Troops Transported 500

St. Camille[7] Troops Transported —

Total 2,290

Trawlers and M.F.Vs. Total 59 of which at least 3 were sunk. (Reg. No., if any, in brackets)

Alfred Paul Troops Transported 50

André Marcel Troops Transported 50

Angelus de la Mer (B. 1339) *Troops Transported* 17

Antoinette Michel (C. 137(5) *Troops Transported* 93

Ave Maria Gratia Plena (C. 1298) *Troops Transported* 111

Barbe Auguste (D. 812) *Troops Transported* 65

Blei Mor (L. 312(5) *Troops Transported* not known

Caporal Peugeot (Maître Josselin) Troops Transported 105

Ciel de France (C. 5598) *Troops Transported* 108

Credo (DG. 924) *Troops Transported* 53

Du Guesclin (DG. 910) *Troops Transported* 18

Duperre Troops Transported 307

Edmond Rene Troops Transported 210

Emile Deschamps[7] Troops Transported —

Etoile Polaire (L. 4125) *Troops Transported* not known

Gabrielle Georges Troops Transported not known

Gaston Rivier (Officier des equipages H. Wallyn) *Troops Transported* 100

Henriette Troops Transported not known

Jean Bart (Doublecourt, Skipper) *Troops Transported* 208

Jean Ribault (Premier-Maitre Dupiénois) *Troops Transported* 100

Jeanne Antoine Troops Transported not known

Jésus Flagelle (B. 1853) *Troops Transported* 98

Jeune France (Di. J 213) *Troops Transported* 186

Jolie Mascotte (C. 1347) *Troops Transported* not known

Joseph Marcel Troops Transported 150

La Colombe (C. 1322) *Troops Transported* 111

La Mouette (C. 1441) *Troops Transported* 53

Lauritz (DG. 574) *Troops Transported* not known

Les Trois Cousins (DG. 350) *Troops Transported* 48

Lutteur (tug) *Troops Transported* 308

Marcel Paul (C. 5530) *Troops Transported* not known

Margaux (D. 092) *Troops Transported* not known

Maria Elena (Enseigne de vaisseau Fatout) *Troops Transported* 120

Marie (Enseigne de vaisseau J. Aguttes, Patron Leprêtre) *Troops Transported* 100

Mimi Pierrot (L. 3968) *Troops Transported* not known

Monique Camille Troops Transported 302

Nôtre Dame de la Salette (B. 1832) *Troops Transported* 48

Nôtre Dame des Miracles (Di. 1194) *Troops Transported* 50

Noune (DO. 694) *Troops Transported* 66

Patrie Troops Transported 659

*Pierre*⁷ (Patron P. Elran) *Troops Transported* —

Pierre et Marie (Enseigne de vaisseau Royer in charge Peine A me lie (DG. 668) *Troops Transported* 393

Reine Amélie Troops Transported 48

Rose Effeuillée (C. 2716) *Troops Transported* 65

Saint Cyr (L. 4183) *Troops Transported* not known

Saint François de Salles (B. 1738) *Troops Transported* 31

Saint Michel (B. 1388) *Troops Transported* not known

Saint Pierre IV (C. 1418) (Enseigne de vaisseau E. Le Coniat) *Troops Transported* not known

Saint Saulve (B. 1581) *Troops Transported* 45

Saint Sophie (I)G. 715) *Troops Transported* 66

Ste. Germaine (B. 1790) *Troops Transported* 34

Ste. Isabelle (Patron Boudard) *Troops Transported* —

Ste. Marie Protégez Nous (B. 1510) *Troops Transported* 30

Ste. Thérèse de L'Enfant Jésus (DG. 230) *Troops Transported* not known

Soizic (L. 4107) *Troops Transported* 16

Stella Maris Troops Transported 1

Surcouf (DG. 921) *Troops Transported* 17

Thérèse Louis (B. 1741) *Troops Transported* 174

Yvonne et Moabe⁷ Troops Transported not known

List of Belgian Ships. Part III

Trawlers, unless otherwise stated. Total 45 ships of which 4 of them were sunk.

A.5 (Patrol boat) (Lieut. J. D'Hauwer, Belgian Navy) *Troops Transported* 229

Abel Dewulf (N. 58) *Troops Transported* 17

Alex Rachel (H. 23) *Troops Transported* 25

Aline-Bertha-Antoinette (Z. 26) *Troops Transported* 93

André Lucienne (N. 53) *Troops Transported* 18

Anna (N. 38) *Troops Transported* 97

Anna Léopold (H. 76) *Troops Transported* 289

Anna-Marguerite (Z. 2) *Troops Transported* not known

Buffalo Bill (Z. 4) *Troops Transported* not known

Constant Léopold (Z. 35) *Troops Transported* 43

Cor Jésu (O. 227) (Capt. J. Delbal, Master) *Troops Transported* 191

De Ruyter (Z. 25) *Troops Transported* 84

Elona-Constance (Z. 6) *Troops Transported* not known

Frieda (H. 13) *Troops Transported* 150

Gaby (O. 87) *Troops Transported* not known

Georges Edouard (O. 86) (Capt. M. Coppin, Master) (Master of the Belgian S.S. Julia) *Troops Transported* 401

Gerard-Léon (H. 64) *Troops Transported* not known

Getuigt vor Christus⁷ (N. 59) *Troops Transported* —

Gilda (H. 77) *Troops Transported* 120

Gods Grenade (H. 75) *Troops Transported* 100

Goliath (tug) *Troops Transported* 183

Graaf van Vlaanderen (O. 92) *Troops Transported* not known

Guido Gazelle (O. 225) (Capt. R. Lusyne, Master) *Troops Transported* 145

Gustaaf (Z. 31) *Troops Transported* not known

Henri (Z. 40) *Troops Transported* 33

Indépendence (O. 308) *Troops Transported* not known

Irma (Z. 71) *Troops Transported* 54

Irma-Germaine (Z. 3) *Troops Transported* not known

John (O. 210) *Troops Transported* not known

Jonge Jan (O. 200) (M. Nys, Master) *Troops Transported* 215

Louise-Iréne (H. 80) *Troops Transported* not known

Lydie Suzanne (Z. 50) (G. F. Ragaert, Master) *Troops Transported* 416

Madeleine Kamiel (H. 81) *Troops Transported* 90

Maréchal Foch (O. 274) (Capt. P. Lusyne, Master) *Troops Transported* —

Navis-Maria (H. 51) *Troops Transported* 44

O.L.V. van Vlaanderen[7] (N. 49) *Troops Transported* —

Onder Ons (O. 318) *Troops Transported* 139

Pharailde (H. 42) *Troops Transported* —

Prins Boudewijn (O. 153) (Kolb-Bernard, Second-Maître de Manoeuvre, Commanding Convoy No. 7) *Troops Transported* 138

Raphael-Raymonde (H. 43) *Troops Transported* not known

Rockall (O. 323) *Troops Transported* 150

Sunny Isle[7] (H. 5) *Troops Transported* —

Victor-Erna (H. 63) *Troops Transported* not known

Yvonne (Z. 41) *Troops Transported* not known

Zwaluw (Z. 11) *Troops Transported* not known

List of Polish Ships. Part IV

Blyskawica (destroyer) *Troops Transported* —

List of Dutch Ships. Part V

Demok I (yacht) *Troops Transported* 214

M.74 (motor boat) (Lt. Cdr. H. G. Boys-Smith, R.N.R. from Kestrel 1st June) (L/Sea. R. W. Legg, Coxswain) *Troops Transported* —

List of Norwegian Ships. Part VI

S.S. Hird (Capt. A. M. Fredhjem) *Troops Transported* 3,500

Appendix B

Named Ships and Vessels Lost and Damaged during Operation "Dynamo"

(Dates in brackets)

Note: Large numbers of unnamed boats were also lost and damaged.

Ships and Vessels Lost Part I

By Air Attack

Destroyers

Basilisk (1/6), *Grenade* (29/5), *Havant* (1/6), *Keith* (1/6)

Minesweepers

Brighton Queen (1/6), *Devonia* (31/5), *Gracie Fields* (30/5), *Skipjack* (1/6), *Waverley* (29/5)

Personnel Vessels

Clan Macalister (29/5), *Crested Eagle* (sp. S/V) (29/5), *Fenella* (29/5), *Lorina* (29/5), *Normania* (29/5), *Queen of the Channel* (28/5), *Scotia* (1/6)

Motor Lighters

X.149 (31/5), *X.213* (31/5)

Trawlers

Calvi (29/5), *Nautilus* (29/5), *Polly Johnson* (29/5)

Hospital Carrier

Paris (3/6)

Landing Craft

A.L.C. 16 (29/5)

Barges

Lady Rosebery (1/6), *Doris* (1/6)

A.B./V.

King Orry (30/5)

Seaplane Tender

S.T. 243 (2/6)

Gunboat

Mosquito (1/6)

Drifters

Boy Roy (27/5), *Paxton* (27/5)

Tugs

St. Abbs (1/6), *St. Fagan* (1/6)

Small Craft

Commodore (31/5), *Mirasol* date not known, *Southern Queen* (P.L.17), date not known

By Torpedoes (E–Boats)

Destroyers

Grafton (29/5), *Wakeful* (29/5)

Trawlers

Argyllshire (1/6), *Stella Dorado* (1/6)

By Mines

Trawlers

Blackburn Rovers (2/6), St. *Achilleus* (1/6), *Thuringia* (28/5), *Westella* (2/6)

Personnel Vessels

Mona's Queen (29/5)

Blockship

Gourko (4/6)

Small Craft

Renown (1/6)

Yacht

Grive (1/6)

By Gunfire (Shore)

Personnel Vessel

Sequacity (27/5)

Drifter

Lord Cavan (1/6)

Skoot

Horst (31/5)

Small Craft

Gallant's Motor Boat (2/6), *New Prince of Wales* (31/5)

By Collision and other Misadventure

Minesweeper

Brighton Belle (28/5)

Skoots

Alice (28/5), *Lena* (4/6), *Sursum-Corda* (31/5)

Blockship

Holland (3/6)

Trawlers

Comfort (29/5), *Thomas* date unknown, *Bartlett*[1] (28/5)

Yachts

Amulree (1/6) *Pellag II* (1/6)

Tug

Fossa (2/6)

Drifters

Eileen Emma (1/6), *Fair Breeze* (1/6), *Gervais Rentoul* (1/6) *Girl Pamela* (night 28/29 May)

Exn. Serv. V.

Ocean Reward (28/5)

Seaplane Tenders

S.T.243 (31/5), *S.T.254* (31/5), *A.M.C.3* (31/5)

---

1 Blew up on Allied minefield.

Small Craft

Albatross², *Aljanor²*, *Aloa-Oe²*, *Ambleve* (30/5), *Aura³* (2/6), *Black Arrow* (29/30 May), *Bobeli* (2/6), *Bonnibell* (2/6), *Bullpup⁴*, *Canvey Queen* (30/5), *Court Belle²*, *Cyb²*, *Dreadnought II²*, *Frightened Lady³ ⁴*, *Golden Spray II* (31/5), *Good Hope²*, *Grace Darling IV²*, *Gwen Eagle²*, *Handy Billy²*, *Hanora³ ⁴*, *Iote* (1/6), *Island Queen²*, *Josephine I²*, *Lansdowne³* (1/6), *Letitia* (M/B) (4/6), *Little Ann²*, *Madame Sans Gene* (4/6), *Maid of Honour²*, *Ma Foie* (30/5), *Maldon Annie IV* (31/5), *Margherita²*, *Mary Rose* (31/5), *Mary Spearing⁴*, *Minikoi* (29/5), *Minoru II²*, *Pioneer²*, *Queen of England* (29/5), *Roberta²*, *Rocinante⁵ ⁶*, *Rosabelle²*, *St. Patrick* (31/5), *Santosy³* (3/6), *Scene Shifter* (29/6), *Sea Falcon* (31/5), *Seamew²*, *Semois²*, *Shamrock* (30/5), *Silver Queen¹* (30/5), *Skylark II²* (S.M.281. II), *Skylark L.L.II²*, *Stonehaven²*, *Sunshine³* (31/5), *Thetis²³* (2/6), *Triton³* (31/5), *Two Rivers* (31 /5), *Vanitee²*, *Dreadnought III²*, *Eastbourne Queen* (1/6), *Empress³* (1/6), *Enchantress²*, *Enterprise* (31/5), *Escaut²*, *Eve²*, *Moss Rose²*, *Nemo IV²*, *New White Heather²*, *Peggy IV⁴*, *Princess Lily* (31/5), *Venture²*, *Viewfinder* (31/5), *Viscountess Wakefield* (31/5), *Wave Queen⁷* (5/6), *Westerley³* (1/6), *Yser²*

Wherries, Punts and Boats

Aimée² (wherry), *Carama* (punt) (30/5), *Clara Belle²* (wherry), *Dinky²* (10 ft. boat), *Doris²* (wherry), *Dumpling²* (boat), *Edina²* (wherry), *Lark²* (punt), *Medora²* (wherry), *Miranda²* (No. 58), *Sarah & Emily²* (boat), *Viking III²* (dinghy)

Barges

Aidie³ (1/6), *Barbara Jean³* (1/6), *Claude* (water-boat date and cause of loss not known), *Duchess³* (1/6), *Ethel Everard³* (1/6), *Lark³* (1/6), *Royalty³* (1/6), *Warrior³ ⁴*

Landing Craft

A.L.C.4 (29/5), *A.L.C.8³* (31/5), *A.L.C.15* (31/5), *A.L.C.18* (29/5), *M.L.C.12³* (2/6), *M.L.C.17⁵* (3/6), *M.L.C.22³* (2/6)

Ships and Vessels Damaged Part II

By Air Attack

Destroyers

Anthony (30/5), *Gallant* (29/5), *Greyhound* (29/5), *Intrepid* (29/5), *Ivanhoe* (1/6), *Jaguar* (29/5), *Sabre* (30/5), *Saladin* (29/5), *Vivacious* (31/5) (28/5), *Wolfhound* (27/5), *Worcester* (1/6)

Minesweepers

Hebe (31/5), *Pangbourne* (29/5), *Ross* (1/6), *Salamander* (1 /6), *Westward-Ho* (1/6)

---

2 Date and cause of loss not known.

3 Abandoned.

4 Date of Loss not known.

5 Cause of loss not known.

6 Returned from Dunkirk damaged beyond repair.

7 Returned to England in sinking condition.

A.A. Cruiser

Calcutta (2/6)

Personnel Vessels

Canterbury (29/5) *Prague* (1/6) *Royal Daffodil* (2/6)

Sloop

Bideford (29/5)

A.B/V

Mona's Isle (27/5)

Hospital Carriers

Isle of Guernsey (29/5), *St. Julien* (29/5), *Worthing* (2/6)

By Gunfire

Personnel Vessels

Biarritz (27/5), *Princess Maud* (30/5)

Trawlers

"Kingston"[8] (2/6), *Spurs* (2/6)

A.B/V.

King Orry (21/5)

By Mine

Hospital Carrier

St. David (1/6)

By Collision or Grounding

Destroyers

Icarus (2/6), *Impulsive* (31/5), *Mackay* (29/5), *Montrose* (29/5), *Vimy* (1/6), *Whitehall* (31/5), *Wolsey* (31/5)

Minesweepers

Leda (4/6), *Sharpshooter* (30/5)

Hospital Carrier

Isle of Thanet (28/5)

---

8 Probably either the *Kingston Alalite* or the *Kingston Olivine*.

Personnel Vessels

Ben-my-Chree (2/6), *Maid of Orleans* (1/6), *Roebuck* (31/5)

French Ships Sunk during Operation "Dynamo" Part III

Bourrasque, Torpedo boat, sunk by shell fire, (30/5)

Foudroyant, Destroyer, sunk by air attack, (1/6)

Siroco, Destroyer, sunk by E-Boat, (31/5)

Denis Papin, M/S trawler, sunk by air attack, (1/6)

Joseph Marie, M/S trawler, sunk by air attack, (29/5)

La Majo, M/S trawler, sunk by air attack, (29/5)

Moussaillon, M/S trawler, sunk by air attack, (1/6)

Venus, M/S trawler, sunk by air attack, (1/6)

Douaisien, Cargo ship, not known, not known

St. Camille, Cargo ship, not known, not known

Emile Deschamps, Fleet auxiliary, sunk by mine, (4/6)

Pierre, Trawler, sunk by shell fire, (31/5)

Yvonne St. Moabe, not known, sunk by air attack, (1/6)

Belgian Ships Sunk during Operation "Dynamo" Part IV

Getuigt V or *Christus*, Trawler, not known how sunk, (2/6)

Marechal Foch, Trawler, sunk by collision, (4/6)

O.L.V. Van Vlaandaren, Trawler, not known how sunk, (2/6)

Sunny Isle, Trawler, not known how sunk, (2/6)

Appendix C

No. 11 Group Fighter Patrols

26th May – Patrols 22, Total Daily flying hours, 480,

Enemy aircraft destroyed 30, Enemy aircraft driven down 20

27th May – Patrols 23, Total Daily flying hours, 536,

Enemy aircraft destroyed 48, Enemy aircraft driven down 32

28th May – Patrols 11, Total Daily flying hours, 576,

Enemy aircraft destroyed 20, Enemy aircraft driven down 6

29th May – Patrols 9, Total Daily flying hours, 674,

Enemy aircraft destroyed 78, Enemy aircraft driven down 8

30th May – Patrols 9, Total Daily flying hours, 704,

Enemy aircraft destroyed —, Enemy aircraft driven down —

31st May – Patrols 8, Total Daily flying hours, 490,

Enemy aircraft destroyed 36, Enemy aircraft driven down 4

1st June – Patrols 8, Total Daily flying hours, 558,

Enemy aircraft destroyed 69, Enemy aircraft driven down —

2nd June – Patrols 4, Total Daily flying hours, 231,

Enemy aircraft destroyed 16, Enemy aircraft driven down 6

3rd June – Patrols 4, Total Daily flying hours, 339,

Enemy aircraft destroyed —, Enemy aircraft driven down —

4th June – Patrols 3, Total Daily flying hours, 234,

Enemy aircraft destroyed —, Enemy aircraft driven down —

Total flying hours 4,822

Appendix D

Signals Re Build-up of Destroyers

Between 27th May and 1st June

Note (i) The 213 signals in Appendices D to Z have been collated from the copies of some 2,500 "Dynamo" signals in Admiralty Record Office Enclosure Box No. 370 which accompanies Admiralty Record Office Case 5458.

Note (ii) 15 destroyers from the Nore Command, 10 from the Western Approaches Command, 10 from the Portsmouth Command, and 6 of the Dover Command.

– a total of 41 British destroyers – were employed in Operation "Dynamo".

Monday, 27th May

1. Vice-Admiral, Dover to Admiralty (R) C.-in-C. Nore

Request Dover Forces may be strengthened forthwith by six additional destroyers but not at the expense of Nore Command. 1036/27

2. Admiralty to C.-in-C. Western Approaches, C.-in-C. Portsmouth (R) Vice-Admiral Dover, C.-in-C. Nore, C.-in-C. Home Fleet, F.O.I.C. Humber, R.A Dover.

Request four destroyers from Western Approaches and two from Portsmouth be sailed for Dover as soon as possible.... . 1317/27

3. Vice-Admiral, Dover to *Grafton* (R) S.O. 10th M.S.F., *Greyhound, Calcutta.*

Close beach in vicinity of La Panne at 0100 and send in boats for British troops. You should withdraw at your discretion and anyhow not later than 0330. Paddle minesweepers and small craft will be in vicinity. Acknowledge. 2054/27

> [V.A. Dover informed (between 2015 and 2055/27) that embarkation was only possible from the beaches, and that evacuation on the night of 28th-29th May was problematical (see Apps. M.3 and M.4)].

4. Vice-Admiral, Dover to *Grafton, Greyhound, Blyskawica*[1] (R) S.O. 10th M.S.F.

Close the beach at La Panne at 0100 tomorrow Tuesday and embark all possible British troops using your boats. This is our last chance of saving them. 2127/27

---

1 Was not available

4a. The Polish destroyer *Blyskawica* was not in company but she replied at 2242/27:

"We have two pulling boats only. Can accommodate 3 in each."

Monday, 27th May

5. Vice-Admiral, Dover to *Gallant, Vivacious, Windsor, Vimy, Calcutta, Anthony, Impulsive.*

Close beaches one to three miles east of Dunkirk with utmost despatch and embark all possible British troops using your own boats. This is our last chance of saving them. *Maid of Orleans, Lormont,* 17 drifters and other craft will be operating. 2142/27

6. Vice-Admiral, Dover to *Wolfhound, Wolsey.* 17 drifters arriving Dunkirk tonight. Direct to beaches as necessary. 2158/27

7. Vice-Admiral, Dover to *Vimy*

Close the beaches one to three miles east of Dunkirk at 0100 tomorrow Tuesday and embark all possible British troops using your boats. This is our chance of saving them. 2238/27

8. Vice-Admiral, Dover to *Sabre*

Last chance of saving B.E.F. is tonight. Proceed with all despatch to beach one to three miles east of Dunkirk and embark troops using own boats. Route from Dover is by No. 6 Calais buoy, south of Dunkerque B.W. buoy and French coastal route. Return by Zuydcoote Pass Q.Z.F.3. and Q.Z.S.60. Other British ships will be off the beach. You should leave at your discretion and anyhow not later than 0330. 2305/27

Thursday, 30th May

9. Vice-Admiral, Dover to Admiralty, C.in-C. Nore

Dover 30th May, departures: *Javelin, Impulsive, Havant, Harvester, Icarus, Intrepid, Ivanhoe,* at 0515, for Sheerness. 0538/30

Note: This followed a decision to withdraw the 7 modern destroyers from Operation "Dynamo".

10. C.-IN-C. Nore to *Harvester, Havant, Ivanhoe, Impulsive, Icarus, Intrepid* (R) C.S.

S/H, V.A. Dover.

Raise steam forthwith and proceed to Dunkirk by Route X for X-ray. 1531/30

Note: The decision to withdraw the modern destroyers was revoked.

11. Admiralty to C.-in-C. Nore (R) *Ajax, Hotspur,* V.A. Dover, *Lynx*

A spare destroyers crew is to be sent to Dover as soon as possible to provide temporary reliefs in crews of destroyers operating off Belgian coast... . 2341/30

Appendix E

Signals Re Build-up of Minesweepers

Note: 30 minesweepers took part in Operation "Dynamo" and were drawn from the following flotillas: 1st, 4th, 5th, 6th, 7th, 8th, 10th, and 12th.

Sunday, 26th May

1. Admiralty to C.-in-C. Home Fleet, (R) A.C.O.S., V.A. Dover, M/S 1, M/S 6

Owing to casualties, 10 M.S.F. at Dover has been reduced to two effective ships. Oil-burning fleet sweepers are urgently required there to maintain channel for communication with B.E.F.

Request two ships of 1st M.S.F. may be spared from your command and sailed to join 6 M.S.F. at Dover forthwith[1].

1833/26

[1] *Hebe* and *Sharpshooter* arrived Dover 1723/28.

Monday, 27th May

2. C.-in-C. Nore to Vice-Admiral, Dover

5th M.S.F. can sail from Harwich at daylight.

Would they be of use to you at Dunkirk. 2345/27

Reply

3. No thank you very much. 0044/28

Tuesday, 28th May

Note: Admiralty message 1003/28 [not available] ordered the 7th and 8th M/S Flotillas (which were at Rosyth) to Harwich, under the orders of the Vice-Admiral, Dover.

---

1 Was not available

4. C.-in-C. Nore to F.O.I.C. Harwich , (R) V.A. Dover, Admiralty

12th M.S.F. is to proceed to arrive off La Penne at 2200 today, Tuesday ...

5th M.S.F. is to proceed to arrive off beach between Zuydcoote and Malo-les-Bains at 2200 today ... 0939/28 T.O.R 1036

5. Vice-Admiral, Dover to *Emperor of India*, *Princess Elizabeth* [10th M.S.F.] (R) C.M.S.

Emperor of India is to proceed direct over minefield to La Panne to embark troops.

Princess Elizabeth is to proceed over minefields to Dunkirk keeping well clear to northward of Gravelines Point where enemy batteries may be in place. Then embark troops. Return route to be at your discretion depending on the state of the tide. 1607/28

Appendix F

Signals Re Build-up of Skoots

22nd May

F.1. Admiralty to C.-in-C. Portsmouth, (R) F.O.I.C. Portland, F.O.I.C. Southampton, V.A. Dover

From the following list of Dutch coasters lying in Poole, four empty and of about 200-300 tons, are to be sent immediately to New Docks, Southampton, where they will be loaded with military supplies. These will be manned by naval crews after arrival at Southampton, and will work under the War Office.

2. As many of the remainder as are in light condition will be taken over and manned by naval crews and when ready will be at the disposal of V.A. Dover.

3. C.-in-C. Portsmouth, is requested to arrange for the organisation and assembly of these vessels reporting names of vessels as they became ready for service.

4. Arrangements are being made for sets of charts to be sent to Portsmouth Chart Depot.

5. Further signal will be made regarding provision of naval personnel and disposal of Dutch crews on taking over.

6. It is a matter of great importance that these vessels should be got ready for service as soon as possible.

7. *Despatch II*[1], *Horst, Jaba, Brem*[1], *Sursum Corda, Ruja, Boekelo*[1], *Abel Tasman, Java, Hebenobel*[1], *Kaapfalga, Friso, Virgo*[1], *Alice, Dourswold*[1], *Aldo*[1], *Fredanja, Nottingham*[1], *Hebe II*

1703/22

F.2. Admiralty to C.-in-C. Nore (r) F.O.I.C. London, V.A. Dover

1. From the following list of Dutch coasters lying in the Port of London, four in ballast and of about 200-300 tons, are to be sent immediately to Victualling Wharf Deptford to load military supplies. These will be manned by naval crews after arrival at Deptford, and will work under the War Office.

2. As many of the remainder which [Pas] are in light condition are to be taken over and manned by naval crews.

3. C.-in-C. Nore is requested to arrange for the organisation and assembly of these vessels which when ready will be placed at the disposal of V.A. Dover.

---

1 Was not available

4. Names of ships to be reported as they became ready for service.

5. Arrangements are being made for sets of charts to be sent to Chart Depot Sheerness.

6. Further signal will be made re disposal of Dutch crews and provision of personnel for manning.

7. It is a matter of great importance that these ships should be got ready as soon as possible.

8. *Twente, Brabant, Bart, Tilly, Antje, Hondsrug, Brandaris, Reiger, Delta, Lena, Princess Juliana, Borneo[1], Caribia, Oranje, Liberty[1], Vrede, Gorecht, Bernina[1], Rika, Fiducia[1], Limburg[1], Patria, Junior[1], Bornrif, Amstelroom[1], Deneb, Martha[1], Express[1], Mercurius[1], Aegir, Jutland.* 1704/22

F.3. Admiralty to Vice-Admiral, Dover, C.-in-C. Nore, C.-in-C. Portsmouth (R) F.O.I.C. London, F.O.I.C. Southampton, F.O.I.C. Portland Admiralty 1703/22 and 1704/22 to certain addressees only. The operation for which these ships are being prepared will be known as Dynamo. 1944/22

Appendix G

Signals Re Lack of Small Craft

Sunday, 26th May

1. Admiralty to A/S Chatham, A/S Portsmouth, (R) C.-in-C. Nore, C.-in-C. Portsmouth, V.A. Dover.

Investigate and report how many cutters and whalers can be made available for immediate service under V.A. Dover. 2028/20

2. Admiralty to C.-in-C. Portsmouth, Vice-Admiral, Dover (R) Combrax Portsmouth, Commandant 1st D.C. Fort Cumberland.

8 A.L.C's. with crews complete are available and will be embarked in S.S. Clan Macalister at Southampton a.m. 27th May … 2337/20

Monday, 27th May

3. (Admiralty) D.S.V.P. to Commodore, Sheerness (R) C.-in-C. Nore V.A. Dover.

About 40 motor launches have been ordered to Sheerness of which 30 should arrive at daylight tomorrow Tuesday. The rest during the day. These will be manned on arrival at Sheerness … Request you will inform V.A. Dover when boats are ready for service. 2035/27

Tuesday, 28th May

Note: (At 0430. S.N.O. Dunkirk asked for all vessels to be sent alongside east pier).

4. Vice-Admiral, Dover to S.N.O. Dunkirk (R) Fighter Command.

Further destroyers and small craft are being sent now to Dunkirk. 0630/28

Signals Re Build-up of Small Craft

5. N.O.I.C. Ramsgate to Vice-Admiral, Dover.

1st Mine Recovery Flotilla Vessels *Lord Cavan, Fidget, Jacketa, Silver Dawn* and *Fisher Buoy*. Tug *Java*. Drifters *Lord Collingwood, Lord Rodney, Lord Keith, Lord St. Vincent*. Motor boats *New Britannic, Walker I, Walker II, Angler, Nayland*, sailed Ramsgate for Dunkirk.

6. D.M.O.[1] to Vice-Admiral, Dover (R) C.-in-C. Nore, N.O.I.C. Ramsgate, Admiralty.

17 motor boats and 17 whalers left Sheerness for Dover between 1830 and 1900 escorted by trawler *Asama*. 1916/28

7. Vice-Admiral, Dover to C.-in-C. NORE (R) Admiralty.

Request you will send every available shallow draft power boat capable of ferrying from beaches to ships, direct to ships lying off beaches to eastward of Dunkirk stocked with fuel and provisions for 2 days. 2002/28

8. (Admiralty) D.S.V.P. to C.-in-C. Nore, S.N.O. Dover, S.N.O. Sheerness.

Additional motor boats up to a possible 40 are being sent from Thames to Dover to arrive before tomorrow night 29th.

Some boats will come by lorries direct to Dover. 12 crews are being sent to Dover and 20 to Sheerness to await arrival of boats. Runner crews take boats to Sheerness but will not proceed further. 2031/28

9. N.C.S.O. Thames to Commodore Sheerness, C.-in-C. Nore, Vice-Admiral, Dover, N.O.I.C. Ramsgate.

All small craft are being routed direct to beaches east of Dunkirk provided they have charts, food, fuel, etc. If not complete they will be sent to Sheerness first. 2301/28

Wednesday, 29th May

10. Admiralty to Commodore in Charge, Sheerness (R) C.-in-C. Nore V.A. Dover. N.O.I.C. Ramsgate.

All motor boats being prepared for service under V.A. Dover are to be sent immediately they are ready to Ramsgate where they will receive orders from the Naval-Officer-in-Charge. 0120/29

11. *Wolfhound* to Vice-Admiral, Dover.

Have you any orders for fleet of motor boats now tied up alongside *Wolfhound*. 0224/29

Reply

12. Make utmost endeavour to hasten departure of motor boats to La Panne beach. 0256/29

13. (Admiralty) D.S.V.P. to C's-in-C. Portsmouth, Nore, S.N.O.'s Yarmouth, Newhaven, Vice-Admiral, Dover.

Officers from S.V.P. are proceeding to requisition suitable motor boats reported to S.V.P. under Emergency Statute[2] and otherwise, for immediate service on coast from Portsmouth to Yarmouth.

---

1 Dynamo Maintenance Officer (Admiral Taylor) at Sheerness.

2 This emergency statute was *Statutory Order No.* 718, dated 10th May, 1940, entitled *Small Craft (Information) Order,* 1940. It was issued at the request, on 16th April 1940, of Admiral Sir Lionel Preston, Director of the Small Vessels Pool, Admiralty, in view of the probable requirements for small motor craft.

The order, briefly, called on all owners of self-propelled craft between 30 and 100 feet in length, to send particulars of their craft to the Admiralty within 14 days. The Order was published in the press in the usual way, and on 14th May it was broadcast on the B.B.C. At the time of the conception and issue of the Order, however, there was clearly no question of a possible evacuation

In all about 140 are anticipated of which 40 have already been requisitioned in the Thames Estuary for special service and ordered to Dover.

It is requested that boats when collected are placed under control until their crews arrive as follows:

Area 1—Lymington to Littlehampton including I.O.W. assembling at Hamble.

Area 2—Littlehampton to Rye, assembling at Newhaven.

Area 3—Brightlingsea to Harwich, assembling at Harwich.

Area 4—Southwold to Gt. Yarmouth, assembling at Yarmouth. 0940/29

14. Admiralty to C.-in-C. Portsmouth, C.-in-.C. Nore (R) V.A. Dover, N.O.I.C. Ramsgate, Cdr. i/c Sheerness.

Investigate as a matter of urgency provision of additional small craft which can be made available within 48 hours from all ports in your command for Operation "Dynamo" including X-lighters and other self-propelled lighters. Any available in Portsmouth Command to be sent to Dover forthwith.[3] Those in Nore Command to be sent to Ramsgate. V.A. Dover to be kept informed.

All craft are to be provided with charts and if necessary manned by naval crews.

S.T.O.'s have been informed and have full requisitioning powers. 1115/29

15. (Admiralty) D.S.V.P. to C.-in-C. Portsmouth, Nore, Vice-Admiral, Dover (R), N.O.I.C. Ramsgate, C.S. Sheerness, S.N.O. Yarmouth, S.N.O. Newhaven.

My 0940/29 and Admiralty 1115/29:

Officers of S.V.P. now in area mentioned have been ordered to co-operate with your organisations.

They are to supply records from S.V.P. of boats available, and to send boats as ordered in Admiralty 1115/29 and not repetition not as in my 0940/29. 1130/30

10. Admiralty to Vice-Admiral, Dover (R) C.-in-C. Nore.

20 Thames barges in tow of 5 tugs expected to arrive Ramsgate 1700 today May 29th ... It is for consideration that they be used as piers. 1255/29

17. Vice-Admiral, Dover to *Hebe* for Captain Bush.

20 Thames barges in tow are being sent. Can they be usefully used as piers for loading troops at points on the beaches or do you consider they would be more usefully employed for ferrying troops ... 1456/29

18. C.-in-C. Nore to A/S Chatham, Commodore in Charge, Sheerness, D.M.O. (R), N.O.I.C. Ramsgate.

All available X-lighters which can be released without disorganising dockyards are to be sent to Ramsgate forthwith ... 1210/29

19. Vice-Admiral, Dover to C.-in-C. Portsmouth.

All small craft should be route-ed direct to Ramsgate and not repeat not to Dover. 1618/29

---

from the Continent.

3 See Appendix G 22.

Thursday, 30th May

20. C.-in-C. Portsmouth to Admiralty, N.O.I.C. Ramsgate, Vice-Admiral, Dover.

Small craft for Belgium operations due Ramsgate approximately as follows:

0600 3 fast M/B's.

0700 Dutch *Mok I*.

0900 2 fast paddle steamers, 1 M/B, 1 Picket boat.

1000 H.M.S. *Dwarf*, tug *Grappler* towing lighter and launches, tug *Emprise* towing launch, and 2 coaling tugs.

1100 3 Hopper barges.

1200 2 picket boats, 1 diesel boat.

1300 2 small cargo carriers, 3 launch, 1 small tug.

1400 1 Dutch M/B and 2 M/B's.

1500 2 I.O.W. car ferries and 2 drifters.

1600 1 small tug towing launch.

1900 5 Hoppers.

2400 2 launches.

All above times are 30th May. No ships are degaussed.

0005/30

21. Vice-Admiral, Dover to *Hebe*.

Rear-Admiral [Dover] from 1st Sea Lord.

Report conditions on beaches and whether boats are distributed to best advantage. 1019/30

22. Vice-Admiral, Dover to Admiralty for 1st Sea Lord.

Your 1019. Beaches crowded. Hardly any ships are here for loading. Request

destroyers and sloops ... Until more small boats (are available for ferrying) strongly

of opinion ... essential to concentrate on evacuating from Dunkirk itself. 1107/30

23. Admiralty to F.O. Dover Straits (R) V.A. Dover.

Understand pulling boats are weak link please confirm. Every step is being taken to send as many as possible. 1141/30

24. Admiral Taylor, Sheerness to D.S.V.P. (R) D. of S.T.

Thames river steamers have no condensers and cannot run on sea water. Request no more be sent. 1150/30

25. Admiralty to Vice-Admiral, Dover, N.O.I.C. Ramsgate.

War Office have placed seven 30-knot motor launches at your disposal and are sending them to Ramsgate today Thursday. Naval crews are being sent to man them.

Names of launches: *Marlborough, Wolfe, Grouse, Kestrel, Vulture, Swallow, Pidgeon.* 1336/30 *and later*

26 Add to list of fast military launches *Haig* ... 1882/30

27.C.-in-C. Portsmouth to Admiralty, N.O.I.C. Ramsgate, Vice-Admiral, Dover.

Small craft due Ramsgate approx. as follows:

1900/30 Power boat R.F.A. 115 (?)

2100/30 Fast motor boat, Admiral's barge and Examination Serv. Vessel *Llanthony*.

0100/31 F.A.A. Tender Ocean Rover and hopper Foremost 102.

0880/31 Car Ferry *Fishbourne* (previously reported but delayed).

1000/31 One self-propelled lighter.

1300/31 One self-propelled lighter and steam pinnace ...

1852/30

28. F.O.I.C. London to C.-in-C. Nore, Vice-Admiral, Dover, N.O.I.C. Ramsgate, N.O.I.C. Southend, Admiralty.

23 merchant ships motor-lifeboats and 46 rowing ditto in tow of six tugs leaving Tilbury from now till complete, manned by volunteers and naval ratings

On arrival Southend they will be routed immediately to Ramsgate where first tow should arrive about 0600 Friday [31st May] ... 1900/30

Friday, 31st May

29. Vice-Admiral, Dover to C.-in.-C. Nore, F.O.I.C. Harwich, Admiralty, R.A. Dover, N.O.I.C. Ramsgate.

Boat convoy for last flight of B.E.F. departs Ramsgate 1300 Friday 31st for Dunkirk via Route X. Anticipate time of return to Dover and Sheerness 1000 Saturday 1st June. Request all available M.T.B.'s may escort this convoy for as much of the outward passage as possible and for the whole of the return passage.

Anticipated speed of advance outward bound six knots. 0459/31

30. Vice-Admiral, Dover to M.A/S.B.'s *06, 07*, M.T.B.'s *68, 102* (R) R.A. Dover.

M.A/S.B.'s are to rendezvous off Ramsgate at 1200 Friday 31st May with boat convoy to Dunkirk, and escort on outward passage also on return passage, sailing about 0300, Sat. 1st June for Dover.

Off Dunkirk beaches, M.A./S.B.'s and available M.T.B.'s are to embark, under the direction of R.A. Dover, the C.-in.C., B.E.F., and Staff.

M.T.B.'s report when ready to sail.

31. C.-IN-C. Nore to N.C.S.O. Southend, F.O.I.C. London, F.O.I.C. Harwich, Commodore in Charge, Sheerness (R) Admiralty, D.M.O. Sheerness, V.A. Dover, N.O.I.C. Ramsgate.

No more small craft are to be sailed for Ramsgate until further orders. They are to be kept at immediate notice at the places where they now are. 1825/31

32. Vice-Admiral, Dover to Admiralty (R) N.O.I.C. Ramsgate, C.-in-C. Nore, F.O.I.C. London.

For Admiral Preston.

In view of alteration of plan request 30 motor boats and a number of pulling boats up to 40 may be sent to Ramsgate forthwith. Please advise expected time of arrival. 2031/31

33. F.O.I.C. London to Vice-Admiral, Dover (R) C.-IN-C. Nore, N.O.I.C. Ramsgate, Admiralty, N.C.S.O. Thames.

V.A. Dover 2031/31. 30 motor boats sailed; expect to arrive Ramsgate 1100. And 40 lifeboats with 3 tugs should arrive noon 1st June. Crews for lifeboats will be required to join at Ramsgate. 2330/31

Saturday, 1st June

34. Admiralty to F.O.I.C. Harwich (R) Commodore in Charge, Sheerness, V.A. Dover, N.O.I.C. Ramsgate.

All motor boats from Burnham if still detained at Harwich and any others available are to be sent at once direct to Ramsgate for Operation "Dynamo". 0947/1

Appendix H

Signals Re Lack of Small Craft

Tuesday, 28th May

1. *Wakeful* to Vice-Admiral, Dover. Plenty of troops few boats. Conditions good alongside Dunkirk east pier protected by smoke. 0507/28

2. *Calcutta* to Vice-Admiral, Dover (R) S.N.O. Dunkirk ... Conditions for embarkation at La Panne are very bad owing to heavy surf but may improve with rising tide. Have already lost one and possibly both my whalers. 2225/28

Wednesday, 29th May

3. *Leda* to Vice-Admiral, Dover. Message from Brigadier-General i/c embarkation. Present rate of embarkation from shore to ship quite inadequate. Beach bombed throughout the day. 0210/29

4. D.16 (*Malcolm*) to Vice-Admiral, Dover. Destroyers motor boats are inadequate to deal with number on beaches. More boats urgently needed. Weather is now difficult for boat work. 0428/29

5. *Calcutta* to Vice-Admiral, Dover. Evacuation at La Panne being seriously delayed by lack of boats. 0805/29

6. *M.S.10* to Vice-Admiral, Dover. Motor landing craft urgently required Bray strong tide. 1455/29

Thursday, 30th May

7. S.N.O. Afloat to Vice-Admiral, Dover. There is a serious shortage of ships and boats. I have no destroyers. 0039/30

8. V.C.I.G.S. to Vice-Admiral, Dover. Beaches well organised. Troops in good heart. There has been no bombing since dark. There is still a great shortage of small craft which are urgently required. T.O.R.0044/30

9. Rear-Admiral in Charge, Base to Vice-Admiral, Dover. Beaches are filling up rapidly. More ships and boats are an essential requirement. 0744/30

10. Rear-Admiral in Charge, Base to Vice-Admiral, Dover. Can you ... send over 5 ships life boats with skeleton crews to work from beach ... as soon as possible. 0916/30

Friday, 31st May

11. Rear-Admiral, Dover to Vice-Admiral, Dover (R) Admiralty. Urgent need for boats particularly power boats still paramount at La Panne and Bray. Presence of motor boats will be decisive in final evacuation. Request I be informed of action taken on this signal. 0045/31

12. *Icarus* to Vice-Admiral, Dover. Situation at Bray impossible. No power boats ? evacuation 10 an hour. At least 2,000 men still ashore. Troops being bombed and shelled. Dunkirk being bombed continually. If no power boats become available propose withdraw at dawn. 0047/31

13. Colonel Hutchison, *Impulsive*, to Admiralty (R) V.A. Dover. Conditions ideal at present for embarkation but pulling cutters urgently required also more power boats. 0945/31

14. Admiralty to Vice-Admiral, Dover (R) C.-in-C. Portsmouth, C.-in-C. Nore. War Office request maximum possible number of Carley floats and similar devices be left lying on beaches together with paddles after other craft have withdrawn. 1152/31

15. Rear-Admiral, Dover to Vice-Admiral, Dover. Boats not yet arrived. Most available vessels are evacuating from Dunkirk. Minesweepers will not be here in time. I will do what I can. 1736/31

16. Vice-Admiral, Dover to Rear-Admiral, Dover. La Panne reports 6,000 troops to clear urgently and they lack boats and ships. 2130/31

Saturday, 1st June

17. *Gossamer* to Vice-Admiral, Dover. Troops arriving now. Send more boats. 0132/1

18. Vice-Admiral, Dover to *Niger, Gossamer, Halcyon.* Use own boats. Utmost despatch essential. 0204/1

Reply from *Gossamer.*

19. Your 0204. Hardly any boats available.

20. *Gossamer* to Vice-Admiral, Dover. 6,000 British marching from La Panne through Bray on Dunkirk. 0235/1

21. *Gossamer* to Vice-Admiral, Dover. We must have more boats west of La Panne. 0243/1

22. Vice-Admiral, Dover to *Gossamer.* It is now impracticable to send more boats. You must do your utmost with yours. 0334/1

23. *Niger* to Vice-Admiral, Dover, Rear-Admiral, Dover. Situation on beaches is critical. Third Division marching to Dunkirk. More boats urgently required. 0346/1

24. *Gossamer* to Vice-Admiral, Dover. Thousands more (?moving) from La Panne westward. No boats. 0358/1

25. General Whitaker to General Dill, War Office. Absolutely essential provide many more small boats with motor boats to tow if grave losses are to be avoided and remainder B.E.F. cleared. Matter utmost urgency. 0430/1

26. Rear-Admiral, Dover to Vice-Admiral, Dover. All craft used for towing boats have returned in the night. They must be sent back. 0611/1

27. Niger to Vice-Admiral, Dover. Number of towing and small boats are returning empty. Warn following ships to stop them. 2150/1

28. Vice-Admiral, Dover to Force K and Minesweepers (R) Admiralty. Reported that number of towing and small boats are returning empty. Essential to arrest this. Keep good lookout and force them back. 2201/I

29. Vice-Admiral, Dover to Admiralty. Owing to severe conditions and enormous wastage on Dunkirk coast, small boat flotillas, vital for beach work, can no longer be relied upon even in fair weather. Information just received that at least two such flotillas have turned back tonight Saturday. 2328/I

30. Vice-Admiral, Dover to Force K and Minesweepers (R) Admiralty. False information and orders to return are being given to our inshore units by 5th Column skoots or other vessels. Endeavour to keep our small vessels to their duty on the coast. 2336/I

Sunday, 2nd June

31. Admiralty (D.N.I.) to Vice-Admiral, Dover. Your 2335/1: Please supply any information regarding the ships suspected of 5th Column activities. 1834/2

Monday, 3rd June

32. Vice-Admiral, Dover to Admiralty. Your 1834/2. Following is information to date:

On the morning of the 1st June it was reported that a number of small craft had left Dunkirk beaches. An M.T.B. was sent out to round them up and send them back. A signal was intercepted from *Leda en route* to Dunkirk saying that she had met boats returning, and she was ordered to send them back.

During the evening of the 1st June a report was received from S.N.T.O. Margate to the effect that a skoot was going along the beaches at Dunkirk telling boats to return to England.

The *Antje* was hailed and told to return. A warship was in the vicinity, and *Antje* intended to get confirmation from her, when the troop carrier *Scotia* was sunk close to her; so *Antje* filled up with survivors and returned. It is understood that skoot *Oranje* with boats in tow was told to return to England and complied.

In view of these reports, message 2335/1 was sent out. On an earlier occasion another skoot was informed that Dunkirk was in German hands. It has not been possible to get confirmation of these details. 2332/3

Appendix J

Signals Re Patrols in the North Sea South and on the Routes to Dunkirk

Sunday, 26th May

1. Admiralty to C.-in-C. NORE, (R) V.A. Dover, F.O.I.C. Harwich, F.O.I.C. Humber.

All available forces are to be used for covering Operation "Dynamo" tonight Sunday. 1937/26

2. *Widgeon* to C.-in-C. Nore. *Siroco* was torpedoed by 2 M.T.B.'s 0200/31

Saturday, 1st June

3. *Malabar* to Any-British Man-of-War.

Argyllshire sunk by torpedo. Survivors report submarine submerged before explosion 2 miles ? S buoy. 0310/1

4. *Kingston Galena* to Vice-Admiral, Dover (R) Capt. A.P. *Stella Dorado* torpedoed. Picked up 5 survivors, 1 badly injured. Proceeding to Dover. 0430/1

5. Vice-Admiral. Dover to Ships & Authorities Nore & Dover Command. Magnetic mines reported to have been laid vicinity of buoy F.G. on route X. 2310/1

Sunday, 2nd June

6. Vice-Admiral, Dover to *Epervier* (R) *Léopard, Savorgnan de Brazza*.

Three aux. patrol vessels reported out of action at 1214 B.S.T. in position 090° N. Goodwin L.V. 8 miles. Caused by shell fire. Vanquisher left Dover 1305 B.S.T. to investigate and report. 1315/2

7. Vice-Admiral, Dover to *Calcutta*, (R) C.-in-C. Nore, Admiralty, *Savorgnan de Brazza*. Return to Sheerness and revert to 1 hours notice for steam. An exactly similar patrol to that carried out today Sunday is to be carried out tomorrow Monday, provided C.-in-C. Nore can provide a screen. Inform the French vessels on your patrol line. 1247/2

8. *Calcutta* to Vice-Admiral, Dover. Your 1274. French ships apparently left patrol when bombing started at 1035 as I have not seen them since. 1442/2

9. *Saon* to Captain A.P. *Blackburn Rovers* struck by torpedo. Going to her assistance. 1618/2

Monday, 3rd June

10. Vice-Admiral, Dover to C.-in-C. Nore (R) Admiralty, *Calcutta*. As withdrawal from Dunkirk tonight 3rd/4th is planned for 0230 instead of 0300, do not propose to employ *Calcutta* as A /A escort. 1419/3

Appendix K

Signals Re Routes to Dunkirk

Monday, 27th May

1. Vice-Admiral, Dover to Ships operating under orders of Vice-Admiral, Dover. Routes to Dunkerque are as follows:

Route Z, via No. 6 Calais bell buoy and south of Dunkirk AW buoy.

Route Y, via Downs, West Hinder, North Channel and West Deep, Q.Z.S.80 and 60.

Route X, via Downs from North Goodwin 115 degrees, 24.5 miles to light buoy, F.G., and thence 164 degrees to No. 6 W buoy. New light buoys[1] are 115 degrees 7.8, 15.0, and 22.3 miles from N. Goodwin.

Route X may be used in emergency when state of tide permits, or when ordered. *Route Z* should only be used at night.

Route Y is in general use. i.e. "U", "V" and "W" buoys. 1107/28

2. Vice-Admiral, Dover to Ships operating under orders of Vice-Admiral, Dover. My 1107. Add to *Route Z*: "passing south of chartered position of Dyck Light Vessel". 2006/28

Wednesday, 29th May

3. Vice-Admiral, Dover to Ships and Authorities, Nore and Dover Commands. Route Y is to be amended to run from Middelkerke Bank buoy 320 degrees 9½ miles to position north of Dyck whistle buoy. Transports are to be instructed accordingly as opportunity offers. 0631/20

Saturday, 1st June

4. Vice-Admiral, Dover to Admiralty. Owing to magnetic mines ships evacuating troops may be using *Route Y* as well as *Route X*. Request Fighter and Coastal Command be informed.

5. Vice-Admiral, Dover to Admiralty. Channels to Dunkirk now all under fire of German batteries. New battery came into action this evening suspending traffic on only remaining daylight route,

---

1 A skoot informed *Oranje* that beach evacuation was complete, that there were already sufficient ships in Dunkirk harbour and that the *Oranje*'s tow of 4 boats, was not required. About an hour later the *Oranje* returned to England.

namely *X*, maintaining heavy barrage ... 2329/1

Sunday, 2nd June

6. *Venomous* to Vice-Admiral, Dover. Dunkirk approach channel is under fire from the shore guns. 2110/2

Monday, 3rd June

1. Vice-Admiral, Dover to Ships and Authorities, Nore and Dover Commands. Route X. From F.G. buoy steer 172 degrees for No. 3 W buoy and thence keep close to Southern channel buoys.

Appendix L

Signals Request for Fighter Covers

Monday, 27th May

1. B.N.L.O. Dunkirk to Vice-Admiral, Dover. Pass to War Office from O.C. Dunkirk: Complete fighter protection over Dunkirk now essential if a serious disaster is to be avoided. 1655/27

2. Air Liaison Dunkirk to Fighter COMMAND (R) Air Ministry. Unless fighter protection is provided continually from dawn tomorrow result will be very serious. Embarkation on beach east of 892 [?] Dunkirk. 2350/27

Tuesday, 28th May

3. (C.A.S.[1]) Air Ministry to Fighter Command, Costal Command etc. Today is likely to be the most critical day ever experienced by the British Army. The extreme gravity of the situation should be explained to all units. I am confident that all ranks will appreciate that it is the duty of the R.A.F. to make their greatest effort today to assist their comrades of both the Army and Navy. 0125/28 Chief of the Air Staff[1]

4. B.N.L.O. Dunkirk to Vice-Admiral, Dover. Continuous bombing and machine gunning on beaches. Only maximum air protection can alleviate situation at dawn. 0225/28

5. Admiralty to Vice-Admiral, Dover. The Air Ministry are fully in the picture as to requirements at Dunkirk and are doing all they possible can. If any particular requirements turn up, such as group of ships being attacked, report to Admiralty as soon as possible. 1240/28

6. Vice-Admiral, Dover to S.N.O. Dunkirk. Can personnel ships still go alongside Dunkirk. 1135/28

---

1 These letters refer to an arrangement, whereby at the commencement of "Dynamo" the Dunkirk beaches were described by a letter code referring to Map G.S.G.S. 4040, Sheet 29, 1/50,000. The lengths of beach lying in each 1000 metre map square were lettered, west to east, commencing with "A" at square 2686 in sequence to "O" at iquare 3990. (Appx. N. 10). Under this arrangement, A.B.C.D. actually refers to the beach at Malo-les-Bains.

This arrangement appears to have fallen into disuse on and after 29th May, when the stretch of beach, one mile east of Dunkirk to one mile east of La Panne, was divided into equal parts, referred to as *La Panne, Bray* and *Malo*, from east to west, with a mile gap between each part. (Appendix O. 11).

Reply

7. B.L.O., C.-in-C. Northern Naval Forces to Vice-Admiral, Dover Your 1135. Yes when fighters are actually keeping off bombers. 1337/28

Appendix M

Signals Re Evacuation 26th and 27 May

(Additional to those in Appendices D to L)

Sunday, 26th May

1. Admiralty to Vice-Admiral, Dover C.-in-C. Nore, C.-in-C. Portsmouth. Operation "Dynamo" is to commence. 1857/26

2. Admiralty to C.-in-C. Nore, Vice-Admiral, Dover C.-in-C. Nore, C.-in-C. Portsmouth, B.N.L.O. Marceau, B.N.L.O. Dunkirk. Captain W. G. Tennant has been appointed S.N.O. Dunkirk. He will proceed to take up his duties tomorrow Monday, May 27th. 2321/26

Monday, 27th May

3. S.N.O. Dunkirk to Vice-Admiral, Dover (R) Admiralty. Port continuously bombed all day and on fire. Embarkation possible only from beaches east of harbour A.B.C.D. Send all ships and passenger ships there to anchor. Am ordering *Wolfhound* to load there and sail. T.O.O. 2005/27 T.O.R, 2025

4. S.N.O. Dunkirk to Vice-Admiral, Dover. Please send every available craft east of Dunkirk immediately. Evacuation tomorrow night is problematical. T.O.O. 1958/27 R.O.T. 2055

(See also, Appendix D3 to D8)

Appendix N

Signals Re Evacuation on 28th May and Night of 28th–29th May

(additional to those in Appendices D to L)

Tuesday, 28th May

1. Vice-Admiral, Dover to S.N.O. Dunkirk. Report now and every hour the approx. number of men waiting to be embarked from Dunkirk. Acknowledge. 0758/28

2. S.N.O. Dunkirk to N.O.I.C. Dover. Your 0758. There are at present 2,000 men on Dunkirk beach, and 7,000 men on sand dunes for whom I have had no ships. They are now in need of water which Army cannot supply. Unlimited numbers are falling back on this area and situation in present circumstances will shortly become desperate. I am doing my best to keep you informed but shall be unable to report hourly. 0935/28

3. Vice-Admiral, Dover to S.N.O. Dunkirk. Your 0935. Steady transport by 15 destroyers1 will continue by day, spread evenly between beaches. Maximum effort by every type of craft from all beaches and from Dunkirk if practicable is intended for 2200 tonight. 1140/28

16 destroyers were evacuating troops from Dunkirk and the beaches on 28th May.[1]

---

1 V.A. Dover's 1748/29 cannot be traced. Probably Admiralty Message 1748/29 (see Appendix O, 9c) is meant.

Appendix O

Signals Re Evacuation 29th May

(Additional to those in Appendices D to L, and in Appendix Y)

Wednesday, 29th May

1. Vice-Admiral, Dover to S.N.O. Dunkirk (R) Admiralty. Owing to surf on beach most important move as many troops as possible from La Panne and Bray to Dunkirk. 0431/29

2. S.N.O. Dunkirk to Vice-Admiral, Dover (R) Admiralty. No enemy interference at present. Embarkation going at 2,000 an hour. This can be kept up provided supply transport is maintained. Swell prevents use beach; all ships to Dunkirk. Any air attack would be disastrous. Maximum fighter protection essential. Passenger transport, inflammable loaded, mined and sunk about 2 miles east Dunkirk pier light. 0709/29

3. S.N.O. Dunkirk to Vice-Admiral, Dover (R) Admiralty. Embarkation is going on well; enemy is leaving us alone. The situation ashore is obscure and ominous. I have sent Capt. Bush by M.T.B. with an appreciation. There is little food or water in Dunkirk. This should be sent as soon as possible … Armies are quite unable to help or organise anything. Keep on sending any ships … A good medical officer with staff should be despatched. 1001/29

4. Admiralty to Vice-Admiral, Dover C.-in-C. Portsmouth. Rear-Admiral Wake-Walker has been appointed as R.A., Dover for command of seagoing ships and vessels off the Belgian coast, and is to hoist his flag in such ship as V.A. Dover shall direct. 1748/29

5. Vice-Admiral, Dover to Ships & Authorities Nore & Dover (R) Admiralty. C.-in-C. Portsmouth, C.-in-C. Nore

> My 1748/29, 1321/29 and 1832/29 to *Hebe* only. Authority for Operation "Dynamo" under V.A. Dover is as follows:
>
> R.A. Wake-Walker has been appointed as R.A. Dover for command of seagoing ships and vessels off the Belgian coast.
>
> R.A. Dover has hoisted his flag in *Hebe*. Captain Tennant has been appointed as S.N.O. Dunkirk and is responsible under R.A. Dover for all shore organisation. 1328/30

6. Admiralty to Ships & Authorities in Area A (R) C.-in-C. Portsmouth C.-in-C. W.A. During present operations on Belgian coast where many small craft are present, destroyers are not repetition not to stop to render assistance to ships in distress. 1105/29

7. *Ivanhoe* to Vice-Admiral, Dover. From S.N.O. Dunkirk – enemy shelling pier with shore batteries from S.E. Request bombers to counter. Vital. 1105/29

and later

8. B.N.L.O., C.-in-C. Northern Naval Forces to Vice-Admiral, Dover. My ... 1105 cancel request. Consider possible retaliation would be to our disadvantage. 1200/29

9. Major General Lloyd to Major General DEWING, D.M.O., War Office. Morale of troops landing is remarkably high partly no doubt due to arrival home. Approximately half armed. Percentage of officers small. All drawn from units promiscuously, mostly Third Corps ... 1204/29

10. Vice-Admiral, Dover to General Lindsell [Q.M.G.], S.N.O. Dunkirk. Stores and supply craft have had to return undischarged owing to lack of assistance from shore. Must press you to organise parties for unloading purposes; Naval beach parties will indicate when and where required. 1432/29

11. Vice-Admiral, Dover to S.N.O. Dunkirk (R) Admiralty. Evacuation of British troops to continue at maximum speed during the night. If adequate supply of personnel vessels cannot be maintained to Dunkirk east pier destroyers will be sent there as well. All other craft except hospital carriers to embark from beach which is extended from one mile east of Dunkirk to one mile east of La Panne. Whole length is divided into 3 equal parts referred to as La Panne, Bray, Malo, from east to west with a mile gap between each part. La Panne and Bray have troop concentration points each end and in middle; Malo at each end. These points should be tended by inshore craft. Pass this message by V/S to ships not equipped W/T as opportunity offers. 1900/29

12. S.N.O. Dunkirk to Vice-Admiral, Dover. [Your 2057] No. Hope to get a good move on tonight but it is doubtful if much more can be done in daylight hours.

2150/29

Note: The authority for the above signal is S.N.O. Dunkirk's Report (R.O.III, p. 350). V.A. Dover's 2057 is not available. It asked whether the harbour was blocked.

Appendix P

Signals Re Evacuation on 30th May

(Additional to those in Appendices D, E, G – L, and Y)

Thursday, 30th May

1. Military Dunkirk to Vice-Admiral, Dover (R) War Office. Great opportunity missed during night when only 3 drifters arrived. No water or food yet provided on Dunkirk beach for large number of troops. Sporadic bombing. 0755/30

2. B.N.L.O. to N.O.T.C. Dover. From S.N.O. Dunkirk … Have sent [Captain] Howson take charge La Panne beach under G.H.Q … T.O.R. 0835/30

3. S.N.O. Dunkirk to Vice-Admiral, Dover. Troops are concentrated in unlimited numbers just east of Dunkirk beach, on Bray beach, and at La Panne. Please do your best to distribute … 0930/30

4. S.N.O. Dunkirk to Vice-Admiral, Dover … I have no M.T.B. and can only communicate with U.K. by French W/T station or when destroyers are in sight. If conditions remain as at present a destroyer alongside continuously for embarkation would be a magnificent help. The moment bombing starts all must shove off. 0943/30

5. S.N.O. Dunkirk to Vice-Admiral, Dover. If this weather persists I want a ship every half hour. 0950/30

Appendix Q

Signals Re Evacuation on 31st May and Night of 31st May 1st June

Friday, 31st May

1. Vice-Admiral to *Gossamer, Leda, Speedwell, Halcyon, Skipjack, Salamander, Niger, Ross, Albury, Kellett, Fitzroy, Sutton, Saltash, Lydd, Dundalk,* (R) C.-in-C. Nore, F.O.I.C. Harwich. Ships addressed are grouped as follows for special embarkation today Friday:

Group one. *Gossamer, Leda, Ross, Albury.*

Group two. *Halcyon, Skipjack, Speedwell, Dundalk.*

Group three. *Niger, Salamander, Fitzroy, Sutton.*

Spare. *Kellett, Saltash, Lydd.*

Each ship is to adjust programme forthwith as necessary to rendezvous empty with Senior Officers of groups at W buoy … at 2200/31. Object final evacuation of covering force of five thousand troops.

Execution. Groups are to proceed so as to arrive off beach eastward of Dunkirk in following positions vide chart 1872 as close as possible to the shore at 2400/31.

Group One. Bray Dunes Hotel, 5 cables apart.

Group Two. La Panne light 4½ cables apart.

Group Three. *Niger, Salamander, Rosendael.*

Fitzroy, Sutton, battery longitude 02° 27' E.

Kellet, Saltash, spare ship between Groups One and Three and Groups One and Two respectively. *Lydd* is to make rendezvous, and if not required to complete Groups, to lie off Braye.

Troops will be brought off in three groups by waiting motor boats commencing at 0130 or earlier. Maximum speed of embarkation essential. Seven ocean tugs will lie to seaward of minesweepers to take overflow but maximum loading of ships is necessary to ensure complete evacuation. Group One is to return to Sheerness, Groups Two and Three to Dover. Spare ship to Harwich. Acknowledge.

0400/31

Note: The above signal was amended later – see Appendix Q.18.

2. S.N.O. Dunkirk to Vice-Admiral, Dover. Every available ship will be required at Dunkirk during next 2 hours to evacuate rest of Army. 0445/31

3. Rear-Admiral, Dover to Vice-Admiral, Dover. Conditions on beach bad. On-shore wind. Whalers capsized. 0051/31

4. Vice-Admiral, Dover to Admiral [Landriau], *Savorgnan de Brazza*. Request you will send in all your available destroyers and ships to Dunkirk and to beaches at once. 0819/31

5. Admiral [Landriau] to Vice-Admiral, Dover. C.-in-C. Dover from French Admiral, Pas de Calais:

> This night and tomorrow I continue maximum effort. I request support of aviation on Dunkirk tomorrow as today.

6. Rear-Admiral, Dover to Vice-Admiral, Dover (R) Admiralty. Majority of boats are broached to and have no crews. Conditions on beach are very bad owing to freshening on-shore wind. Only small numbers are being embarked even in daylight. Under present conditions any large scale embarkation from beach is quite impracticable. Motor boats cannot get close in. Consider only hope of embarking any number is at Dunkirk. Will attempt to beach ship to form a lee to try to improve conditions. 1035/31

7. S.N.O. Dunkirk to Vice-Admiral, Dover. Your 0855. We have been continuously and heavily bombarded and they are gradually finding the range of our loading berth. I would rather only enter ships which are necessary for the flow of troops. 1044/31

8. Rear-Admiral, Dover to Vice-Admiral, Dover. Dunkirk our only real hope. Can guns shelling pier from westward be bombed and silenced. 1105/31

9. Vice-Admiral, Dover to *Saltash, Queen of Thanet, Westward Ho, Devonia, Plinlimmon, Brighton Queen, Niger, Dundalk, Fitzroy, Speedwell*, N.O.I.C. Margate, C.S. Sheerness. Ships carrying out Sheerness – La Panne ferry are now to run to Dunkerque beach and Margate instead. This service is to be maintained as long as possible while conforming to my 0400/31 (i.e. Appendix Q.1.). 1114/31

10. Admiralty to Rear-Admiral, Dover (R) V.A. Dover, S.N.O. Dunkirk. A paddle minesweeper suggests that much time could be saved if she puts her bows ashore on rising tide and she is then used as a bridge for deeper draught ships coming to her stern. 1134/31

11. Vice-Admiral, Dover to Rear-Admiral, Dover. Admiralty's 1134:

Act on this if you judge conditions suitable. 1151/31

12. Vice-Admiral, Dover to Rear-Admiral, Dover (R) S.N.O. Dunkirk. Officers and men of beach parties have returned to Dover under instructions from Dunkirk. All repeat all beach parties must be retained to the last. 1229/31

13. Vice-Admiral, Dover to *Worcester*. Embark beach parties and proceed when ready by *Route X* with all despatch. Land them as allocated and then continue evacuation from La Panne. 1308/31

14. Vice-Admiral, Dover to Rear-Admiral, Dover. Fresh beach parties are being sent in *Worcester* and have been allocated to beaches. 1405/31

15. Vice-Admiral, Dover to Destroyers (R) R.A. Dover. When there is room in Dunkirk harbour destroyers are to enter there in preference to beaches. R.A. Dover pass to S.N.O. Dunkirk. 1910/31

16. Vice-Admiral, Dover to Rear-Admiral, Dover (R) S.N.O. Dunkirk. Army wish to recommence evacuation at 2030. Instruct boats and ships to close beaches at this time. 1640/31

17. Rear-Admiral, Dover to Vice-Admiral, Dover. Weather off beaches now good. Many more boats should come into use again as tide rises. General movement of troops to westward towards Dunkirk. No petrol supply yet and many motor boats are getting short off La Panne and Bray. Movement from Dunkirk continues. Great air activity. 1707/31

Note: Actually, drifters with petrol arrived at 1815/31.

18. Vice-Admiral, Dover to *Gossamer, Halcyon, Niger, Lydd*. My 0400/31 [i.e. Appendix Q. 1]. Cancel words "final" and "covering" Cancel positions off beaches. Embarkation will take place from beach between long. 02° 29'E., and long. 02° 36' E.[1] Ships are to be evenly spread along this beach in order of Groups from east to west, Two, One, Three. First flight will leave beach at 0030 repetition 0030. *Lydd* take place of *Saltash*. Senior officers of Groups pass to remaining ships and acknowledge. 1904/31

Note: Between Zuydcoote Sanatorium and 1 mile east of La Panne. [*See also* next signal].

19. Vice-Admiral, Dover to Ships and Authorities Nore and Dover Commands. Military now desire that tonight's special evacuation should take place from beaches covered by 1 and 2 [? Groups] starting at 0030/1. Groups should be closed up to conform to this. Embark naval personnel from beaches 1 and 2 if practicable. Embarkation of French will continue tomorrow Saturday from the harbour and from Malo beach by British and French Ships. The final evacuation of the B.E.F. is expected on the night 1st/2nd June. R.A. Dover acknowledge. 1920/31

20. D.19 [Keith] to Vice-Admiral, Dover. V.A. Dover, Captain Tennant, from R.A. Dover. Impossible to embark except Dunkirk and beaches immediately east. 1929/31

21. S.N.O. Dunkirk to Vice-Admiral, Dover. No ships for the French and us. Please despatch. 2235/31

22. General Lloyd to Director of Military Operations. Following is new plan:

General Alexander has been placed in command of final phase of evacuation. Composition of force not known. Tonight, the special transport force designed for lifting last flight of 4,000 is being concentrated on 2 eastern beaches. Tomorrow efforts are to be concentrated on French evacuation. It is impossible now to say how long this will take, but Alexander Force remains till last. V.A. Dover will provide maximum capacity for Alexander on beach just east of Dunkirk on night 1st/2nd June, or later if necessary; details being arranged between Admiral Wake-Walker and Alexander. Naval Liaison Officer is being provided at Alexander's H.Q. 2309/31

---

1 Note: The minesweeper *Devonia* was beached at about 1600.

Appendix R

Signals Re Evacuation on 1st June and Night of 1st-2nd June

Saturday, 1st June

1. Rear-Admiral, Dover to Vice-Admiral, Dover. Parachute mines are being dropped all over west of Bray. Request sweep of Dunkirk road. 0047/1

2. Rear-Admiral, Dover to Vice-Admiral, Dover (R) Admiralty. Yesterday ships off Bray were under fire. Today's shorter front will bring dangerous area westward. For this reason, and mining, consider any beach work too costly and evacuation must be confined to Dunkirk. Small craft will be moved westward at dawn. 0235/1

3. Vice-Admiral, Dover to Rear-Admiral, Dover (R) *Halcyon, Skipjack, Speedwell, Sharpshooter.* Troops from La Panne now marching towards Dunkirk. Act accordingly. 0300/1

4. Vice-Admiral, Dover to Rear-Admiral, Dover. We must take full advantage of low visibility to use beaches. Keep me informed on this point. 0630/1

5. Vice-Admiral, Dover to General Alexander, Dunkirk (R) R.A. Dover, S.N.O, Dunkirk. On the likely assumption that complete evacuation will be ordered tonight the problem of transport makes it essential to use both sides of harbour, pier and eastern beach. I am planning on these lines and for evacuation to start at 2200/1. 0951/1 (as amended by 1044/1)

6. Vice-Admiral, Dover to Destroyers. All destroyers are to return to harbour forthwith. 1345/1

7. Vice-Admiral, Dover to C.-in-C. Nore, N.O.I.C. Harwich, Commodore in Charge, Sheerness, N.O.I.C. Ramsgate, 1st, 4th, 5th, 6th M/S Flotillas. All available ships operating under V.A. Dover of the minesweeping flotillas addressed, are required to assist in evacuation tonight Saturday. Ships to sail to arrive off the beach between Dunkirk and a point 1½ miles east, at 2200/1. Ships which have not D.G. equipment are not to sail. Ships report forthwith whether they can comply. 1510/1

8. Vice-Admiral, Dover to General Alexander, S.N.O. Dunkirk, C.-in-C. Northern Naval Forces (R) Admiralty. Evacuation will take place tonight Saturday from:

(a) Beach between Dunkirk and 1½ miles to the eastward, between 2100/1 and 0300/2, for 9,000 men.

(b) East Pier, between 2100/1 and 0330/2, for 7,000 men.

(c) East side inside harbour, between 2200/1 and 0330/2, for 1,000 men.

AH naval personnel are to be withdrawn this Saturday night.

Reference (B), time of termination of this evacuation may be extended and will be signalled. 1609/1

9. Vice-Admiral, Dover to Destroyers. Following destroyers are required for duty tonight. Remainder revert to 2½ hours notice for steam:

Esk, Codrington, Icarus, Windsor, Venomous, Winchelsea, Whitshed, Sabre, Shikari. 1711/1

and later

10. Destroyers named in my 1711 will be addressed Force K. 1745/1

11. S.N.O. Dunkirk to Vice-Admiral, Dover. Things are getting very hot for ships. Over 100 bombers on ships near here since 0530. Many casualties. Have directed that no ships sail during daylight. Evacuation by transports therefore ceases at 0300. If perimeter holds, will complete evacuation tomorrow Sunday night, including most French. General concurs. 1754/1

12. Vice-Admiral, Dover to FORCE K (R) R.A. Dover. Destroyers are to proceed in pairs at hourly intervals to berth on east pier Dunkirk harbour, returning to Dover when loaded. If no vacant berth, V.A. Dover and next pair to be informed, and the destroyers to assist at beach instead. The personnel vessels will also be berthing at east pier and have priority. Destroyers to leave Dunkirk vicinity not later than 0300/2, *Route X. Route Z* may be used during dark. First pair to arrive Dunkirk 2200.

Pairs: *Windsor, Icarus.*

Codrington, Sabre.

Shikari, Esk.

Winchelsea, Whitshed.

Caution is necessary owing to wrecks in Dunkirk harbour. 1810/1

13. Vice-Admiral, Dover to Rear-Admiral, Dover (R) S.N.O. Dunkirk. Enemy action bombing and shell fire make it impossible for personnel ships enter harbour in daylight. 1859/1

14. Air Ministry to Fighter Command, Bomber Command, Costal Command, BACK C. B.E.F., WAR Office, Admiralty, Vice-Admiral, Dover. Confirming conversation between C.-in-C. and D.H.O.X. 153 1/6.

Situation at Dunkirk. Two divisions French territorials reduced strength still to be evacuated. Evacuation will continue in any event until tomorrow morning. Strong continuous patrols should therefore be carried out over Dunkirk and beaches from 0430 to 0830 hours 2/6.

Last boat in the morning will leave Dunkirk before 0700 hours. If part of garrison still remains evacuation will recommence in the evening. If so, strong continuous patrols should be carried out over area from 170.0 to 2100 hours, when operations will terminate night 1st/2nd June. Night fighters should patrol same area during hours of darkness. Fighter patrols should be routed out over area in which our ships are working between N. Foreland and Dunkirk, and on return journey should fly low on the same routing to give vessels maximum protection against low flying bomb and machine gun attack. 1930/1

15. Admiralty to Rear-Admiral, Dover Straits, S.N.O. Dunkirk (R) V.A. Dover.

(a) Should there be a channel which it is possible to use during daylight hours, it is intended that evacuation from Dunkirk should proceed continuously from 2130 tonight Saturday until 0700 tomorrow Sunday.

(b) Continuous air protection will be provided from daylight tomorrow Sunday until 0830 by fighters, and from 0830 until 1100 by Coastal Command.

(c) It will be decided tomorrow Sunday forenoon in the light of the naval and military situation as to whether evacuation is to continue tomorrow Sunday night.

(d) It may also be necessary to carry out evacuation from 1730 tomorrow Sunday until dark, should evacuation in daylight still be possible.

(e) From the above it will be seen that there will be no ships proceeding to Dunkirk between 0700 and 1730 tomorrow Sunday.

(f) Request you will inform Admiral Abrial and General Alexander of the above arrangements.

(g) Should it be impossible to use any of the 3 Channels from Dunkirk owing to shell (R) shell fire from coast batteries you are to inform Admiralty ... T.O.D. 2021/1

16. Admiralty to Vice-Admiral, Dover.

(a) Embarkation of troops from Dunkirk is to proceed continuously from 2130 today Saturday until 0700 tomorrow Sunday.

(b) Strong and continuous fighter protection will be provided from 0430 until 0830 tomorrow Sunday.

(c) Protection by Coastal Command will be provided from 0830 until 1100.

(d) It is hoped that the evacuation may be completed tonight but should this not be possible, you should be prepared for further evacuation tomorrow Sunday night.

(e) It may be necessary to carry out evacuation from 1730 tomorrow Sunday in addition to the night evacuation.

(f) Should it be decided that the conditions are such that evacuation cannot be carried out between 0300 tomorrow Sunday and 0700 tomorrow Sunday, you will be informed. T.O.D. 2025/1 T.O.R. 2044/1

17. Vice-Admiral, Dover to S.N.O. Dunkirk. Evacuation tonight Saturday from west end of beach and from harbour only, to cease at 0300. Can embark about 9,000 from beach if weather remains calm. Lighters and destroyers will enter harbour. 2045/1

18. Vice-Admiral, Dover to Admiralty, C.-in-C. Northern Naval Forces General Alexander, S.N.O. Dunkirk.

My 1609/1 [Appx. R.8] and S.N.O. Dunkirk 1754/1 [Appx. R.11]:

Casualties to shipping are now being caused by heavy artillery. All shipping has been ordered to withdraw before daylight tomorrow Sunday. 2214/1

19. Vice-Admiral, Dover to Admiralty. A.M. 2025/1 [Appx. R.16] paras, (a) to (f), S.N.O. Dunkirk 1754/1 stating General concurs that evacuation for transports is to cease at 0300:

Channels to Dunkirk now all under fire of German batteries. New battery came into action this evening, suspending traffic on only remaining daylight route, namely *X*, maintaining heavy barrage, sinking transports *Mona's Queen* and *Brighton Queen*[1] and a trawler in the fairway near No. 5 buoy.

---

1 No transports were sunk by gunfire on 1st June. The *Mona's Queen* was sunk by magnetic mine on 29th May; the A.B/V *Mona's Isle* was straddled by shore guns on 1st June and sustained some damage. The minesweeper *Brighton Queen* was sunk by aircraft on 1st June. The minesweeper *Sandown* came under fire of Nieuport guns on 31st May.

French destroyer nearby turned back *Royal Daffodil* and "*Royal Scot*" [? *Royal Sovereign*). Eight transports have now been lost and eight disabled. Crews of others difficult to keep on service.

The above facts coupled with recent naval losses and also military losses by drowning have convinced me that any attempt to continue evacuation during the day is unwise. Permission is therefore requested in accordance with A.M. 2021/1 [Appx. R.15] para. (G) to withdraw all forces at 0300 until the following night. 2329/1

Sunday, 2nd June

20. Vice-Admiral, Dover to S.N.O. Dunkirk. Admiralty has directed that evacuation by personnel steamers from Dunkirk pier shall continue until 0700. 0055/2

21. Admiralty to Vice-Admiral, Dover (R) R.A. Dover Straits, S.N.O. Dunkirk. Your 2329/1:

(a) Evacuation up to 0700 in accordance with Admiralty telegram 2025/1 to V.A. Dover, and 2021/1 to R.A. Dover Straits and S.N.O. Dunkirk, is to be carried out using destroyers only.

(b) Destroyers to be ready to open fire on any batteries.

(c) If further experience shows that the channel is prohibitively dangerous due to gunfire, evacuation by day is to cease and Admiralty informed immediately. 0115/2.

22. Vice-Admiral, Dover to Force K. Evacuation by destroyers is to continue until 0700 from Dunkirk harbour. Transports are to leave Dunkirk at 0300. Destroyers inform transports. Fire of shore batteries should be returned. 0125/2

23. *Winchelsea* to Vice-Admiral, Dover. Your 0055 and your 1729/1 not passed to S.N.O. Dunkirk.

24. S.N.O. Dunkirk to Vice-Admiral, Dover (R) Admiralty, War Office. Your 1609/1/6 [Appendix R.8] not received until 0430. Large proportion naval personnel evacuated. Estimated approximately 20,000 British and French evacuated, greater (proportion ?) being French. There remain to be evacuated night 2/3 probably 5,000 British and approximately 30,000 French. Request more transport for tomorrow's operation than was provided for tonight. Request ... M.A/S ... boats. Sappers, General, S.N.O. and remainder naval personnel (will leave ?) 2300 hours. T.O.R. 0704/2

25. General Lloyd to War Office M.O.4. Information is difficult to obtain and often contradictory. General Martel reports little pressure on his front yesterday but there is less reliable evidence to show that pressure on some points elsewhere was severe.

Most personnel evacuated last night were from pier. Shell fire on beach was apparently bad as have been given names of 3 officers killed there. Estimated numbers so far reported landed Dover and Ramsgate since midnight 10,600 of which about 1/3 French. Three personnel ships and many smaller craft not reported 0800 hours. Numbers remaining 458 area impossible estimate. Might be in region 2,000 British. 0815/2

Appendix S

Signals Re Deliberate Attacks on Hospital Ships on 2nd June

Sunday, 2nd June

1. Dunkirk to Dover W/T [Sent *en clair*]. Wounded situation acute. Hospital ships should enter during day. Geneva Convention will be honourably observed. It is felt that the enemy will refrain from attack. 0730/2

2. Vice-Admiral, Dover to Admiralty. Hospital carriers *Worthing* and *Paris* have been deliberately bombed and severely damaged today by Germans in circumstances admitting of no mistake of their identity. 2016/2

Appendix T

Signals Re the Evacuation of the British Rear Guard on Night 2nd/3rd June

Sunday, 2nd June

1. H.M.S. *Lydd* to Rear-Admiral (R) V.A. Dover, Force K, Minesweepers. Brigadier tells me that C.-in-C. says it is essential that rear guard B.E.F. embarks from beaches east of mole on account of French congestion on mole. Considerable number of British troops still on mole. Military are (? expecting) further arrivals there. Rear guard expects to arrive on beach by 0230. 0040/2

2. S.N.O. Dunkirk to Vice-Admiral, Dover (R) War Office ... About 5,000 British remain ... Sporting chance of embarking tonight. Maximum number of fast motor boats at 2130 at inner end of long pier would assist. T.O.R. 0830/2

3. Vice-Admiral, Dover to Destroyers and Minesweepers. The final evacuation is staged for tonight, and the Nation looks to the Navy to see this through. I want every ship to report as soon as possible whether she is fit to meet the call which has been made on our courage and endurance. 1052/2

4. Vice-Admiral, Dover to Destroyers, Paddle Sweepers, Personnel Vessels (R) S.N.O. Dunkirk. Evacuation tonight 2nd June will be from Dunkirk harbour, ships berthing on east pier. Following berths established if required (?) from north to south:

> Berth A: from lighthouse to trawler wreck.

> Berth B: from wreck to gap in pier.

> Berth C: from gap in wall to hut at end of pier.

> Berths D & E: smaller berths extending to the inner end of pier.

In addition, berth on east side of east pier. This berth will not normally be used unless all inside berths are occupied.

Pier master will direct berthing from east pier, and ships entering will be guided by a motor boat. Ships are to work special brows and ladders which will be supplied at Dover, and have boxes ready to form steps ... Intention is to keep berths A to E constantly filled. 1430/2

5. Vice-Admiral, Dover to Destroyers. My 1430/2. Destroyers are to sail to arrive at Dunkirk as follows:

> 2100 – *Shikari and Sabre*

> 2130 – *Venomous*

2200 – *Windsor*

2230 – *Icarus*

2300 – *Winchelsea*

2330 – *Esk*

2400 – *Vanquisher*

0030 – *Codrington*

0100 – *Express*

0130 – *Vivacious*[1]

0200 – *Whitshed*

0230 – *Malcolm*

Acknowledge. 1715/2

6.Vice-Admiral, Dover to Minesweepers (R) C.-in-C. Nore, F.O.I.C. Harwich, Cdre. i/c Sheerness. Ships evacuating tonight Sunday are to sail to arrive off Dunkirk as follows:

From Margate: 2100 to 2230.

From Sheerness: 2230 to 2351

From Dover: 0001 to 0130

From Harwich: 0130 to 0200

Times of arrival of ships in each group to be staggered. Ships to berth at inner end of eastern arm as directed by traffic control motor boat. Red Very's light stops entry. Green Very's light allows entry. 1548/2

7. S.N.O. Dunkirk to Vice-Admiral, Dover (R) Admiralty. B. E.F. evacuated. Returning now. 2330/2

---

1 *Vivacious* had, however, been detailed to take part in a blocking operation.

Appendix U

Signals Re Evacuation on 3rd June

Monday, 3rd June

1. Air Ministry to Fighter Command, Coastal Command, Back Violet, V.A. Dover (R) Admiralty, War Office. X.334 3/6.

This signal confirms arrangements made by telephone for providing fighter protection for Dunkirk and shipping in evacuation over the period 1930 hours 3rd June to 0800 hours 4th June. Coastal Command to provide protection for shipping between Dover and Dunkirk during period 1930 hours till dark. Fighter Command to maintain continuous patrol – strength one Blenheim fighter – over Dunkirk area during hours of darkness. Fighter protection to be provided over Dunkirk area and shipping in the channel from 0430 hours to 0800 hours 4th June, protection to be provided by Fighter Command followed by Coastal Command; times to be arranged with C-in-C, concerned by Back Violet. 1850/3

Appendix V

Signal Re the Decision to Terminate the Evacuation After the Night of 3rd–4th June

Monday, 3rd June

1. Vice-Admiral, Dover to Admiralty (R) C.-in-C. Nore. After nine days of operations of a nature unprecedented in naval warfare, which followed on two weeks of intense strain, commanding officers, officers and ships companies are at the end of their tether.

I therefore view a continuance of the demands made by evacuation with the utmost concern as likely to strain to breaking point the endurance of officers and men,

I should fail in my duty did I not represent to Their Lordships the existence of this state of affairs in the ships under my command, and I consider it would be unfortunate, after the magnificent manner in which officers and men of the surviving ships have faced heavy loss and responded to every call made upon them, that they should be subjected to a test which I feel may be beyond the limit of human endurance.

If therefore evacuation has to be continued after tonight I would emphasise in the strongest possible manner that fresh forces should be used for these operations, and any consequent delay in their execution should be accepted.

2. Admiralty (1st Sea Lord) to B.N.L.O. Marceau (R) V.A. Dover. Pass to Admiral Darlan from 1st Sea Lord.

I urge most strongly that evacuation be completed tonight, as after nine days of continuous work of this nature officers and men of both H.M. Ships and merchant ships are completely exhausted. Request early confirmation that evacuation will be completed tonight, and number to be evacuated. 1512/3

3. B.N.L.O. Marceau to Admiralty (1st Sea Lord), Vice-Admiral, Dover. French Admiralty agree that evacuation should be terminated tonight, if possible, and estimate approximately 30,000 men remaining.

In French opinion, only competent authorities are now Admiral Abrial and V.A. Dover.

Captain de Revoir[1], and officer from V.A. Dover are *en route* Dunkirk to inform Admiral Abrial of plans for termination evacuation. These officers should keep V.A. Dover informed of numbers involved as French Admiralty unable to communicate Dunkirk. 1651/3

---

1 French Naval Attaché

Appendix W

Signals Re the Build-up of Ships for the Night of 3rd/4th June

Destroyers – Monday, 3rd June

1. Vice-Admiral, Dover to Destroyers, Minesweepers, Auxiliary Vessels. I hoped and believed that last night would see us through but the French who were covering the retirement of the British rearguard had to repel a strong German attack and so were unable to send their troops to the pier in time to be embarked.

We cannot leave our Allies in the lurch and I must call on all officers and men detailed for further evacuation tonight to let the world see that we never let down our ally.

The approach will be made later and the retirement earlier. The night protection of our fighters which stopped all bombing of the harbour last night will be repeated. 1009/3

[see Appendices Y.18, Y.19 and Y.22.]

Disposition of Ships

2. Vice-Admiral, Dover to Force K, Minesweepers, *Locust, Guillemot, Kingfisher.* Dunkirk evacuation tonight Monday.

From East Pier by personnel vessels, destroyers and paddle minesweepers.

From West Pier, new outer port by other minesweepers, corvettes, skoots and French vessels.

Inner harbour by drifters and small craft.

All ships to leave by 0230/4. *Locust* will remain outside entrance receiving loads ferried out by small boats. Tugs will be available outside Dunkirk. 1440/3

Appendix X

Signals Re Evacuation on 4th June

Tuesday, 4th June

1. Admiralty to C.-in-C. Home Fleet, Vice-Admiral, Dover, V.A.S., C.-in-C. Rosyth, C.-in-C. Nore, C.-in-C. Portsmouth, C.-in-C. Western Approaches, C.S.2, C.S.

Operation "Dynamo" now completed

Appendix Y

Signals Re Evacuation of French and Belgian Troops

Wednesday, 29th May

1. Admiralty to Vice-Admiral, Dover (R) N.O.I.C. Ramsgate. There are a certain number of Belgian troops at La Panne who ask permission to embark in British ships in order to join Allies. As we are using Belgian ships and crews for our own embarkation this request must be acceded to and instructions should be given accordingly. 1347/29

2. S.N.O. Dunkirk to Vice-Admiral, Dover (R) Admiralty. Bombing of beaches and Dunkirk pier has now commenced without opposition from fighters. If they hit Dunkirk pier embarkation will become very jammed. Beach at La Panne covered with troops congregating in large numbers. Very slow embarkation taking place from eastern beach. The French staff at Dunkirk feel strongly that they are defending Dunkirk for us to evacuate which is largely true ... 1358/29

Note: The above signal was made by S.N.O. Dunkirk when he was in the *Express* off La Panne.

Friday, 31st May

3. Admiralty to Vice-Admiral, Dover, Rear-Admiral, Dover Straits, S.N.O. Dunkirk. The policy of H.M. Govt, is that both British and French troops be given equal opportunities for being evacuated in British ships and boats. 0104/31

4. S.N.O. Dunkirk to Vice-Admiral, Dover (R) Admiralty, R.A. Dover. Am now receiving a number of Frenchmen. I have at present raised no objection to their embarking in British ships and am allowing them to do so. 0638/31

Saturday, 1st June

5. Secretary of State for War to C.-in-C. 1st Corps. You will appreciate importance from point of view of future Anglo-French relations embarking as large a proportion of French as is humanly possible today. I am sure that we can count upon you to help us in this. 0131/1

6. War Office to Madelon (R) British Commander, Dunkirk. Following for General Weygand from C.I.G.S. All evidence, naval and military, shows that every effort must be made to complete evacuation tonight. Strongly urge that Admiral Abrial be instructed to co-operate in this effort in the interest of our two Armies. Only remaining channel now coming under fire of German guns, which will put an end to all evacuation by day indefinitely. 1330/1

7. I.G.S. to S.N.O. Dunkirk. Following for General Alexander. We do not order any fixed moment for evacuation. You are to hold on as long as possible in order that the maximum number of French and British may be evacuated. Impossible from here to judge local situation. In close co-operation with Admiral Abrial you must act in this matter on your own judgement. 1729/1

8. S.N.O. Dunkirk to Vice-Admiral, Dover for C.I.G.S. Ref. 1858 from C.I.G.S. Withdrawal now proceeding according to plan. Shall have certain reserves here tomorrow to assist French. Intend to complete evacuation tomorrow by midnight. 2315/1

9. S.N.O. Dunkirk to Vice-Admiral, Dover (R) Admiralty. Reference S.N.O.'s 2315 from General [Alexander];

> Request again maximum number transports for British and French at 2130 June 2nd. It is intended that all British shall be evacuated by midnight. Request M.A/S.B. if possible for General at 2300. 0400/2

Sunday, 2nd June

10. French Admiral Pas de Calais to Admiral, C.-in-C. Dover. Message received Savorgnan:

> Received new orders from French Admiralty to try resume evacuation by day-time. I ask opinion Admiral Dunkirk. Do you intend to operate by daytime as well as night. 0525/2

11. Vice-Admiral, Dover to French Admiral Pas de Calais (Pass via Savorgnan). Your 0525. No. By night only. 0811/2

12. Vice-Admiral, Dover to S.N.O. Dunkirk, Admiral du Nord (R) Admiralty. Following are the arrangements for final evacuation British and French tonight Sunday. Maximum numbers of transports, destroyers and minesweepers will be employed to evacuate from pier and harbour; the first ships arriving at 2100 the remainder following at close intervals. In addition the French are making own arrangements for embarking from beach and west pier in new harbour.

Transport for General will be sent as you asked for.

Arrange for Lewis to direct ships at entrance again. Clouston[1] is coming over as pier master with details of plan. Good luck to you all. 1251/2

13. S.N.O. to Vice-Admiral, Dover (R) War Office. French still maintain front line except for front east of Bergues where the Germans have penetrated 2 miles on a 2 mile front. Counter attack being made at 1500. In port, no movement. Present situation hopeful. 1538/2

and later

14. Military situation: French counter-attack postponed until 2000. Remainder of front quiet. Bombers will probably be (playing ?) evening (hymn ?). 1840/2

15. Admiral Nord to Admiral Dover.

> **Part One**. If during night of 2nd/3rd June 30,000 men can be evacuated, I hope to be able to try on the night of 3rd/4th June to withdraw the 35,000 men who are defending the bridgehead.

> **Part Two**. In order to embark these troops quickly after retirement, numerous boats will be required along east pier, Embecquetage, and Quai Felix Faure; also boats and small craft to

---

1   *Seaplane tender 243,* in which Cdr. Clouston was taking passage, was bombed en route and sunk. Cdr. J. C. Clouston, R.N., was lost.

embark 6,000 men on the beach between Malo-les-Bains and Malo Terminus.

Part Three. This evening all British officers will leave Dunkirk but the help of British naval Officers will be essential during the night of 3rd/4th June to direct British ships.

Part Four. If this programme could be carried out, the blocking of harbour could take place at the end of the night of 3rd/4th June.[2] I will keep you and Rear-Admiral Dover Straits advised of my intentions.

Part Five. I shall require help of British fast motor boats to assist in the conduct of operations of evacuation, a great number of French fast motor boats being damaged. 1610/1

16. S.N.O. Dunkirk to Vice-Admiral, Dover. Have promised French I will press for shipping for them tomorrow night when they hope to evacuate 15,000. Reply Admiral Nord. 1735/2

17. War Office to General Alexander (R) S.N.O. Dunkirk. Understand from French that another night will be required to complete the evacuation altogether. If British troops are entirely evacuated tonight, conclude this is with concurrence of Admiral Nord. 2037/2

Monday, 3rd June

18. Rear-Admiral, Dover in M.A /S.B.10 to Vice-Admiral, Dover Four ships now alongside east pier but no French troops.

[see Appendix Y.22].

19. Rear-Admiral, Dover to Vice-Admiral, Dover. Plenty of ships cannot get troops. 0115/3

and later

20. Ships in harbour will not be filled by 0300. Am returning to Dover. Waiting outside. 0200/3

21. Captain D.20 [Express] to Vice-Admiral, Dover. Ordered to return. No troops. 0250/3

22. Admiral Nord to Admiral Landriau, Pass to Admiral Dover. 2140/2/6.

Primo. Enemy attacked yesterday from East Berghes [? Bergues] and again today and advanced as far as Teteghen.

We have counter-attacked and regained ground. Counter-attack will continue tomorrow.

Secundo. On bridgehead partial attack has been repulsed.

Tertio. Enemy has occupied Berghes [? Bergues] without advancing further.

Quarto. General Jansenne killed.

Quinto. Last British elements have embarked.

Sexto. As attacks most probable today, situation concerning munitions may become critical and may oblige evacuation troops to which (group undeciphered) embarkation of all advanced troops (group undeciphered) and obtainable.

Note: The above signal was timed 2140/2/6, and was passed to V.A. Dover, with the following addition.

Admiral Landriau understands that this attack explains delay in bringing French troops to the pier.

---

2 See Appendix Z.3.

French destroyers *Bouclier* and *Flore* delayed for one hour forty. Admiral Landriau begs on account of delay to send if possible more fighters this morning. 0403/3/6

[see Appendix W.1].

23. Vice-Admiral, Dover to Admiral Nord (R) French Admiral in harbour. My intentions for tonight 3rd/4th are to provide a maximum effort with available remaining ships between 2230/3 and 0230/4.

We shall send ships to entire length of eastern pier as fast as possible capable of accommodation for 14,000 men. We will assist with ships at the western pier in the Avant Port to the extent of accommodation for 5,000 men. In addition, French ships will be responsible for evacuation from the Malo beach, Quai Felix Faure, and the New Avant Port for which I cannot estimate numbers.

I will land officers and men on the eastern pier. A British M.T.B. will be at your disposal from 2200.

I will be deeply grateful if special arrangements could be made to evacuate as many British wounded as possible in return for the British effort on behalf of the French Army.

Appendix Z

Signals Re Operation C.K. – the Blocking of Dunkirk Inner Harbour

Sunday, 2nd June

1. S.N.O. Dunkirk to Vice-Admiral, Dover. Admiral Nord requests that blockships will arrive at entrance at 0300 tomorrow night. He will signal if their placing is to be postponed. 0405/2

2. Admiralty to Vice-Admiral, Dover, Rear-Admiral, Dover Straits, S.N.O, Dunkirk. My 1000/31st May, not to S.N.O. Dunkirk. Operation is to be carried out, forces sailing from the Downs about 1900 today Sunday. E.T.A. Dunkirk roads 0200 3rd June. Final order to block is to be given by Captain Dangerfield who will enter Dunkirk ahead of forces and consult with Admiral Nord as necessary. Owing to the tide, blockships cannot enter Dunkirk harbour after 0300 on night 2nd/3rd Tune. 1300/2

3. Admiralty to S.N.O. Dunkirk (R) V.A. Dover, R.A. Dover Straits. French now state that following has been received from Admiral Nord.

"Evacuation will not be completed during the night of 2nd/3rd. Blocking of Dunkirk must not take place for the moment".

We hope, however, to complete evacuation tonight and blockships are being sent. Captain Dangerfield has orders to proceed to Dunkirk in advance of blockships and get in touch with Admiral Nord and arrange time of blocking with him. 1552/2

[see Appendix Y.15].

Monday, 3rd June

4. *Vivacious* to Admiralty (R) Vice-Admiral, Dover. Operation C.K. completed. Two blockships sunk between breakwater, but regret obstruction of channel not achieved. T.O.R. 0445/3

The two blockships were the *Westcove* and *Edvard Nissen*. The third blockship, the *Holland*, was lost *en route*.

5. Admiralty to Vice-Admiral, Dover, Rear-Admiral, Dover Straits. My 1300/2 [Appx. Z.2]. Operation is to be repeated tonight June 3rd, forces sailing from the downs about 2000 today Monday. E.T.A. Dunkirk roads 0130/4. 1158/3

RESTRICTED

Dunkirk Sources

The principal sources on which this account of Operation "Dynamo" is based, are as follows:

M.011883/40 Operation "Dynamo." Report of Proceedings. (Report of Vice-Admiral Ramsay, F.O.C. Dover, referred to in this narrative as D.R.)

M.020721/40 List of ships which took part in Operation "Dynamo," 26th May to 4th June (From F.O.C. Dover, 26/10/40).

M.017681/40 Ships lost during Operation "Dynamo" - Report (From F.O.C. Dover, 5/9/40).

M.017978/41 Report of Rear-Admiral Wake-Walker on the evacuation from Dunkirk, 29th May to 4th June, 1940. (Rear-Admiral Dover's Report).

C.W. 29685/40 Operation "Dynamo." Recommendations for Honours and Awards. (From F.O.C. Dover, July 1940).

Case 5458 [6 volumes] Admiralty Record Office Operation "Dynamo." Evacuation of troops from Dunkirk, May to June 1940. (Contains reports of individual ships, "Dynamo" Maintenance Officer, S.N.O. Dunkirk, etc.) Referred to as "R.O.I - VI."

Enclosure Box No. 370 Admiralty Record Office Contains signals connected with the operation.

M.011431/40 Admiralty War Diary. (Signals).

M.010977/40 Blocking of Dunkirk Harbour (Operation C.K.)

Case 6256 Admiralty Record Office Demolitions carried out at Dunkirk (Operation X.D.)

H.M. Ships lost during the evacuation of troops from Dunkirk.

H. & A.8/42 Evacuation from Dunkirk Norwegian S.S. *Hird*. Recommendations for awards.

M.016146/40 Dutch coasters. List of commissioned for "Dynamo," etc.

M.010932/40 Report of Proceedings of Riflemen landed to cover Demolition Party at Boulogne on 23/5/40.

M.010824/40 Evacuation of Boulogne. Report by Major C. F. L. Holford, Royal Marines (with M.010932/40).

M. 3422/40 Particulars of [Belgian] men and craft from the Dartmouth area who assisted in Dunkirk evacuation. (From C. in C. Western Approaches, 14/7/40).

M.011882/40 Operation "Dynamo" Work of Personnel Vessels. (From F.O.C. Dover, 18/6/40).

M.014793/40 Reports of Operations off Dutch, Belgian and French Coasts [Evacuation of Boulogne.]M.013316/40 Operations conducted by F.O.C. Dover during period 10th- 15th May on Dutch, Belgian and French Coasts.

T.0.9436/40 Operation "Dynamo" Small Craft. (Ministry of Shipping 5/6/40).

T.M.6213/40 Voyage reports by Masters or crews of ships and small craft which took part in the evacuation of the B.E.F. from Dunkirk. (From Ministry of Shipping, Sea Transport Dept., 2/8/40).

T.0.9144/41 (Small craft taken up for "Dynamo" Operation). Letters (part I) received giving account of operations. (Ministry of Shipping, Sea Transport Dept., 17/11/41).

T.0.9144/40 Provision of certain small craft for special service (pooled at Sheerness) "E" Scheme. (Ministry of Shipping, Sea Transport, Dept., 27/5/40).

T.0.9436/40 Operation "Dynamo" – small craft. Procedure for settlement of claims.

N.L.5097/40 Compulsory reporting of small craft – Proposed order. (From small vessels pool, 16/4/40).

S.T.N.4B (Director of Sea Transport). Vessels dealt with by S.T.N.4B which took part in "Dynamo."

D.Y./1/01 Operation "Dynamo" (from Commodore in Charge Sheerness). (Pack of signals and letters).

R.E./2/014 Operation "Dynamo". (Reports and Recommendations. From Commodore in Charge Sheerness).

R.A.F. Narrative The Campaign in France and the Low Countries, Sept. 1939-June, 1940. (Air Historical Branch (1) Air Ministry).

The following sources contain some first-hand information which is not in Official Records:

Statements made by Masters of tugs engaged in the evacuation from Dunkirk (From William Watkins Ltd., Steam tug owners, London).

Account by the R.N.L.I. of their work in the evacuation of the B.E.F. from Dunkirk.

Reports made by crews of vessels engaged in "Dynamo" operation. (From Pickfords' Ltd.)

"Little ships of Dunkirk)" [in manuscript]. (Reports of small craft collected by Mr. J. D. Casswell, K.C.)

Statements made by Masters of tugs engaged in Operation "Dynamo." (From W. H. J. Alexander Ltd., tug owners, London).

French Admiralty records of French ships at Dunkirk.

The following books provide a background to the operation:

Dunkirk. By A. D. Divine, D.S.M. London. Faber & Faber Ltd. (Mr. Divine took part in the operation).

The Epic of Dunkirk. By E. Keble Chatterton. London. Hurst & Blackett Ltd. (Contains some vividly illustrative photographs).

Michael Pearce

Mike Pearce served with the Ministry of Defence (Navy) for nearly 40 years and was on the staff of the Britannia Royal Naval College, Dartmouth for 12 years. Closely involved with the Royal Navy throughout his career, he held management and planning roles within many different fields of MoD activity and on numerous projects for the Royal Navy in London, Hampshire and at the Naval Base at Devonport in addition to BRNC. As a naval historian, he has been a trustee of the Britannia Museum since its inception in 2008 and is a series editor for the Britannia Naval Histories of World War II; in 2012 he co-authored, with Dr Richard Porter, the introduction to *Fight for the Fjords*, and in 2013 wrote the introduction to *Between Hostile Shores, Mediterranean Convoy Battles 1941-42*, both in the series. Following the series re-launch in 2019, he wrote the introduction to *Confronting Italy, Mediterranean Surface Actions in 1940*. His particular area of expertise is the period 1860-1960 and he continues to undertake research, both on behalf of the Trust and in his own areas of interest.

He traces his first spark of interest in naval matters back to the age of four, when his father lifted him shoulder-high on the Isle of Wight ferry so that he could see HMS *Vanguard*, the last British battleship. His interest in naval history took off in his teens when he started reading and buying naval history books – he has never stopped. At school, he was often found tucked away in corners, avidly reading naval history and he counts himself fortunate that his career enabled him to put his knowledge to effective use.

Married to Anne, they have two grown-up children and live in South Devon where Mike is also a qualified watchkeeper with the National Coastwatch Institution at Prawle Point.

Admiral Sir James Burnell–Nugent KCB CBE MA

James Burnell-Nugent joined the Royal Navy at Britannia Royal Naval College, Dartmouth, in 1971 after the award of an Honours Degree in Mathematics at Corpus Christi College, Cambridge. He was awarded the Queen's Gold Medal while under naval general training and the Admiral Sir Max Horton Prize for excellence in submarine training. He commanded in every rank from Lieutenant to Admiral.

After the "Perisher" qualifying course for submarine commanding officers, his first command was the conventional submarine HMS *Olympus* 1979-80. He then served on the staff at Dartmouth, teaching leadership, navigation and seamanship. This was followed, as a Lieutenant Commander, by command of the nuclear powered submarine HMS *Conqueror* 1984-86, carrying out many Cold War patrols hunting down Soviet ballistic missile submarines. After time in the MoD and the Joint Service Defence College, he had the triple command of the 2nd Frigate Squadron, the frigate HMS *Brilliant* and Captain Initial Sea Training 1992-93. In this latter role he had oversight of all Officers Under Training from Dartmouth for their first experience of 8 weeks at sea in a warship of the squadron. HMS *Brilliant* was part of a Task Group in the early stages of the Bosnia Crisis, one of whose roles was to be ready to withdraw UK troops. After a somewhat unusual secondment to HM Treasury working on areas other than defence, he was appointed in command of the aircraft carrier HMS *Invincible*. In his time she made two joint operational deployments to the Gulf for air operations over Iraq and then conducted further air operations during the Kosovo War. These were the first operations for an integrated RN and RAF Joint Harrier Force, with 16 jet aircraft and 6 helicopters embarked.

As a Rear Admiral, Commander UK Maritime Forces 2001–02, he was in command of a large deployed RN Task Group at the time of the New York Twin Towers attack by Al Qaeda. Having opened his Headquarters alongside the US Navy in Bahrain, this then evolved into him being the Maritime Commander of the UK Joint Force and the Deputy Maritime Commander of the Coalition for the early stages of the campaign in Afghanistan. This was a combined force of 40,000 men and women in 104 ships, including 5 aircraft carriers.

In 1999 as a Rear Admiral, he joined the Admiralty Board as the Assistant Chief of the Naval Staff. On promotion to Vice Admiral, he became Second Sea Lord and Commander-in-Chief Naval Home Command with responsibility for all personnel matters. He flew his flag in HMS *Victory*, making frequent use of Nelson's Great Cabin. From 2005 as Commander-in-Chief Fleet, he was responsible for the preparation and operation of all the ships, submarines and aircraft of the Royal Navy and Royal Marines. During this time he redirected a major forward deployment of the Fleet, including implementing the concept of long term basing of ships overseas and rotating their ship's companies. At the same time he held the NATO appointment of Maritime Component Commander (Northwood), initiating the first maritime deployment outside the "NATO Area". He left the Navy in 2008 for a broad range of chairmanship, non-executive and strategic advisory roles.

He was awarded the CBE for inspirational leadership in 1999 and knighted with particular reference to encouraging diversity in the Royal Navy in 2004. He is a Younger Brother of Trinity House, a Freeman of the City of London, a Companion of the Institute of Leadership and Management, an Honorary Fellow of Corpus Christi College, Cambridge and a Governor of Stowe School. He is married with 4 married children, 10 grandchildren and with his wife runs a smallholding in South Devon.

Britannia Naval Histories of World War II

Historical material, newly commissioned commentary, maps, plans and first–hand accounts of specific battles. Each foreword is written by naval veterans of the highest order, including HRH Prince Philip, Duke of Edinburgh.

Never previously published in this format, World War II Battle Summaries are documents once stamped 'restricted' or 'confidential' and held in the archive of Britannia Royal Naval College in Dartmouth, South West England. They are unique records written up by naval officers during the conflict, and soon after 1945. Events are recorded in minute detail, accompanied by maps and plans drawn up during the period by serving officers. Where Führer Conferences are featured, these contain Hitler's words as they were minuted and typed at the time. These historical texts have been reorganised into a contemporary format. The first–hand accounts are from worldwide sources and contain invididuals' reactions, emotions and descriptions, making fascinating reading.

Introduction by
G H Bennett

Hitler's Ghost Ships
Graf Spee, Scharnhorst and Disguised German Raiders

Paperback
ISBN 978-184102-308-3
Hardback
ISBN 978-184102-307-6
Extent
224 pages
Format
156 x 234 mm
Category
JWMV2 Military and Naval Ships

Foreword
Admiral Sir Jonathon Band,
former First Sea Lord and Chief
of Naval Staff

%% The German Navy's tactics of disguise to oust the British fleet and isolate island Britain.

%% Includes tracking maps drawn when the Battle Summary was compiled.

Disguised Auxiliary cruisers could sidle up to merchant vessels undetected as they were flying a neutral flag, similar to 17th century pirate ships. Completion of the disguised ships was difficult and took its toll on the German dockyard workers and crews, sailing in waters dominated by the Royal Navy. The Battle Summaries chart how the Royal Navy dealt with the threat of these raiders of 70 years ago.

Introduction by

M J Pearce and R Porter

Fight for the Fjords

The Battle for Norway 1940

Paperback

ISBN 978-184102-306-9

Hardback

ISBN 978-184102-305-2

Extent

408 pages

Format

156 x 234 mm

Category

JWMV2 Military and Naval Ships

Foreword

Admiral Lord Alan West, a former First Sea Lord and Parliamentary Under-Secretary of State at the Home Office

※ Contains the wartime British and German documents that detail this famous sea battle.

※ Includes tracking maps drawn when the Battle Summary was compiled.

The fierce naval battles fought in Norwegian waters during the spring of 1940 were recorded in documents that were once subject to restrictions under the Official Secrets Act. Fight for the Fjords includes the German account, written within three years of the end of World War II, and the British report, which compiled previously unavailable Royal Navy records to produce one complete account. The combination of these two summaries forms a unique record.

Introduction by
J E Harrold

Dark Seas
The Battle of Cape Matapan

Paperback
ISBN 978-184102-304-5
Hardback
ISBN 978-184102-303-8
Extent
160 pages
Format
156 x 234 mm
Category
JWMV2 Military and Naval Ships

Foreword
Written by HRH Prince Philip
who served in the action

※ The only publication to have a first-hand account of the battle by HRH Prince Philip.

※ Includes original hand-drawn maps and diagrams.

Written shortly after World War II, the summary of the Battle of Cape Matapan draws on first-hand accounts of action on both sides. Unearthed from archives, the vivid and compelling detail is reproduced and newly published as Dark Seas. During the battle, the enemy was hunted, trailed, avoided and engaged. Accurate intelligence combined with the inaccurate and misleading in the 'fog of war'. This is a unique insight into one of the last fleet engagements in naval history.

Hunting Tirpitz
Naval Operations Against Bismarck's Sister Ship

Introduction by
G H Bennett

Paperback
ISBN 978-184102-310-6
Hardback
ISBN 978-184102-309-0
Extent
304 pages
Format
156 x 234 mm
Category
JWMV2 Military and Naval Ships

Foreword
Admiral Sir Mark Stanhope,
First Sea Lord and Chief of
Naval Staff

- Operation Chariot, Operation Source, Operation Tungsten are detailed and analysed.
- Includes original hand-drawn maps and diagrams.
- Contains newly translated first hand accounts by German crew members of Tirpitz.

While it was the RAF that delivered the final coup de grâce, it was the Royal Navy, from 1942 to 1944, that had contained, crippled and neutralised the German battleship in a series of actions marked by innovation, boldness and bravery. From daring commando raids on the coast of France, to the use of midget submarines in the fjords of Norway and devastating aerial attacks by the Fleet Air Arm, the Royal Navy pursued Tirpitz to her eventual destruction.

Introduction by
P D Grove

Turning the Tide
The Battles of Coral Sea and Midway

Paperback
ISBN 978-1-84102-333-5
Hardback
ISBN 978-1-84102-334-2
Number of Pages
240 pages

Foreword
Capt. John Rodgaard USN
During his 41 years with the
US Navy, Captain Rodgaard
also served on navy and joint
intelligence tours including
Submarine Group 8, Carrier
Group 4 and the J2 Defense
Intelligence Agency. He is an
author and has contributed
to the Discovery Channel's
Unsolved History series. He is
a graduate of the United States
Naval War College.

%% Includes tracking
   maps drawn when the
   Battle Summaries were
   compiled.
%% Explains the turning
   point of the Pacific
   War.

The Battles of Coral Sea and Midway in 1942
were the conflicts which resulted in the first naval
victories for the United States. The tide turned
for the US, following their amphibious landings
on Guadalcanal. Japanese losses were devastating
and many of the Japanese airmen who had carried
out the attacks at Pearl Harbor would meet their
end at the Battle of Midway.

Introduction by
G H Bennett, R Bennett
and E Bennet

Bismarck
The Chase and Sinking of Hitler's Goliath

Paperback
ISBN 978-1-84102-326-7
Hardback
ISBN 978-1-84102-327-4
Number of Pages
160 pages

Foreword
Commander 'Sharkey' Ward
DSC Author of *Sea Harrier over the Falklands*, Sharkey Ward is known as something of a maverick who led 801 Naval Air Squadron during the Falklands War in 1982. Ward retired from the Royal Navy in 1989 and lives in Grenada.

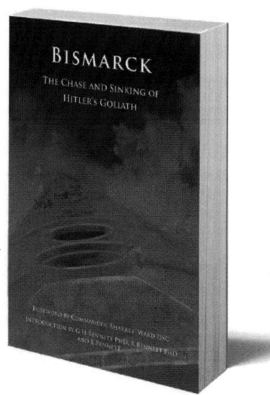

- Contains both a German and British first-hand account.
- Includes tracking maps drawn when the Battle Summary was compiled.
- Quotes from the minutes of Führer Conferences, alongside signals sent to and from *Bismarck*.

Bismark – the most formidable surface ship in Hitler's fleet – was chased and finally sunk by the Royal Navy. This news, relayed at the time, later became a matter of speculation: did the mighty battleship sink during action or was she scuttled by her crew in a final act of defiance? Containing extraordinary detail from 1941 Führer Conferences on Naval Affairs.

Introduction by
M J Pearce

Confronting Italy
Mediterranean Surface Actions in 1940. Exploding the Myth of Mussolini's 'Mare Nostrum'

Paperback
ISBN 978-1-84102-439-4
Hardback
ISBN 978-1-84102-442-4
Number of Pages
192 pages

Foreword
Admiral Sir John Cunningham Kirkwood "Jock" Slater, GCB, LVO, DL. A former first Sea Lord and great-nephew of Admiral Sir Andrew Cunninghm, Commander-in-Chief of the Mediterranean fleet during this period when the actions covered in this volume took place.

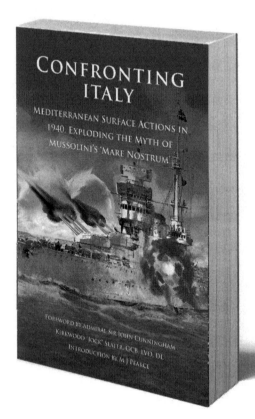

- Contains both a Italian and British first-hand account.
- Includes tracking maps drawn when the Battle Summary was compiled.
- Includes the supplement to the London Gazette

Actions in the Mediterranean were fought when the Royal Navy was still evolving its use of naval air power and when radar at sea was primitive and fitted to only a few ships, while Italy's Regia Marina was handicapped by having access to neither.

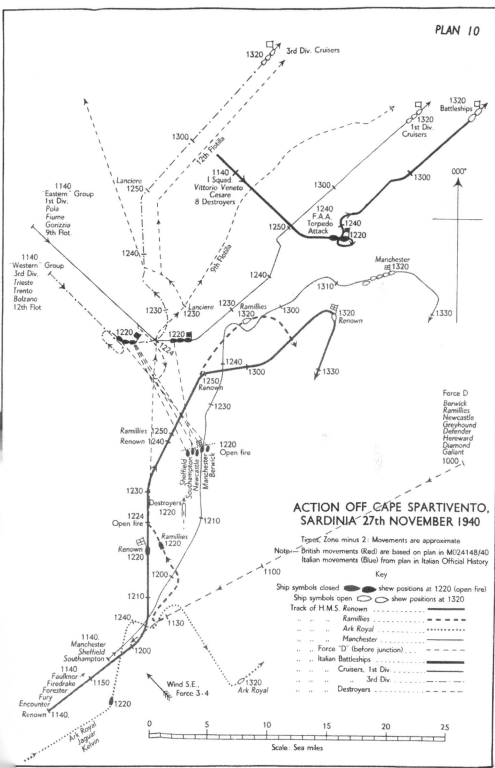

PLAN 10

1320 ⟶ 3rd Div. Cruisers

1300

12th Flotilla

1320 Battleships
1320 1st Div. Cruisers
1300

000°

1140 1250 Lanciere

1140
"Eastern" Group
1st Div.
Pola
Fiume
Gorizia
9th Flot.

1140
I Squad.
Vittorio Veneto
Cesare
8 Destroyers

1240
F.A.A.
Torpedo
Attack

1240

1220

1250

1140
"Western" Group
3rd Div.
Trieste
Trento
Bolzano
12th Flot

1240

9th Flotilla

Manchester
1320

1240

1310

1330

1230   1230
1230 Lanciere   Ramillies
1220   1320
1230 Lanciere   1320
1220 1220   Renown
1224

1330

1240

1250
Renown

1230

Force D
Berwick
Ramillies
Newcastle
Greyhound
Defender
Hereward
Diamond
Gallant
1000

Ramillies 1250
Renown 1240

1230

1220
Open fire

Sheffield
Southampton
Newcastle
Manchester
Berwick

ACTION OFF CAPE SPARTIVENTO,
SARDINIA 27th NOVEMBER 1940

Destroyers
1220

1224
Open fire

1210

Times, Zone minus 2: Movements are approximate
Note:— British movements (Red) are based on plan in MO24148/40
Italian movements (Blue) from plan in Italian Official History

Ramillies
1220

Renown
1220

1200

1210

1100

Key

Ship symbols closed ▰▰ shew positions at 1220 (open fire)
Ship symbols open ▱▱ shew positions at 1320
Track of H.M.S. Renown . . . .
 ..   ..   ..   Ramillies . . . . . .
 ..   ..   ..   Ark Royal . . . . . .
 ..   ..   ..   Manchester . . . . . .
 ..   Force "D" (before junction) . . .
 ..   Italian Battleships . . . . . .
 ..   ..   Cruisers, 1st Div. . . . .
 ..   ..   ..   3rd Div. . . . . . .
 ..   ..   Destroyers . . . .

1240
1130

1140.
Manchester
Sheffield
Southampton

1200

1140
Faulknor
Firedrake
Forester
Fury
Encounter
Renown 1140.

1150

1220

Wind S.E.,
Force 3-4

1320
Ark Royal

Ark Royal
Jaguar
Kelvin

0   5   10   15   20   25

Scale: Sea miles

. 22724

Special Limited Edition

Warships at a Glance, 1914: A Naval Cadet goes to War Foreword is by Capatain Henry Duffy, RN, Captain, Britannia Royal Naval College 2014.

Cloth bound ISBN 978-1-84102-376-2

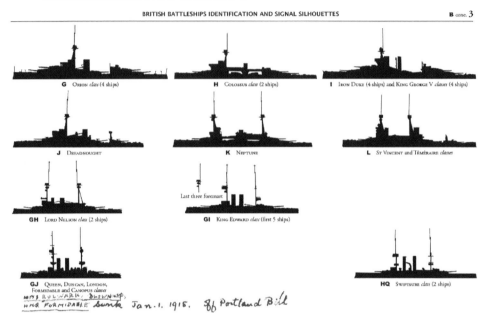

G Orion *class* (4 ships)   **H** Colossus *class* (2 ships)   **I** Iron Duke (4 ships) and King George V *classes* (4 ships)

J Dreadnought   **K** Neptune   **L** St Vincent and Téméraire *classes*

GH Lord Nelson *class* (2 ships)   Last three foremast   **GI** King Edward *class* (first 5 ships)

GJ Queen, Duncan, London, Formidable and Canopus *classes*   **HQ** Swiftsure *class* (2 ships)

HMS BULWARK, BLOWN UP, HMS FORMIDABLE Sunk Jan. 1. 1915. Off Portland Bill

This special limited edition of *Warships At A Glance* issued to graduating cadets to mark the centenary of the outbreak of the First World War. It is a tribute to the cadets and midshipmen of the Royal Navy in 1914, some of them very young, who fought and died for their country in that conflict.

One copy in the Archive at BRNC, Dartmouth bears the name 'A L Tidd', written in the immature hand of a 14 year-old. Alec Lister Tidd was born on 12th April 1900 in Guildford, Surrey, and joined Osborne in Drake Term, in January 1914, leaving in April 1915 to join St Vincent Term of Britannia Royal Naval College at Dartmouth. Christmas 1916, he passed out from Dartmouth and was commissioned as a Midshipman with a seniority of 1st January 1917, joining the battleship HMS *Neptune* in the Grand Fleet at Scapa Flow, where he served until after the end of the First World War, being given the acting rank of Sub Lieutenant on 15th November 1918 and witnessing the surrender of Germany's High Seas Fleet seven days later. HMS *Neptune* was the only ship of her class and her silhouette is prominent in *Warships At A Glance*, among the newer battleships of the Royal Navy.

BMT Press

Britannia Museum Trust Press

Printed in Great Britain
by Amazon

8bc22e37-dd81-435f-9825-47633695a212R01